SPAIN

ALGECIRAS   GIBRALTAR

TANGIER   MEDITERRANEAN SEA
            SEBTA
    ABD EL KRIM
    TETOUAN
ARCIL
                                ALHOCEIMA   MELILLA
LARACHE   CHEFCHAOUENE   MESTAZA   NADOR   NEMOURS
                                        AZROUNT
BOU SELHAM   KSAR EL KEBIR-TAZA   ZEITA   BERKANE
        OUEZZANE   AKNOUL   OUJDA
            RHAFSAI   TAOUNATE   DEBDOU
    OURIDA   SIDI KACEM   TISSA
EL KANSERA   MLY IDRISS   FES   TAZA   GUERCIF   JERADA
TIFLET 140   MEKNES   DEBDOU   ENGUSNT
LAHEMISSAT   SEFROU   DOUAR EL HAJ
                120   IFRANE   EL TERADID
ROMMANI   AZROU
IZZ HJJA   OULMES   MICHLIFEN   MISSOUR
            AGUELMANE SIDI ALI
OUED ZEM   KHENIFRA   BOULMANE
KASBA TADLA   IZZER   MIDELT   BOU AREA
EL KSIBA   MENGOUB   TENIET ZASS
BENI MELLAL   BIN EL OUIDANE   RICH   ROUANANE   FIGUIG
            ASSOUL   KSAR ES SOUK   BOUDENIB
M'SEMRIR   LAB   GOULMIMA   COLOMB-BECHAR
    TINERHIR   ADUFOUS   KENADZA   TARHIT
DOUMANE   ERFOUD   BENI ABBES
KELAA DES M'GOUNA   RISSANI   ABADLA
        NEKOB   TAZARINE   TAOUZ
AGUZ
OUT N'MANE
    ZAGORA
MHAMID   TAGOUNITE

Streams
Principal Routes   ★ Lakes
Secondary Roads   ★ Artificial Lakes
---- Tertiary Roads   Palm Groves
Railway   Cedar Forest

Realm of the Evening Star
A History of Morocco and
the Lands of the
Moors

by Eleanor Hoffmann

CHILTON BOOKS

A DIVISION OF CHILTON COMPANY
Publishers   Philadelphia and New York

Realm of The Evening Star

A History of Morocco and
the Lands of the Moors

To my Moroccan friends, the merchants of Fez, whose hospitality during the summer of 1931 introduced me to the charms of their country and the Arab world.

PREFACE

My love affair with Morocco began in April, 1929. The Arab world and the north African landscape were not new to me. I had already fallen under their spell in both Algeria and Tunisia. I knew the hospitality of the people, the pattern of sea-green minarets rising from the flat roof tops of white cities against blue African skies. I knew the beauty of spring wild flowers, the charm of mountains, desert and beaches and the majesty of Roman ruins. To know Africa from Carthage to Tlemcen was enough to have to know it from Tlemcen to Rabat.

In 1929, in the outward calm and order left by the great Lyautey, the tourist was unaware of the fighting still existent in the heart of the Middle Atlas and beyond the crest of the High Atlas. The deceptively submissive Mohammed V, aged twenty, had held the nominal title of Sultan for two years while behind the scenes the French Resident General pulled the strings. It was the year in which the Sultan's eldest son Moulay Hassan, now Hassan II, was born. The rebel patriot Abd el Krim had begun his long Indian Ocean exile on the Island of Réunion. The first faint stirrings of nationalism had set in unnoticed by the outside world.

Like other tourists, I moved from city to city enchanted by all that I saw; enchanted by all that I bought as future souvenirs—rugs, jewelry, pottery and the famous leather—over glasses of mint-tea from friendly merchants. Suddenly, unexpectedly and by purest accident I became an importer of Moroccan rugs. I had sent three of the beautiful Berber weavings back to my family in California as presents. They had been seen and admired by friends and I began receiving letters and checks begging for similar ones.

For the next few years my life became entangled in skeins of Moroccan wool. In Paris Le Corbusier had already introduced the rugs woven by the Beni M'Guild tribe of the Middle Atlas—striking in their thick pile of white wool and over-all diamond pattern of black—as perfect accent for his ultra-modern décor. My favorites came from the looms of a High Atlas tribe, the Beni Ouzguita. In mine horizontal stripes of black and white (white sheep's wool, black goat hair) were crossed by vertical bands of long pile in colors so delicate and subtle and of wool so silky that their origin in the crude huts of primitive mountaineers seemed inconceivable. The merchants from whom I bought them became my good friends, especially the merchants of Fez. Like an "Open Sesame" their hospitality led me into a world of *A Thousand and One Nights*. It seemed like a dream then. It seems even more fabulous now after the passage of so many years and after the old Morocco has given way to the new.

When I changed professions from importer to writer, I wove Morocco and the Arab lands into my books for children and into articles of history and travel for adults. In this last book I have tried to tell the story of Morocco, its land and its people, from the beginning to the present. It is, of course, not only the story of the Arabs and their great surge out of the East in the seventh century but also that of the Berbers whose roots go back in the north African land into the misty past of pre-recorded history.

Throughout the long months of research I have longed for far greater skill and knowledge than any I possessed. I longed, especially, to be one of those magnificent French Arabists of past and present—a de Slane or a Houdas able to read the Ibn Khaldouns, the Ibn Batoutas, the El Bekris in the original, or an E.-F. Gauthier knowing the Sahara from shore to shore, a Prosper Ricard able to trace art and architecture from the rock paintings and cromlechs of primitive north African man to the intricate arabesques and carved marble of Merinid medersas and Saadian tombs, or a Charles-André Julien, historian with a lifetime devoted to the records of the Moghreb.

These men and many more like them have made my book possible. I owe them endless gratitude. If it were not for the fact that today no book in English, and as far as I know, none in French, covers the whole story of Moroccan history, I would never presume to intrude in fields surveyed by such experts. Budgett Meakin's *Moorish Empire,* the only English account of Morocco from earliest days on, ends in 1899. Charles-André Julien concludes his excellent *Histoire de l'Afrique du Nord* in 1820. Coissac de Chavrebière published his *Histoire du Maroc* in 1931. In America Rom Landau, friend of the late King Mohammed V, has kept the English-speaking world conversant with Moroccan history from the beginning of the century to the present. I have found all of his books most helpful.

To the Moroccan Ministry of Information in Rabat I am greatly indebted, not only for their kindness in supplying me with their publications but for their help during my last visit to their capital. From Douglas Ashforth in his *Political Change in Morocco* and from Horace Miner and his *Primitive City of Timbuctu* I have learned with fascination how the modern political scientist dissects human society in Moslem and Black Africa. For my earliest chapters Gibbon of course was invaluable. To Samuel Parsons Scott I owe much of my material on Moorish Spain.

For the story of Timbuctu past and present and the region south of the Sahara my especial thanks go to the superb *Guide Bleu* of west Africa with its preface rich in articles by such scholars as Theodore Monod, Director of the *Institut Français d'Afrique Noire* at Dakar; it even includes pen and ink drawings of west Africa's antelopes and gazelles. Galbraith Welch, through her accounts of the medieval Niger empires and Caillié's discovery of Timbuctu, was largely responsible for my own visit to the Niger and the realization of a lifelong ambition to reach its fabled city, whose roofs were once said to be of gold.

Family and friends have been of immeasurable help. My brother Walter Wesselhoeft Hoffmann, through a careful reading of the manuscript and copious notes, has saved me much time and work by pinpointing many needed changes. My sister Gertrude (Lady Bliss) has provided me with invaluable research material from London bookstores. My mother, Gertrude Wesselhoeft Hoffmann, at the age of ninety-four has cheerfully put up with not only two years of neglect and frozen food but also with my absence in Timbuctu and Morocco.

Friends to whom I owe gratitude include Ashley Montagu who kindly read the first chapter for me on the pre-history of northwest Africa. Carl Raswan has checked my Arab glossary. To Margaret and Frederick von Soosten I am deeply indebted not only for kindnesses of many sorts but especially for help in typing and for their warm interest in the manuscript from start to finish. Prynce Hopkins has been most generous in giving me access to his splendid library rich in material on the Arab world. And from Jay Monaghan I have had invaluable help and advice. Reaching back into the past, my thanks go to Sidi Mohammed Barada who did so much to make me feel at home among the merchants of Fez during the summer of 1931 when I had a house between the medieval walls of Fez-Bali.

In Rabat, during an all-too-short visit in 1962 Mr. Territ and Mr. Stuart of the United States Embassy were most kind and helpful. Marvine Howe, then Moroccan correspondent for *The New York Times* and author of *The Prince and I,* aided me greatly in getting a picture of the new Morocco. But above all my deepest thanks go to my good friend, Ivan T. Sanderson—and to his wife Alma—for suggesting the undertaking of this book and for the delight of his encouragement during the long, difficult and sometimes despairing months of writing it.

CONTENTS

⦃⊰⦄

Contents

A NOTE ON THE TRANSLITERATION OF ARABIC WORDS INTO EUROPEAN LANGUAGES

When Lawrence of Arabia was rebuked by his publishers for inconsistency in spelling the name of his camel, he answered that there was no correct way of spelling Arabic words in English, that three ways were better than one and that she was a splendid camel! Trouble in this field lies in the path of every writer who deals with Arab lands. This trouble springs, of course, from the dissimilarity between the Arabic alphabet with its twenty-eight consonants and three vowels and our own with twenty-one consonants and five vowels. Anyone who has ever looked up the name of the Prophet will be aware of the confusion arising from trying to approximate the sound of an Arabic word in English. He will find Mahomet, Mahommed, Mohammed, Muhammed and a score of other variations. There is a saying that from the time of the Crusades on, every traveler to the Middle East came back with a different spelling of the Prophet's name. In the Thirteenth Edition of the **Encyclopaedia Britannica** one finds the Prophet under **Mahomet** but Institutions, Law and Religion under **Mahommedan.**

To add to the confusion each European language has its own way of transliterating Arab words. The dry river-bed which the English call **wad** or **waddy** the French call **oued.** The English **suk** becomes the French **souk; sheik** becomes **cheik; jinn** becomes **djinn** and so forth. Because Morocco is an ex-French colony and the Moroccans themselves use the French form of transliteration I, too, have used it throughout the book. There are, however, a few exceptions. Where a word has already become familiar through a Middle Eastern origin, for example **pasha, Sufism** (the mysticism of Islam), **Wahabism** (the puritanical doctrine of Saudi Arabia), **jihad** (Holy War), I have kept to the English way.

The result is impossible consistency. The reader whose eye is used to the **wadis, suks** and **sheiks** of ex-British Arab countries will not like my spelling but, on the other hand, those who made their first contacts with the Arab world in the former north African colonies of the French will, I hope, be happier with my **oueds, souks** and **cheiks.**

GLOSSARY

Unless indicated as Berber (B), Spanish (Sp.), Latin (L), or French (Fr.), the words are Arabic.

ABBASIDS: Second dynasty of Arab Caliphs succeeding the Prophet, 750–1258.

ABD: Slave.

ABD EL OUADIDS: Princes of Tlemcen during thirteenth and fourteenth centuries.

ABOU: Variant of **bou;** possessor or father of.

ACHARITES: Orthodox believers in Koran as identical with word of God.

ADRAR (B): Mountain or mountainous mass.

AGADIR (B): Fortress.

AGHLABITES: African dynasty, 800–910; conquerors of Sicily; capital —Kairouan.

AGUELLID (B): Tribal chief or native king.

AHMAR: Red, masc.; fem., **hamra.**

AID: Feast.

AIT (B): Sons of.

ALAOUITES: Ruling Moroccan dynasty of Arab descent from the Tafilalet; founded 1640.

ALIM: Singular of **oulema;** theologian or professor.

ALMOHADS: Berber dynasty from High Atlas ruling ex-French North Africa and part of Spain, 1148–1269.

ALMORAVIDS: Berber dynasty from southwestern Sahara, ruling Morocco and part of Spain, 1062–1148.

AMAN: Demand for peace.

AMGHAR (B): Elected chief of Berber assembly.

ARABESQUE: Generic name for Moslem ornamentation.

ARBA: Four, or Wednesday.

AYYUBITES: Egyptian dynasty founded by Saladin (of Turkish-Armenian descent), 1174–1250.

AZALAI: Saharan salt caravan.

xvii

BAB: Gate.

BALI: Old.

BARAKA: Supernatural power thought to be in descendants of Mohammed, holy men, sacred words, and certain inanimate objects.

BASILICA (L): Roman building serving as meeting place, exchange, tribunal, and promenade.

BEN: Son of; plural, **beni.**

BIDONVILLE (Fr.): Shantytown made of flattened gasoline tins.

BLED: Country; **bled es siba,** country of insolence; **bled el maghzen,** country under government control.

BORDJ: Fort or fortified settlement.

BURNOUS: Hooded woolen cloak.

CADI: Moslem judge.

CAID: Chief of a tribe.

CALIPH: Successor; temporal and spiritual successor of Mohammed.

CHAOUIA: Coastal plain east of Casablanca.

CHEIK: Religious chief; chief of a tribal faction.

CHORFA OR CHERIF: Patrilineal descendants of Mohammed.

CHRA: Islamic law derived from Koran.

COUSSCOUSS: Stew of steamed grain, vegetables, and meat.

CRAM-CRAM: Prickly weed whose northern growth limit marks southern botanical limit of Sahara.

CROMLECH: Megalithic monument of upright stones in a circle or avenue.

CUFIC: Arabic script in which the characters are angular.

CURSIVE: Arabic script in which the characters are rounded.

DAHIR: Cherifian or royal decree.

DJELLABA: Short, hooded woolen cloak with wide sleeves.

DJEMAA: Berber assembly.

DJINN: Supernatural beings which can take many shapes, human, animal, and inanimate.

DJOUF: Depression in desert.

DOLMEN: Megalithic monument composed of a table supported by vertical slabs.

DOUKALA: Hinterland of El Djedida (Mazagan).

EL: Or **al;** the.

EMIR: Prince.

ERG: Sand dune region of desert.

EVOLUÉS (Fr.): Moroccans of two cultural worlds—France and Islam.

FATIMITES: African dynasty founded on ruins of Aghlabites of Kairouan and Idrisids of Fez; eventual capital—Egypt; 916–1171.

FETOUA: Conjoint legal decree of Islamic scholars.

FIGUIG: Defile.

FIQH: Assembly of chiefs of Moslem law.

FONDOUK: An inn for man and beast.

FORUM (L): Marketplace and promenade of Roman cities.

FQIH: Teacher, scholar, jurist.

GHARB: Region of alluvial plains between Rabat and Larâche.

GONDOURAH: Long flowing garment, frequently hooded.

GOUM: Native militia during Protectorate.

GOURBI: Native hut of reeds, branches, or stone.

GUICH: Tribes giving military service instead of taxes.

HAD: Scrubby thornbush whose southern natural limit marks southern botanical limit of Sahara.

HADITH: Documents embodying traditions concerning the Prophet based on remembered acts and conversations.

HADJ: Pilgrim or pilgrimage to Mecca.

HAFSIDS: Moslem dynasty of Tunisia, 1228–1574.

HAHA: Region between Es Saouira (Mogador) and Agadir.

HAIK: Great sheet of white cotton or wool covering Moroccan women, now largely replaced in cities by tailored gondourah.

HAMMADA: Desert rock denuded by wind erosion.

HARKA: Military expedition.

HAOUZ: Plain of Marrakesh between Oum er Rebia River and High Atlas.

HEGIRA: Mohammed's flight from hostile Mecca to friendly Medina.

IDRISIDS: First Moroccan dynasty, 789–987.

IFRANE: Plural of **Ifri;** precipice; summer residence of Moroccan King in Middle Atlas.

IMAM: Prayer leader.

ISLAM: The word of Allah revealed to the prophet Mohammed by the Angel Gabriel; also the collective countries practicing this religion.

ISTIQLAL: Independence; **El Hisb el Istiqlal,** the Party of Independence.

JIHAD: Holy War.

KAABA: Building housing sacred Black Stone, goal of Mecca pilgrimage.

KHALIFA: Variation of **Caliph,** successor to the Prophet.

KHAREDJITES: Heretical Moslem sect arising in opposition to Ali's caliphate with kingdom in central and eastern Moghreb.

KHOTBA: Friday prayer.

KITAB: Book.

KOHL: Powdered antimony used for darkening the eyes by Moslem women and Touareg men.

KRIM: Generous.

KSAR: Plural **ksour;** fortified habitation; Saharan village.

LALLA: Princess, madam.

LITHAM: Face veil of women or Touareg.

MAGHZEN: Cherifian government.

MAHDI: Deliverer, messiah.

MALEK: King.

MALIKITE: One of the four principal schools of Sunni law, the one followed in Morocco.

MAMELUKES: Arabic for slaves; an Egyptian dynasty, 1250–1517; power totally destroyed in 1811.

MANSOUR: Victorious.

MARABOUT: Member of a brotherhood; a saintly person; also tomb of a saint.

MARIGOT (Fr.): River branch through swampy region such as the flood area of the Niger bend.

MECHOUAR: Vast esplanade attached to a palace.

MEDERSA: School, college, college dormitory.

MELLAH: Jewish Quarter.

MENDOUB: Sultan's representative in Tangier.

MERINIDS: Berber dynasty ruling the Moghreb, 1248–1420.

MIHRAB: Decorated niche in mosque indicating the direction of Mecca.

MINARET: Tower of a mosque for the call to prayer.

MINBAR: Pulpit of a mosque.

MITHKAL: Measure of gold; an eighth of an ounce.

MOGHREB: Land of the setting sun; the North African West.

MOOR: Vague term meaning in general people of northwestern Africa and Moslem Spain.

MOULAY: Title of nobility for sultan or cherif.

MOULAYA: Tortuous; the Moulaya River.

MOUMIN: True Believer.

MOUNA: Food formerly exacted from tribes for travelers under the sultan's protection.

MOUSSEM: Berber festival in honor of a saint.

MUEZZIN: Person who calls the Faithful to prayer.

MUTAZILITES: Believers in unity of a God without divine attributes, in the creation of the Koran, and in free will and the right to reason.

OMMAYIDS OF SPAIN: Head of Cordova Caliphate, 756–1013.

OMMAYIDS OF DAMASCUS: Second Moslem dynasty of the East, 661–750.

OU (B): Sons of.

OUATASSIDS: Branch of Merinid dynasty ruling Morocco 1420–1550.

OUED: Dry river bed except during seasonal rains; English transliteration **wadi.**

OULED: Son, child.

OULEMA: Singular **alim;** body of theologians or professors.

PASHA: Mayor of a city.

QAIDA: Sacred custom.

RAHMAN: Compassionate; **Abderrahman,** Slave of the Compassionate (God).

RAMADAN: Month of fasting from sunset to sunrise; important Islamic practice.

RASHID: Orthodox, just.

RECONQUISTA (Sp.): Reconquest of Spain from the Moors.

RIBAT: Monastic border fortress for spreading Islam through Holy War.

RIF: Mountainous central and eastern Mediterranean coast of Morocco.

SAADIANS: Cherifian dynasty from region of the Dra River ruling Morocco 1550–1668.

SAHEL: Littoral of ocean or desert.

SANHADJA: Great Berber confederation with northern and Saharan branches. Enemies of Zenata.

SEBT: Seven and Saturday.

SEGUIA: Canal.

SELJUK TURKS: Dynasty ruling Middle East from 1055 to c. 1300. Sultans at Baghdad during spiritual rule of last Abbasid Caliphs.

SERIR: Small.

SHIITES: Believers in the divine succession of Ali and his descendants to the Caliphate; the sect of the Fatimites and modern Iran.

SOUDAN (Ar. "Country of the Blacks"): Region south of the Sahara from Atlantic to Red Sea of brush, savanna and parkland. Plural, **Soudoun,** black.

SOUIRA: Small rampart; post-independence name of Mogador.

SOUK: Rural market or market section of city.

SOUS: Valley of the river Sous south of the High Atlas.

SUFISM: Mystical doctrine with belief in the union of the soul with God.

SUNNITES: Followers of sacred custom **sunna** as opposed to Shiites.

SURA: Chapter of the Koran.

TABOR: Native regiment with French officers.

TAFILALET: Oases along the river Ziz southeast of the High Atlas; caravan head of the trans-Saharan trail to Timbuctu; cradle of Alaouite dynasty.

TANEZROUFT: "Land of thirst." The most arid and dreaded region of the central Sahara.

TASSILI (B): Mountains, primarily foothills of the Hoggar.

TAWID: Unity of God.

TAZEROUALT: Region northeast of Spanish Ifni; home of Berber acrobats seen in European and American circuses.

TERTIB: Land tax.

TIT (B): Plural **tetouaine;** eye or spring.

TOUAREG: Moslem Berber nomads of Sahara from Libyan Desert to Timbuctu; men veiled, women unveiled; only Berbers with a written language.

TOUAT (B): Oases.

TOUBIB: Doctor.

VIZIR: Minister of state.

ZAIM: Leader.

ZAKA: Almsgiving.

ZAOUIA: Monastic community of Moslem Brotherhood.

ZENATA: Great Berber confederation. Enemies of Sanhadja.

EMIRS, SULTANS AND KINGS OF MOROCCO

THE IDRISIDS (Arab)
Capital—Fez

789–791	Idris I
791–804	Rashid (regent)
804–828	Idris II
828–836	Mohammed I
836–848	Ali I
848–881	Yahya I
881–894	Yahya II
894–904	Ali II
	Yahya III
904–917	Yahya IV
917–922	INTERREGNUM. Fez lost to Meknassa 925.
922–935	El Hajjam
935–948	El Kennoun
948–954	Aicha el Fadhel
954–961	El Hassan
961–970	Abdallah
970–987	Mohammed II

THE MEKNASSA (Berbers)
Capital—Fez and Meknès

925–938	Mousa ben Abitafia
938–952	Meddine (Founded Meknès and made it capital)
952–973	Ibrahim I
973–1014	El Kasem

THE MAGHRAOUI (Berbers)
Capital—Fez

928–1000	Ziri ibn Atia
1000–1026	El Mouaz
1026–1039	Hamama
1039–1060	Dounas

1060–1065	El Fatih		**THE MERINIDS (Berber)**
	Ajisa		**Capitals—Fez, Meknès and**
1065–1067	El Moannasir		**Marrakesh**
1067	Tamin		

THE ALMORAVIDS (Berber)

Capital—Marrakesh

		1248–1258	Abou Yahya
		1258–1286	Abou Youssef
		1286–1307	Abou Yacoub
		1307–1308	Abou Thabit
		1308–1310	Abou Rebia
1062–1106	Youssef ben Tachfin	1310–1331	Abou Said Othman
1106–1143	Ali	1331–1348	Aboul Hassan (The
1143–1145	Tachfin		Black Sultan)
1145–1146	Ibrahim	1348–1358	Abou Inan
1146–1148	Ishak	1358–1359	Said (Infant)
		1359–1361	Abou Selim
		1361	Tachfin (An idiot)
		1361	Pretenders:

THE ALMOHADS (Berber)

Capitals—Marrakesh and Seville

			Abd el Halim
			Abd el Moumen
			Abderrahman
		1361–1366	Abou Zian Moham-
			med
1148–1163	Abd el Moumen	1366–1372	Abd el Aziz
1163–1184	Youssef the Wise	1372–1374	Es Said (A child)
1184–1199	Yacoub el Mansour	1374–1384	Aboul Abbas (Fez)
1199–1214	Mohammed en		Abderrahman (Mar-
	Nasir		rakesh)
1214–1223	El Mostansir	1384–1386	Mousa and Ahmed
1223–1224	El Makhlou		el Mostansir
1224–1227	El Adhel	1386–1387	El Ouatek
1227–1232	El Mamoun	1387–1393	Aboul Abbas
1232–1242	Er Rashid		(Restored)
1242–1248	Es Said (Fez lost to	1393–1396	Abou Faris
	Merinids 1248)	1396–1408	Faris II
1248–1266	El Mortadha	1408–1420	Abou Said Othman
1266–1269	Abou Debbous		III
	(Marrakesh lost		
	to Merinids		
	1269)		

THE OUATASSIDS (Berber)

**Capital—Fez
(Regents 1420–1472; Rulers
1472–1550)**

1471–1501	Mohammed ech Cheik
1501–1526	Mohammed the Portuguese
1526–1548	Ahmed
1548–1550	Mohammed X

THE SAADIANS (Arab)

Capitals—Fez, Meknès and Marrakesh

1550–1557	Moulay Mohammed ech Cheik
1557–1574	El Ghalib
1574–1576	Mohammed the Flayed
1576–1578	Abd el Malek
1578–1603	Ahmed el Mansour el Dehbi (The Victorious and the Gilded)
1603–1608	Rivals: El Mamoun Abou Faris Zaidan
1608–1627	Zaidan
1627–1631	Abd el Malek (Marrakesh) Aboul Abbas Ahmed (Fez)
1631–1636	El Oualid

1636–1655	Mohammed ech Cheik el Seghir (First to assume title of "Sultan")
1655–1658	Ahmed Abbas
1658–1668	Abd el Karim (in Marrakesh)

THE ALAOUITES (Arab; known also as Filalians and Hassanians)

Capitals—Fez, Meknès and Marrakesh

1666–1672	Er Rashid
1672–1727	Moulay Ismail
1727–1728	Ahmed el Dehbi
1728–1729	Abd el Malek
1729–1734	Abdallah
1734–1736	Ali el Aredj
1736–1738	Mohammed ben Arbia
1738–1740	El Mostadhi
1740–1745	Abdallah (2nd rule)
1745–1746	Zaid el Abidine
1746–1747	El Mostadhi (2nd rule)
1747–1757	Abdallah (3rd rule)
1757–1790	Mohammed II
1790–1795	El Yazid
1795–1822	Soleiman
1822–1859	Abderrahman
1859–1873	Mohammed XVII
1873–1894	Hassan
1894–1908	Abd el Aziz
1908–1912	Hafid
1912–1927	Youssef
1927–1961	Mohammed V
1961–	Hassan II

Realm of the Evening Star
A History of Morocco and
the Lands of the
Moors

CHAPTER I

෫෮෫෮෫෮

HERCULES, ATLAS AND THE ESCARGOTIÈRES
(The Prehistoric Years)

෫෮෫෮෫෮

Our earliest map of the world, created by the myth-making Greeks, was a simple disc surrounded by "River Ocean" and cut from east to west by "The Sea," our Mediterranean. Of its four boundaries, only two tie in with our present maps. To the south lay Ethiopia. On the outmost fringe of the Western World stood the Pillars of Hercules, our Straits of Gibraltar. King of the Western World was *Hesper*, the Evening Star, and here the giant Atlas, forced by Perseus to gaze on the fatal Gorgon's Head, became changed from a god to a mighty mountain range, supporting the Heavens on his shoulders.

Hercules, during his famous twelve labors exacted by Eurystheus, made two visits to the land of the Farthest West and of the Evening Star. During the tenth labor, in search of the oxen of the three-headed monster Geryon, he reached the end of ancient "Libya"—another name of the Greeks for this Western World. There, as a monument to his progress, he divided a massive mountain into two, forming the Pillars of Hercules —pillar number one, Moroccan Mt. Acho; and number two, the [British]

1

Rock of Gibraltar. On his eleventh task, he traveled again to the edge of the flat earth in search of the Golden Apples of the Sun. These were guarded by the daughters of Atlas in the Garden of the Hesperides. Holding the Heavens on his shoulders, to satisfy the condition by which Atlas would deliver the treasure, Hercules slyly tricked Atlas into taking back the Heavens, by saying that he wanted a minute to rearrange the pad on his shoulders.

In Spain, the city of Seville claims: "Hercules built me; Julius Caesar encircled me with walls and high towers; and St. Ferdinand liberated me." In Morocco, a city in sight of the famous "Pillars" also traces itself back to the Greek hero-god. Perhaps it was on his way to seize the Golden Apples that he met the beautiful Tinga, whose father, Antaeus, he had strangled. Their son founded Tingis, the present Tangier. Another reminder is the Caves of Hercules, a few miles out of the city, on the road to Cape Spartel.

Atlas, like his cousin and enemy Hercules, also left his name in this realm of the Evening Star, which we know as Morocco. He gave it not only to the mountain range that stretches across the northern shore of Africa's bulge (or *Africa Minor*) but also to the ocean on its western coast and to Atlantis, that enigmatic island (fable or reality?), scene of Plato's perfect society.

Modern Morocco is that corner of northwest Africa separated from Spain by Hercules' Pillars, or the Straits of Gibraltar. Geologically speaking, the separation is a recent one. It is supposed to have occurred toward the end of the third great geologic era, the Age of Mammals, covering a span of sixty to seventy-five million years. By the time *Homo sapiens* appeared on the face of the earth (according to present thought only something like 100,000 or so years ago), the land bridge had already vanished. The Straits, however, were narrow and, in the course of the great migrations of the Stone Age, proved a negligible barrier between Europe and Africa. To the east of the Straits for three hundred miles, the concave curve of the Rif Mountains edges the Mediterranean to the Algerian border. South of the Straits the Atlantic coast—first in a second concave curve, then bulging out into the ocean—runs south for about six hundred miles to the Spanish Sahara. Inland, beyond the alluvial plain of the river mouths, the Atlas Mountains with their forests of cedars and peaks of 12,000 ft. slant diagonally northeast to the Mediterranean, joining the eastern end of the Rif.

At the foot of the rugged Atlas lies a smoother region. Here, among the former rivers and lakes, the rhinoceros, the hippopotamus, the giraffe, and other tropical fauna were hunted by primitive man. It was a region, however, that had dried out to sand and gravel, polished rock, and lakes of salt and soda by the time the Arabs called it by their word for desert, the Sahara.

In contrast to the other great divisions of the Sahara, those of Algeria,

2

Mauritania,* Mali, Niger, Chad, and Libya, Morocco's share is microscopic. But cross the rocky plateaus or *hammada,* between the oases of the *Oued* or river Guir to the oases of the *Oued* Ziz, and from the Ziz to the upper reaches of the *Oued* Dra, and you couldn't ask for a more desolate region of rock, sand, and empty river beds.

On the huge map of Africa, Morocco is a small country, about the size of California. Algeria is far larger. Tunisia is smaller. The vaguely rhomboid outline of Morocco suggests one of those minute stone implements or microliths known as Capsian, which belonged to the late Stone Age and were first found in Tunisia.

The Atlas range does not stop at the Algerian border, but follows the Mediterranean shore to that angular jog where the Tunisian coast runs south along the Gulf of Gabès to the Tripolitanian border. These three countries, lumped together so simply until their recent independence as French North Africa, merged and still merge into each other as a physical whole. Political boundaries in what we must now call northwest Africa took their first vague shape under Carthage and Rome.

But before northwest Africa entered history, there were the five billion years of the world's existence. If we go back to the late Carboniferous period, about 350 million years ago, when our coal beds were forming, we find, according to the Austrian geologist Eduard Suess, that Africa and India united to form a large continent named by him Gondwanaland. Some 150 million years later this separated into two. The one to the west was modern Africa.

Geologists call the last million years the Pleistocene, from the Greek meaning "most new." They also call it the Glacial Epoch or the Ice Age, because of the four tremendous advances south, and alternate retreats of the Polar ice during its course. Anthropologists call it the Palaeolithic, from the Greek *palaios,* "old," and *lithos,* "stone." The stones they are concerned with are, of course, the worked tools and weapons that tell the story of man's development.

At the end of the Palaeolithic period comes the last division of prehistoric time, the Neolithic, or New Stone Age. Now we are talking in terms of thousands of years instead of millions. The length of this period varies in different parts of the world. Among the Guanches of the Canary Islands off the coast of Morocco it lasted up until the fifteenth century of our own era. There are still primitive peoples in various parts of the world. The Australian bushmen, for instance, are still scarcely out of it. For northwest Africa and the western Sahara, the rough estimate is about four thousand years before the Phoenicians began to explore and found settlements along the Mediterranean shores, or 1200 B.C.

* The Roman country of antiquity is spelled Mauretania. The modern nation is Mauritania.

If the spades of the archaeologists started digging later in northwest Africa than in the northern countries of the glacial advances and retreats, it was for the very good reason that, while scientists were at liberty to comb the caves and river terraces of Europe, this Moslem land before it came under French control, was forbidden to the "Christian dog."

The story of early man in Algeria and Tunisia began toward the end of the last century to form a pattern that is still changing with new discoveries. Algeria had been in French hands since 1848, and Tunisia since 1881, the former as a part of France, the latter as a protectorate. In Morocco a Christian would have been in danger of his life, even in disguise, until the Algeciras Conference in 1906.

When the celebrated French prehistorians started work, they came up against the difference between pinning a time label on Stone Age remains in Europe and on those in northwest Africa. In Europe there were convenient layers and stratifications, brought about by the great grinding ice masses with their melting torrents. There, archaeologists took the four great glacial epochs and the intervals between them to date the cultures they discovered. Working from the top down, in cave and river terrace, they descended, horizon by horizon, from polished stone, bone and pottery shards of the Neolithic, past the finely-fashioned but unpolished stone of the late Palaeolithic, to artefacts that grew simpler and simpler in their workmanship, until they reached the lowest level of all, where they could hardly be sure whether a man of a million years ago had merely picked up a rough stone to hurl at his enemy or had actually fashioned it into a crude shape.

In northwest Africa, on the other hand, there were no great glacial winters, measured in tens of thousands of years, to produce stratifications to indicate the periods. Ice caps on peaks of the Atlas here and there, yes, but what had been snow and ice in Europe had been torrential rains in Africa, pluvial periods (instead of glacial) when thousands of years of cool rain changed to warmth and dryness in recurring cycles. The Sahara was savanna country with the fauna of the tropics; and northwest Africa, which today has almost the same climate as subtropical California, was semi-jungle. When the archaeologists started their searches, almost everything was on or near the surface.

Above all there were the *escargotières*.

Like the kitchen middens or the shell mounds of Europe, or the "greasy Indian soil" of North America, they mark the camp sites of early man. They take their name from the French word *escargot* or "snail," and our closest translation would be "snaileries," from the millions of discarded snail shells. The gastropod *Helix pomatia* (a well known delicacy in Paris restaurants) and its relatives appear to have been the staple diet of Stone Age man in this part of Africa—easier to hunt down than the stag and wild ox. Even today their brittle and empty shells in countless numbers whiten the soil and the asphodel fields.

4

On the surface and in the rock shelters from Morocco to Tunisia, the *escargotières* hold many of the answers to prehistoric cultures. Out of the campfire ashes and refuse, snail shells, animal bones, human bones, and the worked stone weapons and tools that gave the age its name comes the story of these primitive snail-eaters. Fortunately for the scientist, each mound, set off from the surrounding soil by its grey color, represents a uniform culture. By his clever detective work in linking the river terraces of glacial Europe to the river terraces of pluvial Africa, by his knowledge of the shifting of man and prehistoric beast back and forth according to climate across the ancient land bridges at Gibraltar and Sicily, the scientist can date these age-old African refuse heaps.

The results of this dating, not only of the *escargotières* but also of grottos and other prehistoric finds, came as a surprise to the scientific world. A three-toed horse (*Hipparion*), associated with human remains, and a mastodon, for instance, found near Tunis, antedated the earliest known Stone Age culture in this area. Evidence of man and his tools, prehistoric beasts and their bones appeared from the southern shores of the western Mediterranean south across the Sahara to the Niger.

The various cultures, all well represented, moved up through the great divisions of the Lower Palaeolithic with their primitive hand axes, rough scrapers and crude points, in a manner paralleling that indicated by the same tools in European sites. Even more exciting than the tools are discoveries of fossil man himself. Ashley Montagu in his *Introduction to Physical Anthropology* traces the findings in Algeria and Morocco.

The first of these discoveries, in 1954, consisted of two mandibles in a pit near Mascara, Algeria. One appeared to be male, the other female. And through the size and shape of teeth and jawbone they were assigned an age of a half million years and included in the group of "apemen who walk erect" (*Pithecanthropus erectus*). These Algerian jaws, however, differed enough from the Javanese specimens to warrant giving them a name of their own. By their finder, Professor C. Arambourg of Paris, they were labeled *Atlanthropus mauritanicus* (Atlantic man of Mauretania—Mauretania being Rome's name for northwest Africa).

In the same year, a third jaw was found near Casablanca, Morocco—again an *Atlanthropus mauritanicus*—this time associated with stone implements dating about a hundred thousand years or so later.

In Rabat, Morocco, there have also been found skull fragments of this Middle Palaeolithic age.

Famous successors to these "apemen who stood erect" before the appearance of *Homo sapiens* were Neanderthal Man, widely distributed throughout the world, and the Cro-Magnon of Europe. Of these two, no remains have yet turned up in northwest Africa.

With the start of the age known as the Upper Palaeolithic came the greatest surprise. At this point, it was discovered, northwest Africa had apparently developed a culture not only uniquely her own but one that had been spread by migrating man to Spain in the north, Syria to the west, and Sahara to the south. Cultures take their names from the places where they are first discovered. This one was called Capsian, from a place not to be found on any modern map. Capsa was the Roman name for a town in southern Tunisia, now called Gafsa. Veterans of World War II will remember it.

Even to the untrained eye, these minute implements with their neat geometrical symmetry, called microliths and found in great profusion in the environs of Gafsa, appear different from the larger, coarser and more shapeless implements that belonged to the coeval cultures of Europe. Of these European cultures, the Magdelanian is perhaps the easiest for us to remember, as the period of the splendid cave paintings with their bison and reindeer of southern France and northwestern Spain. The French prehistorian who decided that the findings near Gafsa needed a new name was Jean de Morgan.

The use of many of these microliths, like that of the "doughnut stones" of the California coastal Indians, is one of science's many mysteries. Imagine a double-pointed slender piece of finely worked flint, half an inch to two inches long. Fishhooks? There are no notches to hold a line, and there are not always fishbones in the refuse heaps. Picks to remove marrow from bones, and snails from their shells? A splinter of wood or bone would have done as well and involved less labor. Needles for tattooing? Who knows? A grooved oxbone suggests that a row of razor-like microliths might have been inserted into the groove to form a saw. These are the inconclusive explanations imagined by archaeologists working an *escargotière* in the neighborhood of Constantine, Algeria, in 1928 under the auspices of the Logan Museum, Beloit, Wisconsin. The same questions are asked from Spain to Syria wherever these small, finely-worked Capsian flints are found.

Out of the snail mounds also came tools with obvious uses, and bone artefacts, probably for decoration, skillfully fashioned from the leg bones of large animals. There are awls and daggers, long and short points, and rough needle-like shapes without eyes. This is still the Upper Palaeolithic. The true needle made its first appearance in Neolithic times. There are also blades cut from the shells of ostrich eggs. The modern African still delights in putting the ostrich egg to use and covering it with fine decorations.

We lose these Capsian tool-makers during the period that bridges the old Stone Age and the new. On both shores of the Mediterranean, the Neolithic Age was the giant step toward the civilization to come. It took eight thousand years or more; but, in the course of it, *Homo sapiens* of both Europe and northwest Africa learned to till the soil, to breed domestic animals, to make pottery, to weave, to live in settled communities, and to raise giant stones over the graves of his dead.

Probably the most dramatic discovery throwing new light on the New Stone Age of the Algerian Sahara was Lt. Brennans' finding of the Tassili rock paintings in 1933 in the Tassili-n-Ajjer Mountains northeast of the Hoggar on the Libyan Border, and the remarkable copies made of them by Henri Lhote and his expedition in 1956.

Americans who know the deserts of their own southwest in all the infinite variety of structure, surface, color, flora, and fauna will not expect to find in the Sahara three thousand miles of unbroken undulating yellow sand dunes from the Atlantic to the Nile. To those who know the naked mountainsides of Death Valley, the red sandstone carvings of the Grand Canyon, the black volcanic sand and gravel of the Mohave, the Chocolate Mountains and yellow dunes of the Imperial Valley, it will come as no surprise to learn that the Sahara is also a gigantic patchwork of soft dunes and harsh gravel, polished rock and narrow gorges, of depressions below sea level, and volcanic mountain masses more than 10,000 feet in height. There are salt mines and oil deposits, and oases of palm trees. Under the palm trees there are figs, apricots, melons and grain. From the winter snows of the southern slopes of the Atlas, seasonal rivers pour down to dry and vanish underground in the hot summer sands. There are fossil rivers that once watered the Sahara from the Atlas to the Niger and Lake Chad, with the hippopotamus a familiar sight to Neolithic man. It is their intermittent underground waters that keep many of the oases green.

The modern geologist does not believe that the Sahara was at any time an arm of the Mediterranean. In studying the possibility of letting this ocean into the fertile oases of southern Tunisia (known as the Djerid), engineers came up against a solid barrier now known as the Gabès Ledge. This showed no evidence of ever having been pierced by a river mouth. There is, however, the supposition—based on the finding of fossil sea urchins and oyster shells—that in the Cretaceous or Chalk Age of 132,000,000 years ago an arm of the Atlantic extended into the Sahara as far as the central Hoggar and Tassili-n-Ajjer Mountains.

As a rule, the striking climatic changes that have come over the world in its five billion years have been measured in periods of a length difficult to grasp. With the Sahara it is different. Proofs of a recent humid past in this present "Land of Thirst" are many.

Georg Gerster, in his *Sahara, Desert of Destiny*, describes one of the strangest in a chapter called "The Green Desert." This is the microscopic examination of the fossil manure of the prehistoric rock badger in the Hoggar Mountains in the heart of the desert—an inferno of heat and volcanic rock that today suggests the lifeless landscape of the moon. The manure or guano found in Hoggar caves contained, among other unassimilated bits of food, pollen grains—the male germ cells of plants. Within the past fifty years or so, the palaeobotanist with his microscope has been using his ability to identify the pollen of various plants to reconstruct the

7

prehistoric flora of a region. In this particular case, Carbon-14 dating fixed the age of the excrement at about four thousand five hundred years. The rock badger had been feeding on the succulent twigs of such plants as maple, willow, beech, woodbine, buckwheats, grasses and reeds. These familiar plants of our temperate zone have long since been pushed back to the rain-rich littoral of the Mediterranean Sea.

In addition to proof of this familiar flora from the mountain slopes of the Hoggar, we also have proofs of a tropical savanna flora and fauna at lower levels. These lie not only in the beautiful Tassili rock paintings of well-fed cattle and men hunting the hippopotamus from canoes but in other rock paintings and engravings of the same river-loving creatures scattered across the desert to the edge of the Atlantic. They lie also in the first records of history, when horse-drawn chariots joined the pack ox on the trans-Saharan caravan trails. This was before the day of the camel, which probably made its appearance from farther east at some time between the first and sixth centuries of our era; there are no exact records. Henri Lhote, author of *Search for the Tassili Frescoes*, believes (from the rock paintings and carvings both in the Tassili and elsewhere and from his vast research into the Sahara's story) that, when in A.D. 19 the Legate Cornelius Balbus extended Roman rule beyond Biskra at the Sahara's edge, he actually crossed the Sahara and reached the Niger by way of the ancient native caravan routes. Somewhere, Pliny, from whose account of Balbus Lhote deduces the Saharan crossing, tells us that the horses of Rome's desert outposts had to carry their own water. By the time the camel assumed the role of desert mount and pack animal, wells and waterholes were too far apart for horses to carry enough liquid slung beneath their bellies to keep them alive. As Pliny the Elder was killed in Pompeii in the eruption of Vesuvius, A.D. 79, we know that the climatic changes of the Sahara can be measured almost by centuries.

If the story of crocodiles appearing in 1926 in underground pools of the Hoggar, the Tassili and the Tibesti mountains of the Central Sahara had not come from such great Saharan authorities as Henri Lhote and Professor E.-F. Gauthier, they might be hard to believe. Imagine your skepticism if someone spoke of alligators in Death Valley! Here again is proof of the Sahara's humid and river-rich past. These small degenerate, six-foot beasts, true crocodiles nevertheless, belong to what the geologists call residual fauna—animals left over from another age. In addition to the crocodiles that may still be lurking in unexplored subterranean pools, there are also in the neighborhood of the Biskra oasis a tropical cobra and a tropical catfish.

Now to go back to the Tassili frescoes of the Algerian Sahara east of the Hoggar Mountains. With the discovery and the remarkable life-size copyings of these prehistoric rock paintings—hundreds and hundreds of them—the oldest Negro art so far known has been revealed to the world. According to Lhote, the skill in portrayal of the human figure was not equaled again until the day of the classical Greeks.

This is the Neolithic age of the Sahara, eight thousand years of Negro life moving from the most primitive of stone tools to the dawn of history. We see these lithe, long-limbed people of the Tassili as mighty hunters with arrows flying from their bows. We see them fishing and herding cattle, dancing and worshipping immense, fantastic gods. We see the beasts they hunted, often life-size or larger—the elephant and the ostrich, the hippopotamus in midstream, antelopes leaping, giraffes fighting. We see them surrealistically depicted, with fantasy running joyously wild. Little horned devils dance across the rocks. The human figure is given thread-like limbs. Heads are triangular or bluntly round, and all but featureless.

The style changes. The black hunters vanish, and with them the surrealism. Black herdsmen take their place with an art as naturalistic as the other was inventive. They show us their great sleek herds of lyre-horned cattle. At the edge of history they leave us, driving their horse-drawn chariots at a flying gallop.

We say they are Negroes, but even in those days there was no such thing as purity of race. The animistic masks characteristic of west Africa, the thread-like figures and dynamic archers matched in the cave paintings of eastern Spain, the flat figures of Egypt, the flying gallop of Mycenae suggest outside influences. There was no time or place in that ancient world when restless peoples were not on the move, mingling their blood and their way of life with enemies and neighbors.

With the Tassili discoveries, the prehistorians were more convinced than ever of two important theories: one, that the Neolithic Sahara was a region of great rivers and tropical fauna, and the other, that the population was predominantly black or Nigritic. The latter theory meant that the ancestors of the native northwest Africans, or Berbers—a white people unable to adapt themselves to humid tropical heat—had been confined to the brisker climate of the bordering Atlas mountains. And as the Sahara lost its tropical fauna and rivers, the Negroes withdrew southward to the streams that were still flowing—the Senegal, the Niger and the watered marshes of Lake Chad. Many of these tough white Berbers, especially the ancestors of the modern Touaregs, pushed forward and evolved a unique way of life in a waste of sand, rock and sparse water holes.

While the Negroes of the Tassili and other regions of the Sahara were recording their activities in paint and line carvings on the faces of caves and rock shelters, the Berbers of the slanting Atlas range were leaving a very different kind of record. In addition to rock carvings, they took the great unhewn rocks themselves and set them up on end as tombs for their dead.

Eli Faure in his *History of Ancient Art* speaks of Athens rising to the peak of history while the moors of Brittany were being covered with their "dull flowers of stone." We know these "dull flowers of stone" best by their Celtic names—menhirs, cromlechs and dolmens. The menhirs, the tall isolated stones, take their name from the Breton, meaning "high stone." A cromlech, from the Welsh "crooked flagstone," is a group of menhirs used to enclose a space as in the great wonder of Stonehenge. In the dolmen— again from the Breton *men*, "stone"; *dol*, "table"—three to five menhirs stand close together to support a table or capstone. What better proof of the bond between Europe and northwest Africa than the fact that menhirs, cromlechs and dolmens march in an unbroken line from Scotland via Brittany, southern France and Spain to the Atlas Mountains!

And what a step toward civilization in this concern for the dead in contrast to the casual tossing of human bones into the refuse heaps of the *escargotières!* Whether it was born of awe and reverence for, or fear and dread of, ancestral spirits, it showed at least an awareness of something beyond mere animal existence.

The exact religious uses of the cromlechs are as mysterious for this region of northwest Africa as they are for Europe; but the dolmens were obviously tombs—tombs with the skeletons arranged in the foetal position, head between drawn-up knees ready to move into the next world in the position in which they had entered the first. There are many of these massive prehistoric tombs between Tangier and Cape Spartel. Follow the old Roman road via M'Zora and El Ksar el Kebir southeast to Fez, and you can still see these relics of Neolithic Age man in all their variety; and in menhir and cromlech the first reachings toward the sky before the shimmering, gold-topped minarets of the Arabs.

Caves, too, both natural and artificial, played their part in the burial of the dead from Tangier to Tunis. In a wild pocket of the Middle Atlas known as the Tadla, where the Berbers held out long and savagely against the French, the early Moroccan explorer Vicomte Charles de Foucauld (later Père de Foucauld, murdered by the Touaregs in the Hoggar Mountains) was the first European to come upon a region of Morocco's ceremonial caves. De Foucauld, disguised as a Jew for safety, found high and inaccessible openings in the rocky walls of a deep ravine. He also found legends peopling the caves with buried treasure and guardian *djinns*.

Other caves, honeycombed with burial chambers and still rich in legends of dragons, djinns and human sacrifices, have been explored. Skeletons have been found; but any treasures or objects that might have been buried with them have long since fallen to the grave robber.

In these legends of sacred caves, and in superstitions of springs and of magic-working trees, we see traces of the pagan beliefs that belong to the age of cromlech and dolmen. In these remote mountain fastnesses and in the tents of the nomads, we see a way of life not too far removed from the days of the *escargotières*.

These then are the beginnings of man in Africa northwest of the Niger. With the desiccation of the Sahara, the black man retreats to his rivers and savannas. We meet him again at the height of his great medieval splendor in civilizations built on salt and gold. The white man of mountain and desert enters the first pages of history under various names—Libyan, Mauri, Numidian, Getuli, Berber. All but the last disappear or take on other meanings. Berber is the name he goes by today. The Berber was the proud indigenous tribesman of northwest Africa at the time of the Arab conquest.

CHAPTER II

ᏛᎾᏤᎾᏤᎾᏤᎾᏤ
ᏛᎾᏤᎾᏤᎾᏤᎾᏤ

PEOPLE OF THE PURPLE DYE AND THE HOUSE OF MASINISSA

(Phoenicians, Carthaginians and Numidian
Princes, 1200 B.C.–A.D. 41)

ᏛᎾᏤᎾᏤᎾᏤᎾᏤ
ᏛᎾᏤᎾᏤᎾᏤᎾᏤ

Northwest Africa, and with it the future Morocco, first enters history with the establishment along its shore of trading posts by the seafaring Phoenicians. They were the people of the purple dye, the traffickers in ivory, apes and peacocks and the gold of Ophir. Their cities were Tyre and Sidon, and their highlands were the cedar-rich mountains of Lebanon. Like their neighbors the Israelites, and like the Arabs who followed them to North Africa fifteen centuries later, the Phoenicians were Semites, deeply and fiercely religious. They were shipbuilders, daring sailors, ardent merchants and makers of objects precious in their day—glass, vessels of brass and gold, finely woven wool, engraved gems and, above all, from the secretions of the spiral shells of *Murex* and *Boccinium*, the richest purple dye known to the ancient world. *

* "The purple of the ancients," according to Julian Huxley in *From an Antique Land*, "was not all purple in the restricted colour-sense in which we use the word today. It ranged through intense red, rose, heliotrope, violet and a deep sea-blue, to almost blackish purple, and, with special treatment, even to green."

12

To the Phoenicians also goes the credit for establishing and spreading a simplified form of the Mediterranean alphabet. For the Babylonians and the Egyptians, writing was a secret and priestly art; for the Phoenicians, it was an everyday necessity for carrying on business in their trading posts. Through the Greeks, this alphabet of theirs, with the addition of vowels and other changes, passed into the Latin and so to us.

The early trading posts were not cities. Some histories refer to them as "factories." This may sound anachronistic until we stop to think that the primary meaning of the word "factory" is a trading station where factors or agents reside and transact business.

Carthage—*Kart-hadsht*, "New-town"—was probably founded about 814 B.C. by immigrants and possibly, as the legend claims, by political refugees from Tyre headed by the King's sister, Dido.

The hill site, whether or not it was measured off by the strips of a bull's hide, was a steep height easily fortified and easily provided with a harbor. El Aouina, the airport of modern Tunis, lies at the foot of it. Because the newcomers were there to trade, not to conquer, they survived despite their small numbers. In the beginning they paid tribute to the native chiefs. Later, as they grew powerful, they exacted tribute, but always with the same clever restraint and standards of fair trade that enabled their small "factories," now reaching the Atlantic, to exist safely among belligerent Berber tribesmen. With this increase in power, Carthage not only soon outshone the older settlement, Utica, fifteen miles to the north near the present Bizerte, but dominated all that was Phoenician along the African shore, and influenced all that was Berber to the fringes of the Sahara.

If we take 814 B.C. as the approximate date of the founding of Carthage, the obvious end of the period would be the year of its destruction, 146 B.C. This was the historic year when Rome burned and massacred the conquered city for seven terrible days; then, still not satisfied, ploughed up the soil and sowed it with salt. For the proud people of the Byrsa hill, for the Barcas, for the priests of Moloch and of Tanit Baal, for the ships in the harbor and the elephants in their stables, it was of course the end; but, for the mass of Berber tribes beyond the vanished walls, life went on at first very much the same. Roman proconsuls ruled at Utica. Like Carthage, they exacted tribute; like Carthage they made the *aguellids* (tribal chiefs or native kings) responsible for collecting it; otherwise they left the Barbarians more or less alone to lead their wild free life until the rebel Jugurtha needed punishment.

They interfered again when they took a conquered king's small son to Rome to adorn Caesar's triumph after the battle of Thapsus, educated him, married him to the daughter of Marc Antony and Cleopatra, and sent him back as Juba II to rule his father's kingdom. No king succeeded

13

Juba's son Ptolemy, strangled in A.D. 41 by his cousin Caligula. The Mauretanias—Caesariensis (western Algeria) and Tingitana (northwest Morocco)—became two imperial provinces.

Because our story concerns the native Berbers rather than their conquerors, the Carthaginians and the Romans, the end of their semi-independence under their own Mauretanian and Numidian kings marks the end of an era before the yoke of colonial rule under the emperors. This Roman period, beginning in A.D. 41 with Claudius who succeeded his murdered nephew Caligula, ends abruptly in 429 with the eruption out of Spain of Genseric (Gaiseric is another spelling) and his Vandals, followed by a hundred years of Vandal rule. When these Northmen were finally crushed, it was not by decrepit Rome but by the eastern capital, Constantinople, and the Emperor Justinian. Toward the end of the seventh century, the Byzantines lost their feeble hold on Africa. Only the city of Ceuta opposite Gibraltar acknowledged their rule. The Goths of Spain, crossing the Straits, held Tangier. By the time the first of the Arabs reached this city toward the end of the seventh century, the Roman and Christian patterns of life, where they had existed at all, had become nothing but a thin veneer.

It might be wondered why the story of Morocco, a country so apparently Arab in its religion, customs and language, should not begin with the coming of the Arabs. The answer is that the story of Morocco is as much the story of its native Berber tribes as it is of the invading Arabs.

The visitor to Morocco who travels from city to city sees very little of the remote mountain villages of Rif and Middle Atlas, or of the oases at the desert's edge. He is unaware that forty per cent of the language of the country is Berber; and, above all, he is ignorant of the age-old antagonism between natives and invaders.

It might also be wondered why in the story of Morocco (in Roman days Mauretania Tingitana) we concern ourselves with the territory that is today Algeria (in Roman days Mauretania Caesarea and Mauretania Sitifiensis, or the Kingdoms of East and West Numidia) and of Tunisia (the Republic of Carthage) instead of confining the story to ancient Mauretania, the land of the Mauri (present Morocco) stretching between the Moulaya River and the Atlantic. To that the answer is that all the recorded history of northwest Africa is too tightly interwoven and too homogeneous to be broken down into separate units until we reach the year A.D. 789 and Morocco's first entity as an independent kingdom. The extraordinary Numidian and Mauretanian kings who fought for and against Rome are as much part of the Berber picture as the Moroccan rulers to come. As for Masinissa, the greatest of these, he easily takes his place at the side of such giants as the famous Moroccan Almoravid, Youssef ben Tachfin, and the Almohad Abd el Moumen.

The problem of the actual origin of these Berbers of northwest

Africa, with whom first the Phoenicians and then the Carthaginians traded so profitably, has given historians a great deal of trouble. They are usually divided roughly into two groups: the Libyan-Berbers between Egypt and the present Tunisia, and the Berbers of the western Mediterranean. Libyan-Berbers first play their part in Egyptian records as far back as the First Dynasty (c. 3300 B.C.). By Carthaginian times they are distinguished from the western group by their mixture of northern Mediterranean and Semitic blood. The western Berbers are a more homogeneous Hamitic (white) people—with dark hair and brown eyes as a rule, though tribes showing red hair and blue eyes like the Algerian Kabyles are puzzling exceptions.

In Roman times, and even more so during the two explosive Arab invasions, there was a constant displacement of eastern Berbers toward the west. Nothing was ever static in that tormented land. The far side of the Moulaya River, with its wild valleys and mountain pastures of the High and Middle Atlas, became a temporary refuge from the great powers of Carthage, Rome and Mecca; and, with the coming of the camel about the time of the Christian era, the desert itself became a refuge for the tough, fierce nomads who learned how to live with its austerity.

During the first centuries of Carthage, when lion and leopard, elephant and stag roamed freely through north African forests and plains, the Berbers combined the life of hunter and herdsman. They hunted the wild beasts for food and protection; they bred splendid horses and pastured great flocks of cattle, sheep and goats. They fought each other as savagely as tomcats, yet practiced a democracy in their agglomerations of straw and stone huts that still sets an example to the smug world of today. Any male not answering the roll call at weekly village meetings to vote on community business was fined. The elders of the village presented the agenda of the day, but needed a unanimous vote to carry it through. Out of the banding together of village or tent community grew the tribe and, out of the uniting of tribes, the confederations. Only at this level was a chief or *aguellid* chosen—a temporary leader during a period of war. Out of those *aguellids* clever enough to perpetuate their power, even make it hereditary, arose the first kings whose names have come down to us at the time of the Second Punic War (218–201 B.C.): Masinissa of Numidia and Syphax of Mauretania.

It is not difficult to imagine what these early Berbers looked like. The old records match what we see today in Morocco in a mountainside village of the Rif or Atlas, for instance, or even at Marrakesh in the great market square of the Djemaa el Fna. The rough homespun cloaks, protection against sun and cold, rain and snow, a sleeved and hooded *djellaba* or long, hooded *burnous* have not changed, nor have the tough goatskin *babouches* for their feet.

15

As a rule the Berbers are the short figures among the taller Arabs. The desert Touaregs are among the exceptions. In contrast to the bird-of-prey look so common to the Arab with his hooked Semitic nose, Berber noses are small, often fine; the faces neatly modeled, rounded rather than long. Dress a Berber in European clothes and he could pass for any weather-beaten Latin peasant north of the Mediterranean. They must have stood out with the same contrast to the swarthy aquiline-nosed Carthaginians, when they came into the city market with their ivory and ostrich plumes and wild beast skins, and gaped at the purple cloaks and gold jewels, the stone temples and the bronze statues to the gods, and the beaked-nosed vessels lined up in the harbor of the Admiralty.

One wonders what they thought of these rich and polished lords of their land, who looked down on them as crude savages and yet appeased their own god Moloch with the sacrifice of their infants. Did every rough tribe from the Gulf of Gabès to the Pillars of Hercules know the details of the grisly ceremony? Did they know how parents laid an infant in the outstretched arms of the brazen bull-headed monster, controlling all sobs and cries as it rolled down into the fire inside?

For three hundred years, the Carthaginians had been planting their trading posts along the North African coast before any of their navigators left a written record. There is no exact date for Hanno's *Periplus*. Perhaps it is about 470 B.C. Moreover, the account is second hand, coming to us from a Greek translation carved on the walls of the temple of Melkarth. And yet to historians it is of enormous interest. For centuries they have been speculating, arguing and disagreeing about the location of the most southern point on the west African coast that Hanno really reached. Did he get beyond the southern border of modern Morocco? Some think not. But he speaks of crocodiles and hippopotamuses, and neither crocodiles nor hippopotamuses are seen on the banks of the rivers Dra or Nun. Were the creatures he thought to be "hairy" men and women, which therefore he described as *gorillas* (the word for them in the Punic language), truly gorillas in *our* sense of the word? As no gorillas have ever been found north of the Cameroons, they were probably baboons, chimpanzees or primitive human beings.

According to the Playfair-Brown *Bibliography of Morocco* quoted by Budgett Meakin, *gorilla* is the only Punic word in general use that has come down to us; and, also, according to the same source, Sir Richard Burton believed that Hanno passed both Cape Verde and Cape Palmas and reached the Bight of Benin, only five degrees above the equator. All historians agree that he founded a colony near the present sister cities of Rabat and Salé adding it to earlier Phoenician settlements such as the present Tangier, Asilah and Casablanca. They also agree that he could easily have seen herds of elephants on the banks of a river identified as the Tensift, reaching the Atlantic coast west of Marrakesh. The elephants were still there five hundred years later, in Pliny's day.

After this nugget of recorded history, Mauretania, land of the Moors, drops out of sight until it reappears two hundred and fifty years later, during the second war between Carthage and Rome. We do know, however, that as Carthage enlarged her territory beyond her triple city walls there were fierce wars with both Numidians and Moors. We know, too, that she sent her senators to her various trading posts to bargain with native chiefs for mercenary troops. The fame of Berber or Numidian cavalry as mercenaries has come down in history from Carthaginian and Roman days to the late colonial conquests of France and Spain.

Neither Carthage's early wars with Greece nor her first war with Rome are really vital to the story of Morocco. The First Punic War was fought for the possession of Sicily. Rome came out of it not only victorious but, thanks to her invention of the crow's bill or grappling hook, the supreme power of the Inland Sea. If this were primarily the story of Carthage, our chief interest in the Second Punic War would be in following the magnificent Hannibal and his elephants through the Italian triumphs, the African defeats and the final exile and suicide. And if it were the story of Rome we should consider the noble Scipio Africanus the Elder, scholar and general, his annihilation of Barca power in Spain, his alliance and friendship with the Numidian King Masinissa, the invasion of Africa from Italy with his self-created army, and the final crushing of Hannibal at Zama with Masinissa's cavalry on his right wing. But, because this is the story of the Berbers, our main interest lies in the personality and role of Masinissa, King of the Massyli, or Eastern Numidia.

Masinissa, like many other rich young native princes, was educated at Carthage. The luxury of city life, the refinements of Latin, Greek and music, of which he was particularly fond, had no softening or deteriorating effect on the tough Berber fibre of his character. He only added these new interests to his passion for huge wild dogs, fiery horses and the freedom of his country. He was born about 238 B.C., and was therefore close to twenty in 218 B.C. at the beginning of the Second Punic War. When he died in 148 B.C. at the age of ninety, he had within four years produced the last of his fifty-four sons, and also the downfall of his enemy Carthage.

The Second Punic War began, it will be remembered, when the Carthaginian power in Spain represented by the Barca family defied the Roman command to keep south of the Ebro River and respect the city of Saguntum as an ally of Rome. While Hannibal was ripping through Italy, a smaller Carthaginian force with Masinissa and his cavalry—before his feud with Carthage—as ally defeated the Roman army sent to cut off supplies in Spain.

A second Berber ally of Carthage was Masinissa's enemy Syphax, King of West Numidia. When Carthage, breaking a former promise, gave Sophonisba, the beautiful and gifted niece of Hannibal, to Syphax in marriage, instead of to Masinissa, the furious prince switched his allegiance and invaluable cavalry to the side of Rome. Near Utica he helped Scipio Africanus destroy the enemy's combined forces and take Syphax prisoner. At the final curtain of Zama, his cavalry fighting on Scipio's right wing sealed the victory over Hannibal and Carthage.

Rome was not wholly generous in her rewarding of Masinissa. To be sure, she made him king of all Numidia, his own as well as the western lands of Syphax, and much of Morocco. Instead, however, of giving him his beloved Sophonisba as queen, Rome demanded the Carthaginian princess as an enemy prisoner. To save the latter the disgrace of ornamenting Scipio's Roman triumph, Masinissa himself, after a brief and tragic marriage, provided his bride with a cup of poison.

The reader familiar with French classical drama will remember that the historical tragedy *Sophonisba* by Jean de Mairet inaugurated the form perfected by Corneille. For his plot, de Mairet turned to Carthage and the broken romance of the young Numidian king and the niece of Hannibal. It was the perfect material for subordinating passion to honor in the grandiose style of the classical dramatists.

Masinissa now had a capital, the city of Cirta (the present Constantine in eastern Algeria), one of the dramatic, natural rocky citadels of the world, high above the protecting gorge of the River Rummel. There he regaled his guests off services of gold and silver to the accompaniment of music from the Greek island of Delos. To improve on his own Carthaginian education, he sent his sons to Greece for theirs.

To the east, Masinissa's boundary was the Carthaginian Republic or modern Tunisia; to the west, the Moulaya River—or roughly modern Morocco; to the south, the land of the desert robbers known to the Ancient World as the Getuli, ancestors of the modern Touaregs. The tribes that he held together in two great loose confederations—his own and the former subjects of Syphax—were the semi-nomadic or sedentary hunters and herdsmen of the high plateaus, mountains and fertile coastal strip. In his great ambition he saw them molded into an empire as powerful as Carthage, and with a Berber-ruled Carthage its capital. His is the first name that comes down to us to hold out for an Africa for the Africans. And yet, as he appraised his primitive land through eyes educated by both Rome and Carthage, he saw how little it resembled the desirable settled farmlands. To create a kingdom capable of furnishing stable and reliable taxes, he would have to create grain fields, olive orchards, and permanent communities.

With his dream clearly defined, Masinissa bent his iron will to changing both the way of life of his people and the face of their land. Little by little, forests, brushwood, and asphodel fields gave way to grainfields and orchards. Like the Romans who had translated and benefited by the famous agricultural treatise of the Carthaginian Magon, Masinissa also learned from its teachings, put his people behind iron ploughshares, and tied them to the threshing floor. Villages, market towns and small cities sprang up as the cultivation of the soil held the former nomads captive. In addition to his unmatched, free wheeling cavalry, he developed not only an army of infantry along Roman lines, but also a small navy. He became, as he had planned, a monarch to be reckoned with, safe from his friend and ally, Rome, only as long as the strength of Carthage exceeded his own. To his own Africans he became a god, with temples erected in his honor.

In the treaty that ended the Second Punic War, one of the stipulations forbade Carthage to engage in either offensive or defensive warfare without the permission of Rome. For fifty-two years Masinissa took advantage of this. Whenever he clawed at her territory and she struck back, he promptly notified Rome that she had violated her agreement. When Carthage complained of his attacks and begged for help, Rome looked the other way. Carthaginian post-war prosperity had grown much too fast to please her conqueror. Finally in 153 B.C. Rome sent the sanctimonious Cato the Elder to Africa to report on the situation. Everyone knows how he returned with figs fresh from Carthaginian gardens, to prove to the Senate the dangerous nearness of the old enemy, as he began to hammer his parrot phrase of "Carthago delenda est." His psychological attack served its purpose. The year of his death, 149 B.C., marked the beginning of the Third (and last) Punic War. In the next year Masinissa died, at ninety still the great Berber chief, the supreme *aguellid*, the agile rider of barebacked barbs. Two years later, Scipio Africanus the Younger, adopted great grandson of Hannibal's victor, ordered and directed his country's ungallant annihilation of a conquered enemy.

With Carthage reduced to ashes and her ploughed soil strewn with salt and curses, and Masinissa dead, Rome made Utica capital of her "Province of Africa," and soon began to feed her people with its grain. To forestall future danger, Scipio quickly divided the administration of Masinissa's empire among three of his sons, giving the government of the capital to the eldest, Micipsa. With the death of Micipsa's two brothers, both power and land soon reverted to him. Though we have no date for Micipsa's birth, we can assume that the eldest son of a prolific ninety-year-old father would not, on reaching the throne, have the necessary youthful vigor to defy Roman power recklessly, especially after having witnessed the vicious blotting out of Carthage. Under his peaceful and quasi-independent rule, cities grew, foreign merchants were made welcome, and the grain export increased. His Greek education had given him a preference for organization and philosphy over campaigning and war. The first thirty years of Rome in Africa rolled smoothly along until Micipsa's death.

Micipsa must have known that no good would come from letting his nephew Jugurtha (son by a concubine of his brother Mastanabal) share the kingdom with his own two sons. Public opinion, however, forced him to legitimize this hotheaded young grandson of Masinissa and include him as an heir. Jugurtha had served on the military staff of Scipio the Younger in Spain. There, handsome, fiery and intelligent, he had become the idol of the young Roman officers. At home, among Numidians, both young and old, he was worshipped as a future leader like his grandfather—a god-prince who might some day with their help throw the Romans out of Africa.

In the eyes of many of his followers, he began his rule well by killing one of his cousins and sending the other in terrified flight to Rome, thereby restoring the unity of the empire that had been redivided at Masinissa's death by the cautious governor, Scipio.

Jugurtha defied Rome at a time when the fine old virtues of the Republic had given way to materialism, corruption and dishonor. Clever and cynical himself, he met his opponents on their own grounds. As long as there were consuls, senators and generals to be bought or blackmailed, he made fools of all who were sent to punish his rebellion. So sure was he of the power of his bribes, he even appeared in Rome to answer charges against him. On leaving, he flung back over his shoulder his famous remark: "Rome is a city for sale and condemned to perish, if she can find a buyer."

For nine years things went Jugurtha's way. In 109 B.C., however, Rome elected as a consul a soldier of the old incorruptible stamp. Against Metellus and his army, the rebel's purse was as useless as it would have been against Scipio the Elder or Tiberius Gracchus.

In land west of the Moulaya River (modern Morocco) the tribes had united under an *aguellid* by the name of Bocchus. With this Mauretanian king, Morocco steps into recorded history, though not, unfortunately, with the credit one could wish her. Bocchus was Jugurtha's father-in-law and helped in his struggle against Metellus and again when Metellus was replaced by S. Cornelius Sulla of future fame. For four years Jugurtha, aided by Bocchus, kept Roman armies chasing back and forth between Cirta and the Moulaya, in an effort to run him to earth. When the end finally came it was due to no honest warfare on the part of the Romans but to the sly diplomacy of Sulla and the treachery of Bocchus. Bocchus, secretly won over by bribes and persuasion to the side of Rome, delivered Jugurtha by ambush to the enemy. On the second and last journey of the Numidian king to Rome in 104 B.C., all the past bravado, riches, and cunning were of no avail. He was first starved, then strangled. In Africa Bocchus was acclaimed friend and ally of Rome and the Roman people, and given the western half of Jugurtha's kingdom.

Too cynical and tricky to arouse the admiration of posterity, Jugurtha was nevertheless one of the early African Berbers who struggled fiercely for his country's freedom, when it was threatened by an imperialist conqueror whose moral standards at the time were anything but an example to semi-barbarous people.

The treacherous Bocchus became a docile vassal of Rome, spending his later years collecting lions, leopards, elephants, wild boars and stags for the Roman arena. In 93 B.C., Sulla delighted the populace of Rome with a display of a hundred lions. They may well have been part of Bocchus's contribution. When the Moorish *aguellid* died in 70 B.C., he left his kingdom to two sons, Bocchus II and Bogud. East Numidia was held, nominally, of course, by Masinissa's great grandsons.

For the bewildered Mauretanian and Numidian rulers to pick the winning side in Rome's domestic wars, now spilling over into Africa, would have been beyond human ability: Marius versus Sulla; Sulla versus Pompey the Great; Caesar versus the Pompeys, both Gnaeus and Sextus; Octavian versus Antony.

In Julius Caesar's great African victory over the followers of the dead Pompey at Thapsus in southern Tunisia in 46 B.C., he had the two Mauretanian kings, Bocchus and Bogud, on his side; against him, on the side of the Pompeians, was Juba I, great-grandson of Masinissa. After Caesar's victory, Juba committed suicide. Six years later, Bogud made the mistake of siding with Antony against Octavian—thereby losing not only his share of Mauretania, to his brother Bocchus, but his life as well.

When Juba I committed suicide after Thapsus, his four-year-old son was taken to Rome to swell the prizes of Caesar's triumph. When Octavian defeated Antony and Cleopatra at Actium in 31 B.C., the three children of their torrid love affair—a girl (Cleopatra Selene) and twin boys—enhanced the excitement of the triumph of the future emperor. Thanks to Octavian and his sister, all four of these little exiled African orphans received as fine an education as if they had belonged to the Julian house itself. When Juba and Cleopatra were of a proper age, Octavian married them to each other and returned them to Africa as King and Queen, first of Numidia, then of Mauretania.

Juba had absorbed education like a sponge. His new capital with the Phoenician name Iol, changed by him to Caesarea, is the present Cherchell, sixty miles west of Algiers and three hundred miles from the present Moroccan border. In Cherchell's modern museum, much of Juba's treasure is on display. Part of it may be seen in the Museum of Algiers and in the Louvre. The wealth of Greek statues—both originals and fine replicas —columns, masks and mosaics, shows that Juba II was not only a lover of Greek art but a collector with a trained eye for the best of past and present in Athens and Rome. Today the ruins bring back before our eyes this ancient city associated with Juba. Though it lies beneath the modern Arab town, all the finds of the archaeologists point to its former grandeur,

The Arch of the Basilica in the ruins of Volubilis. / *O. N. M. T.*

to its well deserved title of an "oasis of Greek culture." To the east and west are the Thermes (the Baths) rich with fragments of marble and onyx. The theatre provided most of the Museum statues. Circus and amphitheatre complete the Roman pattern.

Though not proved, it is thought probable that Juba enjoyed a second capital in the central Moroccan city of Volubilis. There the ruins stand out splendidly free of any superimposed Arab settlement. But, as the principal monuments visible today date from the time of the Severi, Septimius and especially Caracalla, two centuries later, Volubilis belongs to the story of Roman rule under the Middle Empire.

When Rome thought of the rebel Jugurtha, she must have been immensely relieved to watch her puppet king Juba not only contentedly collecting statues but so absorbed in the world of books, so fertile in producing them, that he became known as the African Varro—the equivalent of saying that he was the equal of the most learned scholar and prolific writer of his day. Nothing but fragments have come down to us; but we know that Pliny in his *Natural History* drew freely on this Berber king's knowledge of botany and zoology. We know that Juba visited the Canary Islands off the Moroccan coast to investigate the dye-producing lichen, *Rucella tinctoria*. In the Moroccan port of Mogador, he established works producing purple dye. As to whether it was the purple of the deep sea *Murex trunculus* or of *Rucella tinctoria* there is no record. We do know, however, that his son Ptolemy wore to Rome a purple cloak of Moroccan dye, so magnificent that it aroused the jealousy of his cousin, the Emperor Caligula, to such an extent that he had the African king strangled.

Juba's Queen Cleopatra, who by all the laws of heredity should have been a woman as enchanting as her by-name, Selene or Moon, has no record of beauty either in the coins that were struck of her head or in the accounts of those who had known her.

And no charm seems to have been attributed to her son Ptolemy, the last of the line. On the contrary, history pictures him as a dissolute playboy, disgusting his simple Berber subjects with the oriental splendor, extravagance and depravity of his court. Yet when the news of his murder reached Mauretania it fired a rebellion that produced serious trouble for Caligula's successor, Claudius.

With Ptolemy, who succeeded his father in A.D. 20 and died in A.D. 42, we reach the last of Masinissa's known descendants, the last of the colorful pagan Berber princes. There was to be nothing like them again under the alien rule of imperial procurators, Vandal kings and Byzantine exarchs. When north African Berbers again seized the center of the stage, they were spreading Islam from the southern Sahara to the Pyrenees, one thousand years after Ptolemy's murder.

In the great coin collections of the world, the House of Masinissa comes strikingly alive. There is a small cabinet in the farthest right hand corner of the Room of Coins and Medals in the Bibliothèque Nationale in Paris, devoted to Rome's African colonies and the Numidian Princes. The names that at first meeting seemed as dim and legendary as gods, when spelled out in bronze or gold encircling the proud profiles become as real as the galloping horses of the reverse. Masinissa and his enemy Syphax, Jugurtha with a laurel crown, Bogud, Juba II with Cleopatra Selene, and Cleopatra Selene with bull and moon. Ptolemy is characteristically one of the few coins struck in gold. Portraits—all of them more than twelve hundred years before the great days of portraits in paint— link us to the first great personalities of northwestern Africa.

CHAPTER III

ROMANS, VANDALS AND BYZANTINES
(A.D. 41–A.D. 684)

To extinguish the Mauretanian revolution that flared up after Ptolemy's murder, Claudius sent out several generals during his reign, among them Suetonius Paulinus. Paulinus has the distinction of being the first Roman military leader to cross the Atlas. In a grueling, ten-day march, he chased the rebels out of the cedar forests, across volcanic uplands to the black sands and parched rocks edging the river Guir, before turning back to the comparative safety and civilization of Volubilis. At home in Rome his success aroused delight and celebration. The next assignment of this same Suetonius Paulinus was an expedition to Britain, where his victory over Queen Boadicea led to her suicide by poison in A.D. 62.

The fact that the Roman army reached the Guir and the neighborhood of the great desert caravan-head known as the Tafilalet does not mean that Roman rule extended at any time to the date-bearing slopes of the desert. On the contrary. Romanized Morocco (Mauretania Tingitana) was a surprisingly small triangle, with Tangier as the apex, the coast line to Rabat-Salé as the hypotenuse, and Volubilis the angle south of Tangier (Tingis) and east of Rabat. Not only was it too far away from the African capital, the newly built Roman Carthage, to control easily but also too many rugged mountains, too many hostile tribes lay between the region of grainfields and olive orchards to the east to make the effort of intensive colonization worth while. Instead of serving as part of the new Roman bread basket, Mauretania Tingitana played the part of buffer zone for Spain against the African hinterland tribes of mountain and desert.

Three things from this savage country brought delight to the Romans: animals for their arenas, purple dye for the robes of their emperors, and citron-wood for their tables. Of Tingitana, Gibbon says: ". . . the more southern parts were seldom explored except by the agents who searched the forests for ivory and the citron-wood and the shores of the ocean for the purple shellfish," adding in- a disapproving footnote: "The foolish fashion of this citron-wood prevailed at Rome among the men as much as the taste for pearls among the women. A round board or table four or five feet in diameter sold for the price of an estate (*latifundia taxatione*), eight, ten, or twelve thousand pounds sterling."

This historic citron-wood or arbor vitae (*Callistris quadrivalis* or *Thuya articulata*) was, of course, not a true citrus but a conifer, useful not only for its beautiful and enduring wood but also for its gum or resin.

Wherever native Tingitanian chiefs, either within this small Tangier–Rabat-Salé–Volubilis triangle or on its outskirts, proved themselves sufficiently Romanized and loyal to rule their own territory, they were given the title of prince (sometimes king) and, as insignia, ivory staffs and red cloaks. For two hundred and fifty years, the Pax Romana lay over the Province as it lay over most of the Empire. It could hardly have been much more of a true peace than the so-called peace of our own day, as we read of sporadic revolts and rebellions. Moreover, we know the wild independent spirit of the Berbers and can easily imagine their resentment of the imperious and orderly Romans. On their western side of the Moulaya River, no Romanized Masinissa and his descendants had forced them to abandon their hunting and their herding to raise grain. But the records are dim. Only Volubilis with its ruins and its inscriptions represents a clear picture of ancient Rome in Morocco.

The great cities of Roman Africa, magnificent in their temples, theatres, basilicas and triumphal arches, are of course, in Algeria—Timgad and Lambaesis guarding the gates of the desert; and in Tunisia—Djemila, Dougga, Thuburbo Majus and Bulla Regia. And yet no one who has come upon Volubilis, especially in the spring, with its white ruins framed in blue skies and silvery green olive orchards, and with the flower fields of lupines and poppies creeping in between the fallen marble, will ever forget it.

26

Broken columns lead to Caracalla's Arch. / *Kostoma-roff, Service des Antiquités, Rabat*

As one approaches from the little river valley winding under what was once the southern wall, the solid Triumphal Arch, the tall ends of the basilica and a grove of columns—a few complete with capitals, the majority fragmented to a multitude of different lengths—stand out against the blue sky. On the tallest column a stork is usually nesting.

When the first relic of Roman days that one encounters within the ruins turns out to be an oil press, and one finds that it was one of at least fifty others, one can imagine that the landscape of olive orchards has not changed in almost two thousand years. That it was a flourishing city in Juba's reign is proved by the temples and altars under the dated Roman monuments. Inscriptions in Punic prove that it went back long before Juba's day. Relics of the Stone Age indicate a settlement of pre-historic times.

Because of the irregularity of the terrain, Volubilis is not one of those checkerboard Roman cities born of the military camp with the two main streets—the *decumanus maximus* and the *cardo maximus* cutting squarely across each other at the forum. Instead, there is a pleasant wind-ing and jogging of lanes and paved roads leading into the heart of the city. There, in the large, irregular, stone-paved space of the forum, the citizens gathered to conduct the business and pursue the pleasures of the day, to listen to speeches under the rostrum to the left, to visit the adjoin-ing baths, to seek the shade of the two-storied basilica, to pray and sacri-fice to Jupiter, Juno and Minerva in their temples, and to admire the massive triumphal arch built in honor of the Emperor Caracalla. Here the rich Romans of the villas, the House of the Nymphs, the House of Orpheus, the House of the Nereids—with garden courts, fluted columns, mosaic floors and splendid statues of bronze and marble—rubbed shoulders with humble artisans from oil mills, potteries, brickyards and bakeshops, and with the foreign merchants, Jewish, Syrian and Greek, who shared their city. And always, of course, the soldiers, not from the famous Third Legion of Augustus, which was at Lambaesis, but auxiliary corps and loyal natives, and the red-cloaked chiefs whose descendants in our own day served Spain and France. From the length of the walls and the density of the foundations, it is estimated that the inhabitants could have numbered between fifteen and twenty thousand.

In the forum opposite the rostrum, there is an interesting and important inscription identifying the lost statue that once stood above it. The name is that of a Berber, with the Romanized name of Marcus Valerius Severus, chief of Volubilis at the time of the Emperor Claudius. During the rebellion following Ptolemy's murder, this Severus appears to have given help of such value to Rome that he won for Volubilis not only the rights of citizenship but the right of valid marriages with native women.

Inside the triangle of Tangier, Salé and Volubilis, many traces of other Roman settlements exist. A road ran from Tangier to Volubilis; another near the coast from Tangier to Salé. The frontier or *limes* with its fortified system of trenches, earthworks and protecting network of roads, so often well defined in parts of Algeria from aerial studies, is non-existent west of the Moulaya.

The first European to report on the ruins of Volubilis was an Englishman named Windus, who visited Morocco in 1721 at the time of the sadistic Alaouite Emperor, Moulay Ismail. His sketches and descriptions do not match what we see today. In the first place, Ismail in his mania for building a Moroccan Versailles robbed Volubilis of much of its carved marble and dressed stone; and in the second place the great earthquake of 1775, felt from Scotland to Asia Minor, bringing half of Lisbon down in rubble, destroyed ceilings, snapped columns and dislodged huge blocks from basilica, temple, porticoes and villas.

The first important digging was done by German prisoners of war in 1915, at the order of General Lyautey. Since then the excavation has been in the hands of experts, and the most valuable finds deposited in the museums of Rabat.

It is not surprising that the most outstanding monuments should belong to the reign of the Severi. Septimius Severus (193–211), founder of the house, was the first African Emperor of Rome. He was born in Leptis Magna in the present Libya, and his native language was Punic. Both he and his infamous son—Caracalla of the famous Roman Baths— and the upright Alexander Severus favored Africa especially with their exuberant scattering of triumphal arches, temples, theatres and other monuments. Moreover, during the strong rules of Septimius and Alexander, the people of Volubilis were still at peace. The rich could still pave the

28

floors of their villas with mosaic legends of gods and half-gods, collect such treasures as the famous Bronze Dog of Volubilis, the youthful Aesculapius and his lively serpent, the enchanting head of a "Sleeping Cupid," marble busts of Juba II, and Cato of Utica.

As the second half of the third century developed into a period of decline and confusion for Rome, with the Senate powerless as the Legions chose emperors not for their virtue but for their exorbitant excess of pay and loot, and as the Barbarians pushed against the frontiers from the Rhine to the Euphrates, boundaries shrank and with them the riches and good life of outposts as distant as Volubilis.

Drastic changes for Tingitana took place under Diocletian (285–305); other parts of the Empire seemed more important to this Dalmatian Emperor than westernmost Africa. Not only was the defense of Volubilis abandoned, and the frontier moved north to within fifty miles of Tangier, but the rule was transferred to the Diocese of Spain and its Spanish Vicar.* In military affairs the province was still governed from the African side of the Straits.

With the withdrawal of Rome from Volubilis, a murky enveloping cloudbank rolls in over the mountains and valleys west of the Moulaya, while east of that great dividing river, in a blaze of light, not even the Eternal City itself unrolls a more exciting drama of life. Who in all the early history of Christianity stands out more clearly than those African bishops and martyrs—St. Cyprian, St. Perpetua, and St. Felicitas—as well as the unnumbered nameless ones brave enough to die rather than acknowledge the Emperor as their God and the countless nameless ones weak enough to conceal their faith only to meet persecution from their self-righteous fellow Christians?

Carthage was the stage. In the Roman amphitheatre the young Perpetua and her companions were thrown to the wild beasts. In Carthage, St. Cyprian, before the loss of his head, rewarded the executioner with a piece of gold. St. Augustine presided over synods and condemned heresies. As Rome grew weaker, the Church grew stronger. Rome was paying the penalty for exploiting the land and the people. The masses had long been tied to the soil of the rich landowners, especially as the Empire shrank and slave labor diminished. For the poor and the downtrodden, a religion that offered the Brotherhood of Man, a loving God, and eternal bliss was worth dying for, just as five centuries later another religion out of the East, stressing the equality of man, a just and merciful God and the delights of Paradise, won them over with even more lasting success.

* Both "diocese" and "vicar" are, of course, used in the early civil sense without ecclesiastical connotation. Diocletian, along with Decius and Gallienus, was among the most determined persecutors of Christians. No official toleration of this new religion took place until after Diocletian's death, under his successor, Constantine the Great.

29

For the educated and subtle-minded—the Tertullians, the Cyprians, the Augustines—Christianity stood on its own merits, binding them as tightly to its new concepts as it bound the most miserable slave. To the cynical Romans, whose pantheon by now was of little meaning, this new religion with its triad of queer Gods would have been of no more interest than any of the myriad pagan beliefs of their various Barbarian subjects, if it had not been a threat to their political and military authority. Christians directed their obedience to their threefold God instead of to the Emperor and the officers of his Army. Military Rome could not control her provinces with increasing numbers of conscientious objectors. For this reason, the emperors from the temperate Trajan to the ruthless Galerius persecuted the followers of Christ in the hope of wiping them off the face of the Empire.

To what extent Christianity spread westward across the Moulaya from the land of saints and martyrs, it is hard to estimate. Unsubdued and un-Romanized tribes held the "Taza Corridor," a natural mountain pass from the Algerian border into central Morocco. Intercourse with Rome came from across the Straits in Spain via the roads running south from Tangier. In Volubilis, the spades of archaeologists have turned up a few lamp fragments with Christian signs. From A.D. 298, there are two records of martyrdoms: one of a soldier, the other of a clerk. As the soldiery of Tangier was recruited from among the natives, the former was probably a Berber. In 345 an epitaph marks the death of the virgin and "handmaiden of Christ, Aurelia Sabina, *ancilla Cresti.*" A few other Christian tombs of this same period indicate that Christianity was not uncommon near the edges of the Atlantic; but neither was it widespread nor lasting.

Though Constantine the Great established Christianity as the state religion, this did not mean peace for the Christians of North Africa. Of the many schisms and heresies that bred hatred and vicious persecution in a religion based on brotherly love, only two concern us here: the Donatism of the Fourth century, and the Vandal Arianism of the Fifth.

Donatism, not because of the fine points of theology, but because of the effect on future history from the Pillars of Hercules to the Gulf of Gabès, split the country on the subject of punishment for those who had refused to suffer for their faith during the persecutions. To Donatists, priesthood and life within the church were forever forfeited by: the *lapsi,* who weakly avoided martyrdom by refusing to confess their faith; the *libellacati,* who refused to hand over the Sacred Books; and the *sacrificati,* who made sacrifices to Roman gods. For the orthodox Catholics backed by St. Augustine, forgiveness for these sinners was the approved policy. The righteous Donatists opposed this forgiveness. In the course of the bitter and cruel persecutions against them, the Donatists drew into their camp a powerful group of natives rebelling against forced labor on the land of the rich Roman proprietors. These rebels went by the name of *circumcelliones*—those who "prowled around (*circum*) granges (*cellae*)" with the purpose of looting them.

Rage against established authority, seething in the spirits of Donatists, *circumcelliones* and freedom-loving Berber tribes, explains to a great extent the lightning-like ten-year conquest of the Arian Vandals from Tangier to Carthage.

Few phases of history are more confusing than the early migration of Germanic tribes in their erratic southward wanderings across the face of Europe. Those that are of special import in the story of Morocco are the Goths from Sweden and the Vandals from the Baltic. There is no need to follow them as they milled around on the shores of the Black Sea, in the basin of the Danube and in northern Italy where they met as enemies. Stilicho was the Vandal general of the Emperor Honorius against Alaric I, king of the West or Visigoths. In 405 Honorius had his Vandal general murdered. While the exultant Visigoths sacked Rome in 410, the Vandals moved out of their reach into Spain. Or so they thought. But soon the Visigoths were also on the move again, first into Aquitania, then over the Pyrenees into Spain, as self-appointed defenders of the Roman Empire.

In twenty years of energetic activity in Andalusia or Vandalusia (Roman Baetica at the time of their arrival) the restless Vandals had been preparing themselves to strike the flimsy power of Rome on its least protected flank. It is not certain how much the arrival of the Visigoths at their heels affected this crossing into Africa over twenty miles of water. And it is also not certain how much an invitation from Count Bonifacius, the Roman governor at Carthage, temporarily at odds with the court at Ravenna, affected Vandal plans. Moving southward on their powerful black horses was a century-old habit with these blond, blue-eyed Northmen. Moreover, all the world knew that no country was richer in the good things of life than Roman Africa.

At the time of the invasion, the Vandal king was Genseric, brother of his predecessor. Of his 80,000 subjects, his fighting force probably numbered not more than 15,000. The present Tarifa was his point of departure; his landing place, in the neighborhood of Tangier, the year 429. There he was welcomed as a liberator by the many victims of political, economic and ecclesiastical oppression.

To quote Gibbon's account: ". . . the Moors, regardless of any future consequence, embraced the alliance of the enemies of Rome; and a crowd of naked savages rushed from the woods and valleys of Mt. Atlas to satiate their revenge on the polished tyrants who had injuriously expelled them from the native sovereignty of their land."

Gibbon lived before the French conquest of Algeria in 1847, and before Baron William MacGuckin de Slane's translation of the great Arab historian-philosopher Ibn Khaldoun's *Histoire des Berbères*. Subsequent modern authorities on the Berbers—Stéphane Gsell and E.-F. Gauthier, for example—stress the extraordinary stability of their customs over the centuries. One might, therefore, visualize these Moroccan Moors as covered with much the same coarse homespun cloaks that one would see today in the remote "woods and valleys of Mt. Atlas."

The immense, conglomerate, looting horde was soon on its way to attack the east Algerian city of Bône—Hippo Regius in Roman days, and famous as the episcopal see of the great St. Augustine. In the course of the siege, 430–431, St. Augustine died at the age of seventy-six. Perhaps his death came as a blessing. To have lived longer and to have seen his country forced into Vandal Arianism, a heresy as abhorrent to him as the many others, Donatism, Manichaeism and Palagianism, which he had fought against with such passion, would have been a tragic end to such a saintly life.

Arianism differed from the Catholic creed declared orthodox at the First Council of Constantinople, convoked by its enemy, Theodosius the Great, in 381. Arianism propounded the belief that before the general creation God had created and begotten a son, the first creature, but neither eternal nor equal with the Father. To the Catholics, this heresy of a Son less of a God than the Father smacked of paganism; but to the rude Germanic tribes, who had absorbed it from their Bishop Ulfilas, it was a simpler and more comprehensible dogma than the mystical conception of a threefold Godhead.

Genseric, a Vandal King born in 390, was close to forty when he began his conquest of northwest Africa. He was lame; he was a bastard; he was as astute, as devious, as cunning as any Levantine steeped in wiliness since the days of the Greeks bearing gifts, or Dido and her bull's hide. His rule spanned the period of Rome's downfall, and he made the most of every chink in her armor. In 476, the year before Genseric died at the age of eighty-seven, the German Odoacer, on his conquest of Ravenna, deposed the last Roman emperor of the West, Romulus Augustulus. For Imperial Rome, the year 476 was as final as 1453 for Imperial Constantinople. Genseric, as master of the western Mediterranean, presented Odoacer with all of Sicily exclusive of Marsala, subject, of course, to tribute.

In six years after his arrival in Africa, Genseric had signed a treaty with Rome in return for agreeing not to attack Carthage. He and his Vandals were made free to settle in the three Mauretanias and part of Numidia. Like other Barbarian allies, they were raised to the status of *"foederati"* and required to pay a light tribute. Four years later, in 439, Genseric attacked and took Carthage. There he closed the Catholic churches, made a forced collection of all the gold and jewels, instigated a drive against sodomy, and began to build a fleet. Rome trembled. Alaric's sack of the city in 410 was still a living nightmare. When the Vandal King attacked Sicily instead, Rome threw him another bone in the form of a second treaty. This time she gave him territory outright as far west as Bône, and an offer of the Emperor Valentinian's daughter Eudocia as wife for his son Hunneric.

For the next thirteen years Genseric, fortunately for Rome which was fighting off Attila the Hun in the North, gave himself up to organizing his new kingdom. In the territory that he ruled by right of treaty, he seized and distributed the land to his own family and people. In the territory beyond, he collected tribute but left the management to its former magistrates. With the exception of those of Carthage, he destroyed all city walls.

In 455, the licentious young emperor Valentinian III, for whom first his mother, then his general Aetius had ruled, murdered the general. Six months later he himself was murdered at the instigation of the senator Marjorian, whose wife he had raped. Valentinian died without sons. Some authorities claim that his widow, Eudoxia, called on Genseric to come to Rome to save her from her enemies. Others call this a legend. At any rate, Genseric came. For two weeks his Vandals pillaged and looted. Jewels, gold, precious metals and captives for ransom were the chief objects of plunder.

As a favor to Pope Leo I, Genseric refrained from burning the city. In comparison to what Rome did to Carthage, the evil was mild;

Caravan crossing a sand area. / *O. N. M. T.*

yet our word "vandalism" has its origin in Genseric's sack of Rome. If there had been a Carthaginian Procopius to chronicle Rome's reduction of a great city to ploughed fields, the word "romanism" might also have come down to us as a synonym for wanton destruction.

Year by year Genseric's power increased. With the islands from Sicily to the Balearics added to his empire, he lashed out at the coasts of Greece, Egypt and Asia Minor. No one could punish him. Not Rome alone. Not Rome and Constantinople together. He was one of the greatest of the Barbarians not "at" but "inside" the "Gates of Rome."

For Genseric, the closing of Catholic churches was a matter of expedience. In molding his kingdom he could not afford to tolerate an intelligent and powerful faction like the bishops, who could conspire with Rome against him. At the height of his power he reopened the churches. His son Hunneric, on the other hand, was both an Arian fanatic and a sadistic tyrant. Under him, African Catholics underwent their cruelest torture. Burning, flagellations, the cutting out of tongues are all on record. Where there were martyrdoms there were also miracles. In the Algerian town of Tipaza, Hunneric ordered all Catholics to become Arians. Though those who refused had their tongues and right hands cut off, it is said that they continued to talk as normally as before.

The Vandal century ended abruptly in 533. In 527 the ambitious Justinian, afterward the Great, became emperor of Byzantium. In his eventful reign he codified Roman law, built the great church of Hagia Sophia, regained Africa and Italy from Vandals and Goths for the Roman Empire, and ushered in the Dark Ages by closing the Schools of Athens. The mean and envious Justinian did none of the great things himself. The jurist Tribonian directed the codification of the laws; Count Belisarius and the eunuch Narses restored his empire; and Anthemius of Tralles and Isodorus of Miletus built the Hagia Sophia. But it was Justinian himself who extinguished the bright flames of learning kindled in the Academy of the Platonists, the Lycaeum of the Peripatetics, the Portico of the Stoics and the Garden of the Epicureans, where the Fathers of Philosophy had once walked and talked.

When Count Belisarius landed his Byzantine army in Africa, the Vandal king was Gelimer, great-grandson of Genseric. A hundred years of decadent African life had softened the tough wanderers of invasion days. Nor were they any longer in Berber eyes the welcome liberators. Their aloof life as conquerors, their strict edict against inter-marriage, their hateful Arianism had lost them their early friends and supporters. Count Belisarius had little trouble in defeating their forces, seizing Carthage, and starving out the fugitive Gelimer from his last stronghold in a mountain village.

In Justinian's reorganization of Roman Africa, the present Morocco scarcely enters the picture. Only the Roman city on the Straits, *Ad Septem Fratres* (changed by the Arabs to Ceuta), was made an important observation post under a governor or exarch of the Emperor. The rest of his efforts in wiping out all trace of Vandal rule, restoring churches to Catholic orthodoxy, and rebuilding the razed walls and defenses of towns and cities were confined to lands east of the Moulaya. When he died in 565, hatred of all that he stood for—his own greedy policy of exploitation, his brutal governors, exorbitant taxes and Arian persecution—bred native wars and rebellions, chaos and turmoil. Swelling under his feeble and equally unpalatable successors, the inborn Berber fury against all invaders gathered momentum and striking power until not only the great orderly empire of the Antonines and the Severi but also its ephemeral revival under the genius of Count Belisarius faded into the past.

Of the Romanization that left its mark on northwest Africa during the eight and a half centuries between the destruction of old Carthage by Rome and of new Carthage by the Arabs, only two aspects lived on feebly into medieval Islamic times—the Latin language and Christianity.

During the eleventh century, the Papal Court at Rome seems to have carried on its correspondence with the African clergy in Latin. During the same century, coins with Latin inscriptions were struck in Moslem Kairouan; and, according to the twelfth century Arab geographer Idrisi, the people of Tunisian Gafsa (the town of the Capsian artefacts) spoke Latin in his day. Scarce as these records are, they indicate that in many spots the languages of Rome and of Mecca lived side by side for three or four centuries after the Arab Conquest.

And Christianity? Here again throughout these undocumented years we draw our conclusions from shadowy clues and the records of the Papal Court. In 1053, during the rule of Pope Leo I, there were still five bishops; twenty years later, only two. In the large cities growing up under the first Arab and Berber dynasties, Christian communities, flourishing in the beginning, begin to drift out of the picture. How many among their members became converts to Islam, how many fled to remote refuges in mountain and desert, there is no knowing. In the 1880's de Foucauld, crossing the High Atlas into the Saharan edge, noted with interest how many settlements went by the name of Ksar Nsara (Nazarene or Christian Village).

In comparing the meager Roman legacy of Morocco in architecture and art, in letters both legal and ecclesiastical, with the glorious riches of the eastern Provinces, Coissac de Chavrebière says sadly: *"La Tingitane, à côté de cette floraison, apparaît sterile. Mais qui sait tout ce que la terre a devoré et ce que les Arabes ont détruit?"* ("In comparison to this splendor Tingitana appears sterile. But who can tell what the earth has devoured and what the Arabs have destroyed?")

CHAPTER IV

ALLAH IL AKBAR
(Mohammed and the Arab Conquest, 622–740)

For the Berber tribes of Morocco, the momentous year of A.D. 622 passed as uneventfully as any other. They fertilized their dates, thrashed their grain, harvested their olives, led their sheep and goats to the high mountain pastures in summer and brought them down again before the winter snows. They knew as little about an Arabian camel driver named Mohammed and his flight from Mecca to Medina as the Britons in A.D. 32 under the Romans knew about the crucifixion of a man named Jesus. They were unaware of the bomb this Mohammed had hurled at the pagan worshippers of Mecca's *Kaaba*, the shrine enclosing the "Black Stone" and 360 idols. They had never even heard of Mecca.

Quickly and in all directions the shock waves of Islam raced out of Arabia through the ancient world, in the form of war-crazed zealots. In the west, the Atlantic, instead of absorbing them, only deflected them across the Straits to the north.

Because this great surge of Islam was to affect the futures of all Moroccan Berbers, whose lives had been left virtually unchanged by the

Carthaginians, Romans, Vandals, and Christians, it is important to trace that surge back to its source and watch the incredible advance before its first century had even ended.

To the devout Moslem, every event of their Prophet's full and dramatic life is almost as familiar as if he had been born in his own century. When a great religious leader, as a young man managing the business affairs of a rich widow fifteen years older, marries her, it catches the imagination of people of all times and faiths. Familiar, too, are the revelations that came to him in the cave from Allah through the Angel Gabriel and became the Koran—the permission for multiple wives, the prohibition of alcohol, the promise of Paradise with sensual delights—and the magic personality that won companions to spread the faith.

But for even a superficial understanding of the Prophet and his laws, so important today to both the Arabs and Berbers of Morocco, more details are necessary.

Mohammed belonged to the important Koreish merchant family of Mecca. He was born after his father's death—probably in the year A.D. 570. After being briefly suckled by a household slave, he was put out to nurse for two years with a Bedouin woman in the black tents of the adjoining desert. When he was six, his mother died and he passed into the guardianship of a devoted grandfather who died two years later. His next guardian was an uncle. For a time during his adolescence, the boy shared the life of Bedouin shepherds; but at seventeen he entered his family's world of caravan and trade.

Khadidja, the rich widow, became his wife when he was twenty-five. He had been managing her business affairs on caravan trips to Damascus and Aleppo. Of their six children, Fatima is the one name that has come down to us. The Prophet's only direct descendants are traced through Fatima and her husband, Ali. (Among these descendants of Ali we find the first and also the last and present Moroccan dynasty, the Alaouites.)

Until Mohammed was forty he lived the normal life of a prosperous Meccan merchant and citizen. At the age of forty he began to have visions, revelations from Allah (God), commands to spread the holy words. These first appeared in dreams, then during waking hours or during trances in the Cave of Mt. Hira outside Mecca.

For seven years he resisted these revelations and commands, and the idea of becoming the Prophet or Messenger of God. After that, he submitted to the voices in the cave, and shared his secret with Khadidja and his companions. With this sharing, Islam (the word means "submission") came into being.

In his native city Mecca he soon had many followers. There were also enemies plotting to murder him. By a secret flight of two hundred miles to the north, he reached the loyal city of Medina. This historic move, in our year 622, became known as the *Hegira* ("Flight"). It marks the Moslem year 1, an era moving forward by lunar instead of our longer solar months.

After successful battles at Medina, there came a return to Mecca, more battles and, finally, control of the city and the whole Arabian peninsula. In Mecca the 360 idols of the Kaaba shrine were wrathfully destroyed. Only the "Black Stone" itself was kept as a Holy of Holies for the people and pilgrims of Islam. Furthermore, as a safeguard against future idolatry, he forbade the reproduction of living forms, human, animal, or plant, thereby limiting Moslem art to arabesque and decorative script.

At the age of sixty-three Mohammed died and was buried in Medina. With Mecca, the city of his tomb became one of the two holy cities of Arabia.

After Khadidja's death in 620 Mohammed had, after the custom of the country, taken other wives—for his followers he limited the number to four.

During his last illness, Mohammed had appointed his closest friend and father-in-law, Abou Bekr, to substitute for him as *imam* or leader of prayer in the mosque. After his death, his followers appointed Abou Bekr as his successor or *caliph*—literally "he who is left behind." Despite his extraordinary insight into human nature, Mohammed, like most of the world's great rulers, had not been sufficiently omniscient to plan a peaceful and permanent succession of power.

At Abou Bekr's death, three more of the Prophet's contemporaries, companions and relatives followed as caliphs. The second caliph, Omar, conquering warrior and organizer, and the third, Othman, husband of two of Mohammed's daughters, were both assassinated by their enemies. The fourth caliph, and last of Mohammed's intimates, was his son-in-law Ali. Like the other two, Ali also died a violent death.

These four men, Abou Bekr, Omar, Othman and Ali, all intimate associates of the Prophet, became known as the four "Orthodox Caliphs." Until Othman's murder in 656, the capital was the holy city of Medina. Ali ruled from Kufa near Baghdad in Irak. The third caliph, Othman, had belonged to an important Koreish family of Mecca by the name of Ommaya. To avenge his murder, a cousin, the governor of Damascus, defeated Ali and seized the rule by force. Thirteen Ommayid caliphs governed the Moslem world from Damascus during the next ninety years.

For another two hundred and fifty years, their descendants ruled the Spanish Moslem world, with Cordova its capital of light and learning.

In A.D. 750 the Damascus Ommayids were defeated, massacred, and all but annihilated by their successors, the Abbasids. This family, though descendants of an uncle of the Prophet, through marriage and association had become more Persian than Arab. The fifth of these Abbasid caliphs was Haroun er Rashid of Arabian Nights fame. We shall find him playing a sinister part in the founding of the first Moroccan dynasty. The Abbasid capital was, for the most part, the great new city of Baghdad with its splendor and its learning. Toward the end of their period, the Baghdad caliphs degenerated into puppets in the hands of the Seljuk Turks. In 1258, Hulagu Khan, grandson of Ghengiz and brother of Kublai, destroyed Baghdad and killed the last of the miserable Abbasid caliphs.

To follow the story of Morocco and Moorish Spain, it is necessary to understand the bloody struggles and shifting power from dynasty to dynasty, and city to city: from Ommayids to Abbasids, Aghlabites to Fatimites; Medina to Damascus, to Baghdad to Cordova to Cairo.

Ten years after Mohammed's death in 632, most of what we know as the Middle East acknowledged Allah and his Prophet. In 732, exactly 100 years after his death, the French under Charles Martel "the Hammer" were stemming the Moslem advance on Paris by the battle of Poitiers.

For many, of course, conversion was a matter of expediency. The cynical Gibbon was right when he said that "many millions of Africans and Asiatics must have been allured rather than constrained to declare their belief in one God and the apostle of God since by repetition of a sentence and the loss of a foreskin, the subject or the slave, the captive or the criminal, arose in a moment the free and equal companion of the victorious Moslems." For many millions, however, the religion itself bit deep into hearts and souls. Today the Moslem population of black and white Africa is close to 90 million; of Asia, 330 million.

The man who learned to talk in a Bedouin camp, who had spent part of his childhood among city people of importance, who had gone back to the Bedouins again to guard their sheep before plunging into the world of war and trade and caravans; the man who had married eleven wives, the traveler who had observed two religions (Jewish and Christian), both acclaiming one God, was well prepared to mould his divine messages into a religion that would fit his people, both nomads and town dwellers, as practically as their loose and flowing robes.

He tore down and he constructed. He tore down idolatry; he shattered the flesh pots of wine and silk garments, of unused muscles and unbroken sleep. He thundered against cruelty to slaves, to the poor, to women and to concubines. He constructed a way of life upheld by five strong pillars.

"*La illah illallah ou Muhammed raisul Allah* . . . There is no god but Allah and Mohammed is the Prophet of Allah." This is pillar number one, the profession of faith.

Number two is prayer: prayer after ablutions with water and, if not water, sand; prayer five times a day—at dawn and at noon, at midafternoon and at sunset, and again at dusk. Kneeling is not enough. The body, turned toward Mecca, bends forward until outstretched palms and forehead touch the ground.

Zaka, "almsgiving," to the amount of a tenth of one's salable property is pillar number three. There was nothing new about this. Tithes were as old as Ur and Akkad. This, however, was not an exaction by the tax collector, whip in hand, but a religious offering freely and piously given.

Most curious to non-Moslems is number four, the Fast of Ramadan. Beside it, the hardships of Christian Lent are negligible. During one lunar month a year, moving through the seasons, the Moslem must abstain from dawn to sunset from food, drink and all carnal pleasures—an abstention hard enough at best, and a particularly cruel and difficult test of character for Saharan caravans when Ramadan falls in midsummer.

Fifth and last is the *hadj,* the pilgrimage to Mecca that every Moslem must perform once, if humanly possible, during his lifetime. How cleverly Mohammed knitted his followers of all times and places together by this ingathering at the holy Kaaba beyond the Red Sea! How he widened their horizons by pulling them out of their provincial towns, their mountain villages, their desert oases and by showing them the great world!

He made travelers out of them centuries before our northern ancestors started out on their Crusades. No wonder that that fabulous fourteenth century traveler Ibn Batuta called his book *A Gift to Those Interested in the Curiosities of Cities and the Marvels along the Way.* And in Ibn Batuta's same century we see the great Kankan Mousa from the black Mali Kingdom of the Niger making the Mecca pilgrimage with 500 slaves, each bearing a staff of gold weighing six pounds, upsetting the gold market on his way through Cairo with his camel loads of gold dust, and luring back from Mecca a Spanish architect to build his mosques in Timbuctu.

These then were the five main pillars: declaration of faith, almsgiving, prayer, fasting, and pilgrimage. There were many others. Chief among them was the *jihad,* or "Holy War," against the Unbelievers, the Unfaithful, the Infidels, the Christian Dogs. Let us follow the *jihad* as it sweeps across Africa into Morocco.

By 642 the conquering Moslems had Egypt behind them. For the soft and dying African provinces of the Byzantine Empire, decimated by Genseric and his Vandals, propped up hopefully, but in vain, by Justinian, these mounted hordes out of the East were a terrifying spectacle. The lusty old Numidian princes—Masinissa, Juba I or Jugurtha—might have given them a fight; but effete Byzantine nobles and bishops and quarreling native tribes were no match for them.

Visualize them whirring out of the East like locusts, tall and fierce

The Great Mosque of Kairouan, begun in 670.

in the saddles of their tough desert-bred horses, bearded, hawk-nosed, weather-beaten, woolen cloaks flying behind them, swords glittering in their hands, voices hoarse from shouting *"Allah il Akbar."* They sent the tribes of Libya fleeing westward. They stormed the ports of the Tunisian coast. Their confidence knew no bounds. Their Allah was all powerful and they shared his power.

When Okba ben Nafi chose the site for the future city of Kairouan, he planted his spear into the ground and addressed the serpents and wild beasts of the region. "In the name of the Prophet," he ordered them, "retire with your children from this place." For forty years not a single serpent dared show itself. St. Patrick had to drive the snakes out of Ireland; Okba, who also became a saint, had only to order them to leave.

Okba founded Kairouan in 670. Eleven years later, to reward his conquests, he was given supreme command of Africa by the Damascus Caliph. In Moroccan history his is the first Arab name. He is the pride of the early Arab historians as he moves westward through their pages. According to some he reaches the shores of the Atlantic where he plunges his horse into the waves shouting: "O Allah, if this ocean did not stop me, I would go on into countries more distant still fighting for thy religion and killing those who did not believe in thy existence and those who adored other gods than thee!" From there he marched south to the land of the Blacks. But according to others his great fighting went no

41

farther west than the mountains of the Hodna north of Biskra where he was killed in battle in 683.

In Sidi Okba, the oasis village named after him on the edge of the desert that he did or did not cross, the mosque contains his tomb, and in all Africa the oldest Arabic inscription, as simple as its beautiful upright Cufic lettering: "This is the tomb of Okba son of Nafi. May Allah have mercy upon him."

Okba's successor was a warrior named Mousa ben Nocier, imbued with the same zeal to push Islam to the ocean's edge. When he returned to his capital Kairouan in 702 after a successful western campaign, he left Tangier garrisoned with 10,000 Arabs and Egyptians under Tarik ibn Zaid en Nafsi, a Berber converted to Islam.

Thirty-five miles from Tarik's garrison in Tangier a man known to history and legend as Count Julian ruled in 710 in what is now the Moroccan town of Ceuta. In the confused and contradictory accounts of the ancient chroniclers he appears at the coming of the Arabs in several roles: Visigoth governor of Ceuta, Byzantine exarch and petty king of Berber origin. It is not even known for certainty whether Ceuta was independent or under Byzantine or Visigothic control. Much is hazy in the beginnings of the momentous Arab conquest of Spain in which this Count Julian played a part.

Visigothic kings of remote Scandinavian ancestry had been ruling Spain for almost 200 years. At first they paid token allegiance to the Eastern Empire. Toward the end of the seventh century, however, they had dislodged the Imperial officers from their last strongholds along the southern coast. On their arrival in Spain they were Arians. Like the Vandals they believed that Christ, though the noblest of all created beings, was not the eternal son of God or of the same substance as the Father. In 587 they became Catholics. Corruption and anarchy in the second half of the seventh century made them an easy prey for foreign invaders.

In 708 (or 709) King Witiza died leaving the throne to his son Agila. In an ensuing revolution Roderick, Duke of Baetica, was elected king by the nobles. Defeated by Roderick, Agila fled to Africa. In Ceuta he and his brothers turned to their father's old friend Count Julian for Moslem help in restoring him to the throne.

Legend has Julian eager to sweep Tarik's forces into Spain in revenge for the rape of a daughter by the usurping king. Historians, however, believe Julian merely acted as intermediary between Agila and the Moslem leaders in gratitude for past help from Witiza and with an eye to his own profit. One thing is certain. He himself accompanied Tarik on the invasion.

With him from his garrison, Tarik took 300 Arabs and 7,000 Berbers. On the first attempt, he had reconnoitered only as far as Algeciras across the Straits, leaving his name at the nearby Rock of Gibraltar,

Djebel el Tarik, Mountain of Tarik. On the second crossing, he sailed up the coast toward Cadiz in the Christian ships, and burned them behind him. A few miles inland on Lake Janda, the battle took place—a battle lasting three long and bloody days, in which Roderick, last king of Visigothic Spain, was defeated.

One account has Roderick slain in the battle; another postpones his death to a battle two years later. Legend has him "slowly devoured by snakes for his sins."

If Agila and his brothers expected the Moslem army to return to Africa after their victory they might as well have expected rivers to reverse their course. The Battle of Lake Janda took place in July, 711. By the end of the year, Tarik, conquering as he went, had marched north to Alcala. Under one of his commanders, Cordova had fallen into Moslem hands.

The spectacular success of a subordinate commander was too much for *his* commander, the African governor, Mousa ben Nocier, in Kairouan. By 712 Mousa, too, was on Spanish soil to share (or rather seize) the booty and the glory. From Cadiz to the present Portuguese border, his path was as easy as Tarik's, while in eastern Andalusia his son, Abd el Aziz, conquered the Christian armies. By 713 the sovereignty of the caliph of Damascus was proclaimed at Toledo.

At this point the greedy and ambitious Mousa made two bad mistakes. His first was a proposal to make Spain a springboard for conquests of the entire northern littoral as far as Constantinople. From the point of view of a distant caliph, success from such an undertaking would give a mere governor far too much power. Mousa and Tarik were summoned back to Damascus. The second mistake was to have Tarik arrested, claim credit for all the booty of the invasion, and, with a flourish, present it from himself to the Caliph. Part of the loot, however, was a famous treasure known as "Solomon's Table," made of gold and emeralds. By stealthily removing a leg before it was loaded onto Mousa's camels, and by presenting it to the Caliph later, the crafty Tarik was able to prove that it was he, not Mousa, who had won the first and best of the loot.

Mousa's career came to an abrupt end and for the next two years his son Abd el Aziz, married to King Roderick's widow, governed Moslem Spain. The first real resistance to the successors of Mousa and his son came, not in Spain itself, but on the French side of the Pyrenees.

In 721 the Moslem advance was checked at Toulouse by the Duke of Aquitaine. The Moslems were not used to defeat. On the other hand, the Christians of Aquitaine felt more horror of the invading infidels than the Christians of Spain had felt. After eleven years of being held in check, the Moslems suddenly swarmed northward again in a great *jihad*. Alone, the Duke of Aquitaine was no match for them. Fortunately for him, the Franks to the north were frightened too. The Moslems were only 60 miles from the holy city of Tours, and Tours was only 160 miles from Paris, capital of the Merovingian kings.

Charles Martel, grandfather of Charlemagne, joined forces with Duke Otho of Aquitaine. The two armies, Christian and Moslem, met between Poitiers and Tours. The year 732 is one of the great dates of history. The Christian world still shudders to think of its fate if Charles the Hammer had not sent the polygamous, infidel Moslems fleeing back to the foothills of the Pyrenees.

In the meantime, trouble for the Arabs in both Spain and Morocco helped the northern Christians in establishing their victory. A bitter feud between Arabs and Berbers was coming to a crisis in both countries. In Spain it arose from the arrogant attitude of the Arab minority to the men of the Berber army and their descendants, who had made the conquest possible. The 300 Arabs of the invasion, for all their leadership, education and religious zeal, could never have overpowered Spain without the 7,000 fighting Berber tribesmen. And yet the Arabs took the best of the loot and the best of the land. Their greedy eyes immediately realized the charm and fertility of Andalusia. In their opinion, the arid plains of La Mancha and Estremadura, and the rugged northern mountains of Leon and Galicia were quite good enough for these crude but useful fighting animals, their Berber allies, who could be kept in their place by clever masters.

In Morocco the trouble started with taxation. In 739 a new governor in Tangier doubled the previous tribute from the subdued Berber tribes. This outrage was enough to unite them in one of their rare flashes of alliance. An army of 7,000 stormed Tangier and slew the governor. Following this success, they marched south and killed the governor of the Sous—the region south of the High Atlas.

Like so many north African Berbers they had become avid converts to an Eastern sect of Islam known as Kharedjism. Kharedjite heretics were as violent in their scorn of the Caliph Ali as the Shiites or Alids were ardent in their worship of their "Lion of God." They were also fierce opponents of the inheritance of the caliphate through a female, even if that female was Fatima, the Prophet's daughter.

The Arabic word *kharedjites* means those who depart. The Kharedjites had deserted Ali during a battle against the Ommayids, in which his action had displeased them. Over the years they came to despise both Ommayids and Abbasids and their worldly courts. They were democrats, and they were puritans. They considered the caliphate not a dynastic but an elective office; an honor for the best man who could fill it, irrespective of blood ties with the House of the Prophet, or of political importance. They were puritans in that they stood for austerity, simplicity and piety— sometimes for the extremes of fanaticism. Ibn Rostem, *imam*, or religious

44

leader, of their most famous domain, never during his lifetime touched with his bare hands anything so sordid as money. Kharedjites today in the Algerian oases of the Mzab look on the use not only of alcohol but also of tobacco and coffee as forbidden vice.

It is easy to see how the Berbers, toughened by the harsh poverty of their existence, took to this ascetic way of life. With their *djemaas,* or village councils, they had been used to democratic self-rule centuries before the Arabs appeared in their land. In Kharedjism they found a rallying point for opposition against the supercilious, domineering and oppressive invading Arabs who threatened their freedom. As Charles-André Julien points out, it cloaked the same class struggle, the same xenophobia that flourished under the name of Donatism at the time of the conquering Romans.

The caliph whom the 7,000 Berbers of assorted tribes had chosen to lead their rebellion was Maisura, originally a poor and ignorant water carrier. Until the Arabs summoned outside help from their own caliph in Damascus, the Berbers triumphed. Even with an army of 30,000 recruited in panic from Syria and Egypt, plus an African garrison of 7,000, the Arabs fled. But the Syrian cavalry of their army escaped to Ceuta. There, with added reinforcements, they at last defeated the Berbers.

In the meanwhile, the bitter Berbers of Spain had grouped themselves into three columns—one to march on Toledo, one on Cordova, and the third to reach Algeciras to seize the fleet, cross to Ceuta and kill off the Syrians. Instead, the Spanish Arabs managed to get the Syrians across to their side, and with their help conquered the three Berber columns.

A short peace in the form of ruthless subjection of the rebels was finally achieved in both countries; but beneath the surface the hatred boiled on, not only for the next years but for the next centuries. The French made the most of it in 1953, when they tried to fasten on the Berbers the blame for the dethronement and exile of Mohammed V.

CHAPTER V

ᑲᑲᑲᑲᑲᑲᑲᑲᑲ

A FUGITIVE FROM THE CALIPH
OF BAGHDAD
(The Idrisids, 789–987)

ᑲᑲᑲᑲᑲᑲᑲᑲᑲ

Vice and corruption, beauty and the arts were the characteristics of the Damascus caliphate. Life at the Ommayid court was a far cry from the austere virtues of Mohammed, who forbade wine, sodomy and silk. There the silk that took its name from the city fell in glittering folds from the shoulders of the Syrian nobles, even of the cooks in the Caliph's palace. Wine flowed in the fountains of the inner courts. The gold of Byzantine mosaics shimmered on the walls of the Great Mosque. Painted dancing boys dressed as girls joined the poets, musicians, buffoons and acrobats of the pleasure-mad court.

The caliphs, who as "Commanders of the Faithful" should have set the example of virtue and piety, often outraged their subjects by vice and impiety. The worst offender, Walid II, though a poet of distinction, insisted that his dogs accompany him on the Pilgrimage to Mecca, while his pet monkey, Abu Kais, dressed like Walid himself in cloth of gold, shared both the drunken revels and the hangovers of his master. No wonder their enemies were waiting to destroy them!

If the sanction of polygamy had the advantage of swelling the ranks of the Faithful, it brought with it the disadvantage of multiplying the claimants to any hereditary post, as one sees again and again in the case of sultans whose sons are numbered by the hundreds. In the case of Mohammed, who left no sons, there were innumerable pious relatives itching to overthrow the detested Ommayids.

This was finally accomplished by a descendant of the Prophet's oldest uncle. In 750, the debauched Ommayids were beaten and brutally slaughtered. The new Abbasid caliphate and dynasty took its name from its first ruler, Abul Abbas. Such was the hatred and fear of the Damascus princes that the new rulers made a point of filling the ditches with Ommayid corpses, after having run the victims down like rats to see that none escaped. In spite of all their zeal, they were not so successful as they thought. Abderrahman, a grandson of one of the Ommayid caliphs, slipped through their fingers and secretly made his way across North Africa to Spain. By 755 he was welcomed by the Spanish Moslems still loyal to his house. As Abderrahman I, he founded the Ommayid Dynasty of Cordova, transferring to Moslem Spain the brilliant flowering of the arts, letters and science, *and* much of the vice and corruption, for which Damascus had become famous. In Damascus the Ommayids had lasted less than a century. In Cordova, where the mental virtues outweighed the physical vices, they were the shining civilization in the dark ignorance of Europe for two and a half brilliant centuries.

In 762 the Abbasids of the East laid the foundation for a new capital on the site of the old Babylonian Baghdadu, on the Tigris a few miles from the great Persian capital of Ctesiphon. This is Haroun er Rashid's Baghdad of the *Thousand and One Nights,* the famous "Round City" of concentric walls with palace and mosque at its center; and, of course, the Baghdad of his son, the great astronomer Caliph El Mamoun, with its library, "House of Science," and magnificent observatory.

Though the Abbasids belonged to the house of Mohammed, they had no bitterer enemies than the partisans of the house of his son-in-law Ali, known as Alids or Shiites. Here, through Ali's son Hossein, were the Prophet's only direct descendants. Here was the most valid of all claims to the great office.

At a moment when the Alids considered the Abbasids weak enough to attack, a great battle was fought, in which the Abbasids were victorious and the Alids slaughtered and hunted down as the Ommayids had been before them. This was during the rule of Haroun er Rashid (786–809).

Paralleling the Ommayid defeat shortly before, one prince of the vanquished side again escaped. Like Abderrahman, grandson of the Damascus Ommayid Caliph Hisham, Idris ben Abdullah ben Hassan ben *Ali,* great grandson of the Caliph Ali's son Hassan, accompanied by a faithful companion, fled across Egypt to the wild mountains of the Moghreb.

For Idris and his loyal servant Rashid, the 3,000-mile flight across Africa was at all times through enemy territory. Those who recognized the fugitive as a prince of the House of Ali dared not help or shelter him for fear of Haroun er Rashid's wrath; at the same time they dared not injure him because of the sacred blood that ran in his veins. Only once did help come to him. The well-to-do postmaster of Egypt managed to get gold to him to smooth his way. For this, the postmaster paid with the loss of his head. Where danger seemed greatest, as among the Berber Kharedjites (the sect that had no veneration for Ali), the loving servant Rashid hid his master in a great peasant cloak of coarse brown wool and led him on through untraveled mountain passes, avoiding the broad but hostile east-to-west corridor of the old Romans.

In unfriendly Tangier, the Atlantic ended the westward flight. North of the Straits, the Spanish Ommayids would not have welcomed an Alid prince, who might have become a rival. There was only one direction left —the old Roman road that ran for six days southeast to the ruined Roman city of Volubilis under the walls of a Berber village by the name of Oulili.

Perhaps it was chance, perhaps it was talk they had picked up along the way that led the two fugitives to Oulili and the realm of the Aouraba. Whatever it was, here was the only Berber tribe from the Red Sea to the Atlantic with the courage and desire to welcome a lineal descendant of the Prophet.

On the surface, perhaps for less than half a century, these Kharedjites had been hostile to the Alids. Beneath the thin and recent layer of Islam, however, there were stronger influences. There was Roman blood in their veins from Caracalla's Volubilis garrisons. In their mental heritage there were civilized Roman ideas that had made them susceptible to Byzantine Christianity and now far more receptive to an educated Moslem leader from the East than were those Berbers who had jumped suddenly from paganism to Islam.

"How can we serve him?" the council of the tribe asked eagerly when their chief, Abd el Mejid, revealed the identity of their guest.

"By proclaiming him our *imam*, our ruler and leader of prayers," the chief answered.

How proud these Berbers were to give their new *imam* the title of *Moulay* ("my Lord"), due him because of his noble *cherifian* descent! Within six months after his arrival he became Moulay Idris, their king, winning their love and allegiance by his learning, his courtesy and his military leadership.

No other Berbers—not even the haughty and disdainful Arab invaders under whose arrogance every Berber smarted—had such a nearness to Allah through the blood of his Prophet.

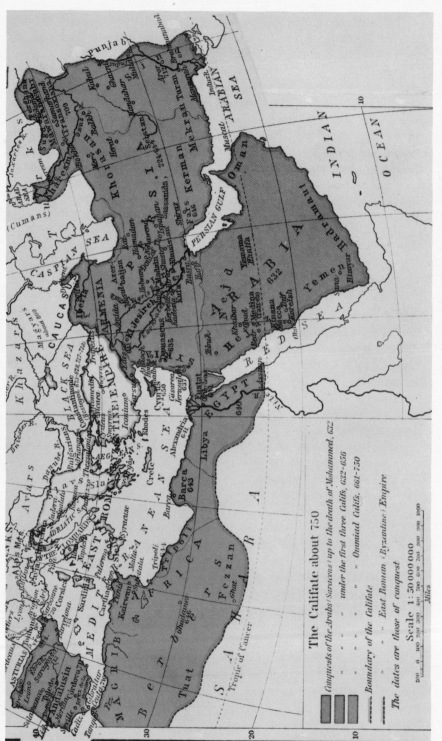

The Califate about 750

Conquests of the Arabs (Saracens) up to the death of Mohammed, 632
"   "   "   under the first three Califs, 632–656
"   "   "   Ommiad Califs, 661–750

Boundary of the Califate

East Roman (Byzantine) Empire

The dates are those of conquest

Scale 1:50000000

200 100 0 100 200 300 400 500 600 700 800 900 1000
Miles

Shepherd's Atlas of Medieval and Modern History, Henry Holt, 1932

For a time and a country where the swiftest transmission of news was by horseback, it was amazing how soon the word of Idris's success traveled back to Baghdad and to the new caliph, Haroun er Rashid.

An independent kingdom in the Moghreb, headed by a hated Alid, was a serious threat to Abbasid rule. Instead of sending an army across the 3,000 miles, the Caliph sent a wily agent impersonating a sympathetic fellow fugitive. The story of how the poisoned drug was administered varies. In a flagon of perfume? In medicine for an earache? Allah alone knows the truth of things. At any rate, in 791, three years after the Aouraba had elected Idris their king, he died a sudden death. On the same day, the stranger from Baghdad left in haste with the undeceived Rashid at his heels. Though the murderer escaped death, he returned to Baghdad leaving by the Moulaya River his right arm, hacked off by Rashid's vengeful sword.

For his Berber subjects (not only the Aouraba but the surrounding tribes that had submitted to his rule and had become the nucleus of a unified Morocco), Idris had become more than a king, a conqueror and a preacher of Islam. He was their beloved saint, more venerated, more adored, even, than the Prophet himself.

They buried him in their midst on the flank of their mountain, and changed the name of their town from Oulili to Moulay Idris. Today, almost twelve centuries after his death, it is still the most sacred city in all Morocco. In May the pilgrims arrive, from Morocco, Algeria and even Egypt. In the honeycomb of flat white houses that climb the steep slope, the shrine with its pointed roof of sea-green tiles beckons them on through orchards of orange and olive trees.

The loyal companion, Rashid, also became a saint with a shrine beside his master's. Often the prayers go first to Rashid—prayers for a son, a harvest, a victory—and then, by his intercession, to the ear of the great saint himself.

If you are a Christian or a Jew, and visit Moulay Idris today, you may join the pilgrims inside the walls by day, but at night (both in May and during all the other months of the year) the gates of this holy city are as tightly closed to you as the gates of Mecca. Unless you have brought a "house of hair" (a tent of woven black goat hair to set up under the olive trees), you must return at sunset to Meknès or Fez for a place to sleep.

Moulay Idris died in 791 without leaving an heir. A favorite Berber concubine named Khamza was, however, well along in pregnancy. At the advice of Rashid the tribal Council waited to discuss the subject of succession. When Khamza's time was up, to everybody's joy, the child born posthumously to their former king was a boy. On the very day of his birth they proclaimed him both *imam* and future king under the regency of the faithful Rashid. If one can believe the old Arab chroniclers this

Idris ben Idris (Idris II) was a genius. At eight he knew by heart not only the Koran but the *sunna*, the traditional wisdom of Islam. At eleven he was proclaimed of age and given the title of king.

Again Baghdad was uneasy and jealous; again a murderer was sent into the distant mountains of Zerhoun. But the Aouraba must have guarded their child king well. This time it was Rashid himself who lost his life to the Caliph's henchman.

Though the unlettered Aouraba chieftains could add nothing to the schooling of their young king's subtle Eastern mind, they could and did train his tough Berber body in the arts of war and horsemanship.

In 806, when Idris must have been still as beardless as a girl, an embassy of five hundred Andalusian nobles crossed the Straits from Spain, bringing magnificent presents and messages of good will from the powerful Caliph Hakim I of Cordova. Both princes held their power and their independence in defiance of the Abbasid East. Both came of families that had fled from its hatred.

"Let us make an alliance against our enemies of Baghdad," Hakim suggested.

Idris agreed with more eagerness and a heartier welcome to the Arab princes than the Aouraba cared for. Idris, the father, with all his learning and princely manners, had fitted into their simple life. Idris, the son, seemed to prefer these rich and worldly kinglets of Spain. First he welcomed Arabs to his court. His next offense was to claim that, for a capital, their Oulili was too difficult a place to fortify, and to explore the countryside for a better site. It is easy to understand that the Aouraba were both hurt and disappointed.

In choosing the site for the future Fez, Idris showed the genius that historians attributed to him. In 808 when he shared the groundbreaking he was barely seventeen. Fez had everything. Like Rome it was a city of hills. From the rising foothills of the Rif to the north and the Middle Atlas to the south, a network of streams brought a luxurious flow of clear sweet water—water to turn gristmills, to wash streets, and to send patio fountains spurting five feet high out of their marble basins. Nearby there were quarries of limestone and gypsum, and beds of fine clay—limestone for the fountains, gypsum for the carved plaster to adorn palaces and great houses, and clay for the potter's wheel. Olive orchards, a legacy of Roman rule, framed the new city. Beyond the olives and the rich garden lands, oaks provided the galls and tan bark that would soon make Moroccan leather famous as far east as Persian Khorasan.

The feuding native tribes (already enjoying the fertility of the countryside), who opposed the Arab intruder, were a mixture of Christians, pagans and fire-worshippers, not at all the kind of polished urbane Moslems Idris envisaged for his new capital. To wipe them out was his first

51

task, one he accomplished quickly and successfully. There were Jews there, too. Far too shrewd to forego their valuable contributions to city life, especially in the form of taxes, Idris made a place for them outside his new walls. Inside the walls, two miniature Arab cities, one from Spain, the other from Tunisia, seemed to have been bodily transplanted to the banks of the River Fez. On the right bank were 2,000 fugitive families from the newly-independent Aghlabite rulers of Kairouan; on the left, 8,000 fugitive families from Cordova, an entire suburb exiled by Hakim. The names still stand today: the *Adoua Kairouiine* and the *Adoua Andalus*, each with its own mosques and its own traditions.

Ten thousand families in Idris's Fez did not mean in terms of numbers what it might today in our own monogamous society with an average of three-and-a-half children each. A family was more like a tribe: the father, the four legal wives, the concubines *ad libitum*, and children like stars in the milky way.

Within a dozen short years, the new capital had become a center of Arab learning and a center of organized trade. Already the tanners had founded the first of the powerful guilds, as famous in medieval Fez as in medieval Europe. Already Idris, pleased and satisfied with his capital, had set out to stave off an advancing horde of heretical Kharedjites and other enemies from the East.

At the city of Tlemcen, a spot to be snarled over like a bone till the Turks made it part of Algeria, he beat back the enemy, established his own residence for three years, and finished building the mosque his father had started. Then, with his ambitions far from satisfied, he turned west again to gather more tribes and territory into his growing empire. But success in this enterprise was not written for him in the Book of Fate. In 828 in his own city of Fez, death came suddenly. Idris II lived only thirty-eight years, but the city he founded grew and flourished. It became the political and, above all, the cultural hub of the Moghreb, "the Boston of the Middle East," to quote the anthropologist Carleton Coon.

For the people of Fez, the shrine of Moulay Idris *el Azhar* ("the Resplendent") in the heart of their city is as venerated as that of his father Idris *el Akbar* ("the Elder") on the far side of the mountains of the Zerhoun. He, too, is a saint who draws to his tomb pilgrims seeking his *baraka* or blessing by kissing or merely touching the carved wood of the entrance, and leaving their offerings for the support of his noble descendants.

The non-Moslem visitor is, of course, forbidden entrance to this holy shrine; but for him the charm of the surrounding *souks* is the essence of Fez. Because it is not possible for him to enter either the shrine or the great Kairouiine Mosque-University with its marble forest of 270 columns and its library of 1,600 ancient manuscripts, or meet the scholars, he will have no share in the spiritual and intellectual atmosphere of this ancient city. What will delight him will be the appeal to his physical senses. The medieval *medersas* or dormitories of the Kairouiine students are enchantments of Moorish architecture. And here in the heart of the souks are the color and the spice-laden air that to our Western world mean "the gorgeous East."

Garlanding the cubicles of the shoemakers' souks, the gold-stamped slippers in their clear fruit colors—lemon yellow, pomegranate red, almond green, plum purple, and orange—hang like a swarm of butterflies. Candles gay with gilt and paint for the Saint's shrine brighten another streetlet. Handwoven silks, Berber rugs from the High and Middle Atlas, "Oriental" rugs from the looms of Rabat, glazed pottery in lustrous shades of seagreen and peacock blue, with designs borrowed from Sassanid Persia, lead one on and on through the colorful maze, fragrant with spices and with the chips and curls of cedar and lemon wood falling from the cabinet makers' lathes and mallets.

Down by the river the chorus of the coppersmiths hammering their great trays rings out, and on the river bank itself the hides fresh from the dye vats hang out to dry like sails in the sunset. As scene after scene gives, as the Arabs say "pleasure to the eyes," the unbelieving visitor may be moved to join the Faithful in an offering of coins at the Zaouia's entrance, in grateful tribute to the second Idris.

The concubine Khamza, Idris's Berber mother, seems to have been the dominating figure in bringing up her eight grandsons, and endowing them each at their father's death with a fair share of the kingdom. Not one of the eight approached his father or grandfather in stature. For the one hundred years that they and their descendants held Fez, cousin snatching from cousin whenever possible, only two names stand out—both Yahya—the first and the fourth. Yahya I loved his grandfather's capital. Under his long rule, the public baths, the caravanserais and the suburbs multiplied. Soon the walls of this orderly and beautiful new city could scarcely hold the newcomers who wanted to call themselves *Fassi,* citizens of Fez.

A hundred years had passed since Idris II founded Fez when Yahya IV swept down out of his Rif mountains to seize the city from his cousin, Yahya III. For sixteen years this strong and learned ruler brought peace to Fez and the kingdom. From all the mosques of the Moghreb the *khotba* or "Friday prayer" was recited in his name—ultimate proof of a Moslem ruler's acceptance.

Strong as he was, the fourth Yahya was nevertheless no match for a great new dynasty, the Fatimites, rising to power in Kairouan and sending out its army to annex the Moghreb. Outnumbering the sixteen years of success, twenty-three years of tragic captivity ended his life. In and out of prisons, the once proud Idrisid king begged for his bread in Asilah, Meknès, and Mahdia, where in 917 Allah (at last taking mercy on his misery) closed his eyes in welcome death.

The new dynasty that brought trouble again from the East had developed under the name of Fatimites as a branch of the old Alid or Shiite party. Ever since the early disputes over the Caliphate, it had existed as a secret sect in Syria, sending out missionary agents to the Moslem world in an effort to undermine the orthodox Sunnite doctrine. The Fatimites promised their converts a *Mahdi* or "Deliverer," who would bring peace, happiness and order to the world.

After great military success and conversion of tribes in Central Algeria through an agent, the Mahdi himself, Obeid Allah, arrived in Ifrikiya, the present Tunisia, in 904. By 909 he had seized the capital, Kairouan, from its Aghlabite *emirs* ("princes"). This ended the independent rule of that early dynasty. In the West the Aghlabites are best known as the first Moslem invaders of Sicily, and the founders of the brilliant Moorish civilization, still existent in spirit if not in control during the Norman era of the eleventh century.

With the help of powerful tribes belonging to the great Berber Sanhadja confederation, Obeid Allah soon gained control of the Moghreb as far as the Atlantic. In 917 his forces had defeated Yahya IV, last lineal descendant of Idris I. In 925 under the leadership of the Meknassa tribe, they had taken Fez.

In this struggle, the enemies of the invading Fatimites were the Zenata tribes and their supporters, the Ommayid Caliphs of Cordova. This was a complicated and confusing struggle on multiple levels. Individuals became insignificant in comparison to tribal rivalries. The Sanhadja (of the North) were the *sedentary* enemies of the *nomad* Zenatas. The Sanhadja-Fatimite combination was composed of Shiites; the Zenata were heretical Kharedjites. Aligned with the Zenata, as against the Fatimites, were the Sunnite Ommayids of Cordova. On the latter level, it was a struggle between Fatimites and Ommayids for temporal power. To simplify (if possible) this intricate and bloody conflict of almost a century, one might say that one side represented an alliance of politically ambitious Fatimite rulers, supported by native sedentary, northern Sanhadja Berbers, claiming the Caliphate in the belief that it should go to a direct descendant of Ali and Fatima; and the other was an alliance of politically ambitious rulers of Moorish Spain of the Sunnite doctrine, supported by native nomadic Zenata Berbers, holding the Kharedjite conviction that the Caliphate was an elective and not a hereditary office. Between the sedentary Sanhadja and the nomadic Zenata the deep-seated enmity centered, of course, around grazing lands and pasturage.

It had better be admitted from the start that the subject of Moroccan tribes is a bewildering maze for both the historian and his reader. In the small country of Morocco, which is about the size of California, the French counted 600 tribes in their zone; after independence, 100 more were added to the count from the small Spanish zone. The great confederations like the Sanhadja and the Zenata break up into fractions and tribes—some nomadic, some sedentary. The Sanhadja, for instance, have sedentary branches in the north, but a nomadic branch, the "Men of the Veil," who roam the Atlantic coast of the Sahara as far south as the mouth of the Senegal and as far inland as Timbuctu on the Niger. These tribes are baffling in their origins and in their movements during what E.-F. Gauthier calls "The Obscure Centuries of the Moghreb."

With the loss of Fez, the descendants of the grandsons of Idris II were limited to a Riffian stronghold known as the "Eagle's Nest" and the seaport of Nokeur, the present Al Hoceima. Five years after the defeat of Yahya IV, one more Idrisid prince, Hassan el Hadjjam, came down out of his "Eagle's Nest" to the rescue of Fez. Defeated outside the walls, he managed to reach a hiding place inside the city. In an attempt to escape by climbing over the walls at night, he fell, broke his leg, and died. His was the last Idrisid name connected with the city that the second Idris had founded.

Throughout the chaos and anarchy of the tenth century, Riffian Idrisids made their intermittent and futile attempts to reestablish their fallen dynasty, switching their allegiance from Kairouan Fatimites to Cordovan Ommayids as often as the old Numidian princes had changed their support from Carthage to Rome. For now, like the Berber tribes, also become fickle in their allegiance, they were nothing but pawns in the great struggle between East and West. Victory for the first three-fourths of the century went most often to the Fatimites. By 973 this dynasty had conquered Egypt and made Cairo their capital.

In Fez the Fatimite allies, the Meknassa, the Berber tribe that had ousted Yahya IV, established Morocco's second, though minor, dynasty. By soon deserting the Idrisid capital for the present city of Meknès, they established the pattern of all dynasties to come—that of scorning or perhaps fearing the capital of their predecessors.

For forty years after the Meknassa left, the miserable Fassi lived a life of terror, never knowing whose army would next crush or starve their city into surrender. If the Fatimite general sent their Spanish governor back to Cairo in a cage, the mighty Cordova commander Ghalib came swooping across the Straits to avenge the insult. Then Cairo again; then Cordova; and so on and on in gruesome succession. As the century ended, it was Cordova lording it over the lawless, feuding splinters of the first Moroccan kingdom; Cordova installing her own allies, the Maghraoua, as the third of the Moroccan dynasties.

Like the Meknassa, the Maghraoua tribe barely deserves the name of dynasty. Only one strong ruler represented them. The rest sat feebly by for half a century until a rumbling storm south of the Sahara gathered enough momentum to sweep them out of power.

Before we cross the Sahara to its southern edge, to watch the stormy "Men of the Veil" spreading their fanatical zeal, another onslaught out of Arabia itself by way of Egypt takes us east to Kairouan and Cairo.

In 1048, when the Fatimite Caliph was ruling Cairo, and his rival the Abbasid Caliph ruled Baghdad, an ungrateful governor of Kairouan enraged his Cairo master. The *khotba*, it will be remembered, is the prayer recited from the pulpit of the mosque in the name of the ruling caliph. Moezz ben Badis, whose family owed its governorship to the Fatimites of Cairo, presumed to change from Shiite to Sunnite allegiance, and out of personal spite to substitute the name of the Abbasid Caliph of Baghdad for that of the Fatimite Mostansir of Egypt. For this flagrant defiance, Mostansir conceived a subtle and far-reaching revenge. Within his territory of Upper Egypt roamed a group of four nomadic and marauding tribes recently transplanted from the Arabian peninsula. By inviting them to cross the Libyan Desert and help themselves to the land and loot of Tunisia and points west, he not only got rid of these unwelcome plunderers but showed Moezz in whose name the *khotba* had best be recited.

Two hundred thousand of these pillagers? Two hundred and fifty thousand? Who can count a swarm of advancing locusts or measure their damage? They took their name from the leading tribe—the Ben Hilal ben Amur ben Sasa—and their depredation has come down in history as the Second Arab or Hilalian Invasion. Morocco, at the end of their thrust, suffered the least; but even there, they seized the plains and the oases, and pushed the Berbers back into the mountains. As primitive, nomadic tribes, they had nothing in common with those early Arabs of the conquest who brought the culture of Alexandria and Persia to Visigothic Spain. With the exception of Budgett Meakin, who credits them with introducing the pure spoken Arabic of the Nedjd (the central Arabian province, seat of the present capital Riadh), Western historians have nothing good to say about them.

In the oases of the Tafilalet, at the edge of the Sahara where the Imperial Highway from Fez meets the main caravan trail from the desert, their name lives on. Remove the framing Berber "T's" common to so many Saharan place names, and you get *Filali* which may also be read *Hilali*.

We shall find the name again as an alternative for the present Alaouite Dynasty—not because the reigning Hassan II was descended from men of that Second Invasion, but because his ancestors moved there from Arabia two centuries later.

THE SPLENDOR OF CORDOVA
(The Ommayid Caliphate, 756–1013)

The familiar expression "Moorish civilization of Spain" is deceptive. It leads one to think that the Moors of northwest Africa—the Moors of Tarik's conquest—brought with them into Spain the civilization that illuminated the darkness of medieval Europe. Actually, the Moors of Tarik's conquest brought nothing out of Morocco to the land which they conquered. There was nothing to bring.

Tarik's Moors consisted of 300 Arabs and 7,000 Berbers. The Berbers were the same magnificent fighting men that they had been in the days of Rome and the Numidian princes, but they were *not* conveyors of the horseshoe arch, the floral arabesque, the illuminated manuscript, the translations of Aristotle, and the cornerstones of modern science. Nor did they dress in silk and jewels and converse in rhymed couplets. By the time a Moroccan ruler of Berber stock could create a minaret such as the Koutoubia of Marrakesh, or discuss with the philosopher Averroes the two-fold path to God, his country had been exposed to the luster of Moorish Spain for close to five centuries and his own dynasty had chosen an Andalusian city as capital.

57

The Arabs who crossed the Straits in 711 with Tarik and took over the city of Cordova as capital of their new conquests had been little more than birds of passage through Morocco. Others followed them from the East, especially from Syria. Nobles and warriors, they were the nucleus of the new Moslem state. In the lovely subtropical valley of Andalusia it was easy to recreate the luxurious palaces and gardens of Damascus.

Much of Morocco would have offered the same charms and advantages of climate and rich soil; but, from the point of view of civilization, that country was as if Rome had never held it. The visitation of the Vandals had left nothing tangible, and the relics of Christianity were almost as rare as the Barbary lion today.

Spain, on the other hand, had a rich century-old background inherited from the days of Rome. Before Rome, Greece and Carthage had mingled their influences. The aristocratic and lovely head of the half-statue of the Lady of Elche in the Madrid Archaeological Museum marks a native Celtiberian art of the highest quality, with some possible influence from Phoenicia. The Barca family of Carthage left its name to Barcelona and the North African city itself left its to Cartagena.

During the centuries of Rome's Carthaginian wars and her own Civil War, the Peninsula was without repose or order; but for the 400 years from the days of Augustus to the coming of the Goths it was a land of peace, prosperity, cultivation and famous men. The Emperors Trajan and Hadrian were born in Roman Italica near Seville. The two Senecas and the poet Lucan were native sons of Cordova. The Silver Age of Rome was also a Silver Age in Spain. Theatres, aqueducts, bridges and the indestructible Roman roads remain even today as tangible signs of an intangible intellectual heritage.

This classical heritage proved powerful enough to continue the Romanization of the wandering Goths who had met Rome before on the banks of the Danube. After their first fling at pillaging and destruction, they began to respect the useful roads and monuments they found. Though they themselves might be warriors who used their hands only to wield a sword or tip a flagon of wine to the lips, they attached the clever artisans of the country to their estates and churches, and lived the luxurious life of the Roman landlords whose property they had despoiled.

Proof of the luxury with which they surrounded themselves was the booty described by their Arab conquerors and taken not only from the capital at Toledo but throughout the land, from the Straits to the Pyrenees and beyond. We remember the solid gold, emerald-encrusted "Solomon's Table" from which the wily Tarik removed a leg when Mousa tried to rob him of his triumph. In the Archaeological Museum in Madrid and in the Cluny Museum in Paris hang jewel-studded votive crowns of the Gothic kings—marvels of the goldsmith's art—meant for the altars of their churches.

Intellectually, too, they had begun to make their own contributions to the culture they had inherited from Rome. Outstanding among these was the Visigothic Code, the famous *Forum Judicum.* Of its virtues, S. P. Scott in his *History of the Moorish Empire in Europe* says: "Every precaution which ingenuity could devise was adopted to insure the fidelity, the honesty, the impartiality of the magistrate whether civil or ecclesiastical." In comparing it with the Justinian Code compiled at the same time, Scott considers "the superiority, upon the whole, largely on the side of the so-called barbarian". Montesquieu and Gibbon also praised this Gothic code of law, though with greater moderation.

Into this Gothic civilization, then, with its roots deep in the traditions of Rome, a small handful of Eastern Arabs at the head of 7,000 primitive Moroccan Berbers came pouring into the Peninsula as the next conquerors.

These first Arabs, and those who followed in the next forty years before the beginning of the Ommayid Caliphate in 756, brought with them the civilization of the Eastern lands they had conquered: architecture from Sassanid Persia with the prototype of the Moorish arch in the ruined and vaulted castle of Ctesiphon; science from Egypt where Ptolemy Soter's University at Alexandria had discarded the purity of theoretical and speculative Greek thought in favor of a new and utilitarian approach to knowledge; and from Syria the soft vices and polished arts of decadent Byzantium.

So they came into Catholic Spain as Persian Arabs, as Syrian Arabs, and as Arabs from their own Arabian Peninsula. They came with men of the Yemen and Medina pitted against men of the Hedjaz and Mecca, dragging their atavistic tribal feuds across the breadth of Africa and across the Straits into Europe. With them came their Moslem converts who had become their scribes and their physicians, their architects and their masons, their astronomers and their astrologists.

Out of what they brought and what they found, with the two elements intertwining as intricately as one of their own convolute arabesques, came that sudden blaze of human achievement known as the Moorish civilization of Spain. A far more fitting adjective would be Moslem or, better still, Saracen—a term that has its roots in the Arab word for east. The splendor of the Cordova period began in 756, lasted throughout the 250 years of the Ommayid Caliphate, and ended in 1013 when the great capital was seized by the Spanish Berbers.

When the Eastern Ommayid Caliphate of Damascus fell at the hands of the Abbasids in 750, and the Abbasids set about destroying every prince of Ommayid blood, it will be recalled that one young noble of the house, Abderrahman, grandson of the next-to-last Caliph, was fortunate enough to make his escape. Like the fugitive Idris, he made his way across Africa to Tangier with a few loyal companions. On news of his arrival, he was welcomed into Spain by a small but powerful faction loyal to his house.

There, his many talents and his military ability enabled him to seize the power from the quarreling Arab nobles, centralize it, and found the dynasty that shone with the first light of learning in the Dark Ages of western Europe.

Though it is customary, it is not exact to speak of the Ommayid Caliphate as beginning with the reign of Abderrahman I in 756. During the first century and a half, the Ommayid rulers called themselves *"emirs"* —princes. The great Abderrahman III (912–961) was the first to assume for himself the supreme title of "Caliph."

Abderrahman I contented himself with subduing and organizing the turbulent land, fending off Charlemagne, and recreating on the banks of the Guadelquivir the counterpart of the beloved Damascus of his youth. Street plans, fortifications, palaces and suburbs all reflected the garden city on the Syrian River Barada at the edge of the Arabian Desert. The first palm tree of Spain grew in his courtyard. Beyond the city he laid out a replica of his grandfather's garden Rusafah, giving it the familiar Syrian name. From his mint, Syrian coins were struck. Poets and philosophers found welcome and encouragement at his court. All that was lacking to make Cordova a second Damascus under his reign was drunkenness, depravity and voluptuous vice. With all his love of beauty and the arts, the first Western Ommayid was both pious and temperate.

In Baghdad of the *Thousand and One Nights,* Haroun er Rashid hated this young Ommayid emir of Cordova and his defiant independence as much as he hated Idris I of Morocco, whom he had tried to have poisoned. He was on friendly terms with the young Charlemagne. To him he sent, among other rich presents, the first clock seen in the West; and to him gave every encouragement to cross the Pyrenees and destroy the new Emirate.*

A few weeks before his death, Abderrahman had the immense happiness of conducting the Friday prayer within the unfinished walls of the Great Cordova Mosque. The mosque fulfilled his dream of creating a shrine second in sacredness only to Mecca itself, where his people were being received with hostility by the Abbasid rulers. Though it rose on the site of the Christian Cathedral, the owners were honorably and generously paid for their loss, and, as added compensation, permitted to rebuild several churches that the war had destroyed.

Though feeble and near death, the Emir worked with his own hands an hour every day on the mosque's walls and foundations. From his nucleus of eleven naves, his successors enlarged it to the north, south and east into

* The *Song of Roland* has its origin in Charlemagne's retreat from his Spanish invasion through the narrow Pyrenees pass of Roncesvalles in 778, when his rear guard, under his nephew Roland, was attacked and annihilated by the Basques. The legend makes Saracens the attackers.

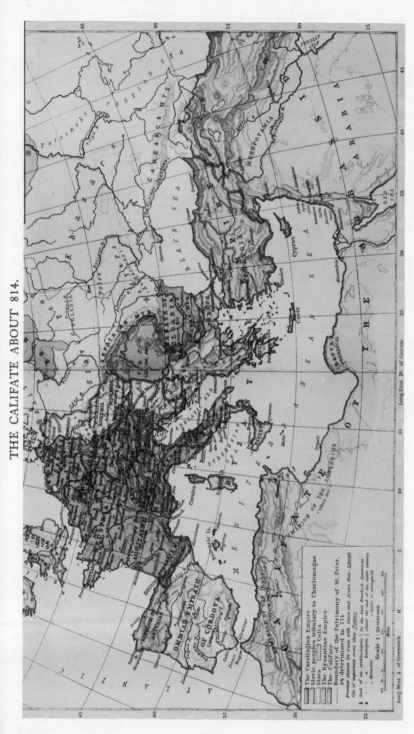

Shepherd's *Atlas of Medieval and Modern History*, Henry Holt, 1932

the nineteen aisles crossed by twenty-nine, forming the impressive forest of a thousand marble pillars arched in red and white that, next to the Great Mosque of Mecca, became the largest mosque in the world. Marble, porphyry and jasper columns came from Roman ruins as far away as southern France and Carthage. Sixteen tons of tesserae for the mosaics of glass and gold, with workmen to assemble them, came as a gift from the friendly Byzantine Emperor Leo IV of Constantinople.

During the short eight years of his reign, Abderrahman's devout and popular youngest son Hisham, who inherited the throne, continued and finished the eleven-nave nucleus of the Great Mosque. Pious and unostentatious in his personal life, he dedicated the sum of 45,000 pieces of gold—his royal fifth of the booty brought back from the conquest of the Languedoc province of France—to the glory of the Holy shrine. His father had begun it with 80,000 pieces of gold from the spoils of the Goths.

Two other features of Hisham's reign stand out as important to Spain and consequently important to North Africa. One was the fact that he introduced Arabic as the obligatory language in the schools of both Jews and Christians. This common tongue did much to foster the extraordinary unity and racial tolerance that existed in many aspects of the new civilization. Without it there would not have been Jewish and Christian scholars teaching at the famous Mosque-University of Cordova. His other act of importance was the introduction of the Malikite rite of Moslem law into Spain as the result of his friendship with, and admiration for, the famous jurist Malik Ibn Anas of the holy Arabian city of Medina.

Malik Ibn Anas was one of the "Four Imams" or "Leaders" who founded the four separate but orthodox Schools of Islamic religious law. All Islamic law was, and is, derived from the Koran and the Traditions of the Prophet. There were, however, different ways of interpreting both of these original sources. Like different religious sects, the four different Schools affected the early politics of the Moslem world.

Today, with the rough edges of their differences smoothed away, they have become a matter of geography. Followers of Malik Ibn Anas, the Malikites, are now the Moslems of North Africa west of Egypt. The followers of Abu Hanifa, Malik's more liberal predecessor, are the Moslems of Turkey, Central Asia and Northern India. Shafiites, disciples of Shafiya, are found in Southern India, Lower Egypt, Syria and Malaya. And the small group of Hanbalites, followers of Hanbal who died in 885, are the fanatic Wahabis of Central Arabia.

In Spain and northwest Africa we are primarily concerned with the Malikites. Ibn Batuta, the great fourteenth-century Moroccan traveler in the footsteps of Marco Polo, served for seven years as Malikite judge in Delhi; and his contemporary, North Africa's illustrious historian-philosopher, Ibn Khaldoun, held the same position for the Mameluke ruler Barqouq in Cairo.

To oversimplify a complicated subject, it could be said that Malik Ibn Anas was a fervent supporter of the literal decrees of the Koran and the Hadith (or Traditions) of the generation of men who had been, or had known, the companions of the Prophet. His code laid down a pattern of life as practiced by the devout but simple and provincial people of Medina. It appealed to the pious Hisham in Spain, who had no taste for pomp or luxury. It also appealed to the simple Berbers of Morocco. With the Abbasid rulers at Baghdad, who had married into the Persian royal house and were under the influence of Persian ministers, its inflexible puritanism found no favor. There, the luxury-loving court found Hanifa's rules of life far more congenial. In Morocco, Malikism had found enemies in the twelfth century when a gentle form of Hindu pantheism crept into Islam from the East, and the word for the unity of God, *tawhid*, became the nucleus of the word *Almohad*. The Almohads or Unitarians became Morocco's third dynasty.

With Hisham's son Hakim I, who succeeded his father in 796, the people of Cordova found themselves living under a bloodthirsty and cruel tyrant. Handsome, well educated, friend of poets and philosophers, he was also vicious and dissolute. The Malikite theologians honored by his father hated him. When the muezzins chanted their *La illah illallah ou Muhammed raisul Allah*—"there is no God but God and Mohammed is the Prophet of God"—they called in the same pious voice, "Come to prayer, O Drunkard!" These theologians were many in number and had become powerful. When they rose against Hakim, he burned their suburb and exiled them and their fellow rebels—8,000 families to Moroccan Fez, the remaining 12,000 families to Crete.

Fez was the new city founded by Idris II. Hakim, it will be remembered, had already sent an embassy to Idris II offering his friendship and alliance against the Abbasids of Baghdad. After the exile, Hakim's Cordovans were given the east bank of the River Fez—an area that became and still remains the "Quarter of the Andalusians." According to the eleventh-century geographer El Bekri, the women of the Andalusian Quarter were more beautiful than those on the opposite bank, whereas the men of the opposite bank—the Kairouiine Quarter—were handsomer than the Andalusians.

This massive influx of Spanish Moors into Morocco was the momentous beginning of the influence that grew throughout the next seven centuries in two distinct ways—one through the exiling to Africa of Spanish Moors, who took with them both their intellectual achievements and their skills as architects, engineers and craftsmen as the *Reconquista* of the Christians advanced to the fall of Granada in 1492; the other, the eleventh- and twelfth-century conquests of Moorish Spain by Moroccan Berber dynasties, whereby leaders and warriors were transformed from rough desert and mountain tribesmen into polished nobles and patrons of the arts.

63

The second Abderrahman (822–852) had a passion for music. In contrast to his father, who spent his last four years in harem debauchery and delirious shrieks of guilt for his past sins and cruelties, the son was one of the four great rulers of the Ommayid House. Those four were the three Abderrahmans and the literary giant and bibliophile Hakim II.

The wars, both great and small, waged by Cordova against Moorish and Gothic rebels, against Frankish enemies north of the Pyrenees and plundering Norman pirates, who made their first appearance on the Spanish coast during the reign of Abderrahman II, do not concern our Moroccan story. Our interest lies in the increasing splendor of the age as ruler succeeds ruler and leaves his mark on this city of light. Under Abderrahman II, the works of Greek philosophers were introduced in translation into the Peninsula. He enlarged and embellished the Great Mosque, and built others with schools and hospitals attached. He brought down waters from the nearby mountains through lead pipes into the fountains and baths of the city. He built public parks, schools and orphanages for destitute children. Like his predecessors, he kept the valuable Roman highways in good repair and added new ones. In times of locusts, drought and famine, he relieved the victims of their taxes, winning the name of "Father of the Poor." At the same time, he was a ruler of extravagant and luxurious tastes, with his monogram woven into his robes of silk, and his face veiled from the public eye.

The lion of Abderrahman's court was the Persian musician Ziryab. At Baghdad in the palace of Haroun er Rashid, his skill, arousing the jealousy of his teacher, had resulted in his banishment. Abderrahman welcomed him to Andalusia with a palace, a retinue of slaves and eunuchs, and 50,000 pieces of gold. In no time, the Persian artist had not only the Emir but all Cordova at his feet. No one had ever heard music like his. He knew the words and melodies of 10,000 songs; he added a fifth string to the lute, giving its notes a new sweetness. But this was far from all. Like the cultivated men of his day, he was a scholar as well as an artist; practical, too, inventing a new drainage system for Andalusian cities. It could well have been said of him, as it was said of the late Jean Cocteau, that he was a "man of twenty heads." He was poet and philosopher, geographer and physician. He was a Beau Brummel, a Lord Chesterfield and a Brillat-Savarin. He introduced new styles in clothes, in court etiquette, and in epicurean dishes. Spain owes to him its spiced meat balls and asparagus; and Ziryab's fricassée is still served in Spanish households.

Abderrahman III (912–961), the Great Caliph, was the remarkable grandson of his weak predecessor, Abdallah. Through his administrative and military genius, he lifted the country from rebellion and war to its greatest prosperity, splendor and fame. In his reign of forty-nine years, no other city west of the Bosporus excelled Cordova as a place to give delight to the senses and joy to the intellect. On a more magnificent scale than Abderrahman II, he satisfied his own love of both luxury and beauty, and at the same time saw to it that his people shared the good life made possible by the overflowing royal treasury with an income of 60 million dollars a year.

Part of the riches came from the spoils seized by his conquering armies; part from the taxes laid upon prosperous Jews and Christians, who became a proud element of his flourishing cities; and part from the commerce of his great merchant fleet. Outbound to the ports of the East the vessels carried, along with precious ores, sugar, wool, and the arts and crafts of Andalusia. In their holds were the carved ivories and tooled leather of Cordova, the silks and brocades of Almeria, the inlaid steel of Toledo, the luster ware of Mallorca, perfumes and vessels of gold and silver. Sailing back into the mouth of the Guadelquivir the ships unloaded a cargo of handsome slaves of both sexes, and eunuchs, marble and porphyry, jasper and lapis lazuli, precious jewels and fragrant wood, gold-dust, spices and rare manuscripts— a cargo destined to dazzle the astonished students from the dank and dirty towns of the north. Dazzled and astonished also were the gaping African Berbers, whose only shelters were sprawling dwellings of undressed stone, reeds woven into huts, or wool woven into tent strips.

For strangers who knew the cities of the East, where magnificence went back to the days of the Sumerians and the Pharaohs, it came as a surprise to find such grandeur at the edge of the Western world. A population of a million was estimated to live within the walled city and its twenty-one suburbs of gardens, villas and palaces. Inside the walls the streets were the same narrow and twisting lanes that you would see in Fez today, but paved, clean, and well-lighted. In summer, awnings stretched across the streets as a protection from the burning sun. Where the streets met in public squares or passed in front of palaces, fountains rose out of carved marble basins. Visitors from the north might have thought the blank windowless street walls of the stone houses disappointing, until the famous Arab hospitality enabled them to enter the inner-garden patios of orange trees, jasmine, dove-cotes and more fountains. Historians of the time tell us that there were more than 113,000 houses of the prosperous middle class in this city of Moorish Spain, 900 public baths, and 700 mosques. Caravanserais took care of the travelers, and inns supported by the public purse housed and fed students too poor to pay their own way while they studied with the scholars of the Mosque-University.

To be a scholar in Cordova or in any great city of Moorish Spain was to taste a life unknown to the learned men of other lands and other times, both past and present. The greatest scholar of the capital was usually the most honored man at the court of the Caliph—not only the most honored but the richest and the most powerful, often the ruler's chamberlain. He

65

was theologian, jurist and philosopher, physician and astronomer, musician and poet. The court chamberlain was usually versed in all the sciences of his day, adding to all his knowledge the courtly charm of the diplomat. The Caliph honored him with palaces and lavish income. A bodyguard of soldiers in silk and gold uniforms accompanied him through the streets. He took precedence over courtiers of noble birth. His daughters became powerful in the royal harem, while his own harem held an outstanding bevy of beautiful women from the slave markets of Europe and Asia, with eunuchs to ensure their virtue.

Like the eunuchs of the Middle East, the eunuchs of Moorish Spain often rose to positions of power in royal households. They kept their own slaves and played significant roles in palace intrigues and revolutions. White eunuchs were chosen for their beauty; black eunuchs for their size, ferocity and ugliness. All were magnificently dressed in rich robes of silk. It is surprising to learn that the principal source for the white eunuchs was the monasteries of southern France, where young peasant boys were bought for the purpose and skillfully altered.

During the reign of the Great Caliph, theological orthodoxy became relaxed. Nothing was more at variance with the austere life of the Prophet who forbade silk, wine and independent thought, and with the austere Malikite pattern of behavior than the fantastic luxury and searching minds of the intellectuals of Moorish Spain. And nothing was so strange as the phenomenal development and achievement of the human mind against this sybaritic background.

In a city that became the wonder of the Western world, three architectural marvels crowned the splendor. These were the Great Mosque, the palace and gardens of Medinet ez Zhara of Abderrahman III, and the library of his son Hakim II. Only the Great Mosque escaped total destruction. Because so much of it still stands as the coeval historians described it, we can believe in their amazing accounts of palace and library.

For the first twenty-five years of his reign, Abderrahman lived in the *ksar*, bordering the river. (The Arabic *al ksar* became the Spanish *alcazar*.) From this fortified palace the Caliph could reach the Great Mosque over a carpet of silk and silver threads and enter it by a private door. During his last twenty-five years he built and ruled from the suburban garden palace that honored in its name his favorite concubine, Ez Zhara. Modern excavations on the mountain slope northwest of the city show the rectangular foundation where more than 4,000 columns of white Italian marble and the verd antique and rose marble of Tunisia marked the walls, arcades and terraces for the Caliph and his seraglio of more than 6,000 women and their attendants. Below this fortified palace building, 400 houses held bodyguard, eunuchs and pages. Below that, the gardens began—a fantastic wonderland of lakes and cascades and summer houses, of cunningly trimmed hedges, of mazes of boxwood and myrtle, of flowerbeds spelling in their designs praises of Allah and his Prophet; fairy grottoes roofed with colored glass played upon by revolving jets of water; rivulets running down the balustrades of marble staircases; a thousand fountains, the most famous with life-size human figures of gilded bronze from Constantinople, and another in the shape of twelve birds and animals of jewel-studded gold, pouring water from their mouths and beaks into a basin of green Syrian marble.

In the palace itself, a circular marble pavilion roofed in alternate tiles of silver and gold amazed the envoys from foreign lands. The columns were of both marble of many colors and rock crystal, with pearls and rubies set into the capitals. Byzantine mosaic filled the spandrels of the arches and the friezes above them, while the walls themselves were of translucent onyx. But the magical device that both fascinated and terrified royal guests was a giant porphyry bowl in the center of the pavilion, filled with quicksilver revolving under the rays of the sun and sending out blinding flashes of light in its circuit.

Abderrahman III, greatest ruler of the Western Ommayids, stands out as a man whose every dream and ambition had come true. And yet in his own evaluation of his life he wrote: "I have reigned fifty years in peace and glory. . . . I have wanted nothing that the heart of man could desire, neither renown, nor power, nor pleasure. During this long life I have counted the days when I have enjoyed complete happiness—and they have amounted to only twenty! Praise be to Him who alone possesses eternal glory and omnipotence, there is no other God than He!"

Perhaps his son Hakim II might have numbered the happy days of his life differently. Like the pious Hisham I, the second Ommayid ruler, he preferred books to concubines; nor did he, like his father, look for pleasure in sodomy. He was a temperate and pious man of great intellect, and may well have been able to look back on many days of happiness in the assembling of his immense library, in the stimulus he gave to literature through rewards and encouragement, and in his own scholarly research and writings.

Hakim's library had all the beauty of a Cordovan palace. Floors and columns of multi-colored marble, ceilings of mosaic and alabaster, cases of rare and fragrant woods inscribed in gold did honor to the manuscripts he treasured. Not a library in Europe or England approached it in the number of its books. Though St. Benedict at Monte Cassino stressed the importance of a library in each new monastery of his order, it was not until after the founding of the Cistercian branches of the Benedictines in 1098 that a separate room in any monastery was set aside for books! This was more than a century after Hakim's death.

Hakim's library is estimated to have held 6,000 volumes, with 44 of them containing the catalogue. Etymologically, of course, volume is the wrong word. The *volumen* or rolled-up manuscript of the past had given way to the codex of the Middle Ages—the book form as we know it now, with pages and covers. The Arabs, who had discovered the secret of paper-making from Chinese captives soon after their conquest of Samarkand, set up their first paper mill in that ancient city in 751. However, as the first paper mill of the Moorish Arabs in Andalusia was not founded until 1150, under the Berber dynasty of the Almohads, it can be assumed that the majority of the manuscripts in Hakim's library were written on parchment. As skillful in transforming the delicate skins of newborn lambs, calves, kids and even gazelles into thin, soft and pliable parchment as they were in tanning, dyeing and stamping the stronger skins of older animals for the famous Moroccan bindings, the Spanish Arabs excelled as manufacturers of the raw materials of books.

In the *scriptorium* of the library—the room set aside for the copying and binding of new or borrowed manuscripts—a great staff covered the fine parchment pages with the ornamental cursive script of written Arabic, inlaid the covers of the choicest volumes with jewels, and closed the covers with clasps of gold. For Hakim, the author's name on the title pages of his books was not enough; his genealogy and the dates of his birth and death were equally important—data often added in the Caliph's own hand.

A thousand pieces of gold was frequently Hakim's reward to an author for a work of outstanding merit. Moreover, it was his habit to advance generous sums to works in progress to ensure the manuscript for his own library. Where other kings and princes of Moorish Spain had their agents in ports of the Near and Distant East searching the markets for Circassian slaves, for the pearls of Oman, the rubies and emeralds of India, Hakim had his spies on the alert for some new translation of a Greek philosopher or the latest heresy of some Persian Sufist.

The broad and inquiring mind of this brilliant bibliophile encouraged freedom of thought in others and, though philosophy and the medical sciences of Moorish Spain reached their crest two centuries later in the great Averroes and Avenzoar, and architecture three centuries later with the completion of the Alhambra, the reign of Hakim II was the golden age of literature during the Moorish occupation of so much of Spain. Seventy libraries beside the great one at Cordova gave the literature of both past and present to the people of Andalusia. For rich and poor, education was as free as the soft subtropical air and the sweet mountain water that splashed in the public fountains. This was a period when the bigoted orthodox were in the minority. Too many scholars of different faiths, races and ideas had been lecturing in the mosques, for minds to be left in the old ruts. The faculty of the University of Cordova had the reputation of pantheism, even atheism—a reputation not entirely without justification.

When we speak of the University of Cordova, we are speaking, of course, of the Great Mosque. In the Moslem world, the mosque and the institution of learning remained one and the same until the most recent plunges of the Arab world into independence and nationalism.

The fountain of all knowledge, therefore of all learning, was the revealed word of Allah in the holy Koran and the Traditions of his "Messenger" Mohammed. Herein for the orthodox lay all theology, all law, all rules for living on this earth and for walking the razor's edge of El Sirat, the bridge into Paradise. For the orthodox Moslem, no other subjects of study were necessary. And yet, as the years passed, the desert Arab with his keen and inquisitive mind came into contact with the clear logic of classical Greece, and encountered the scientific achievements of Hellenistic Alexandria; and, as conquest brought other peoples into his empire, his interests broadened and his mosque-universities enlarged their curricula.

The Baghdad of Haroun er Rashid's famous son El Mamoun was noted for its scientific discoveries, especially in astronomy. Later, under the Seljuk Sultan Malik Shah, the poet, astronomer and mathematician Omar Khayyám reformed the calendar and composed a book on algebra, as well as his blasphemous and enchanting quatrains scorning both "the Prophet's Paradise to come" and the Sufist's "door to which I found no key." In the Mosque-University of Cordova, besides the department of theology where 4,000 students were enrolled, there were classes where 7,000 students studied such subjects as the exact sciences, medicine, music, poetry and art.

Through these students at Cordova and at the other mosque-universities of the Peninsula; through their teachers—Arabs, Jews and Christians; and through the rulers who supported and protected them, the great body of scientific and philosophic knowledge grew in scope. Added to it were the contributions of the Islamic East. Together they formed the gift of Moorish Spain to the Western world.

What was the most valuable in this great and varied heritage? The Arabic digits of Indian origin and the zero, enabling arithmetic to discard the clumsy numerals of Rome? The rational approach and discoveries in medicine, surgery, hygiene, anesthetics and pharmaceutical botany, at a time when the Christian Church forbade such studies, claiming disease was a manifestation of divine displeasure? The invention of sine and cosine, tangent and cotangent for the measurement of giant triangles reaching from earth to moon? The pendulum or the balance? The spyglass or the perfection of the portable astrolabe?

In the twelfth-century geographer Idrisi's map of the world, the latitudes varied only by a few minutes from modern reckonings. Algebra was virtually the creation of the Arabs. Out of alchemy grew discoveries in chemistry, in metallurgy and the art of distillation, giving us, among many benefits: alcohol, sulphuric acid, distilled water and the essence of the rose. Out of a passion for astrology grew knowledge of astronomy. The great cities of Islam—Baghdad, Damascus, Cairo, Samarkand, Cordova—had their observatories. With the astrolabe astronomers were able to determine the hour of prayer and the direction of Mecca. The science of irrigation, with its roots in ancient lands bordering the Tigris and the Nile, turned Andalusia into a great garden of oranges and roses, and the knowledge, passed from Arab to Spaniard, eventually transformed in its turn the semi-arid valleys and hillsides of California into a land of gardens and orchards not unlike the valley of the Guadelquivir.

Hakim II was the last great Ommayid of the Cordova Caliphate; not, however, its last great ruler. The last great ruler was a usurper of over-weening ambition, unscrupulous morals, diabolical cunning and extraordinary military genius, who rose to the top by making the Sultana his mistress, by imprisoning and corrupting the adolescent heir to the throne, and by murdering all rivals. He was known as Al Mansour or Almanzor, the Victorious. Through his rule and brilliant military campaigns, Cordova remained the glittering military capital the Ommayids had made it. He gave the Great Mosque its last splendid addition, bringing its final dimensions to 620 by 440 feet—surpassed in area only by the sacred shrine of Mecca. But what the Great Mosque-University gained in area it lost in its spirit of liberalism and enlightenment. With Hakim's death, the bigoted theologians dared to raise their voices against all that he had stood for, against his sinful love of books over and above the Koran and the *Hadith* or Traditions. To win these bigots over to his side, Almanzor pretended to share their pious orthodoxy, inviting them to destroy any and every book of the world-famous library that met with their disapproval.

After Almanzor's death in 1002, the decline of Cordova began, with the climax in 1038, when the Spanish Berbers seized it, and their Christian allies defiled the Great Mosque by stabling their horses between its marble columns. Though Moorish Spain blossomed again under the Moroccan Almoravid and Almohad dynasties of the eleventh and twelfth centuries, and under the cultivated kinglets of such cities as Saragossa, Toledo and Valencia, and finally under the kings of Granada, Cordova was never again the capital. In 1236 it was seized by Ferdinand III, King of Leon and Castile. Under his fanatic zeal, the Great Mosque, stripped over the years of its treasures, became transformed into the present Cathedral. Gone were the lead roof, the silver floor of the Caliph's chapel, the gold nails of the pulpit, the precious wood and the jewels, the hangings of gilded leather.

Gone was all the material splendor of Cordova; and, by 1492, Boabdil, last King of Granada, had joined the African exiles. But no Spanish zealot, no inquisitor—not Ferdinand the Saint, not the "Catholic Kings," not Jimenez, not Torquemada—could stamp out the quickening flames of human progress that eight centuries of Moorish civilization in Spain had kindled in Western Europe.

CHAPTER VII

ⵗⵗⵗⵗⵗⵗⵗ

THE BLUE-VEILED WARRIORS
(The Almoravids, 1062–1148)

ⵗⵗⵗⵗⵗⵗⵗ

Moroccan dynasties are like the overlapping melodies of a fugue. Before the last one dies away, the next one is rising to its peak. The criterion of the end of one and the establishment of the next is the fall of the capital city Fez, or in some cases of Marrakesh. Long before Fez falls, however, the princes of the last ruling house have become soft and weak in their palaces, while the founders of the next are fighting their way into power with the rugged strength of tent-bred nomad and mountaineer.

In the case of Morocco's fourth dynasty, the Almoravids, Fez falls in 1063 from the brief Maghraoua rule. The Almoravid story, however, begins much earlier.

It begins in 1036 in the Tunisian city of Kairouan, next to Mecca the holiest city of Islam. It begins in the court of the Great Mosque, the one the saint Sidi Okba founded in 671 when he ordered all the serpents and their children to leave the site he had chosen. When the pious Moslems of North Africa made their *hadj* to Mecca, they stopped here with pride to recite their prayers in the noble naves of its marble columns. If their piety

71

was above average, they stayed long enough to enroll as disciples of the illustrious theologians who give to the great mosques the dual role of house of prayer and university.

In the year 1036, Abou Amran el Fassi, a learned teacher from Fez, was used to seeing skins of many colors and costumes of many kinds gathered around him in the open court of the Kairouan mosque, where he was delivering his lectures on the glories of Islam. Turbans and hoods often cast their shadows over the faces, but even so he could distinguish the falcon-beak noses of the Arabs, the short noses of the Berbers, and the broad thick noses of the oases Negroes. One day, however, as he examined his audience, his learned and fluent periods almost came to a sudden stop.

One of the faces before him was, except for the eyes, completely hidden by a veil of dark blue cotton drawn tightly across nose and mouth. More dark blue cotton fell in folds from broad shoulders and a splendid figure. The stranger's black leather sandals were laced with crimson leather thongs curiously embroidered in gold. Every detail down to the daggers at his belt indicated a chieftain of importance. Abou Amram had, of course, heard of the Veiled Men of the Desert. The caravans from Timbuctu brought back talk of them. This was the first one he had ever seen.

For Abou Amran, it was a chance to find out about the progress of Islam at the far edge of the Sahara. For Yahya ben Ibrahim el Djezouli, chief of the Veiled Sanhadja of the Desert, it was the chance to tell how little progress Islam had made there, and to beg the learned doctor for a missionary to enlighten his pagan subjects, who roamed the desert from the mouth of the Senegal River to the buckle of the Niger at Timbuctu.

Abou Amran, shocked and eager to help, asked his disciples for volunteers. No one stepped forward. They, too, had heard the caravan talk about these wild Berbers of the southwestern Sahara, who lived on dead meat and camel's milk, who could pin a man to his horse with their lances or slice him through to the saddle with their swords. Cross the terrible Sahara to go and live with these veiled barbarians to whom bread was unknown, who ate, slept and died without removing their veils, while the faces of their women went uncovered? Surely there were easier and pleasanter ways of earning Allah's Paradise.

In the end, a brave volunteer started out with Yahya on the homeward journey, started but dropped behind at the edge of the Moroccan desert, not, however, without putting Yahya in touch with a more dedicated and courageous holy man of the Atlas, Abdallah ben Yasin.

The veiled Yahya and the unveiled Yasin were both Berbers. Though one came from the northern edge and the other from the southern edge of the Sahara, their language was the same. For Yahya's Sanhadja had migrated in early days from the north to the region of the Senegal and Niger rivers. Yahya's particular tribe in the great confederation was the dominating one, the Lemtuna. They were breeders of camels and hunters of ostriches, who took their name from the desert antelope whose tough hides furnished their shields. Their southern neighbors were the Blacks of what the medieval world called "Negro-land."

By the time the travelers had reached the banks of the Senegal River, they had left the Atlantic shores of the Sahara scattered with converts—but not nearly enough to satisfy them. On an island either in the river, or off the present Mauritanian coast, Yasin established a *ribat*—a fortified hermitage. Yahya could not have brought back a more successful, a more magnetic and dynamic preacher of Islam. Under the teachings of Yasin, the new religion swept like wild fire from tribe to tribe. Sanhadja chiefs sent their sons to learn from him. Rank excused no one from the daily penitential scourgings, or punishment for such vices as sodomy or the taking of more than the four legal wives. As for Yasin—as his power grew and with it his ambition, he took over the role of setting up and pulling down leaders of tribes. Since Mohammed himself had moved from conversion to conquest, what greater virtue could there be than following in his footsteps? With the idea of a jihad or Holy War, Yahya was in perfect accord.

Not many days distant from the Senegal ribat lay the town of Aouadaghast belonging to the pagan Blacks of the Kingdom of Ghana. From these Ghanians came the fabulous gold dust that moved north by caravan; and for the sake of this gold Yasin and Yahya converted them with Book and sword, and destroyed their city.

With the Ghana gold and 3,000 warriors, Yasin and Yahya were now ready to move north across the Sahara. By this time they should be given the name by which they are known to history—the Almoravids—because of the dynasty they founded. To call them *Al Mourabitin* would be closer to the Arabic. The name goes back to the word *ribat*, meaning "one who pickets his horse on a hostile frontier"—a deed of the greatest merit. The ribat on the river island was only one of many on the frontiers of the empire to extend its boundaries. The *marabouts* * who served them were the warrior priests—Islam's Knights Templars. Down through the story of Morocco, including the 1953 exile of Mohammed V, the marabouts have played a significant political role of both good and evil.

The Almoravids were not yet a dynasty as they moved in glorious and easy conquest across the Sahara to the date-bearing slopes of the Atlas Mountains. They were merely a sect and, above all, a magnificently disciplined army—a phalanx of infantry in the center, javelins in front, pikemen behind, camelmen and horsemen along the flanks.

Neither the saint, Yasin, nor the warrior, Yahya, was to see his blue-

---

* The singular, *marabout*, has become a common word in North Africa, designating either a holy man or his tomb.

veiled warriors move from Africa on into Spain and terrify Christian horses with the sound, sight and smell of their desert camels. Yahya was the first to die. In 1056, twenty years after he had brought Yasin to the southwestern Soudan, he fell in battle—not, however, before he had crossed the Sahara and won the important Moroccan city of Sidjilmassa, northern head of the caravan trail. When Yasin died in 1060, the army had moved up into the High Atlas, fighting as skillfully near the winter snow line of the mountain passes as in their familiar desert sand, and subduing and converting the native Masmouda who had successfully resisted both Romans and Arabs. Some say the saint died in the small Atlas kingdom of Aghmat, not far from his own native valley, while the army, moving north, conquered the plain of Marrakesh. Others say he himself took part in the conquest, and fell fighting for the holy cause.

Before he died, Yasin had appointed two leaders—one the gentle Abou Bekr, prince of the Lemtunas, the other Youssef ben Tachfin, cousin of the prince, as his lieutenant. To these two, add a third figure important in molding the ultimate triumph of the invaders—the sorceress Zaineb.

Triangles are rare in Moroccan history. This is the most celebrated of them. When the Almoravids conquered the tiny kingdom of Aghmat on the crest of the Atlas, Abou Bekr claimed the lovely queen, Zaineb, among his spoils of war. To have been listened to in the councils of the leaders, she must have been as beautiful and clever as the historians say she was. On her charms they agree perfectly. On how Abou Bekr lost her to his cousin Youssef, the stories are as different as sand and snow.

In version number one, by her canny appraisal of the man most likely to succeed, she cast her charm over Youssef ben Tachfin, while Abou Bekr was softening up the country to the north for an assault on Fez. On the latter's triumphant return, he was met well outside the capital with praise and presents, and blunt intimations that they came not from a subordinate but from a ruler to his general. Crushed at the loss of both wife and leadership, the gentle Abou Bekr took the hint, acknowledged his cousin as prince, and moved south into the Sahara, where in 1076 he destroyed Kumbi, the capital of the kingdom of Ghana before he died of a broken heart.

In the other version, Abou Bekr became the perfect knight of medieval chivalry. When he was called back to the desert to punish unruly Ghana, his desire for Zaineb's happiness was more important than his own. "Take her," he ordered his cousin Youssef. "I love her too much to think of her becoming a widow in case I am killed." With this generous gesture he renounced his beloved wife and returned to the Niger, where he was killed by a poisoned arrow.

Until now the Almoravids have been the conquering warriors from the Soudan. With Youssef ben Tachfin or Youssef I, the dynasty begins.

Youssef stands out as a giant figure on the pages of North African and Spanish history. Zaineb made no mistake in using her witchery to advance him. His conquests run north like a great river. When he was ready to march on Fez, 100,000 horsemen, his own Men of the Veil and the tribes they had conquered, rode under his standards. The Lemtuna still made the *corps d'élite*, but a great medley of desert and mountain Berbers rode and marched with them.

From the small Atlas town of Aghmat, such an army would have spilled over into valleys and gorges. On the plain below, Youssef bought land and laid out an encampment, a base of supplies, a future capital. He built a mosque for devotions and a citadel to house his treasures, sharing in the labor with his own hands. As a hedge against lions, hyenas, jackals and other marauding beasts, he surrounded the immense space with the spiny branches of jujube trees (*Zizyphus spinacristi*). Seventy years later, in 1131, his son Ali changed the jujube hedge to thick walls. Such was the founding of Marrakesh, capital of the south, in 1062, next to Fez most important of the three Imperial cities. It occurred four years before William the Conqueror landed his Norman troops in England.

When Youssef seized Fez a year later, Tangier, Ceuta and the Riffian coast were already in his hands. In Fez he removed the walls that made separate cities of the Kairouiine and Andalusian river banks. For the next ten years he established such order throughout his land that, except for lions, the roads were safe for travelers from east to west and north to south.

For the people of the Moghreb, Youssef was a new kind of conqueror. Invaders before had burned and robbed, raped and tortured in the name of the Holy War and half a dozen different schisms, rites and heresies. Yet no one was more eager than Youssef to spread Islam. And by Islam he meant the severe, orthodox Malikite rite, the traditional laws of Mohammed that Yasin had taught on the island hermitage.

Like Yasin he broke wine bottles and tore down taverns. He set the example of simple food—barley, meat and milk—and simple wool clothing. From conquered tribes he took only enough to supply his army with arms and provisions. When virtually all of what is now Morocco was under his control, he limited the taxes to the amount prescribed by the Koran. In 1071 he received from the conquered tribes the oath of allegiance. The Arabs accepted him because he did not try to assume the title of Caliph, only Prince of the Faithful. The Berbers were for him because, despite the desert veil, he was one of them and wanted to give them an empire.

Nothing occurred in Morocco that was not watched with hawk-eyed interest by Moslem Spain. Since the death in 1002 of Cordova's last powerful ruler, the Grand Vizir El Mansour, the Caliphate that had glittered before the world like a brilliant pattern of mosaic had lain in fragments as if the bits of shining inlay had been scattered in the dust. In their fortresses in river valley and on mountain peak, the petty kinglets divided their time between listening to the latest poet and fighting and betraying each other. When they first invited Youssef to settle their quarrels for them, he was canny enough to refuse. In the Tadla region of the Middle Atlas there were still forts to be built. There was trouble on the eastern border in the mountains of Tlemcen. There was too much to do in strengthening his rule at home to accept such an invitation from Spain. So Saragossa and Valencia, Murcia and Seville, the *Reyes de Taifa* ("Kings of the Robber Bands") went on fighting each other too absorbed in their own selfish greed to notice the treachery of the despicable and dissolute Prince Kadir, unworthy heir of the splendid King Mamoun of Toledo. He was being besieged by King Motamid of Seville, and was selling out his city to the Christian King Alfonso VI in exchange for the throne of Valencia and the right to keep his treasures.

When the Catholic King marched triumphantly into the Ancient Gothic capital that had been in Moorish hands since Tarik first seized it from King Roderick in 711, the Reyes de Taifa suddenly grew afraid. Alien as it was to their venal natures, they managed to agree on something for their common good. Again they appealed to Youssef of the Holy Wars. This was in 1085.

At first Youssef refused again. Only after King Motamid of Seville, heading a delegation loaded down with presents, crossed the Straits to make the appeal in person, did Youssef consent. With his agreement went conditions. Reluctantly the Spanish princes agreed to give him the town of Algeciras for headquarters; then they returned to their castles and waited nervously while he built a fleet in the ports of the Riffian coast.

The battle of Zalaca in 1086, like the Almohad victory of Alarcos a century later, is the delight of the Arab historians and a black day for the Christians. When the Catholics, protected but weighted down in heavy armour, first struck, they easily routed Youssef's undisciplined Andalusian allies. Instead of advancing to their rescue, Youssef (who was smarting from their supercilious and arrogant treatment of him and his Africans) moved around to the enemy's rear. With a reinforcement of his own army on the Christian front, the enemy was suddenly crushed and slaughtered in a cage of screaming Berbers, snarling camels and blood-mad stallions. The Andalusians turned back to join the carnage, until darkness brought it to an end. The wounded Alfonso barely escaped with his life.

That night, when Christian heads to the number of 20,000 were piled in a high heap, the call to evening prayer rang out from the summit of the grisly mound. The next day the heads were salted and sent back to Morocco to decorate the gates of the Imperial cities. Also on the next day, Youssef learned that his oldest son, favorite of the five he had trained to rule, had died at Ceuta. Leaving his share of the booty to his Spanish allies,

THE MEDITERRANEAN LANDS ABOUT 1097.

Shepherd's *Atlas of Medieval and Modern History*, Henry Holt, 1932

he returned as fast as horse and ships could carry him to Africa to bury his dearly loved son.

Nine years later, Youssef ben Tachfin was again in Spain, again at the request of the groveling Moorish princes. This time it was not King Alfonso who had scared them, but the new Christian prince of Valencia, Roderigo Diaz de Vivar, better known as El Cid. This El Cid is not the noble Castilian warrior, pure of heart and honorable of deed, friend of the poor, defender of the Church, whom we know through *El Cantar de Mio Cid,* and Corneille's famous epic play, *Le Cid,* and recently through Hollywood, but the crafty, double-crossing, treacherous ravisher of virgins and altars, the El Cid of history, the El Cid of only one virtue and that of little value when put to evil uses—courage.

For five years El Cid defied Youssef and his generals. When they finally defeated his army, they broke his proud and wicked spirit. After his death in 1099 his widow, Ximena, held Valencia for a few years more; then, rather than let it fall to the Africans, she burned it to the ground.

By the end of the century, Youssef was in his nineties. Zaineb had been dead thirty years. Both she and Yasin would have been proud of the fiery patriarch. The burning zeal to establish the pure state of Islam, as Yasin had taught it so many years ago and so many miles away, still possessed him. When he looked at the soft princes of Spain, with their silks and jewels, with their pet poets and philosophers who believed in training the mind to question instead of obey, to think along new paths, to respect the beliefs of Christian and Jew, he found them worse than the pagans of the desert because, knowing the face of truth, they turned their backs on it. Ever since he had crossed the Straits at their first screams for help, he had felt their contempt for his nomad ignorance. Surely on that great and awful Day of Judgment, when man's good deeds are weighed in the scales against his evil ones, the fact that he could neither read nor write, that his only Arabic (with an accent these Andalusians scorned) was the prayers and verses of the Koran, would not hurt him in the eyes of Allah, the Just, the Merciful, the Compassionate. On the contrary, he thought, it was these princes who were deserving of punishment; and, Allah willing, in His Name he, Youssef, would administer it to them.

To sanction his plan he called together his doctors of law and theology, who were always on his side against the princes and their freethinking philosophers. Willingly they agreed that Koranic laws were being broken. They drew up a document, a *fetoua* stating that "the Andalusian Princes" were "dissolute, impious and licentious," that their bad example "had perverted the True Believers," that they "exacted illegal tribute and made secret alliances with the Christian Princes."

With this authority approved by the jurists of Islam as far east as Central Asia, Youssef set out on his last major task. The old oath he had taken when he first set foot in Spain—not to harm his Spanish allies—no longer bound him. One by one, under pressure from his general Abou Bekr (not, of course, the Abou Bekr dead in the Soudan, whose wife Youssef had married), the Andalusian princes renounced their rule.

With the fall of Seville in 1091, the wheel spins around again to Youssef's first meeting with the Kings of Spain. The poet-king Motamid— the one who had come to Africa to beg for help and had since plotted against Youssef—was taken prisoner. With his Christian wife and family he was sent to Aghmat, the first Almoravid capital in the High Atlas. While they earned their bread in menial labor, Motamid remembered his retort to his fellow princes when they warned him of the danger in inviting the Berbers to Spain, and he had answered: "If Allah wills that I lose my kingdom to a foreigner, I would far rather be a camel driver in Africa than a swineherd in Castile." When Motamid died, the poets who had shared his exile recited flowery and mournful verses around his tomb.

Abou Bekr's conquests continued. In Baghdad, the Caliph honored Youssef with the title of "Sovereign of Spain and the Moghreb." Though the old desert chief was fast nearing one hundred, he was still, above all, the warrior of Islam. Algeria tempted him, but the campaign ended in failure. A Prince of Bougie, with an army reinforced by the terrible Hilalian Arabs of the Second Invasion, pushed him back beyond Tlemcen. But what did it matter? In the great overall picture of his forty-seven-year rule, and an empire where Moslems in 300,000 mosques recited the *khotba* in his name, this small defeat was no more than a grain of sand in the lofty dunes of the desert. Youssef died in 1106 at the age of ninety-seven. Not far from his simple tomb in Marrakesh, the Koutoubia Minaret of the Almohads, conquerors of the next century, casts its shadow. The Almoravid melody begins to fade away as the notes of the Almohad measures are heard like approaching camel bells in the distance.

If Youssef ben Youssef, the son who died at Ceuta, had lived, there might have been another strong Almoravid ruler. His younger brother Ali, who followed the great Youssef, had none of the genius of the father. Though the house as a whole had become rotten as a wormy date by the soft sweet life of Spain, dissolute living was not Ali's weakness. Prayer and fasting, not government, was his passion. Though he made three invasions into Spain, in the end his losses offset his gains. Worse, however, than the loss of land and cities, was the hatred his corrupt, power-crazed army was building up, not only at home but among both Christians and Moslems of Spain. Ignorant and insolent, stripped of their desert virtues of religious zeal and simple living, they imitated all that was worst in luxury-loving Andalusia. No strong leader, living by the Koranic law, held them in check. They had become pawns of the crafty clergy, of harem intrigues and the vicious plots of palace guards.

Ali's capital, Marrakesh, was now a walled city, though his twelfth-century defenses were not the magnificent seven miles of red walls that the traveler sees today. If he himself was no lover of splendid living, his harem and his court demanded palaces equal to the best in Spain. The sons of the nomad Lemtuna had come a long way from their desert tents. Besides palaces, Ali built mosques as his father had done before him.

Of Almoravid mosques in Marrakesh, none remain.

But the great Kairouiine Mosque of Fez is an Almoravid monument, forbidden, of course, to all Christian dogs. There is another mosque, however, left by this first dynasty, that Christians may visit—the great Mosque of Tlemcen. Tlemcen, Moroccan until the arrival of the Turks in the early sixteenth century, ended up as an Algerian city. With the coming of the French, mosques were soon opened to people of all faiths. In the interior with its colonnades of marble and onyx, the decorations of carved plaster and cedar arabesques are a faithful imitation of the lovely Andalusian style. Unlike their successors the Almohads, the Almoravids had no original ideas for the artisans they imported from Spain.

Though Ali adorned his cities with Spanish mosques and palaces, he shared his father's horror of the tolerant attitudes and inquisitive minds of the liberal Spanish Moslems. Even more than his father, Ali persecuted Christians and, for Moslems, insisted on the orthodox, literal acceptance of the Koran and the Sunna (the Traditions of sacred custom gathered from the companions of Mohammed). For him and his equally narrow-minded clergy, these two books were enough for all pious Moslems. To write others commenting on these two, interpreting their meanings in a fresh light, meditating, thinking, wondering, was an affront against Allah and his Revelations. In great bonfires the libraries of the theologians, especially the works of the Persian Sufist El Ghazali, went up in flames and smoke. To write, to read, to own such books became a sin. Surely Allah would reward his servant Ali for such piety.

But for the expounders of Islam, piety had as many different faces as it had for the early bishops of Christianity. In the midst of his good works, Ali, Prince of the Faithful, received a bold and threatening letter beginning: "To him who is plunged in the seductions of earthly life. . . . It is necessary for us to make war upon you and we shall succeed. . . . The spilling of your blood is lawful, your property is rightful booty."

The letter came from an ugly, misshapen itinerant holy man who dressed in rags, who owned nothing but a staff and a leather water skin, who used the staff to break wine bottles and musical instruments, to push the Prince's sister off her mule into the gutter for appearing unveiled in public—a man by the name of Mohammed ibn Toumert, who called himself "The Mahdi."

THE UNITARIANS OF ISLAM
(The Almohads, 1148–1269)

Of all the many ragged, wild eyed, fanatical marabouts or holy men of Moroccan history who defied sultans and seized power, no one rose to such heights as Abou Abdallah Mohammed ibn Toumert. All were audacious. All hid behind the superstitious belief, as prevalent among the ignorant now as then, that a holy man could do no wrong. If his acts seemed insane, it was because his reason was with Allah. A holy man might appear naked in the street. He might lay violent hands on a girl or woman; in such a case she would profit by his touch or *baraka* and pious passersby would modestly cover the couple with a cloak. Some were charlatans. Some were truly devout. Some were an indeterminate mixture of both.

In the case of Ibn Toumert, the Arab historians put him down as a true servant of Allah. The French historians have their reservations about the selflessness of his astounding career. For effrontery it would be hard to find his equal. He labeled the Almoravids "husbands of whores" because their wives had learned to go unveiled in Spain. Descending from his Atlas village of Tinmel, he strode into the Great Mosque of Marrakesh on a

81

Friday during the holy month of Ramadan and seated himself and his rags on the royal throne. As Ali, Prince of the Faithful, himself appeared, and the congregation rose in homage to their ruler, the marabout (intoning verses of the Koran in a threatening voice) made no move to step down. When Ali banished him from the city after the incident of pushing a royal princess into the gutter, he set up his hovel outside the walls in a graveyard and continued thundering at the people of Marrakesh for their sinful ways.

From this picture, the self-styled *Mahdi* or Deliverer appears scarcely a notch above the ignorant masses who began gathering in increasing numbers around him. Actually he was one of the most highly educated and best-traveled inhabitants of the entire country. It is said that the ruler Ali had scarcely the education of a grammar school boy of Cordova. Ibn Toumert, on the other hand, was the product of the universities of Cordova, Cairo and Damascus. With nothing to help him but a brilliant mind he had pulled himself out of a poor lamplighter's family in a village of the Sous and at eighteen had set out to wrest an education from the great theologians and jurists of Spain and the Middle East. For ten years before returning to his native land he soaked himself in the wisdom of his learned teachers.

Almost one hundred years had passed since the veiled Lemtuna leader, Yahya, had listened to Abou Amran el Fassi lecturing in the court of the Kairouan Mosque and had brought back the orthodox missionary Yasin to convert the pagan subjects of the southwestern desert. Now there were new influences appearing in Islamic thought. Ibn Toumert absorbed them avidly, especially in Damascus at the feet of the great Persian mystic of the Sufist school, El Ghazali. More so than ever "there was no God but Allah," but with a more subtle pantheistic interpretation blossoming out of metaphysical Hinduism.

In Yasin's fundamentalist Malikite doctrine Allah is the one and only god but the Koran says: "He sees and hears." In other words he has human attributes. Among the mystic Sufis, Allah is one but his oneness is allegorical rather than literal. Instead of being able to see and hear, he *is* seeing and hearing, he *is* good *and* evil, the slayer and the slain, the timeless, endless universe itself, of which the soul of man is an indestructible fragment.

It is important to understand this, because it was what Ibn Toumert brought back to Morocco, especially to the Masmouda tribe of the High Atlas who were the first to accept him. When the Almoravids claimed that Allah "sees" and "hears," he accused them of the sin of anthropomorphism. That accusation was a much stronger weapon than merely upbraiding them for their lusts and luxuries. Moreover it made a magnificent impression on his supporters, the Masmouda.

At heart, of course, these Atlas mountaineers were more concerned with appeasing their own fearful world of omnipresent djinns and demons than with making advances to the invisible Allah. If they stumbled against a stone in the dark they apologized to the "Master of the Place"; in dealing with cats, they ran a finger down its ears to see if the hidden slit were present that labeled it a djinn in disguise. Everyone knew of someone (perhaps the frightful experience had been his own) who had been seduced by a woman, soft as a young mouse, of magic voice and dazzling beauty who in the light of day had shown only one eye in the middle of her jasmine white forehead. And everyone hung bits of cloth from venerable trees and from the bushes that encircled the "eye" of a spring, to win friends among the spirits of trees and water.

These acts were as necessary as sowing, reaping and harvesting. How else could one avoid disaster and gain favors? Their Mahdi's Allah was not a god from whom one could ask benefits. But they loved the insults this Mahdi of theirs hurled at the hated Almoravids, the first people who had ever conquered them. Even if their understanding of his metaphysical and theological doctrines was on a level with that of their sheep and goats, they were delighted to agree that the Almoravids were filled with the sins of anthropomorphism, idolatry and heresy. Best of all they loved calling them "husbands of whores." That they understood beautifully.

Twice before we have met Ibn Toumert's Sufist teacher, El Ghazali. The first time was when he was among the theologians and jurists of the Arab world who gave the great Youssef ben Tachfin permission to make war on the backsliding Moslem princes of Spain. Through correspondence he had been a friend of Youssef's, and had even considered a visit to him in 1106, the year of the great ruler's sudden death. He was mentioned again when his books were burned at the order of Youssef's son, the bigoted Ali. El Ghazali and the earlier Sufists of the movement were used to this sort of persecution from the hard-shell fundamentalists of the Middle East; some had paid for their beliefs with their lives. When El Ghazali heard about Ali's bonfire (according to the Arab historian El Marrakeshi) he prophesied as follows in the presence of his Damascus students: "It is sure that his (Ali's) rule will end soon and that his son will be killed. I think it will be none other than one of my disciples who will bring about these changes."

Whether the master's eye rested on the disciple Ibn Toumert or not, naturally the young Moroccan novice felt that he had been honored with a solemn mission.

By the time Ibn Toumert had returned to his native country and established himself in the Atlas village of Tinmel, he had with him a remarkable young Algerian by the name of Abd el Moumen whom he had picked up on his way home. They were the opposites that so often attract each other: Ibn Toumert, the ugly, misshapen, harsh reformer, Abd el Moumen the winning, handsome, future diplomat and warrior. Both came from the humblest backgrounds: Ibn Toumert, son of the lamplighter in the village mosque; Abd el Moumen, son of a village potter. Both ended up, thanks to Ibn Toumert's ingenuity, with noble pedigrees that turned them into *cherifs,* or descendants of the Prophet. Abd el Moumen was given a daughter of Idris II as a lineal ancestor.

Between the years of his arrival in the Atlas, 1121, and his early death in 1128, Ibn Toumert was well on his way to fulfilling El Ghazali's prophecy. Youssef's ineffectual son Ali still ruled at the foot of the Atlas in Marrakesh, but the Mahdi had turned the nearby mountain village of Tinmel into a city—a tremendous ribat—to hold his increasing army. Abd el Moumen, his young vizier and military commander, was winning over tribe after tribe by his battles. The government at Tinmel was reorganized into a Supreme Council of Ten plus two subordinate larger councils of tribal leaders. For his followers the Mahdi found an impressive name— a name that would have pleased his Sufist teacher who felt so strongly about the mystic unity of the universe. He called them Almohads, the Unitarians, those who stood for the Oneness of Allah. (For the reader who finds it difficult to distinguish between Almoravids and Almohads, it may help to remember the root word *ribat* in Almoravid, and *tawid,* the "oneness" or the "unity of God," in Almohad.)

When Ibn Toumert died, Abd el Moumen and his councilors managed to keep the fact secret for two years. By 1130 they felt sure enough of their strength to break the news. Weeping at their loss, the people of Tinmel accepted Abd el Moumen in the Mahdi's place.

Of all the rulers of Morocco, not one is easier to visualize presiding over his council than Abd el Moumen. Not another one of them, with all the grandeur of concubines, slaves, eunuchs and black bodyguards, had a tame lion entering at his side and lying like a loving dog at his feet, or a bird (perhaps a Senegal parrot brought north by caravan) repeating at effective intervals: "Victory and power belong to the Caliph Abd el Moumen!" The uneducated Algerian potter's son, even if his theology was feeble, had his own kind of skill in impressing the simple tribesmen.

Still hanging on to Marrakesh after a thirteen-year-old losing struggle with the new Almohad leader, Ali finally died in 1143. Great sections of the country had transferred their support to his rival. At the same time, Almohad armies under able generals across the Straits had been softening up Spain—not a difficult undertaking because of the hatred the Almoravid governors and their soldiers had aroused. Even the *Mozarabs* or Christians furnished the invaders with provisions and helped them over secret mountain passes of the Sierra Nevadas of Andalusia.

When El Ghazali, who died in 1111, prophesied that the son of the book-burning Moroccan ruler Ali would be killed instead of dying a natural death, his mysticism must have given him second sight. Ali's son Tachfin died a death anything but natural. In 1145, after his two short and hope-less years on the Moroccan throne, the victorious Abd el Moumen chased him eastward out of the border city of Tlemcen. Fleeing for his life on a stormy moonless night, his horse plunged over a precipice, killing the last vigorous ruler of the African Almoravids, to the delight of the Mos-lems of Spain who had spent three painful years under his rule as governor at Seville. An exiled branch of the family hung on for almost a century in the Balearic Isles making minor trouble for the Almohads.

From Tachfin's weakling son, Abd el Moumen soon took Fez, Meknès and Salé. The final triumph in 1146 was Ali's capital Marrakesh. From the very first the lamplighter's and the potter's sons had looked down at it from their Atlas foothold and dreamed of its fall. Abd el Moumen gave the conquered capital a special treatment, perhaps to please the spirit of his dead friend and patron. The city had surrendered. The gates were open. The last Almoravid was dead. Not a soul from the conquerors' camp passed through the gates. "Why?" the elders came out to the camp to ask. "Be-cause your mosques are not properly oriented toward Mecca," was the answer. "Purify your city by destroying them all and building new ones in their places."

This, then, is the reason why the Mosque of Ali ben Youssef, where Ibn Toumert defied Ali from his own throne, and all the other mosques of the Almoravids are as if they had never existed within the walls of Marrakesh.

The modern capital Rabat (again the root word *ribat*) owes the foundation of its *kasba* or fortress, with its ocher walls and gates, to Abd el Moumen. He needed a stronghold north of Marrakesh for controlling the rebellious city of Salé across the mouth of the Bou Regreg after he had destroyed its walls. Even more he needed a fortified center for as-sembling his troops, arms and provisions for the Spanish invasions. Twenty years later, his grandson, the great Yacoub el Mansour, developed this Rabat into a city with broad streets modeled on Egypt's Alexandria. In pirate days it shared the prosperity of Salé; yet until the present century under the French, it never became one of the great Imperial Cities like Fez, Marrakesh and Meknès.

It must always be remembered that until the dominion of the Ottoman Turks at the beginning of the sixteenth century there was no hard and fast boundary between the present Morocco and Algeria (even on the maps of today, parts of the Saharan dividing line are missing). If Abd el Moumen and his army chose to march east beyond Tlemcen, there was always the excuse of punishing some tribe whose orthodoxy fell below Almohad standards, or of rooting out the last of the Balearic Almoravids, who kept sneaking back into Africa in the hopes of regaining their empire.

In 1152 with a huge army that seemed to be headed for Spain, Abd el Moumen suddenly turned east and took Algiers by surprise. With military and administrative genius that the French historian Masqueray compares to that of Charlemagne, he moved farther and farther east gathering in cities—Bougie, Tunis, Sfax, Gabès—along the way until by 1160 his empire stretched beyond Tunisia to Libyan Barca.

As usual the Christian Kings of northern Spain—of Leon, Castile and Navarre—took advantage of their enemy's absence. The last great *jihad* of the conqueror's life was to push them back into their own kingdoms, reorganize the country and install two sons and a trusted general as governors.

Two years later, 1163, Abd el Moumen died in Salé.

It can be safely said that no other Moroccan ruler of past centuries is so sympathetic and endearing a character to read about. In the endless, blood-stained pages of dynastic history that produce a terrible numbness to sadistic cruelty, this first Almohad stands out as sensitive, generous and humane. Cruel people cannot make pets of lions. When the Almoravid ruler Youssef ben Tachfin carried his enemy, the poet Motamid, King of Seville, back to the Atlas as a prisoner, he made him beg for his living. When Abd el Moumen took a former enemy, the cultivated Prince of Bougie, back to Marrakesh, he made him an honored guest at his court. And when the Hilalian Arabs turned against him, and their three chiefs fled after a bloody four day battle, deserting their wives, Abd el Moumen captured them and took them back to Marrakesh, where he not only gave them back their wives (instead of adding them to his own harem) but returned the chiefs to their country with generous presents.

There is also the story that traveling across a dismal and waterless Algerian plateau of dwarf palms he suddenly ordered his army to halt and make camp. When he finished the sunset prayer, he explained to his puzzled companions that once as a youth in this same spot he had spent a night cold, hungry and poor; now he could do no less than stop and thank Allah the Generous, the All Powerful, for his change of fortune.

Youssef the Wise was not his father's immediate successor. For forty-five days there was a Mohammed, the chosen heir. Though during his father's lifetime he had been an able general and diplomat, he was soon disposed of by the Council. Is it possible that the wise and clever Abd el Moumen was unaware that his favorite son had long been a drunkard and a leper?

As usual there was no scarcity of other brothers to take his place. The choice happily fell on Abou Jacoub Youssef. With Youssef, who loved Spain, and with his son, the great Mansour the Victorious, both Morocco and Spain saw a brief renascence of Moorish art and letters. This time, instead of Cordova, Seville was the city of science, philosophy, splendid buildings and luxurious bazaars. It was said that if you craved bird's milk you could find it in Seville.

The unfinished Hassan Tower of the Almohads.

No line can be drawn between the achievements of father and son. What Youssef the Wise began, his great son, Yacoub the Victorious, finished. Mosques and accompanying minarets on both sides of the Straits were monuments not only to their greatness but to a new and original development and, in the eyes of many, the most beautiful of all periods in Moorish architecture and decoration. Where the mosques have vanished,

87

the minarets still stand. The Giralda, once the minaret of the Great Mosque, is known to every visitor to Seville, as is the Tower of Gold, built to house the royal treasure.

In Morocco the Koutoubia Tower of Marrakesh and the unfinished Hassan Tower of Rabat, built by the architect who gave Seville the Giralda, have given fame by their outstanding beauty to the country's rectangular, gold tipped minarets. Historians, however, cannot agree whether their architect was one Sicilian or two Moors. (Perhaps the most recent in the long line going back to ninth-century Fez, and familiar to many who have never visited Africa, is the minaret of the modern Paris Mosque attached to the Moslem Institute.)

The appeal of Almohad decorative art lies in the reduction of the over-elaborate intricacy of the Moorish arabesque to calm and forceful simplicity. In an uncrowded pattern of geometrical and floral elements, stars and hexagons, stylized leaves and tendrils, interlaced arches and their lobes, there are spaces to clarify the design and rest the eye. On four faces of the Koutoubia Tower, recessed rectangular panels form series of delicate arches. Taking fire from the African sun like a kingfisher's wing, a band of turquoise-blue enamel tiles runs under the crenellations of the parapet. Here a second miniature tower repeats the pattern of arches under a melon dome of gilded bronze topped by three gigantic gilded balls of diminishing size. The gold is said to have been applied to the accompaniment of magic incantations, thereby delivering it to the protection of djinns. After experiencing the perfection of the Koutoubia, one cannot look at Seville's Giralda without longing to lop off the incongruous Christian superstructure and restore it to its original Moorish harmony.

Rabat, Marrakesh and the Mahdi's Atlas village of Tinmel, the cradle of the empire, are the places to look for Almohad gates and mosques. In Tinmel, the Mosque, built next to the Mahdi's tomb, lies in ruins; but enough is left of the arcaded interior and *mihrab* (or prayer niche) to prove it a pure and beautiful example of this twelfth-century Moorish art.

Tinmel, about eighty miles south of Marrakesh, lies on the northern slope of the High Atlas near the crest. The road from Marrakesh to Taroudant in the Sous passes within five miles of the ruins, about fifteen miles before reaching the winter snow line and the 7,000 foot col of Tizi-n-Test. A special trip from Marrakesh or a halt on the drive over the High Atlas takes the visitor back 800 years to Ibn Toumert and the birth of the greatest of Moroccan dynasties.

If Tinmel was the cradle of the Almohad dynasty, it was Seville that became the blazing star of the Moslem West under the second Almohad Emir, Youssef the Wise—Seville with its bazaars and palaces, its warehouses along the river quays, its aqueducts and bridges of boats. Beyond

The Koutoubia Tower of the Almohads,
Marrakesh.

the bustle of the worldly city lay the peace of gardens and orchards—all
the wonders of Moorish horticulture. Just as the flashing gold and the
blue-green tiles of the Giralda could be seen a day's journey away, so the
jasmine and orange blossom fragrance of Seville's gardens met the incoming ships almost at the river's mouth as they sailed up the broad waters of
the Guadalquivir.

Youssef the Wise came honestly by his title. He knew his own Koran
by heart, and also knew the works of Plato and Aristotle. To the post
of vizirs, physicians and cadis he had appointed geniuses whose knowledge
and thinking influenced the science and philosophy of medieval and Renais-
sance Europe and indirectly our modern world: Ibn Tufail, Avenzoar,
and (greatest of all) Averroës.

In their stupendous minds, the known knowledge of the material
and spiritual worlds flowed in an undivided stream. Any one of them, as
well as of their less famous colleagues, might have served with equal distinction as philosopher, physician, judge—even poet and musician. Today
we think of Ibn Tufail as author of a philosophical romance that may
have influenced the allegorical aspects of Defoe's *Robinson Crusoe*. Avenzoar stands out as the greatest of Moorish physicians, teacher of a still
greater pupil, the Aristotelian philosopher Averroës.

To his friend Youssef, to the people of the court and to the Arab
world in general, Averroës was known as Ibn Rashd; but to the medieval
Schoolmen—Albertus Magnus, Thomas Aquinas, Duns Scotus, who met

89

Aristotle through his *Commentaries*—he was Averroës. He was Averroës to his admirer Roger Bacon, who recommended the study of Arabic at thirteenth-century Oxford so that he could be read in the original; and Averroës to the Emperor Frederick II, who welcomed Michael Scott, the first translator of Averroës (in Latin, of course) to his Sicilian court in defiance of the disapproving Church.

Before Averroës produced his detailed *Commentaries* on the works of the Greek philosopher whose intellect he considered perfection, the latter was known to the Western world only through fragments, and therefore, of course, scarcely known at all. In addition to the gift of Aristotle, Averroës contributed his own philosophy. Here was no Sufist mysticism such as El Ghazali's, but also no theological tyranny like that of both Christian and Moslem creeds. With the devout and rational Averroës, reason and faith followed parallel paths, arriving at the same goal: faith for the masses; pure reason for those with the mental ability to reach the concept of universal intelligence, or Allah. This defiance of theology was a bold and new step. Thought was liberated. Science could advance. The free inquiring mind could move forward without the blinders of either Rome or Mecca. Roger Bacon experimented. The interest in natural sciences began.

Needless to say, the Church thundered. The Aristotelian *Commentaries*, labeled the "unholy glosses of infidels," were made forbidden reading. The Averroist doctrine of the unity of the intellect opposed both Moslem and Christian belief in the immortality of the individual soul. Petrarch stated that no good could come out of Arabia.

While Youssef the Wise ruled in Spain and Morocco, Averroës found protection from the enmity of the orthodox theologians, who hated him in particular and philosophers in general. When the rule passed to Youssef's son, Yacoub el Mansour, Averroës continued at first to hold positions of honor either as cadi or court physician in Seville and in the capitals of Morocco, at the same time continuing his tremendous outpouring of work. He himself tells us that except for two evenings of his adult life the rest were spent in study. The two exceptions were the night of his marriage and the night of his father's death.

It is strange and sad to read that, though Yacoub el Mansour seems to have valued his famous friend no less than his father had done before him, he nevertheless eventually succumbed to the pressure of orthodox hatred, by stripping the great man of his honors and banishing him from the court. This was in 1185. Two contradictory accounts describe the circumstances of the philosopher's last years: one that he died a beggar in Fez, spat upon by his enemies; the other, a happier one, that Yacoub a year before his death restored him to his former honors.

Though Youssef the Wise was not militant enough by nature to extend his empire, at the same time he had no intention of letting the

Christian Spaniards, the Balearic Almoravids or the Normans of Sicily violate any of the territory. For one thing, every league of it was too valuable. From the distant borders, long gold-laden mule trains delivered taxes to the royal strongholds such as Seville's Tower of Gold. Consequently, like his father, Abd el Moumen, he was spasmodically torn from his capitals of Fez and Marrakesh, and the deep and captivating discussions with his protégé Averroës and the other great scholars of the court on the twofold path to God, in order to put down trouble in Tunisia, in his own Sous, and in Spain.

An alliance of Portugal, the last of Youssef's enemies, with Alfonso VIII of Castile, cost him his life. While his son Ishak was attacking Lisbon with the bulk of the army, he himself laid siege to Santarem. During a savage sortie from the town, Youssef was badly wounded and his son Yacoub, who rushed to his aid from Seville, could get him alive no farther than Algeciras. From there, the body of Youssef the Wise was borne in solemn procession across the country he had ruled so justly and so well— the country to which he and his line had given its finest monuments. In the High Atlas town of Tinmel, he was buried beside the tomb of his father and the revered Mahdi.

Yacoub I, known to history as El Mansour the Victorious, from his victory over Alfonso VIII at Alarcos, succeeded to the throne in 1184. To forestall family intrigue, two brothers and an uncle were summarily disposed of by the electing Council. Members of the Council would have saved their new ruler trouble if they had made it three brothers and two uncles. In Spain Yacoub's brother Yahya and in the Middle Atlas his uncle Soleiman both tried, unsuccessfully, to dethrone him.

The great empire founded by Abd el Moumen rose to its peak under the short but brilliant fifteen-year rule of his grandson, Yacoub el Mansour. During the first ten years, the last of the Balearic Almoravids under Yahya gave him trouble in Algeria and Tunisia. With the help of Karagouz, a Turkish-Armenian and brother of the great Saladin of Crusade fame, they seized the eastern end of the Empire. When the Almohad army of El Mansour pushed them out into the Libyan desert, they struck back as soon as it had turned west again.

Saladin himself, now ruler of Egypt, first supported his brother Karagouz, then switched sides to make overtures to El Mansour. He wanted the help of the Moroccan ruler's fleet against Richard the Lion Hearted of England, who had taken the Syrian city of Acre. El Mansour refused. To help Saladin would have been to break a truce with the Normans of Sicily and the Italian Republics of Pisa and Genoa. By thus honoring his word and avoiding Turkish entanglements he undoubtedly saved Morocco from the future fate of Turkish rule, which later lost both Algeria and Tunisia their independence.

Despite troubles in the East, there was time to build ramparts, gates, mosques, medersas, kasbas, and hospitals—among the last a Marrakesh hospital where the Emir visited the sick every Friday after prayers; time for roads and aqueducts; time for perfecting the orderly government born of his grandfather's genius.

Though war and conquest were not this intellectual ruler's prime interests, defeat by the Portuguese at Santarem, where his father, Youssef the Wise, had been mortally wounded, called for revenge, especially since the Christians were as usual making trouble in Spain, under Alfonso IX of Castile.

In 1195, El Mansour summoned his subjects to a *jihad* or Holy War. The powerful Moroccan army met Alfonso between Cordova and Calatrava, below the castle of Alarcos. This was the third and virtually the last of the spectacular triumphs of Moslems over Spanish Christians. Against the shock of well-disciplined foot soldiers, superb cavalry and the Emir's Black Guard, Alfonso's troops were helpless. The Castilian king himself abandoned the field. Thousands were killed. Twenty thousand prisoners were liberated; forty thousand were sent back to Morocco as captives. Included in the booty were 60,000 coats of mail for the Royal Treasury, and the gilded bronze balls for the summit of the Koutoubia Tower. Yacoub became El Mansour, the Victorious. Among Moroccan rulers there are many El Mansours. None, however, not even the great Saadian, the Gilded Ahmed ("Gilded" from the stolen gold of Timbuctu) is so great as Yacoub.

Alarcos was not only the last great Moslem triumph on European soil, but El Mansour's last victory. If he had had his way he would have marched east to Egypt to punish Saladin's Turks, who were worshiping Allah by means of the heretical Hanefite rite; but this was not written for him in the Book of Fate. In 1199, at the age of forty-nine, the most illustrious of Berber rulers died at Salé, ending the period of greatest Berber power and highest Berber civilization. In the same year, Richard the Lion Hearted of England died in France.

In the chronicles of world history, a direct succession of three such strong rulers as Abd el Moumen, Youssef the Wise and Yacoub el Mansour is a rare occurrence. It is therefore not surprising to find El Mansour's shy, stammering eighteen-year-old son, Mohammed en Nasir, incapable of holding the great Almohad Empire together. A Balearic Almoravid by the name of Yahya was still a powerful opponent in the East, and in Spain the Christian world was still smarting under the defeat of Alarcos.

In the East, the young emir's fleet managed to push the Almoravid Yahya back again into the desert and retake the seized Tunisian cities. In order to hold them while he turned toward trouble in Spain, he installed a strong governor from the High Atlas, Abou Mohammed the Hafsid. In less than thirty years, Abou Mohammed's successors had defied their Moroccan benefactors and set up the independent Hafsid dynasty of Tunisia, which flourished intermittently until the 1574 advent of the Turks.

In Spain a second great fragment of the Empire was destined to crumble away. With encouragement from the Pope, Spaniards and Portuguese massed against the Moors. In a battle as famous for defeat as Alarcos had been for victory, Mohammed and his army were sent fleeing toward the Straits. Las Navas de Tolosa, 1212, marks the beginning of the end of Moslem grandeur in Spain. By 1246, with the fall of Seville, out of all the kingdoms that had paid tribute not only to Allah but to the sciences and the arts, only Granada remained. Even Granada's Moorish kings recognized the sovereignty of Castile until their fall and exile in 1492.

In the Almohad capital, Marrakesh, the elders punished their ruler for his defeat by forcing his abdication in favor of his sixteen-year-old son, El Mostansir. The unfortunate En Nasir thereupon either drank himself to death or was assassinated by palace guards. For an astonishing incident during the wretched Nasir's reign Budgett Meakin gives Matthew of Paris and his *Lives of the Monks of St. Albans* as source. According to the ancient chroniclers, King John of England, frightened by his powerful barons, is said to have sent envoys to En Nasir, begging for help *and promising to become a Moslem* if the help were forthcoming.

Only one event of importance to Morocco marks the ten-year rule of the youthful El Mostansir—the first ominous stirrings of the dynasty to follow.

In El Mansour's great Holy War against Spain that ended in the victory of Alarcos, rival tribes buried their hatreds temporarily and marched side by side. As soon as the war was over and the spoils and rewards of the *jihad* were distributed, the hatreds flared again. The Beni Merin, no lovers of the Almohads to begin with, smarted under the conviction that their immediate enemies, the Beni Abd el Ouadid, had received larger, richer and more fertile lands than they themselves had, as reward for their role in the great battle. From their allotted territory on the Low Moulaya, the great river that enters the Mediterranean near the present Algerian-Moroccan border, the Beni Merin moved westward along the historic Taza Corridor toward Fez, pillaging as they went, and throwing back an Almohad army of 10,000. From then on, in spite of occasional setbacks, their power grew. The last ineffectual Almohads struggled helplessly against them.

Between the defeat by the Spanish at Las Navas in 1212 and the fall of Marrakesh to the Merinids in 1269, nine Almohad rulers followed the deposed En Nasir. There was not a giant among them. Drowned, strangled, beheaded by a son-in-law, murdered by members of their household or their personal guard, most of them met violent deaths. Only one is of interest.

After the drowning of a nonentity by the name of El Adil, two rivals, one in Marrakesh, one in Spain, claimed the throne. Behind the Spanish El Mamoun stood the first Ferdinand of Leon and Castile. With Ferdinand's backing, El Mamoun took Marrakesh. This El Mamoun was not only the son of a Christian slave (with all the captured Christians added to the harems of Moroccan rulers there was nothing unusual about that) but had a Christian among his four legal wives. In this respect he seems to have been unique from the days of Idris I to Hassan II (the great seventeenth-century Sultan Moulay Ismail had an "English Queen," but she had been persuaded to acknowledge Allah as the true and only God by having her feet thrust into burning oil). Whether because of his Christian wife, or Ferdinand's help, or both, El Mamoun permitted the Christian Church of Notre Dame to be built in Marrakesh for the benefit of Christian captives and mercenaries. Though it was destroyed a few years later, the Bishopric of Marrakesh lasted until the end of the century.

In addition to having a sympathy for Christians, El Mamoun turned not only against the Almohad cheiks but against the worship of the revered Mahdi himself. Ever since the Mahdi's death, the cheiks had been the power behind the throne, the electors and deposers of rulers. El Mamoun resented and feared their authority (hadn't one of them declared himself independent and started a kingdom of his own in Tunis!). All those unfortunate enough not to be able to escape his reach, he therefore killed. Besides cursing the name of the Mahdi, without whom his Almohad house would never have existed, he forbade the mention of the founder's name from the pulpits of the mosques.

With El Mamoun's death in 1232, the crumbling of the Empire advanced rapidly. At Tlemcen (today inside the Algerian border) the Almohad vassal Yaghmorasan ibn Ziyan defied the once powerful dynasty and set up his own kingdom. By 1248, the Merinids were masters of Fez; and by 1269 they had thrown the last weakling Almohad, Abou Dabbous, out of Marrakesh. The two imperial cities were in their hands, and with them control of the Moghreb.

CHAPTER IX

෴෴෴

LORDS OF THE MERINO SHEEP
(The Merinids, 1248–1420)

෴෴෴

Merino wool is well known to the Western world. It covers the handsome Merino sheep, with their spiral horns and orange-tinted muzzles, that the Beni Merin introduced from their Atlas pastures into Spain. Now, though these African sheep range from Australia to the Argentine, probably few of their modern breeders associate the name with the sixth Moroccan dynasty of the thirteenth and fourteenth centuries—the Beni Merin or Merinids. This origin of the name of the wool is given by Prosper Ricard, author of the Moroccan *Guide Bleu*. It must, however, be regretfully added that the *Encyclopaedia Britannica*, though admitting that the sheep were introduced into Spain by the Moors, explains the word "Merino" as a corruption of the medieval Latin word *majorinus*—a steward who inspects sheep pastures.

In the beginning, the Beni Merin were not natives of Morocco. Like so many other Berber tribes they had been pushed to the west from the region of Biskra in the central Moghreb by the Hilalian or Second Arab Invasion. During early Almohad rule, they were a proud free people, strong and mobile enough to defy tax collectors. In winter they roamed the high plateaus and semi-arid fringes of the Sahara southwest of Tlemcen; in summer they moved their flocks and tents up into the Middle Atlas pastures south of the slopes of the eastern Rif. Their participation in Yacoub el Mansour's *jihad*, which ended in the victorious battle of Alarcos, was undoubtedly their first encounter with the soft luxury of Andalusian life, its refinements and its decorative arts. A century later, toward the middle of the fourteenth century, they had developed and imprinted on that same Andalusian art their own exquisite expressions of carved plaster and cedar and mosaic tile in the medersas of Fez and Salé.

After Alarcos, when they were still sulking about their share of the loot and land, and when El Mansour's pathetic son En Nasir lost the battle of Las Navas against the Spanish Christians and drank himself to death, they saw their chance for revenge on the stingy Almohads, and marched west.

Though their leader was known for his piety, this invasion had none of the fanatical religious fervor behind it that marked the advent of the Almoravids and Almohads. What the Beni Merin wanted was more fertile land for their flocks. Ahead lay the rich olive orchards of Fez and Meknès. Moreover, their cousins and rivals, the Beni Abd el Ouadid, were not only enjoying superior rewards from Alarcos, but the Ouadid leader had been appointed prince of the city of Tlemcen, for helping one of the Hafsid princes of Tunis against a rival. To make matters even worse in the eyes of the Beni Merin, the second of the Tlemcen princes announced his independence.

The anarchy that ruled throughout the country after the Las Navas defeat (1212) made it possible for the Beni Merin to establish a rough sort of rule over many of the tribes of the north. The cities, however, still recognized the Almohads. With a sudden burst of power, the Emir Es Said defeated the invaders near Fez. This was in 1244. The Beni Merin not only lost their leader but fled so far back into the desert that it seemed to Fez and the Emir to be the end of their insolence.

Though they had lost their leader, they had gained another in one of his sons. Abou Yahya Abou Bekr, famous in battle for carrying a lance in each hand, was both warrior and politician. Out of the three-sided enmity of the Emir Es Said, the rebel prince Yaghmorasan of Tlemcen, and himself, he craftily eliminated the Almohad Emir. By a treacherous offer to side with the latter against the Tlemcen rebel, he appears to have lured the gullible Es Said into a fatal snare. Upon Es Said's death, the Emir's army fled in disorder. Abou Yahya followed, cut it to pieces, and delivered Es Said's corpse to Yaghmorasan. Instead of exhibiting the head over the gate of his city, Yaghmorasan, a prince of noble and civilized disposition, gave his enemy honorable burial.

While Abou Yahya was taking possession of Fez in 1248, and thereby establishing the new dynasty of the Merinids, and his son Abou Youssef was crushing Almohad power forever by the seizure of Marrakesh in 1269, events of importance to the future of Morocco were taking place in Spain. After Las Navas, the Moslem population of Cordova fled in terror. Ferdinand III of Castile and Leon had no trouble in conquering the city in 1236. His first act was to purify the Great Mosque, dedicate it to the Assumption of the Virgin, and butcher its classical Moslem beauty. In Seville, which he took in 1248, he left only the foundations of the Almohads' masterpiece, for his new cathedral. For his crusade against the Moors he was canonized by the Roman Catholic Church. From Seville, too, the inhabitants fled in a great sad exodus—an exile to be repeated many times in the next three hundred and fifty years. Granada, last of the Moorish kingdoms, could not begin to hold them all. Many of the exiles crossed over to the African shore, adding to the luster of the courts of Fez, Tlemcen and Tunis. Some, of course, bitter, jobless and revengeful, became pirates.

Tlemcen, in particular, benefited from the fleeing population of fallen Valencia. In 1238, the remarkable Yaghmorasan had been the ruler three years. He was a Zenata Berber of the same immense confederation of tribes as his cousins the Merinids, with the same roots in the nomad life of tents and flocks, and, like so many Africans, had come under the Andalusian spell, and welcomed not only the scholars and poets of Valencia but also the skillful and industrious artisans. His love for the learned Arabs of Spain was as great as his hatred for the uncouth pillaging Arabs of the Second Invasion. One of his greatest ambitions was to Arabize, in the Andalusian sense, the Berbers of his own Abd el Ouadid tribe, and all other tribes under his rule.

In Fez, the Merinid ruler Abou Yahya had also left the simple world of sheepherding far behind. Only the purest Arabic was spoken at his court; scholars, under his aegis, attached themselves to the great Kairouiine Mosque; and Andalusian architects, with the Alhambra as an ideal, began to substitute the sensuous beauty of intricate lace-like arabesques and honeycombs for the classical restraint of the Almohads.

With the death of Abou Yahya in 1258, the long dynastic struggle between his son Abou Youssef and Yaghmorasan, between Beni Merin and Beni Ouadids, between Fez and Tlemcen, had now begun. Though neither of these civilized Berber rulers who should have been friends was primarily a warrior, the age-old tribal rivalry was too deep-seated to make it possible for either to acknowledge the sovereignty of the other.

For the devout Abou Youssef, who liked to spend his nights in prayer, and to contemplate the lives of saints, there was fortunately also in his make-up the dynamic drive of his father, which enabled him to forge the splintered Moghreb into a submissive whole—all, that is, except the proud and stubborn kingdom of Tlemcen: to make four successful expeditions to Spain; to build a new Fez; to show deep concern for the sick, the blind, the insane and the leprous; and to govern the Medusa's head of rebel tribes and cities with wisdom, justice and strength. Three times he defeated his rival Yaghmorasan in important battles, stripping him of his lands but not of his stout-walled city.

When, at a cry for help from Granada, he turned his back on Africa for the first Spanish campaign, it must have been with the same uneasiness felt by all his predecessors in similar Holy Wars. Of his four successful Spanish campaigns, the first two were against Alfonso the Wise of Castile, friend of Moors and friend of Moorish learning, who was threatening Granada; the third, as King Alfonso's ally when the King's son Sancho, afterward "The Cruel," rebelled against his father; and the fourth, after the noble Alfonso's death, against the despicable Sancho himself. Though not one of the four victories did more than confirm the independence of Granada, they were nevertheless victories fought by men whose grandfathers had fallen at Las Navas, and therefore a small comforting revenge.

In the fourth and last of these minor victories there was particular satisfaction in the terms of the treaty. Among other advantages, thirteen mule loads of invaluable Arabic manuscripts, seized by Spain at the fall of Cordova and Seville, were returned by Sancho. To be sure, Abou Youssef, in his turn, paid two million gold *maravedis* for the damage his armies had done to the Spanish countryside. The gold *maravedi* (a Cordova coin of Almoravid origin, as the name indicates) would be worth about two dollars today. It was a huge sum, but well worth it to the book-loving Abou Youssef for his new medersa in Fez. In 1286 on the way back to Morocco, as Almohad Youssef had done a hundred years before him, he died at Algeciras. His able son Abou Yacoub inherited the throne.

Though Abou Youssef lies buried in the Merinid necropolis of the Chella between Rabat and the river, the "new" city of Fez—Fez el Djedid—was his creation. A city built in 1276 scarcely seems new today. Its ramparts, its mosques, twisting alleys and teeming *Mellah* (the ancient Jewish Quarter) seem of an age with Old Fez—Fez el Bali. Remember, though, that Old Fez was four hundred and fifty years old when the Merinids took it in 1248. Already it was cramped and crowded between its walls. There was no room for a new royal palace, new mosques, barracks, an armory and other buildings and quarters worthy of a new dynasty.

The brothers Jean and Jérome Tharaud, in their *Fez ou les Bourgeois de l'Islam*, compare the two cities to the shape of a bee. The small "New Fez" of the Merinids is the head, the river the narrow waist, and Old Fez the large wide body tilted up against the steep hillside. If, on a visit

The Chella Gate of the Merinids.

to Fez, you are wise enough to choose the Palais Jamai as your hotel—an enchanting remodeled nineteenth-century vizir's palace—you will be situated near the sting of the "bee," just inside the north wall, and can look down on both of the oyster-white cities in their frame of olive orchards. A third Fez, the Fez Nouvelle of the French, lying west of the walled cities, is a modern upstart of only half a century.

Yaghmorasan had died in 1283, three years before his enemy, Abou Youssef. Now the two antagonists were Yaghmorasan's son Othman, and the Merinid Abou Yacoub, with Abou Yacoub becoming doubly bitter when one of his rebel sons was given asylum by the Tlemcen prince. Trouble with Sancho in Spain was of little interest to Abou Yacoub in comparison with the defiance of Tlemcen. Out of his twenty-one-year rule, twelve years were spent working steadily for the downfall of this city, seizing and fortifying the nearby towns and controlling the country as far east as Algiers.

The last eight found him camped in front of its walls. Camped is hardly the word. Abou Yacoub built a city of palaces, mosques and bazaars, where he could rule as luxuriously as at Fez el Djedid, and at the same time tighten the vise on Tlemcen. Confident of success, he called it Mansoura, the Victorious. From Tunis, Cairo and Mecca, ambassadors came to pay their respects. As proof of his own piety, he revived the Mecca pilgrimage, impossible during the long civil wars, sending a Koran copied in his own hand as an offering to the Holy Shrine.

Around Tlemcen itself he built a trench and a wall. According to the Arab historian Ibn Khaldoun, not even a ghost could have penetrated the blockade. The stubborn and starving inhabitants ended by eating dogs and snakes.

This great city, known to the Romans as Pomaria—City of Apples —had been given its first mosque by the first Idris. In all the myriad bloody struggles for power (tribal, dynastic, schismatic, heretical and orthodox) from Cordova to Baghdad, from the shores of the Mediterranean to the banks of the Niger, from the coming of Idris to the coming of the Turks, it stood as the key stronghold. When it seemed on the edge of surrender, the *Deus ex machina*, the hand of Allah, reached out to save it. A eunuch's dagger ended the life and ambitions of Abou Yacoub. The dark cunning of harem intrigue was always as dangerous as the forthright attack of any enemy. "The empire," said Ibn Khaldoun, "was freed of a stain that tarnished it and a rule that made it contemptible." But the French historian Coissac de Chavrebière disagrees. "Great protector of scholars, great builder of medersas and mosques, the sultan did not deserve this wrong."

Fortunately for the besieged Tlemcen, Abou Yacoub's grandson and designated heir, Abou Thabit, only twenty-three years old, had four menacing rivals to contend with. In exchange for support against them, he agreed to raise the siege. At his death a year later, a brother, even younger, took power and also kept the peace with Tlemcen. He, too, died in the second year of his reign.

For the third time, Tlemcen was fortunate. The next ruler, Abou Said Othman, son of Abou Youssef's old age, and a lover of peace and pious works, had no desire to bring Tlemcen to its knees. Posterity is also fortunate in this suspension of the Tlemcen hostilities, as it enabled Abou Othman to build instead of fight. The visitor to Fez, who may not enter the mosques, may and should visit the six beautiful medersas. Of the six, Abou Said Othman's creation, Medersa el Attarin ("of the Perfume Sellers," because of the nearby perfume souks) stands out as the masterpiece.

No English word conveys the exact meaning of the Moslem word *medersa*. Think of it as a college—or rather the college dormitory—attached to the nearby mosque, and somewhat resembling a medieval monastery of the Christian West, but with political as well as theological aspects—a building to house non-resident students during their studies in the great cities. In the case of Fez, the medersas were attached to the

Kairouiine University. Nothing was so simple as, or more austere than, the cells of students looking down onto the court from the second story; but nothing was more elaborately and magnificently decorated than the walls of the court, the vestibules, the hall of prayer and the entrance portico. Elaborate surface decoration and flat architectural simplicity produce the charm of Moorish medersas. The mosaic of floor and sturdy square columns have that shimmer of glazed tiles as cool to the eye as water to the touch. Above them the white arches, smooth, lobed or scalloped, support panels of delicately carved plaster, pierced with smaller arches, honey-combed perhaps, under friezes of flowing (cursive) or angular (cufic) holy script. Above the Arabic script run more carved friezes in the time-darkened cedar moulding and overhanging roof.

In his sensitive book on Mauritania, Sacheverell Sitwell states that no Alhambra filigree is more delicate than the carved plaster of Moroccan medersas, but modifies his enthusiasm by saying that the medersas are all the same. This seems a surprising statement to come from such a connois-seur of art and architecture. Is the explanation, perhaps, that the Western eye finds nothing but sameness in the lace-like patterns of the carved plaster panels? The non-Moslem may examine them carefully enough to distinguish the floral arabesques from the geometrical, the cursive script from the cufic. Unlike the Moslem, however, who has lived with abstract design and nothing but abstract design from the days of Mohammed, he has no eye to follow and appreciate the fine points of its infinite and astounding variations.

When the historians say that Abou Said's reign of twenty-one years was peaceful, they mean, of course, peaceful in comparison to the stormy warpaths of most of his predecessors. He had time to build medersas, raise the ramparts and splendid gate of his family necropolis, the Chella, and above all to restore in his medersas the traditional orthodox Malikite rite of the Almoravids, which had been displaced by the mystical Sufist doc-trines of the Almohads.

Abou Said neither gained new territory nor lost old. To be sure, his favorite son and heir, Abou Ali, rebelled and temporarily deposed him. Forgiven, the monster rebelled again. Most rulers would have regretfully removed the head of such an heir, but Abou Ali was forgiven a second time and sent off to the fringe of the desert as governor. His brother Aboul Hassan now replaced him as his father's appointed heir.

Wise enough to know that the Moslem cause was lost in Spain, the pious and peace-loving Abou Said refused Granada's call for help. A half-hearted expedition against Tlemcen brought neither victory nor defeat. He might even have preferred to live at peace with Tlemcen, if he had not set his heart on a Hafsid princess of Tunis as bride for his son Moulay Hassan. When his ambassador first broached the subject, the alliance was refused. Later, however, when the Hafsid Caliph wanted help from Morocco to fend off a Tlemcen attack, Abou Said was in a position to bargain, and with success. On his way to meet and welcome the princess, suddenly, and most unfortunately for his enemy Tlemcen, since his successor renewed the siege of the city, Abou Said died.

If one considers how widely the peoples of the known world were represented in the imperial harems of the Moghreb, through war, piracy and ambassadorial gifts, it is not surprising to find the color of skins ranging from the prized ivory-white of the Circassians through the tawny shades of mixed blood or the bronze of Abyssinia to the porphyry-black of the Soudan. According to the visiting Englishman John Windus, the sadistic Sultan Moulay Ismail of the seventeenth century, was "of a tawny complexion" through a black mother. Aboul Hassan, the next Merinid, inherited a bronze complexion from his father's Abyssinian concubine, and has come down in history as the "Black Sultan."

Aboul Hassan, as we have seen, owed his throne to his older brother's savage attempts to depose their father, Abou Said. How did this make him regard his own sons, one wonders, as he watched the young horde born of his harem visits grow to manhood as capable of danger as a hatching of cobra's eggs? Did no astrologer warn him against the spirited and ambitious nineteen-year-old Abou Inan, his viceroy in Tlemcen while he himself marched east to add Tunis to his empire?

Aboul Hassan stands out not only as the greatest of Merinid rulers but as one of the great rulers of the fourteenth century. His vitality, his power, his piety and his riches were enormous; but his death was most pitiful, most miserable and most tragic. Only the death of the good tenth-century Idrisid Yahya IV, who died a beggar, can compare with it.

Because his Tunisian bride immediately became his favorite, Aboul Hassan's first act was to carry out his father's promise to help the Hafsids against Tlemcen mischief. Together his own and the Hafsid army dislodged Tlemcen forces from a siege of Bougie. In the south, his rebellious brother Abou Ali had built up the Saharan Sidjilmassa of the Tafilalet region into a small strong kingdom. Aboul Hassan soon put an end to both kingdom and ruler.

Prying the Tlemcen prince, Abou Tachfin, away from the Hafsid Bougie was only a beginning in his scheme to destroy that hereditary rival. His next step was to rebuild the fortified city of Mansoura, created by Abou Yacoub for his eight-year siege. Through Aboul Hassan, Mansoura became one of the wonders of the North African West between the Atlantic and the Eastern Mediterranean. With Tlemcen under siege, this glorified camp usurped the head of the caravan trade for the western Sahara. From the Niger kingdom of Mali, the gold-rich Negro kings sent their ambassadors with presents of giraffes and other wonders of the savanna.

Here took place the exchange of gold dust and slaves, ivory and ostrich plumes, the precious musk of civet cats, the soft fur of the desert fox for such northern treasures as the beads of Venice, hunting hawks and spices, silks and velvets, metals and wine, and white marble for the tombs of black kings. Commerce flourished. As in Tlemcen merchants of each Christian country had their own quarters. Under the pious hand of Aboul Hassan, mosques, medersas and shrines of holy men rose, not only within the walls, but in the adjoining suburbs. Some of them still stand—most famous of these a ruined minaret and the Mosque of Bou Medine. Though today these monuments belong to Algeria, they are essentially both Moroccan and Merinid architecture at its finest, unequalled in that Turkish pirate state, which knew neither powerful ruling dynasties nor great religious passion.

As against Abou Yacoub's siege of eight years, Aboul Hassan's lasted only two. At the final fall of Tlemcen, prince, princelings and viziers died in its defense. Only the *oulema*, the religious leaders, were left alive to beg the conqueror to prevent looting and pillage. The Emir himself rode through the corpse-strewn streets maintaining order and saving a city whose beauty he acknowledged and honored.

While he was returning to Fez as Aboul Hassan el Mansour, the Victorious, news reached him that two sons were in rebellion. One he ordered placed in irons and later put to death; the other, Abou Melik, he forgave and sent as envoy to Spain where the Christians killed him in battle.

The revenge planned by Aboul Hassan for this loss reversed itself into a defeat as deadly as the Almohad defeat of Las Navas in 1212. The massacre at the Rio Salido in 1340, at the hands of Alfonso XI of Castile, lost him his finest chiefs, generals and men, many wives (among them his favorite, the Hafsid Princess), a son and two viziers. It was the last major battle of African Moors on Spanish soil.

When the Hafsid father-in-law of the Merinid Emir died in Tunis, the friendly relations and treaties between the two dynasties snapped. Two rivals claimed the succession. By lending his army to the support of one of them, Aboul Hassan found an excuse to enter Tunis. Once inside the walls he claimed the throne for himself. The historian Ibn Khaldoun, in 1347 a young scholar of fifteen, witnessed the pomp and ceremony of the entrance. He watched the Emir, a hundred standards floating about him, advance through a double hedge four miles long of his Merinid cavalry, heard the earth tremble as the immense army closed in behind him. Inside the palace the conqueror presented both his own cloak, and his own charger, complete with gold-studded saddle and bridle to his appointed governor.

This was in September of 1347. By July of the next year the Emir's empire had crashed to the ground. Resentful Arabs, traitorous Berbers defeated him at Kairouan and besieged him at Tunis. The Great Plague or Black Death raging out of Constantinople ravaged his small but loyal army. His son Abou Inan, left in charge of Tlemcen, hurried to Fez and proclaimed himself emir.

Landing on the Algerian coast from a shipwrecked vessel, the miserable father, a hunted fugitive, with the help of a few faithful tribes, managed to join En Nasir, his only loyal son. Two towns fell to them but in the struggle En Nasir was killed. Now with the monstrous son Abou Inan at his father's heels, a cat and mouse chase began out of Algeria into Morocco, from Sidjilmassa to Marrakesh, and from Marrakesh to the final showdown on the Oum Er Rebia River. Gravely wounded, the maimed old lion took refuge in the High Atlas. Through the bitter winter snows Abou Inan besieged him. At last, tired, sick and desperate, in exchange for warm clothes and a little money Aboul Hassan relinquished his throne. A few weeks later, in May, 1351, he died of pleurisy.

The historians tell us that Abou Inan wept bitter tears over his father's corpse. We know that he buried him with high honors in the necropolis of the Chella. The tomb can be seen today—a marble slab, long and low, mellowed by time and weather, inscribed with touching tributes of filial piety.

We are not sorry to learn that seven years later, in 1358, this unnatural son, deserted by his army, was strangled at the order of an enterprising vizir.

We are, however, for a very important reason, thankful that this murder did not occur earlier. In 1349, the great world traveler Ibn Batuta returned from the East to his native Tangier, journeyed to Fez and presented himself before "our most noble master, the most generous man, the Commander of the Faithful, El Mutawakkil Abou Inan." Though he had reached home after an absence of twenty-seven years, there was still one corner of the world that he had to see with his own eyes before settling down, namely—the gold dust kingdoms on the Niger. On his safe return from the Niger in 1353, he astounded Emir and courtiers with accounts of the wonders he had seen. Some scoffed, insisting that it was all extravagant moonshine; but Abou Inan commissioned a secretary, Ibn Yahzayy, to take down the narrative in Ibn Batuta's own words. With this deed, Abou Inan goes down in history as patron of one of the two first and greatest travel books of all times.

Surpassed in fame as a medieval traveler only by Marco Polo, Ibn Batuta started off to see the Eastern world at the age of twenty-two. He was born in Tangier in 1304, sixty years after the Venetian. Both reached Khan-Baliq, City of the Khan (Peking). Marco's Khan was the great Khublai, grandson of Ghengiz; Ibn Batuta's was Shin-Ti, Khublai's unworthy descendant and last of the Mongol or Yuen dynasty. Both wanderers traveled for a quarter of a century before returning to their native cities, and both dictated accounts of their adventures—Marco in a Genoese prison and Ibn Batuta in the royal palace at Fez.

A Gift to Those Interested in the Curiosities of Cities and the Marvels along the Way makes as good reading today as it did in 1355 at the court of Fez. Except during a few hair-raising escapes from death by robbers and shipwreck, this born traveler seems to have reveled in every moment of seeing the world and never had enough of its "marvels." He was evidently never lonely. On his first stretch between Tangier and Alexandria, he married two wives; in the Maldive Islands he married the legal four. There are casual references to others. Even more frequent are accounts of hospitality presents from his hosts of slave girls and gold, also of sable coats and robes of silk.

This avid traveler came from a family of learned theologians, and was himself a cadi, or judge, of distinction, educating himself along the way with four pilgrimages to Mecca and, at one time, three years of study there. Though travel broadened his outlook on the world and brought him delight in strange customs, he remained at all times a conservative and upright Malikite judge, striving like his contemporary Ibn Khaldoun to root out corruption and evil. (In the Maldive Islands where the bare bosoms of the native Moslem women distressed him, he worked in vain to instill the modesty Mohammed had decreed. And again, on his visit to the Niger, he was horrified by the state of stark nakedness, except for gold ornaments above the neck, of the black princesses at the sumptuous court of the King, their father.)

Ibn Batuta's travels took him zigzagging back and forth across the Middle East, down the coast of East Africa, beyond the Black Sea into the Russia of the Golden Horde and back through Central Asia. After eight years in India as Malikite judge under the Moghul Emperor Muhammed Tughlak, he moved to the Maldive Islands, then Ceylon, with a pious pilgrimage to the mountain of "Adam's Foot." Via Sumatra he sailed to the cities of Sin, or southern China, ending his outward journey with those of Cathay, or northern China, and the Mongol capital, Khan-Baliq. On his way home he found the great Black Death of the fourteenth century at Damascus. When he reached Morocco after an absence of twenty-four years, he found that his mother had died of it.

One of the many facets of interest that stand out in the *Gift* is the extraordinary spread of Islam and Islamic communities along Ibn Batuta's trail. By his time Islam had been adopted by Turks, Tartars and Mongols and had spread sporadically to the shores of the China and Yellow Seas. Moreover, like Marco Polo, this "Traveler of Islam" followed the great medieval trade routes. Along these routes the Arabs of those days shared with the Venetians and the Genoese the talent for turning barter into profit at the far ends of the earth. Though it is known that Ibn Batuta lived on for twenty-three years after dictating his memoirs in 1355, it is only conjecture that he spent those years again in the role of cadi in various Moroccan towns.

While Ibn Batuta was visiting the Niger court of the Mali Emperor Suleiman and his naked daughters, Ibn Khaldoun, an extraordinary man of twenty, of prodigious learning and overwhelming ambition, arrived from Tunis at Abou Inan's court in Fez. The Black Death had left him an orphan, but not before a father, inclined to mysticism, had sent him to the finest scholars of Tunis for his schooling. These were men whom Aboul Hassan, the father of Abou Inan, had brought with him to Tunis in 1347 after conquering the city of the Hafsids.

The education of the day that would enable a young man to earn a living by his wits as theologian, judge or secretary at some royal court began, of course, in childhood with the Koran and the Traditions. This was largely a matter of memorizing, as it still is in most of the Arab world. From this point the student moved on to a sharp division of the sciences or branches of learning: Number one—the Traditional studies or extraction of the laws of Islamic theology and jurisprudence from the Koran's divine Revelations and from the Traditions handed down by the men who had known the Messenger; number two—suspect in orthodox eyes but nevertheless necessary—the so-called Rational philosophic studies where the human mind was in danger of striking out on its own and adding to the wisdom of the past. The latter were the studies of logic, mathematics, natural philosophy and metaphysics. Relevant to these for practical purposes were languages, history, the art of writing scholarly works as well as court correspondence and the handling of administrative affairs.

Admirably trained in all these learned subjects, the young Ibn Khaldoun was appointed secretary in charge of court correspondence at Abou Inan's royal court. Two years later, on charges of conspiracy he was in prison, where he stayed twenty-two months until the unpopular Abou Inan was strangled by one of the power-greedy vizirs.

Out of prison, Ibn Khaldoun plotted with one vizir to overthrow the protégé of another. This was a strange beginning for one who was to develop into the first great philosopher-historian not only of the Moslem people but of all people until the turn of the nineteenth century. Another palace revolution among the vizirs obliged him to leave Morocco. Welcomed at first at the court of Granada, he aroused further court antagonism when he tried to mold the young king into his conception of the ideal ruler. Another exile! This time he went to the court of the Hafsid Prince now ruling the city of Bougie, who had shared his Fez imprisonment. Here he became city manager.

From Granada to Tunis, this second half of the fourteenth century was a period of anarchy and chaos. Ibn Khaldoun, moving from court to court, observing all that was as rotten, corrupt and unstable as in the last days of Babylon, Persia or Rome, put his fine mind to work to discover why dynasties rose, declined and fell in ever recurring cycles. In a lonely castle in the mountains south of Oran, he began work on his universal history. The medieval Arab did not strive for the short concise title. Ibn Khaldoun called his great work: *The Book of Examples and the Collection of Origins and Information Respecting the History of the Arabs, Foreigners and Berbers.* It absorbed the last years of his life, spent between Tunis and Egypt, where he died in 1406, though he also found time in Egypt to lecture at the University of El Ashar and hold the post of Grand Malikite Judge.

When the French made their sudden conquest of Algeria in the middle of the nineteenth century, Ibn Khaldoun became their invaluable guide to North African geography and history. He is still the authority *par excellence* from the Atlantic through the Libyan Desert. French Arabic scholars started to translate him. The Baron de Slane led with the section dealing with the history of the Berbers. In time the philosophical value of the history began to receive its due recognition. In his *Moqaddimah* or *Introduction* Ibn Khaldoun developed what he called the "Science" of history. In 1958 this appeared in an English translation in the Bollingen Series of Pantheon Books. Readers may remember the enthusiastic review by the late A. J. Liebling in the *New Yorker* magazine of November 7th, 1959. Liebling claimed that if the *Moqaddimah* were published in paperback instead of the eighteen dollar Pantheon edition it would be the most popular translation from the Arabic of any book next to the *Thousand and One Nights.*

Ibn Khaldoun was disgusted with the chroniclers whom he found at the courts of princes and kings—all parasites who were paid to sing their master's praises, list his battles and his sons in endless and monotonous adulation. (In Europe his contemporary Froissart was such a biographer, though with a fine literary talent, and an accuracy concerning events, still with the same distortion of character, transforming his questionable heroes into perfect knights of chivalry. All other history of the day, like thought itself, was tailored to fit the doctrines of the Christian Church.) In Ibn Khaldoun's world, no one asked why Moroccan dynasties—the Merinids for example—beginning as proud, free shepherds of the wild uplands, moved into palaces of Fez and Marrakesh, produced a few noble rulers like Aboul Hassan, and then the miserable shabby litter of Abou Inan's 325 worthless sons.

Ibn Khaldoun saw such a decline as one of social organization and natural and economic environment rather than as a problem of individuals. He saw the aggressive "have-nots" of the desert, tough, lawless and on the move, changing first to the easy life of the sedentary "haves," then sinking into the sinful life of the city, and extorting such taxes that the profit incentive disappeared, leaving a vacuum for the next "wild" Arabs or Berbers to take possession and make the same turn of the wheel.

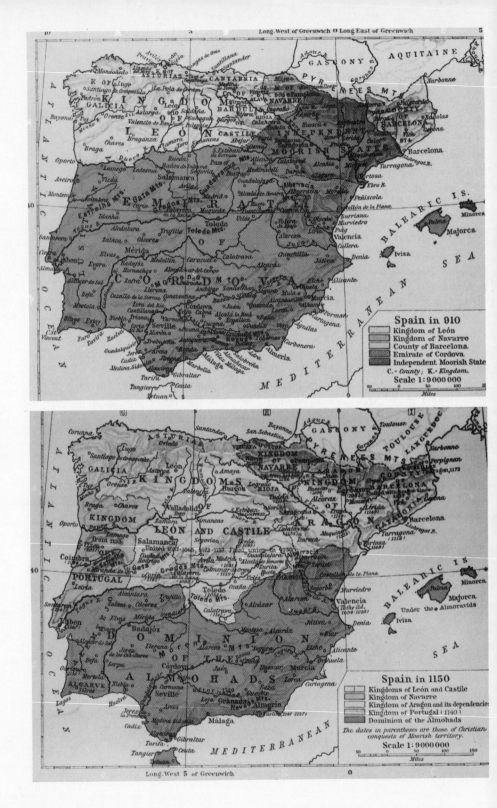

Spain in 910

Kingdom of León
Kingdom of Navarre
County of Barcelona
Emirate of Cordova
Independent Moorish State
C. = County; K. = Kingdom.
Scale 1 : 9 000 000
50   0   50   100   150
Miles

Spain in 1150

Kingdoms of León and Castile
Kingdom of Navarre
Kingdom of Aragon and its dependencies
Kingdom of Portugal (1140)
Dominion of the Almohads
The dates in parentheses are those of Christian
conquests of Moorish territory.
Scale 1 : 9 000 000
50   0   50   100   150
Miles

Long. West 5 of Greenwich   0

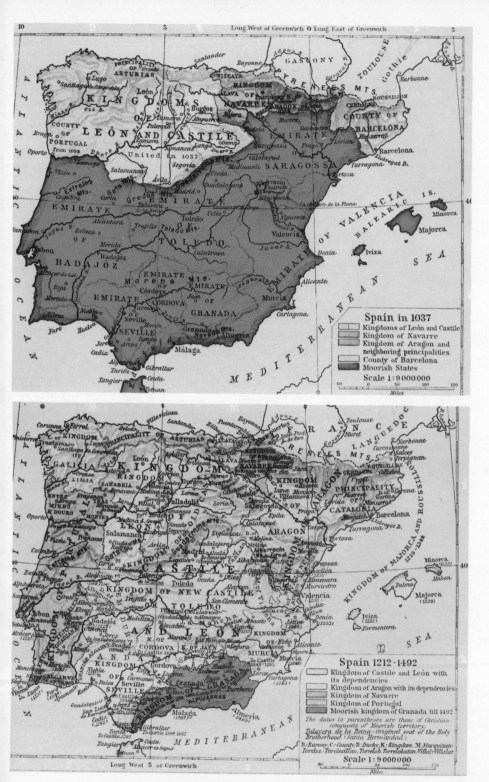

Spain in 1037
Kingdoms of León and Castile
Kingdom of Navarre
Kingdom of Aragon and neighboring principalities.
County of Barcelona
Moorish States
Scale 1:9 000 000

Spain 1212-1492
Kingdom of Castile and León with its dependencies
Kingdom of Aragon with its dependencies
Kingdom of Navarre
Kingdom of Portugal
Moorish kingdom of Granada till 1492
The dates in parentheses are those of Christian conquests of Moorish territory.
Talavera de la Reina : Original seat of the Holy Brotherhood (Santa Hermandad).
B.=Barony. C.=County. D.=Duchy. K.=Kingdom. M.=Marquisate
Tordes.=Tordesillas. Torrelob.=Torrelobaton. Villal.=Villalar.
Scale 1:9 000 000

Shepherd's *Atlas of Medieval and Modern History*, Henry Holt, 1932

It is a detailed analysis of human society as a whole, in the vein of the modern political scientist, cynical, shrewd and centuries ahead of his time, that has given this fourteenth-century adventurer at the courts of Morocco, Moorish Spain, Tunisia and Egypt the byname of the Spengler of the Arab world.

When Abou Inan seized his father's throne, he was only nineteen. When he was murdered at the age of twenty-nine, he left 325 sons. (In 1727 the Sultan Moulay Ismail left more than 500 "old enough," in the words of the chronicler El Oufrani, "to ride horses.")

Even if this barnyard-like progeny had been older, there is little likelihood that they would have been sufficiently united to spread Merinid rule throughout the kasbas of mountains, plains and desert. Cooperation and concord were no more in the blood of such a brood than in the blood of the feuding tribes themselves. No wonder. True, they were born of one father but each one of the many mothers planted the idea of the throne in her son's infant mind, and throughout her whole miserable captive lifetime schemed, plotted and poisoned to put him there.

Scarcely a dozen years had passed since Aboul Hassan's splendid empire stretched in apparently impregnable power from the Atlantic to the Gulf of Gabès. Now suddenly it lay like a dead body with the vultures circling down to pick it to pieces. The vultures were the vizirs and the chiefs of mercenaries, who selected princelings to use as their tools. Not one of Abou Inan's sons succeeded his father as ruler in his own right. The first ephemeral emir (for less than two years), Abou Selim, a son of Aboul Hassan, was backed by Spain, aided by Ibn Khaldoun. In terror of palace revolutions, the royal princelings fled to Granada. Many of them perished at sea. Some of the safe arrivals were served back to the vizirs one by one, with the understanding that Granada should share the power. Vizir fought vizir. Weaklings, idiots and children held the throne. Nothing could be more tedious and unrewarding than to follow them in detail through the last half of the century. During thirty of these years Granada's most brilliant king, Mohammed V, pulled the strings for the puppets at Fez, vizirs and emirs alike.

This was Granada's great century. The Alhambra, begun in 1248, soon after the inception of the kingdom, and finished in 1354, was the wonder palace of the western world. It was an Arabian Nights' dream brought to life in peacock colors, carved white marble and plaster filigree. And the city itself, the richest in Spain, was a city of silk, a city of poets who were architects, and architects who were poets, a city of tournaments and medieval chivalry. In the fifteenth century the charm was still there, but the power began to melt like snow in an Andalusian garden. The year 1492 was, as we know, famous for more than the discovery of America. Their Catholic Majesties Ferdinand and Isabella took possession of the last Moorish kingdom in Spain. More bitter exiles added themselves to the pirate nests across the Straits. King Abou Abdallah, better known to his Spanish enemies as Boabdil, last king of the Alhamares House of Granada, took refuge in African Fez.

The pirates that were to trouble our own young republic at the beginning of the nineteenth century were already, in the course of the fourteenth century, terrorizing the Western Mediterranean. Among the victims to suffer most was the new and vigorous young monarchy of Portugal. By the time John I, founder of the House of Avis, mounted the throne in 1385, Portugal had established herself as a maritime nation. Because the hostile Castilians on her eastern border made her almost as much of an island as Britain, she needed freedom of the seas—especially freedom of the Straits—not only for her commerce but also for her vital cargoes of grain. If her shipping was to become the prey of Moorish pirates, her independence was doomed. Nobody saw this more clearly than King John I.

It can be truly said that throughout history no king was ever blessed with a son so passionately dedicated, both in heart and brilliant mind, to sea and sails and the mystery of undiscovered lands, as John in the Infante Henry. This third son of King John's could as fittingly as his nephew, Alfonso IV, have added the title of "The African" to the one by which we know him—Prince Henry the Navigator. It was his genius that opened up for his country the African coast and its islands from Morocco to Cape Verde, paving the way for Bartholomew Diaz's great rounding of the Southern Cape, and Vasco de Gama's discovery of India before the end of the century.

Henry's four brothers had their own share of distinction. In 1415, the powerful Portuguese fleet commanded by the two Infantes, Henry and Fernando—33 ships of the line, 59 galleys, 110 transports and 50,000 men—surprised Ceuta. Though the fourteenth-century defenses of Aboul Hassan were still strong and the defense itself stubborn, the African "Gibraltar" fell easily to the attackers. In the rejoicing of the Christian world, the Pope ordered a tax on church property to cover the expenses of the Moorish Crusade.

Shocked to the depths of their Moslem souls, Berber and Arab found their country successfully invaded for the first time in seven centuries. Until the fall of Ceuta, their armies had crossed the Straits as the conquerors, the dictators, the lions. Now, in 1415, as they looked about them in their mountains and plains—regions of chaos and anarchy—there was no fiery Abou Yakoub, no fervent Aboul Hassan to throw out the Christian dogs. There was only the weak and dissolute Abou Said Othman, calling himself ruler, at Fez. In a mounting rage of hate and resentment, his palace household finally massacred not only Abou Said himself but most of his family, and violated the members of his harem.

The Portuguese, however, were in Ceuta to stay for the next 165 years.

111

CHAPTER X

ᏜᏜᏜᏜ

ATLANTIC PORTS TO THE CHRISTIAN DOGS
(The Ouatassids, 1420–1550)

ᏜᏜᏜᏜ

The fifteenth century that divided the medieval from the modern world for Western Europe, brought none of its changes, its progress and excitement to Morocco. Through the reborn Western mind, the advances of science and philosophy originating in the medieval Arab intellect developed into forces and events that were to transform men's lives—among them the discovery of new worlds and new paths to the old, of firearms, of cheap paper and its outgrowth, the printing press, and, most significant of all, an inquiring mind freed from religious dogma.

For Morocco it was a century in which the mind stagnated, in which the strong men who seized the power protected no poets or scholars, and left no monuments to embellish the conquered cities, a century in which Spain was a lost and hated land, and a century in which Portugal robbed her of her western sea coast.

The Beni Ouatassi or Ouatassids—of the short and colorless dynasty that followed the Merinids—owe their place in history not to what they themselves did but to what was done to them by Spaniards, Portuguese,

Turks, by their own marabouts and the rising strength of their successors, the Saadians. They were close cousins of the Merinids, and therefore belonged, like them, to that important confederation of tribes, the Zenata, which had been pushed west by the Second Arab Invasion. As Merinid power weakened, their own rose; and when, in 1420, the miserable ruler Abou Said Othman lost his life for letting the Portuguese take Ceuta, the Ouatassi leader, Abou Zakariya (not an intriguing vizir this time but an honorable governor of Salé) was able to seize the position of regent for the infant Merinid heir to the throne, Abd el Haqq, and hold it for a quarter of a century.

Abd el Haqq, during his young manhood, was no threat to the first Ouatassid regent. On the contrary, his interest, like that of his dissolute father, lay in the harem by day as well as by night. It was nothing to him that the Christians held sacred Moroccan soil, that the people were stirred with outrage and, most ominous of all, that suddenly the great swarm of marabouts (call some of them saints, some of them charlatans) was using the Portuguese menace as a bid for political power.

For the saints among these marabouts, this action sprang from an honest desire to come to the defense of Islam and protect the country from the Christian menace. Until the taking of Ceuta in 1415, their activities had been non-political. The role of their *zaouias*, or monasteries, had been to educate the masses, to wean them away from their pagan addiction to trees and springs and stones and demon cats with slit ears, substituting Oriental Sufism, alchemy and their own Islamic form of magic; and also, of course, to train disciples who would multiply the *zaouias* and their teachings throughout the country.

After Ceuta there was a change. Now it was the marabouts, not the emirs, who preached the *jihad*, the marabouts who trained and had at their service a devoted and fervent army, while the miserable emirs were fortunate if their mercenary troops, unpaid and undisciplined, refrained from cutting their leaders' throats. The marabouts not only preached hatred against the invading Portuguese but against all other Christian nations, and inflamed the masses against their rulers for encouraging Christian merchants to settle in their ports. It was the beginning of the xenophobia that, tightening in the seventeenth century, closed Morocco to the Christian world until the victorious intrusion of the French at the beginning of the present century—the xenophobia that staved off the unhappy day of colonial rule but at the same time cut off the Moghreb from the Western world and left it as a feudal island in Western progress.

Most famous, most learned and most powerful of these fifteenth-century marabouts was El Djazuli with a following of 13,000 disciples. The *zaouias* of his brotherhood sprang up everywhere. When he led his armed forces against the Portuguese invaders, he frightened the feeble

Merinid ruler, El Haqq, now free of his regents. (This was the El Haqq who started life under the Ouatassid Abou Zakariya, but had murdered the third of the Ouatassid regents.) El Djazuli had had his formal education at the Kairouiine University of Fez, adding to it the fruits of the Mecca pilgrimage and studies with the Sufists of the East, before founding his "Mother" *zaouia* on the plain between Casablanca and the Middle Atlas. When he died of poisoning in 1465, his disciples in Fez suspected Abd el Haqq, with the result that the last of the Merinids was lured back to the city and beheaded by the powerful Idrisid Cherifs or Chorfa. These descendants of Idris I, and therefore of the Prophet, from the very beginning had despised the Merinid rulers. Now they succeeded in interposing their own leader for a stormy reign of five years. By 1472, the heir of the murdered Ouatassid regent had brought both New and Old Fez into his power, and started rule as Mohammed ech Cheik, first of three bona fide Ouatassid princes.

Mohammed ech Cheik was a brother of the regent murdered by Abd el Haqq. It is important to remember that it was common usage for the leader of the tribe, the Cheik, also to take the name Mohammed. This then is Mohammed ech Cheik of the Ouatassids. The following dynasty begins with Mohammed ech Cheik of the Saadians. At the time of the murder in 1458, he had been fortunate enough to escape to his native town of Asilah, the first Atlantic port south of the Straits. Naturally his obsession had been the recovery of Fez and revenge for his murdered brother. In 1471, after seven years of waiting followed by six of struggle, Fez was in his hands—but at a price. While he had been absent hammering at its walls, the Portuguese with 30,000 men took Asilah, and a few days later, Tangier itself. Among the prisoners whom they carried back to Portugal was the eldest son and heir of Mohammed ech Cheik.

For the fact that the young Ouatassi Prince was eventually returned alive, with a Portuguese education, to reign as Mohammed el Bourtagali ("the Portuguese"—there is no "p" in the Arabic language) in exchange for the bones of the Infante Dom Fernando, the story goes back to an unsuccessful Portuguese attack on Tangier in 1437. By land and sea the expedition had set out from Ceuta under the Infante Dom Fernando —the ships under Dom Fernando himself, the land forces under his brother, Prince Henry the Navigator. For once, marabouts, tribal cheiks, local princelings and their followers had joined forces, and pinched the Christians off from all help until surrender became inevitable.

The terms of the treaty had stated that the Portuguese could return safely to their ships in return for giving up their arms, the city of Ceuta, and Dom Fernando as hostage. In Lisbon, King Edward, backed by the Pope, preferred the sacrifice of his brother to the sacrifice of Moroccan Ceuta. As a result of the broken treaty, Fernando died a lingering and miserable death in the prisons of Fez. The Church added him to its list of Saints, and it was his holy wonder-working bones that were eventually exchanged for the live son of Mohammed ech Cheik.

After Asilah and Tangier, the Portuguese had signed a truce with Mohammed. They had promised not to invade the plain behind the coast. What they wanted was the ports, and enough land surrounding the smooth rectangular walls of their fortified towns to keep them safe from tribal attack. By 1445, their explorers had already reached Cape Verde and the mouth of the Senegal. By 1486, Diaz had rounded the Cape of Good Hope. They needed fresh ports, strung down the coast, to keep their shipping safe from the pirates. The more Moslems Spain and Portugal drove out of the Peninsula, the more pirates there were to seize the fine ships on their way to both the new and the old Indies.

The great news of Columbus's discovery of America must have come swiftly to the courts of Fez and Marrakesh, and to the *zaouias* of the clever marabouts; but of more importance to them in 1492 and, for several centuries, of far more consequence to their country, was the fall of Granada. In the old days of the thirteenth century, when Cordova and Seville fell to Saint Ferdinand, the Moorish exiles were welcome along the African coast from Fez to Tunis; now, however, things were different. In the chaos and anarchy that had ruled ever since 1358 when Abou Inan's 325 sons inherited the country, there was no welcome for extra mouths to feed or for artisans who would take away work where little was to be had. Moreover, the fall of Granada was by no means the end. For Spain and Portugal, both at a high pitch of religious fanaticism, it was not enough to chase out professed Moslems. In the course of the next century, even any Moors whose professed Christianity was suspect had to go, and with them the Jews. During the next one hundred years, a people to whom Spain had been a homeland for more than nine centuries was eradicated as zealously as vermin. It is, however, pleasant to remember that Prince Henry the Navigator, in order to give his mariners the best possible training of the day, appointed both Arab and Jewish mathematicians to the chairs of Lisbon's university.

In 1501, Mohammed the "Portuguese" succeeded his father. Though he had not learned to love his Christian captors, he was by temperament neither vengeful nor warlike, and left the *jihads* against them to the marabouts. His own kingdom was virtually limited to the inland mountain region of Fez, where his capital was briefly happy and prosperous and the people devoted to his peaceful rule. The spread of Portuguese possessions—"stains" in Moroccan parlance—were on the distant Atlantic coast, while to the north the Rif Mountains protected him from Spain.

Unlike the isolationists of Fez, the tribes of the southwest, stirred on by the fanatical marabouts, seethed with fury at the loss of their coast.

Where there were Moorish towns, the Portuguese took them—Safi and Azemmour; where there were ports—Mazagan and Agadir—but no towns, they built their own. From the Moors they bought grain for their own country, and woolen blankets and horses to exchange farther south for gold dust and slaves.

For some of the tribes, relations with the Portuguese intruders were not unfriendly. The latter, in the beginning, behaved decently; but in the eyes of most of the tribes they were Christian dogs to be driven into the sea.

To achieve this, all that the Moors needed was leadership. This they found in Abdallah, Cheik of the Beni Saadi, an Arabian tribe of Cherifian descent, established on the lower reaches of the River Dra in the Saharan region of Zagora.

It must never be forgotten that, however isolated and remote an oasis off in the lonely sands of the Sahara or an eagle's eyrie village of Atlas or Rif might appear, there was always that tight bond with the heart of Islam—the yearly pilgrimage to Mecca. We remember how the young Lemtuna chieftain brought back the pious missionary, Ibn Yasin, to the western Soudan to start the Almoravids on their triumphant conquest, how Ibn Toumert made the *hadj* before he gathered disciples about him in the Atlas village of Tinmel. Throughout the long centuries of the Catholic Church, neither Rome nor Jerusalem was ever so well known to her flock as Mecca to the followers of Mohammed. All that was good and holy and close to the Prophet came out of Arabia. Nowhere else could you find so many direct descendants, so many cherifs, so many men endowed with the powerful *baraka* (sacred magic) that could accomplish ends as dissimilar as expelling the Christian dogs and improving the date harvest of an oasis. It is, therefore, not surprising to find enterprising pilgrims from both Zagora on the River Dra and Tafilalet on the River Ziz luring back magic-working cherifs from the Arabian town of Yenbo, to ensure exceptional crops for their famous dates.

In both cases, they were Hassanian Cherifs—that is, descendants, like the Idrisids, of Hassan, son of Fatima and Ali, and grandson of the Prophet. In both cases, they had been important marabouts in their Saharan oases long before coming into national prominence. First to achieve this was the branch of the Beni Saadi, who became the next powerful dynasty. Succeeding them were the Alaouites, also known as Hassanians or Filalians, who hold the throne today.

In the first years of the sixteenth century, when Mohammed the Portuguese was ruling happily at Fez while the Portuguese were taking his coastal cities and the pirate brothers Barbarossa were seizing Algeria for the Ottoman Turks, the Cheik of the Beni Saadi, Abou Abdallah—*hadj*, warrior and prophet, magician, mystic and marabout—led the tribes of the Sous against the Portuguese settlement of Agadir. Though the attack proved unsuccessful, Abou Abdallah gained in power, and moved north across the Atlas to the region of the Haha. In this coastal strip west of the High Atlas between Mogador and Agadir, he and his two sons established their capital and fought the Portuguese. Palace and gardens described by the coeval historian Marmol have disappeared, along with the city itself.

The Portuguese, who until now had had vassals and allies among some of the tribes, lost them abruptly when their governor of Safi seized the beautiful Berber Itto, wife of one of the tribal Cheiks. The fury and vengeance of the tribesmen sent the Portuguese fleeing back to the shelter of their walled towns. The pirates along the coast preyed on their reinforcements and supplies. The new Cherifs from the Dra established themselves as lords of the coastal plain, even closing in on the Atlas princes of Marrakesh.

When Abou Abdallah died in 1518 and was buried beside his famous forerunner in the family of marabouts, El Djazuli, there could be no great feeling of relief in Fez, in Marrakesh, or in the half-starved Portuguese garrisons of the southern coast. From the beginning, two sons had shared their father's campaigns and the government of conquered territories. There was no reason to hope that, on their father's death, they would relinquish the heady taste of power, and pay willing tribute to the *fainéant* Ouatassids at Fez. It is doubtful if either the old marabout's heir, El Aredj (The Lame), or his younger brother, Mohammed, later known as ech Cheik el Mahdi (The Deliverer), could have doubled anyone's date harvest through their piety or the magic effluvium of sainthood. What they lacked in *baraka*, however, they (especially Mohammed ech Cheik) made up for in military skill—the ability to seize territory and organize their conquests. Within five years, El Aredj had exchanged his father's provincial capital of Tednest for a prize second only to Fez itself, the old Almohad capital of Marrakesh. South of the Atlas, in Taroudant, his brother ruled as governor of the fertile, subtropical valley of the Sous, with a particular interest in the export of the product of its sugar cane.

At Fez the growing Portuguese control of the northern coast now began to impede the commercial prosperity. As usual there had to be a scapegoat—with the result that the poor "Portuguese" Mohammed was forced into unwelcome action. Instead, however, of conducting the popular Holy War against the infidel, the foolish emir marched south toward Marrakesh to settle the usurpers that threatened his rule. Tragically for him, no one rallied to his support. Fez itself rebelled against him. The two Saadian brothers pushed him back to the Oum Er Rebia, a natural river boundary between the Middle Atlas and Azemmour, with the command never to cross it again. According to de Chavrebière "there was nothing for the good Sultan to do but die of grief, a last duty which he performed with dignity in 1526." This Ouatassid Mohammed Emir of Fez was succeeded, not by the brilliant brother whom he had designated as his heir, but by a nephew, Aboul Abbas, who seized the throne by force and lived to regret it.

Sugar, dates, grain, the finest orange blossom water of the Moghreb, copper pots, daggers and ornamental leather were the specialties of the southern province of the Sous under the Saadian Mohammed's rule. Sugar cane had come into North Africa and southern Spain with the Arabs. In a famous thirteenth-century siege of Taroudant, the Almohad Abd el Moumen had set the surrounding cane fields on fire, illuminating the last resistance of the city. Below a line at a latitude of 31° 30′ running from Mazagan to Marrakesh, excavations have uncovered enough sugar mills, furnaces and refineries to leave no doubt of the importance of this industry up to the beginning of the seventeenth century. Some of this crop could, of course, travel south by caravan to the country of the Blacks; yet there was also a market in the north. Europe had begun to buy sugar for middle class as well as for royal tables. Though Mohammed was more than eager to dispose of this valuable commodity to Christian merchants, provided they paid high taxes for the privilege of doing business in the Moghreb, he was not at all willing to let it go to the Portuguese, who controlled the commerce in their port of Agadir and seized the lion's share of profits. The remedy was to control the port himself.

The six months' siege of Agadir in 1541 came very close to duplicating his father's early failure before this city, until suddenly a barrel of gunpowder exploded in the wall. The Moors poured through the breach. Santa Cruz da Capo da Aguir reverted to its original name of Agadir, a Berber word for fortress. The Portuguese governor and his family found themselves prisoners in Taroudant. There the beauty and charm of Donna Mencia, the governor's daughter, won her the position of favorite wife instead of favorite concubine in the Cherif's harem. But it was only a short triumph, ending in poison for her and her first child, gift of her jealous companions. As proof of his grief, Mohammed freed his Portuguese father-in-law.

The fall of Agadir led to the abandonment on the part of Portugal of both Safi and Azemmour—partly because of the growing strength of the Cherifs, partly because local supplies and tribute had come to an end, partly because Portugal herself was becoming more involved with her Indian conquests.

By this time the reader may be wondering whether at last two Moroccan brothers have appeared on the scene willing to share their father's kingdom without black and jealous schemes for each other's destruction. For the sons of Abou Abdallah, the taking of Agadir marked the breaking point. Mohammed, secure in his success, held back the fifth part of the booty due

A Barbary Galley about 1500.

his elder brother as sovereign. He kept all the artillery, all the munitions, all the arquebuses (ancestors of our modern guns), and 400 Christian slaves. And not only that. Instead of fulfilling his role as governor of the Sous, and collecting taxes for El Aredj, he began to collect them for himself. After that, there could be no peace between them. In the struggle, Mohammed emerged the stronger. Ten sons helped him beat "The Lame One" back into the desert and take over Marrakesh.

Now the Ouatassi enemy at Fez was Ahmed, a more belligerent ruler than his uncle, the mild "Portuguese" Mohammed. Well equipped not only with the Portuguese arms of Agadir but also with contraband weapons supplied by the French, British and Dutch merchants in the open ports, Mohammed ech Cherif felt well equipped to set foot on the last step of the ladder. The Cherifian Mohammed and the Ouatassid Ahmed had met before in indecisive encounters. This time the Ouatassid forces lost their leader. Ahmed was wounded and taken prisoner. His army, rescued from its confusion by Hassoun, the uncle from whom Ahmed had stolen the throne, retreated to Fez. There Hassoun appointed a sixteen-year-old nephew of Ahmed's as emir, and proclaimed himself regent. In desperate need of allies, he turned by means of tribute and homage to Soleiman the Magnificent, Sultan of the Ottoman Turks and Caliph of the Moslem world.

In 1453, the Turks had taken Constantinople from the last of the Roman emperors, Constantine Paleologus, who, according to Gibbon, "so feebly sustained the name and majesty of the Caesars," yet perished

119

in noble combat among his own subjects, refusing to live after the capture of the city. By the beginning of the sixteenth century, the Turkish empire encircled the eastern Mediterranean as far as Italy. With the coming of the Brothers Barbarossa, those red-bearded corsairs of the Island of Lesbos, the Spaniards were being pried out of their ports on the Algerian coast, and Christians trembled at the very thought of Arouj of the Silver Arm, and Kheir ed Din, admiral of the Turkish Navy, with the three Horsetails of the Beylerbey floating from his standard. There was a border now between Morocco and Algeria, beginning near the mouth of the Moulaya; and the cities east of it—Tlemcen, Algiers, Bougie, Tunis—said the Friday prayer in the name of Soleiman the Magnificent.

If Abou Hassoun at Fez was willing to make an ally of these Turks, Mohammed ech Cherif at Marrakesh preferred them as an enemy. When an ambassador from the Porte commanded that he, too, say the *khotba* in the name of the "magnificent" Sultan, Mohammed met the order with defiance. No mare's-milk-drinking upstart out of Asia was going to give orders to a Saadian Cherif with the sacred blood of the Prophet in his veins!

Instead of a second attack on Fez from his distant southern capital, Mohammed made a crafty bargain with the prisoner Ahmed. "In exchange for your freedom and a five year truce," he said, "give me the city of Meknès." The gullible Ahmed, eager for the return of his throne, agreed. Meknès was less than forty miles from Fez and a splendid base for the siege of the city.

For the restored ruler Ahmed, there was no loyalty from either the Fassi themselves or the people of the *bled*—the countryside. He had sold them down the river when he gave Meknès to the enemy. Worse, however, in their eyes than their own craven ruler was the enemy himself. When the proud Fassi Cherifs, descendants of the true line of the Prophet, smooth and cultivated, boasting the greatest university of the Moghreb, cursed the Beni Saad, they cursed them as impostors, descendants of the Prophet's Bedouin wet nurse with no more claim to the title of Cherif than the Christian dogs themselves. They also sneered at their uncouth ways, as they sneered at all unlettered warriors who had come up out of the desert sands.

It took the Saadian Mohammed and his 15,000 mounted partisans a year under the walls of Fez to starve the people and weaken the defenses. In the cold of the winter, 5,000 horses of the besieging army died. The men would have died too, if they had not built themselves shelters, even houses.

With the final breakthrough on the walls by the southeast gate, Ahmed again became a prisoner. This time he was soon beheaded. Again his uncle Hassoun escaped. While Mohammed was taking over Fez (1549), the last of the Ouatassids began a court-to-court tour of Europe—Lisbon, Madrid and, in the hope of help from Charles V, even Augsburg.

120

In Fez, according to El Oufrani in his History of the Saadians called *Pungent Amusement*, Mohammed and his entourage were not too self-assured to take lessons, from the vizirs still attached to the luxurious court, in such matters as fashionable dress, drawing a sword from a gold-encrusted sheath, and mounting a horse with grace. By the mistress of the palace, their women were instructed in such arts as the fine cuisine of Fez, the covering of mattresses and cushions with silk and delicate embroidery, and the subtle use of perfumes.

To consolidate his new conquests, Mohammed needed a strong, well-paid army. For a well-paid army he needed taxes. In the High Atlas the tribes resented the *kharadj*, or land tax. In the *zaouias* of both cities and bled, the marabouts who had brought him to power considered that their services warranted all tax exemption. With so many forces against him, the first Saadian and his ten spirited sons, who governed cities and campaigned to the east against the Turks, were ruling the land, not through popular acclaim, but by means of an iron hand.

For this reason, Hassoun, the last Ouatassid, was able to make a brief comeback. Though Charles V had done nothing for him, Spain, Portugal, and even the Algerian Turks backed his undertaking. The Turks were with him because two of Mohammed's sons had seized Tlemcen. The Turks had succeeded in killing the elder of these two and had sent his head back in a cage to Algiers. Hatred between the city of the Beylerbeys and Fez was as deep as the chasms of the Upper Moulaya.

With Turkish help, Hassoun took Fez. The Fassi welcomed him back with joy; but did *not* enjoy his arrogant allies. At the city's demand, he was soon compelled to bribe his pillaging supporters to leave. Then Mohammed struck again. This time the victory was final. With the death of Hassoun during the battle, no more Ouatassids blocked the path. The Saadian branch of the Cherifian dynasty began its rule over the western Moghreb.

Between Marrakesh and the desert, the High Atlas thrust its snow-capped peaks into the sky; and yet there was an air of the desert within and without the red walls of "Morocco" (on early maps the name "Morocco" represents modern Marrakesh). There were the scorching heat of summer, the forest of date palms, and always such a constant coming and going of desert folk across the mountain trails that the great open space of the Djemaa el Fna, with its story tellers, snake charmers, tumblers and dancing boys, might have been the magnified market scene of a Saharan oasis. For Mohammed, this desert-touched city had charms that Fez could never offer. Like rulers before him who had sprung from a land of sun and sand, he made it his capital. A secondary reason may have been his awareness of how he was both hated and despised in sophisticated Fez.

For thirty-six years since his father's death, Mohammed ech Cheik had waged war back and forth across the mountains, plains and deserts of the land, before establishing his rule. Now, like all previous strong rulers, his ambitions turned across the Moulaya River to the east. Well aware of his desires, his enemies in Algiers succeeded in planting assassins among a special contingent of Turkish mercenaries. Due to them, his rule was cut to three short years. Not far from Taroudant, where he had first shown his skill as soldier and governor, they cut off his head and escaped with it to Algiers. From there it was forwarded to Constantinople, where it hung in triumph on the walls until time reduced it to rotted shreds.

Thanks to a devoted wife, his headless body met with a more honorable disposal. In the Saadian Tombs at Marrakesh, the carved marble monument of Ahmed el Mansour el Dehbi, the Gilded, who sacked Timbuctu for its gold, its salt and its slaves, is the usual focus of interest; but lying also beneath the honeycombed arches of delicate carved plaster is the headless body of Mohammed ech Cheik, first of the Saadian dynasty.

The pious wife who buried what was left of the headless corpse was also the mother of El Mansour, the most famous of her husband's ten sons. Ahmed el Mansour el Dehbi took his titles "The Victorious" from his defeat of the Portuguese and "The Gilded" from his conquest of Timbuctu. In order to share the lure of that fabulous city where the roofs were said to be of gold, one must turn briefly away from Morocco in both time and space, and follow the caravan trails south to the land of the Negro on the Niger.

From left to right: a Riffian; a man of the Réguibat; a man from the Meknassa. /
Moroccan Government

122

CHAPTER XI

THE LAND OF THE NEGRO

(Ghana, Mali and the Songhoi Empire,
c. 800–1591)

ᏕᏍᎿᏬᏍᎿᏍᎿᏕ

The Saadians were by no means the first Moroccan dynasty to lust after the gold of the Niger region and seize it by brute force. In the eleventh century the Almoravids had financed their northward thrust with the gold of the conquered savanna. Later when Youssef ben Tachfin was extending his rule from Marrakesh to Fez, Abou Bekr had hurried back across the Sahara to put down black rebellion in the Kingdom of Ghana.

Even that was not the beginning. Long before the coming of the Arabs, Niger gold went north by Berber caravan to Atlantic ports between Cape Juby and the river Dra, where the Phoenicians took it in exchange for their own Mediterranean offerings.

Basil Davidson, in his *Lost Cities of Africa*, states the belief that the three great gold kingdoms of the Niger—Ghana, Mali and the Songhoi Empire—owe their formation to the civilizing effects of iron and have their beginnings with its West African discovery in about 300 B.C. But because, with all their gold, the three states lacked the civilized riches of a written language, these beginnings of theirs are lost to history.

123

The records begin with the arrival of the Arabs. By the middle of the eighth century Islam was beginning to be introduced into the central and western Soudan by its fervent warrior missionaries. Legend, as we know, has Okba ben Nafi, the first Arab to arrive in Morocco, swinging down to the Niger and founding the famous Bekkai family of Timbuctu. Even if this is only legend planned to enhance the greatness and sanctity of the revered Okba, traffic with the Soudan, both north and south from the Mediterranean and east and west from upper Egypt to the Atlantic, goes back to prehistoric days, as proved by the Tassili frescoes and chariot rock paintings of the western Sahara. More recently the Songhoi city of Djenné, about 200 miles west of Timbuctu on an affluent of the Niger, goes back to A.D. 800, and the Egyptian flavor of its architecture suggests that its Songhoi founders were originally nomads from upper Egypt.

By the beginning of the ninth century the fame of the gold had spread throughout the Moslem world. In A.D. 800 the Arab geographer El Fazari speaks of "Ghana, country of gold." In 833, the Persian geographer El Khwarizmi adds the cities of Ghana and Goungou (Gao), south of the Sahara, as well as the Moroccan caravan port of Sidjilmassa on the north to his map of the inhabitable world—the *oecumene*. Out of Cordova, the Ommayids were digging water wells along the most western of the caravan trails south of Morocco across modern Mauritania, to facilitate their own approach to the gold, the slaves and the ivory of Black Africa.

The account of Yasin's conversion of the Almoravids shows how easily the Saharan Berbers took to Islam. Their nomadic desert life with their herds of camels, sheep and goats had, in spite of a difference in race, bred in them a likeness to the nomad herdsmen of the Arabian desert. Mohammed's religion made the same appeal to both. Above all, the *jihad*, with its interwoven raiding and proselytising, appealed to the very depths of their robber souls. With their southern neighbors, the Blacks, it was a different story. Many of them clung fiercely to their pagan animism with its witch doctors and *grisgris*, as they still do to this day. Some became half-hearted converts under force; some, of their own free will, themselves spread Islam as fanatically as any Arab.

The three countries that successively had the spotlight turned on them by the gold-greedy medieval world between 800 and 1600 were the kingdoms of Ghana and Mali and the Songhoi Empire. In some confusion, they coexisted and overlapped; but each had its centuries of glory when its rulers dazzled the white world with their own black skins, their slave girls, their horses and their dogs glittering in gold and silk.

Longest to hold supremacy was Ghana. It was Ghana that ruled when the Arabs first arrived and that, according to unwritten history, had been ruling since the third or fourth century. In the eigth century the Arab writer El Farazi mentions it by name. Its decline began with the

Almoravid conquest of its two principal cities, first Aoudaghast and in 1076 the capital (also with the name of Ghana). Its fall came in 1240 with conquest by the rising kingdom of Mali.

For the next 200 years, Mali flaunted her pomp and gold before the world in an even greater spectacle, until the supremacy of the Songhois in 1465 made the area famous not only for its gold but also for the learning of its scholars at the Mosque-University of Timbuctu. In his time, the great Negro scholar Ahmed Baba, with 600 manuscripts, considered himself poor in comparison to his friends who had 1,600; and, in the words of a fifteenth-century proverb: "Salt comes from the north, gold from the south, but the word of God and the treasures of wisdom are only to be found in Timbuctu."

For the first detailed account of Ghana, history is indebted to a Moorish geographer of Cordova. El Bekri wrote his *Description of the West, the Land of the Blacks, of Egypt and of Spain* in 1068. Though he had never visited the sub-Saharan land he wrote about so vividly, he had every opportunity of collecting firsthand information concerning its peoples and its kings, not only from merchants, slaves and masters of caravans but also through the great new link between the Niger and the Moghreb represented by the advancing Almoravids. By 1068 these Blue Men of the Sahara, under Youssef ben Tachfin, had built Marrakesh and were threatening the walls of Fez. Their southern branch under Abou Bekr had destroyed Ghana's second city, Aoudaghast. It can well be imagined that talk of Ghana and the desert robbers who had seized its gold was on the tongue of everyone in Moorish Spain from the Reyes de Taifas to the melon vendors in the market place.

Perhaps no one in Spain needed El Bekri to tell him that the King of Ghana used an enormous nugget of gold as a hitching post for his horse. One can imagine the speculation with interest and awe about how much the lump would have to weigh to hold the horse securely. El Bekri said it was as big as a large stone.

A hundred years later another famous Moorish geographer described Ghana's gold hitching post. Idrisi, a Moroccan from Ceuta, at the brilliant Norman court of King Roger of Sicily (1105–1154), entitled his book, written to accompany a silver globe of the world, *The Amusement of Him Who Desires to Traverse the Earth—The Relaxation of a Curious Mind.* Fascinated like El Bekri by Ghana, he too described the famous nugget. In his opinion it weighed thirty pounds. Two hundred years later Ibn Batuta speaks of the Ghana gold lump as having come into possession of the Mali kings and of being sold by the greedy Mansa Maghán to an Egyptian merchant for half its worth. Neither El Bekri nor Idrisi needed to see that fabulous mass of gold to believe in it. To those two famous medieval geographers and to the people of their world, it was as real as the Taj

Mahal, the turquoise domes of Samarkand and the crown jewels of Persia are to those of us today who know them only from the tales of travelers.

El Bekri at Cordova, Idrisi in Palermo represented the Moorish civilizations and grandeur built on the gold and slaves that crossed the Sahara by its great spider web of caravan trails (Moorish Spain and Norman Sicily shared the same glories of science and literature). These desert trails met the Mediterranean at Tangier, Tlemcen, Tunis, Tripoli, Benghazi and Alexandria, but for each of these seaports the western starting point was the same—the marshy buckle of the Niger River where the black kings of Negro-land exacted a heavy tax on every load of gold-dust the Moorish merchant fastened to the back of his couched camel, as well as on every load of salt brought into the kingdom from the mid-Saharan mines of Taghaza.

The cities where these kings first ruled were Ghana, the capital, and its tributary, Aoudaghast. El Bekri described a scene at the Ghana courts. "Their king," the geographer tells us, "when he gives audience sits in a pavilion surrounded by his horses draped in cloth of gold; behind stand ten pages holding shields and gold mounted swords; on his right hand are the sons of princes with gold braided into their hair. The gate is guarded by dogs of an excellent breed who wear collars of gold and silver." Idrisi said that the king on parade was preceded by elephants and giraffes. Again El Bekri: "The best gold is found at Ghiarou, eighteen days from Ghana. All nuggets go to the king; the gold dust to the people."

Though El Bekri pinpointed the source of the gold, no white-skinned Moor ever succeeded in finding it. Ghiarou, like other spots also mentioned, was a will-o'-the-wisp of a place, and the true source of the gold was probably far to the southwest where the headwaters of the Senegal and Niger Rivers took their rise.

If Ghana was famous as the capital of the king, Aoudaghast, 180 miles northwest of Timbuctu, was famous for the excellence of its cooking. One hundred pieces of gold could buy a Negress expert in such regional specialties as macaroni with honey, nut cakes, and snakes in absinthe. With such a diet it is not surprising to learn that magnificent buttocks, too decorative to be sat on, were the greatest asset of the women of the city. They always either lay on their sides or stood supported.

This was no mud city to be washed away by violent cloudbursts but one of multi-colored sandstone quarried from the surrounding Rkiz Mountains. By the time El Bekri wrote, there were a dozen mosques and learned men to teach the Koran. Date palms and gardens of melons and henna grew outside the walls. Besides slaves and gold, the people of Aoudaghast sent acacia gum to Andalusia to add luster to its silks. The city lay close to the line dividing the true desert from the scrub country of spiny acacias and jujube trees (today gum Sénégal is one of the chief exports of the Mauritanian Moors).

Aoudaghast was the first of Ghana's cities to be seized by the fanatic Almoravids. Thirteen years later, in 1076 they controlled the capital and the country and intensified their mission of forcing Islam on the unwilling Blacks.

With Abou Bekr's death, Almoravid power south of the Sahara died away, but Ghana never regained her grandeur and, in 1240, lost all semblance of independence to Soundiata, the belligerent King of Mali, south of the Niger.

In the ruins of Koumbi-Saleh, archeologists believe that they have found the old capital of Ghana. Koumbi-Saleh lies about 230 miles north of modern Mali's capital, Bamako on the Niger. Like Aoudaghast, it is within modern Mauritania, but much closer to the Mali border. The ruins show, in an area of more than half a square mile, capable of holding a population of 30,000, the division into two separate cities described by El Bekri. These were the King's city in its ring of sacred woods, royal tombs and cemeteries, and the Moslem merchant city with stone houses and mosques. It is the merchant city that has been brought to light in the diggings of the last decade. Among the many ruins of the Mauritanian *Sahel*, Koumbi-Saleh stands out as the most important.

Mali was the next state to seize the hegemony of the Niger bend and dazzle the outer world with its riches. Among the many slippery Arab and African names to track down in library indexes and encyclopedias, Mali stands high on the list. It is found as: Mali, Malle, Melle, Mandingo, Malinke and even Wangara! And *mali* or *mande* means hippopotamus or manatee or fish or crocodile. No one is quite sure which of these animals the Mandingos chose as their tribal totem. But the name Mali is the choice of the present inhabitants of the region—one of the new African republics since April, 1961. The republic's totem animal is the crocodile. One can see three tiny crocodiles *couchant* on the china of the charming Grand Hotel in the capital, Bamako; and two crocodile statues guard the approach to the President's Palace.

In 1324 the Cairo gold market received a shattering jolt. A glut of gold flooded the Mameluke capital. Prices dropped lower than the Nile before the autumn floods. Eighty camel loads of gold dust, each weighing 225 pounds, had entered the city from the Niger area. The Mali Sultan, Kankan Mousa, was making the hadj, the pilgrimage to Mecca, by way of Cairo. Gold was part of his baggage. Gold in such quantities may sound like a tale of the market place, invented to astonish, but we have the word of Ibn Khaldoun, sober historian, that this is truth and not fiction. To Kankan Mousa's eighty camel loads of gold dust Ibn Khaldoun adds ". . . two thousand young slaves in brocades and silks from the Yemen."

Two other historians, both from the Mali Sultan's own country furnish further details of this fabulous *hadj*. Es Sadi, author of the *Tarikh es Soudan* (History of the Soudan), said "Sixty thousand men in front of the caravan, then five hundred slaves each with staff of gold weighing seven pounds." And Mhmoud el Kati in his *Tarikh el Fettuch* (another history of the Negro Empires) added, "Eight thousand guards, five hundred women not counting wives, live fish, vats of growing green vegetables and" (most astonishing of all for a fourteenth-century trans-Saharan caravan trip) a means for hardening depressions in the sand to hold water for bathing.

If Cairo was dazzled by Kankan Mousa, the Black Sultan was also dazzled by Cairo. This was Cairo's great period. The Mameluke Sultans were building many of her finest mosques and tombs, among them the Mosque-University of El Azhar the Splendid, the Mosque of Kuluan, the Mosque of Nasir. Baghdad was still the mass of ruins left by Hulagai Khan and his Mongols; but Cairo was the Moslems' Paris, as Mecca was their Rome. These were the years when the tales of *Alfa Lailai ou Lailai,* *"A Thousand and One Nights"* with their roots in Persia and India, were being collected and given their Arabian flavor by some genius of Cairo. Kankan Mousa was impressed with what he saw and, being rich enough to buy what he wanted, he added an architect, whom he met in Mecca, to his entourage for the homeward journey.

Abou Ishaq es Saheli, the architect, was not a native of either Mecca or Cairo but of Granada, Spain. He was also a poet, a "meritorious poet" according to Ibn Batuta who visited his grave in Timbuctu in 1353, seven years after his death. In his native Granada Es Saheli had seen the Alhambra in the process of building, and the Generalife was finished five years before he made his journey to Timbuctu. But limited to adobe mud and local sandstone, the mosques and palaces he built on the Niger for Kankan Mousa have nothing to suggest the delicate beauty of Granada's carved marble and plaster. Whatever he did, however, must have satisfied his patron, because Ibn Batuta writes that Kankan Mousa, "a generous and virtuous prince, gave Es Saheli four hundred *mithkals* of gold in a single day." A *mithkal* was an eighth of an ounce—fifty ounces of gold was no mean present.

It was while Kankan Mousa was making his famous *hadj* to Mecca that his general took the Songhoi capital of Gao and the town of Timbuctu. By this time Timbuctu had risen from its modest beginnings in the eleventh century, as a Touareg encampment on the highest point of the Niger bend, to an important center of exchange between the caravans of the north and the river-borne traffickers of savanna and jungle. As the caravans began converging there, the clever merchants of Djenné, another Songhoi town 300 miles up the river, had foreseen its future, peopled it with their agents, and turned it into the great trading center of the next five centuries. Timbuctu became best known to the world; but Djenné, already a city of schools, scholars and precious manuscripts, was the brains behind it.

Djenné built, and still builds, splendid boats for the Niger river trade.

Today, when the flat, mud-baked city of Timbuctu has crumbled to a fraction of its former size and its streets are choked with sand, the trim, baked-clay buildings of Djenné rise invitingly above its ring of bright water. The name, too, may be more familiar than we think, since there is the theory that the name Guinea, if not derived from Ghana, is derived from Djenné. In addition to Djenné, Moroccans also helped build the new trading post of Timbuctu. Their caravans followed the trail leading through the Thagazza salt mines and Araouane, and their merchants established branches and agents in the growing town.

On his way back from Mecca to his own capital, Melle, Kankan Mousa inspected his two new conquests and set his architect, Es Saheli, to work on palaces and mosques and the first flat-roofed houses of the region. By now the territory that he controlled was enormous—Ghana to the northwest, the Songhois to the east, plus his own kingdom south of the "Great River" —giving him a land as large as Western Europe. In local measurement it was territory a year long and a year wide. This implied a twenty-five mile day—the distance a camel and his driver could cover from twilight to sunrise. (When the Franciscan Fathers laid out the California Missions they set them a thirty-mile day apart—man and mule reckoning instead of man and camel.) This remarkable Negro king was the first of his race to establish diplomatic relations with Morocco. During the rule of the Merinid Sultan Aboul Hassan, envoys from Kankan Mousa with giraffes and other fabulous presents appeared at the Mansoura court during the siege of Tlemcen. In Europe the black King's portrait filled the map space occupied by his country. He was the "Golden Emperor of Africa."

Upon Kankan Mousa's death in 1332, a weak son succeeded—the one who sold the great gold lump to an Egyptian merchant. But, under Mousa's brother Suleiman from 1336 to 1359, Mali regained most of its power. During this period Ibn Batuta contributed the first eyewitness account of the extraordinary pomp of a royal audience, the lavish display of gold and silver, and the vices and virtues of the people.

Twenty-four years of crisscrossing the lands between Mecca and Khan-baliq had not satisfied a "curiosity in cities and marvels of the way" for this "Traveler of Islam." Except for its northern rim, he had seen little of his own continent; and now people were talking about the wonders of the Negro Kingdoms. Two years after his return to the Moghreb in 1352 he was in Sidjilmassa at the Sahara's northern edge, buying camels and a four-months' supply of forage for them in order to join a merchant caravan to the regions of salt and gold. By his two-year journey to the Kingdom of Mali, going via the salt mines of Thagazza and returning by the Hoggar Mountains of the central Sahara, he joins the half dozen medieval chroniclers, both Negro and Arab, through whose eyes we can see the gold glittering against black skins, the precious manuscripts in the medersas of

129

the mosques and, most fascinating of all, a Negro world prosperous, civilized and free.

It took Ibn Batuta's caravan almost a month to reach the Thagazza salt mines a little beyond the halfway mark to Timbuctu. Of all the desolate and grisly places of the world where man is still forced to slave for his living, there are probably none more terrible. Ibn Batuta called it an "unattractive village," a proof that he was not given to exaggeration. E.-F. Gauthier, on the other hand, in his *Sahara, The Great Desert* said: "It is hardly possible that even under the most merciless regimes there has ever been an industrial hell comparable to this one anywhere on the face of the earth."

Why? Because after a few years the imported Negro slaves die from the saline water and the savage desert sun. And if we think slavery is extinct today in the Sahara we have only to read Lord Robin Maugham's *The Slaves of Timbuctu*, with his description of buying a slave from the Touaregs in 1960(!), photographing the transaction as proof and then freeing him.

Thagazza, with its salt mines worked in the middle ages and then abandoned, was not a Saharan oasis of water and palm trees, nor is nearby Taoudeni, the modern mine from which fortunes are made today by the middlemen of Timbuctu because Saharan salt is still the only kind that the Soudanese and people south of the Niger will touch. In Timbuctu today, on the sand-covered ground floors of the two-story houses one can see the great three-foot slabs of salt leaning up against the walls. At the Hotel Timbuctu, the salt comes to you grated in a little pile on a saucer beside the pepper and adds its peculiar flavor to the pungent and memorable sauces for pigeons, lamb and river fish.

Twice a year in December and March the *azalai* or salt caravan of 1,200 camels brings the three-foot slabs of Taoudeni salt into Timbuctu. This caravan itself was and is something of a hell on earth. It is nothing like travel with Kankan Mousa and his green vegetables and contrived swimming pool. Read the account by René Caillié, the young French discoverer of Timbuctu in 1828, of his Saharan crossing via the Thagazza mines, or the excellent book written about him, *The Unveiling of Timbuctu* by Galbraith Welch. Read how the strictly rationed water was distributed only once a day in temperatures nearing 160°, of sand storms and dried-up water wells, lost trails and danger of Touareg attack, of dying camels, of leather patches sewn to the cracked and bleeding pads of foot-sore camels, and the same kind of patches sewn to the cracked feet of their barefoot drivers. Or read *Azalai* [published in 1956] by the American John Skolle, who joined the modern caravan of camels out of reckless curiosity, and see what men must still endure to earn a living from Saharan salt.

The caravan of Ibn Batuta, led by a guide "blind in one eye and diseased in the other but with the best knowledge of the road of any man," entered the kingdom of the Blacks at the town of Oualata about 250 miles due west of Timbuctu.

In books on the medieval Soudan, sooner or later the author will quote Ibn Batuta on the subject of the women of Oualata. It is as irresistible as quoting Es Sadi and El Kati on the subject of Kankan Mousa's pilgrimage to Mecca. After twenty-five years of world-wide travel this pious Moslem found a pattern of morals that seems to have surprised and shocked him more than anything else he had ever met.

Here is Ibn Batuta on the women of Oualata in H. A. R. Gibb's translation from the Arabic:

> The women there have "friends" and "companions" amongst the men outside their own families, and the men in the same way have "companions" amongst women of other families. A man may go into his house and find his wife entertaining her "companion" but he takes no objection to it. One day at Oualata I went into the qadi's house after asking his permission to enter, and found with him a young woman of remarkable beauty. When I saw her I was shocked and turned to go out but she laughed at me, instead of being overcome by shame, and the qadi said to me, "Why are you going out? She is my companion." I was amazed at their conduct for he was a theologian and a pilgrim to boot. I was told that he had asked the Sultan's permission to make the pilgrimage that year with his "companion" (whether this one or not I cannot say) but the Sultan would not grant it.

To get the full impact of this scandalous behavior on Ibn Batuta, who himself, both in Delhi and in the Maldive Islands, had held the post of qadi (an office combining the rank and duty of bishop and judge), it is necessary to see through Moslem instead of Christian eyes. It is necessary to be as deeply convinced that women should be at all times veiled as that they should not appear naked, and equally convinced that for the heinous crime of female adultery no punishment is too severe.

In the Sultan's capital, the vanished town of Melle, the traveler describes the pomp of royal audiences. Mansa Soleiman would be seated on a silk-carpeted platform under a silk pavilion surmounted by a gold bird the size of a falcon. "The armour-bearers bring in magnificent arms— quivers of gold and silver, swords ornamented with gold and with golden scabbards, gold and silver lances and crystal maces. At his head stand four *amirs* driving off the flies, having in their hands silver ornaments resembling saddle stirrups. The commanders, qadi and preachers sit in their usual places. The interpreter comes with his four wives and his slave girls about four hundred in number. They are wearing beautiful robes, and on their heads they have gold and silver fillets with gold and silver balls attached. . . ."

Seven months in Melle enabled Ibn Batuta to sum up both the vices and virtues of its citizens. Among the "admirable qualities of the Negroes," he listed: they were seldom unjust and had a greater abhorrence of injustice than any other people; there was complete security in their country (Could any tribute be higher?); they had the habit of wearing clean white garments on Friday, and they brought up their children to attend prayers. "I visited the qadi in his house. His children were chained up so I said to him: 'Will you not let them loose?' He replied: 'I shall not do so until they learn the Koran by heart.'" (The Koran in George Sale's English translation is 336 pages of fine print.) In his short roster of bad qualities nakedness tops the list. "Women servants, slave girls and young girls go about in front of everyone naked without a stitch of clothing on them. Women go into the Sultan's presence naked and his daughters also go about naked."

On the road to Timbuctu, which he traveled by night to avoid mosquitoes, he saw his first hippopotamuses, sixteen bulky monsters pasturing along the river bank in the moonlight, and mistook them for elephants. Of Timbuctu itself he had next to nothing to say except to mention the grave of the architect of its mosques—the Granada poet Es Saheli brought by Kankan Mousa from Mecca. Gao with its twelfth-century royal tombs of Spanish marble was the final "pearl of the Niger Cities" visited by this avid traveler before he returned for good to Morocco, the land of his birth.

Mansa Soleiman, whom Ibn Batuta considered avaricious because of his meager hospitality gifts, and whose daughters appeared naked, was the last powerful ruler of the Mali empire.

The fourteenth century belongs to Mali, but the fifteenth and sixteenth belong to the Songhoi. As soon as Mali lost its hold on the cities of Gao and Timbuctu, the Mossi of the savannas clawed at them from the south and the desert Touaregs from the north. Djenné, a Songhoi city from first to last, achieved independence. But year by year the Songhoi were growing stronger.

The Songhoi were, and still are—660,000 of them—a people as black-skinned as the tribes about them, but tall and slender; in their non-Negritic features the nose is straight and clean cut, and the lips are thin and non-protruding.

The only clear picture in their confused origin is their own statement that their first king was a great fish with a golden ring in his nose who held morning audiences. When the kings became human, we are not sure whether they were black or white; white Berbers, perhaps, from upper Egypt who were eventually killed off or absorbed by their black subjects. One legend has their first rulers coming from the Yemen across the Red Sea from Egypt. Thirteen pagan rulers preceded the first one who acknowledged Allah and his Prophet in 1010.

For the geographical picture of these three early Western Soudanese empires, think of Ghana and Mali with their centers to the west of Djenné and the Niger bend, expanding eastward when they were powerful enough to exact tribute from the Songhoi, and think of the Songhoi with Djenné and the capital Gao as the western edge of a kingdom stretching eastward toward Lake Chad and comprising parts of what today are the new independent states of Mali, Upper Volta, Niger and Nigeria, ready, of course, to engulf their neighbors to the west at the first sign of weakness.

Two formidable personalities stand out as creators of Songhoi greatness—the Sultan Sunni Ali, and the usurper of his throne, Askia the Great. The word Askia means usurper. His real name was Mohammed ben Bekr. He was Sunni Ali's prime minister and brilliant general, who had helped his sultan subdue the vast western Soudan. At Sunni Ali's death, Mohammed took a scornful look at the many and miserable sons the Sultan had sired. Not one of the soft and vicious lot was worth his serving. The simplest thing to do was to wipe out the despicable Sunni heirs, take the throne for himself, and start a new dynasty.

As a military genius, Sunni Ali had been tremendous. Tribute from the subdued tribes poured into Gao and Timbuctu. As a pious Moslem he wasn't much better than the cannibals down in the humid, jungle country where his mother came from. He lumped the five daily prayers into one, or omitted them altogether; he scarcely knew the difference between Allah and Mohammed; and he paid much more respect to witch doctors and sorceresses than to the scholarly cheiks and imams of Islam.

In Askia, on the other hand, the holy men, the marabouts, found all they could ask for in the way of piety and reverence for the laws of the Prophet. Like Kankan Mousa, Askia made the *hadj* to Mecca in the grand style—300,000 *mithkals* of gold for traveling expenses, leaving 5,000 *mithkals* behind to establish a hostelry surrounded with gardens for Western Soudanese travelers. On the way back he stopped at Cairo to pay homage not only to the Caliph but to the learned men of the city—men with whom he corresponded after his return to Gao. Depending on their advice, he modeled his government on what he had learned from the East. He may have been one of the first Negroes to organize a centralized government, divided into provinces, where his own family and sons-in-law held the posts of viceroys, governors and cadis. He also divided his subjects into civilians and soldiers. The army took care of collecting the taxes; the civilians tripled the commerce, and the gold piled up so high that the envious Moroccan sultans 1,500 miles away could almost see it glitter. At Timbuctu, the great Mosque-University of Sankoré became almost as famous as the gold and drew scholars from all over the Arab world. From the Atlantic to Lake Chad, from the salt mines to the cannibal country, the tribal chiefs sent their sons to Sankoré for a Timbuctu education. Timbuctu was more than ever Queen of the western Soudan, and Askia the Great, like

Kankan Mousa, was one of the most extraordinary Negro rulers in African history.

A hundred sons waited greedily to succeed him. As his faculties grew feeble, they pushed him roughly from the throne and fought the usual battle among themselves to seize the power. They were no better, perhaps even worse, than the sons of Sunni Ali. The cheiks and marabouts reproved them in vain for their drunkenness and adultery, sodomy and incest.

On the far side of the Sahara the Saadian Sultans of Morocco watched hopefully. Moulay Abdullah el Ghalib sent a message to Askia Ishak claiming the Thagazza salt mines, on the pretext that they were nearer to his capital than to that of the Songhoi ruler. With commendable defiance, Askia Ishak dispatched a band of Touaregs to pillage the Moroccan oases of the Dra. Twenty years passed before the Sultans at Marrakesh made their next move. From now on the story of the Songhoi is also the story of Morocco. We shall pick it up again with El Mansour the Gilded of the Saadian Dynasty.

CHAPTER XII

THE RAPE OF TIMBUCTU

(The Saadians, 1550–1668)

Of the first four Saadian princes whose rule covered the second half of the sixteenth century, three were sons of the beheaded Mohammed ech Cheik—men of whom their father and their pious marabout grandfather would have been proud. El Ghalib, the oldest living son, became his father's heir and successor. Before the customary bloody disposal of possible pretenders—brothers, cousins, and other relatives, including his old uncle and father's enemy, El Aredj—three younger brothers had wisely crossed the Algerian-Turkish border. Two had even pressed on to the distant safety of Constantinople. Who can blame them, with such a fountain of blood spurting from family necks!

As soon as the dangerous underbrush had been cleared away, El Ghalib settled down to the object uppermost in his mind—vengeance against the Algerian-Turks for his father's death. After an unsuccessful encounter against them with the Spaniards as allies, he turned his attention to Mazagan, the only Atlantic port left to Portugal. Contraband Christian weapons, especially artillery from both Spain and France, almost brought him the

Mazagan (El Djedida), the Portuguese fort
begun in 1506.

success they had brought his father at Agadir; but the thick walls (six horse-men could ride them abreast), the heavy cannon, the everflowing springs of sweet water inside the town, plus reinforcements from the sea gate, de-feated him in the end. Mazagan remained Portuguese until the fatal Battle of the Three Kings sixteen years later.

In 1571, Pope Pius V, distinguished for having fiercely denounced Protestant Queen Elizabeth's claim to the English throne, proclaimed a crusade against the Turks. No one who knows G. K. Chesterton's ballad on the battle of Lepanto will ever forget the hero who led this last crusade to victory. Don Juan of Austria, bastard brother of King Philip II, fought (". . . the last knight of Europe takes weapons from the walls . . .") while the crowned heads of Christendom—Philip, Elizabeth, Charles—waited with indifference, letting others risk their lives. It was the battle in which Cervantes lost an arm, the battle that broke Turkish power in the western Mediterranean and diminished without destroying the menace of the Barbary pirates.

> Vivat Hispania;
> Domine gloria.
> Don John of Austria
> Has set his people free!

Our El Ghalib, loyal to his faith in spite of his murdered father, added a force of 400 Moroccans to strengthen the ranks of Soleiman the Magnificent's miserable son, Selim the Sot.

This insignificant gesture against the Unbelievers, as well as other pious works such as a new mosque for Marrakesh, was far from enough to

136

endear El Ghalib to his enemies the marabouts. They considered him far too tolerant of both Christian and Jew, and they deeply resented his efforts to establish Christian merchants with their middlemen, the Jews, in Moroccan ports. They also disapproved of his interest in alchemy; but like his father before him and the two brothers who came after him, he was too strong for them. The marabouts were forced to postpone their comeback until Timbuctu gold and soft living had weakened the next generation.

The year that El Ghalib died, 1574, was the year that the Turks gained Tunis from Spain. The two Saadian brothers, Abd el Malek and Ahmed, who had fled to Constantinople in 1557 when El Ghalib came to the throne and began to lop off family heads, took part in the Sultan's conquest and returned to the Turkish capital with the triumphant expedition, bringing Murad III the good news. There, Abd el Malek, the older of the two, learned through his spies that he would be enthusiastically supported in an attempt to seize the Moroccan throne from his brother's son Mohammed (later "The Flayed"). Together the two exiled brothers returned and, with Turkish help, chased their nephew up and down the country until he fled in terror of his life to Portuguese Ceuta. There, Mohammed began his treacherous intrigue with the headstrong King Sebastian, offering the Moroccan port of Asilah in exchange for Portuguese help.

Abd el Malek was by no means an unlawful usurper. Succession by the next oldest brother lay deeply rooted in tribal custom. Brief though his two-year rule turned out to be, it swept across the country like a fresh and beneficial breeze. At the Turkish court, both he and his brother Ahmed had absorbed all that was good, enlightened and tolerant in the rule of Soleiman the Magnificent.

More than ever, Abd el Malek disdained the xenophobia of the marabouts, and welcomed relations with the Christian world. In his brother Ahmed, whom he appointed governor of Fez and placed at the head of his army, he had both a loyal supporter and a devoted friend. For the first time we have the pleasure of recording a warm relationship between brothers which in that polygamous society appears to have been as rare as desert rain. Abd el Malek was the first Moroccan prince to have served a foreign ruler; the first to be considered an accomplished linguist—fluent in Turkish, Spanish, and Italian, as well as his own Arabic; and the first to promote diplomatic relations with Turkey, Spain, France and England.

While Abd el Malek was establishing his sane and orderly government, his ousted nephew Mohammed was hard at work exploiting King Sebastian's crazed ambition to become the saviour of Christianity, and to win Morocco for Portugal. In the face of wise advice and the disapproval of his counselors, including the great poet Camoës and his own uncle, Philip II of Spain, Sebastian assembled his armies at Asilah, the Moroccan town Mohammed had given him. From there, with Mohammed as ally, he marched south to the River Loukos between the town of Ksar el Kebir and the port of Larâche to meet the two Saadian brothers.

In this day of atomic attack, it seems fantastic that Abd el Malek should have suggested to the enemy to wait until the fierce midday heat of the August day had ended before starting the battle. Sebastian refused—a mistake. He is said to have died of sunstroke, toward the end of the terrible defeat in which his army was trapped between the two rivers, with the bridge cut behind it. During the midday heat that he had dreaded, Abd el Malek, desperately ill and conducting the battle from a litter, was the second of the three kings to die. The third, the deposed Mohammed, trying to escape across the bridgeless river, drowned. Because his body was fished out later, skinned, and the skin stuffed with straw by his ghoulish enemies, he goes down in Moroccan history as "Mohammed the Flayed."

This battle, known also as "Ksar el Kebir," closed the pages of Portugal's age of glory. Not only did it bring an end to her North African ambitions but it also wrote *Finis* for many years to her very independence.

Sebastian left no direct heir. A Portuguese uncle succeeded him for three years. At that uncle's death, his Spanish uncle Philip II claimed and took possession of the country. This Spanish captivity lasted for eighty years. For Morocco it opened a minor but glittering role on a stage that stretched from the British Isles to the Golden Horn, from the Straits of Gibraltar to the islands of the New World.

The ambitions of the new ruler, Ahmed (acclaimed on the battlefield where his brother died as El Mansour, the Victorious), were as various as they were unbounded. At the Turkish court he had learned government and diplomacy, the art of conquest and the art of organizing an army. He had learned to expect that there would be, in the divan or council of a sultan, poets and historians, jurists and theologians. He had recited the Friday prayer in the mosques of Soleiman's inspired engineer-architect, Mirmar Sinan, and in the Aya Sofia with its roots deep in the venerable thousand-year-old Byzantine–Greek culture of Justinian's day. With this Middle Eastern background, El Mansour brought back to Morocco a wider vision, and also a greater lust for luxury than any ruler before him. The day after the Battle of the Three Kings, he began plans for his Marrakesh palace, El Bedi.

With the gold that flowed in from Portugal for the ransomed captives, El Mansour could well afford to import his artisans and materials from Christian lands. For the marble of Italy he exchanged, pound for pound, sugar from the Sous. The building of El Bedi took fifteen years. El Oufrani, chronicler of the Saadian dynasty, describes the inauguration of the fabulous palace in all its pomp, oriental splendor, and shimmer of Soudanese gold. A century later, Moulay Ismail of the present dynasty reduced it to ruins, dragging off its marble columns and other treasures for his own Moroccan "Versailles" at Meknès.

Saadian Morocco was now playing a minor role in the Macchiavellian game of European power politics. Queen Elizabeth accredited a Mr. Edmond Hogan as envoy to the "King of Marucos and Fesse" and signed one of her letters to El Mansour "Your sister and relative according to the law of crown and sceptre." In those days it was not Morocco itself that the Christian countries were scheming to control, but the ports—ports for commerce, ports as refuge against the storms of the high seas and against the pirate terror. El Mansour, astute as a desert fox, played them off against each other, and outwitted them all in their schemes to control his ports. In 1588 he had the immense satisfaction of seeing his old arch enemy Spain, despite her great Armada, splendidly beaten by his new friend, England.

In the matter of governing a land of both Berbers and Arabs, it must not be forgotten that the Saadians were essentially an Arab tribe, and that the rulers among them had always at the end of their tongues the venerable names in the long line that led them back through nine centuries to Mecca and Mohammed. In their great pride, their contempt was enormous for the native Berber tribes of Morocco's mountains and plains.

By Ahmed's time, many of the wild and savage nomad tribes of the eleventh-century Second Arab Invasion had been settled on the coastal plain and drawn into politics and government. With them and the Arabized Berbers, also coastal tribes, Ahmed formed the core of his government, the Makhzen. From them, in times of peace he collected regular taxes. From other tribes, known as *guich*, exempt from taxes, he drew his army. Whatever lay outside this group, especially in the inaccessible Middle Atlas and Rif or along the fringes of the desert, became the *Bled es Siba*—the land of Dissidents, the Unsubdued, the insolent—a division that disappeared only in the last twenty years of the French Protectorate.

Any dynamic and ambitious young prince, especially one who could look back to Soleiman the Magnificent and his empire expansion, would naturally, on coming to his own throne, examine every boundary for weakness, for a place to push through and expand his own empire as other El Mansours had done before him. But in what direction, when his country to the north and west was hemmed in by water, when he knew all too well the strength of the Algerian Turks to the east, when south of his mountains lay another sea, a sea of sand? Only the sand offered a chance.

The caravans crossed it and returned. Why not his army? The caravans crossed it and brought back gold. Why not his army? The Portuguese ransom money would not last forever, especially when El Bedi needed such ornaments as eighty marble columns from the quarries of Pisa. El Mansour thought of how his grandfather, Ech Cheik, had claimed the mid-Saharan salt mines, second only to gold itself as a source of riches, and of how the black King Askia Ishak had defied the command and sent his Touareg allies to pillage Moroccan soil. Surely this called for revenge from a pious grandson!

In the year 1583, with the blackest conceivable motives, El Mansour sent a scouting party of spies in the sheep's clothing of ambassadors, taking flattery and presents to Askia el Hadj, Askia Ishak's successor. The party returned from the Niger with presents, so superior in magnificence to the ones that they had delivered, that Ahmed lusted more than ever for the riches of the Soudan. Preliminary probes into the desert took one army to the Thagazza salt mines, and another to the Touat and Gharara oases, about a third of the way to Timbuctu. (In this crescent of oases in the Algerian Sahara, known collectively as the "Road of Palms," the southernmost one, Reggan, has been the site of recent French atomic bomb explosions.)

Ahmed's dispute with the white-bearded patriarchs of his council on the proposed conquest of the Songhoi Empire proved that not all Moroccan sovereigns were laws unto themselves. In the eyes of his council, forty-year-old Ahmed seemed as incapable of mature judgment as a forty-year-old United States president in the eyes of some of our elder statesmen. Their arguments against this hot-headed project were the 1,500 miles of hostile desert, the scarcity of water and provisions, an enemy who not only would outnumber whatever might be left of a weakened army but would also be fighting on its own terrain, defending its own homeland. Stubbornly Ahmed talked them down. His spies had given him confidence, and the splendors of Songhoi presents had added fire to his greed.

Ahmed protested, "They fight with lances, with spears and with swords. Their greatest protection, like that of the Almoravids five hundred years ago, is still their leather shields. Can they stand up against muskets and gunpowder?" In the end he won over the council.

It took the army four months to reach the Niger. Under the command of a renegade Spanish Moslem named Djouder, 3,000 musketeers and another 1,000 men, half cavalry, half foot soldiers with swords and bayonets, marched across the "Land of Thirst." In 1591 Ishak II met them not far from Timbuctu with 30,000 foot soldiers and 12,000 horsemen. Numbers counted for nothing against the noise, the smoke and the fire of gunpowder. Behind a protective shield of stampeding cattle, the Songhoi army, limp with terror, fell to the enemy as corpses or slaves. For the sake of peace, Ishak offered through Djouder annual tribute plus a present of 100,000 *mithkals* of gold and 100 slaves. When the gold reached Marrakesh, though it sent the populace into an ecstasy of excitement and won their prince his title of "The Gilded," the ungrateful Ahmed found Djouder's offering so inadequate that he sent another Pasha to replace him as governor of the conquered empire.

The brutal rule that followed, of Moorish Pashas and their subordinates, is an ugly picture. In Ahmed's mind there was no thought of extending his own empire to include the luster of Timbuctu's Sankoré University. Gold was what he had come for, and gold was all that counted.

Pasha Djouder, renegade conqueror of the South. / *O. N. M. T.*

For four years the Moors murdered, massacred and crucified the people of the Western Soudan, until they were crushed beyond the strength of rebellion.

In Timbuctu, city of books, the books were burned and the black scholars taken in chains to Marrakesh, with little better treatment than was

141

meted out to the slaves themselves. Greatest of them all, Ahmed Baba, peer of Ibn Khaldoun and Leo Africanus, spent twelve long years of exile in Marrakesh, always longing to return to the city of his birth and never afraid to let his captors know his feelings.

"Oh thou who goest to Gao," he lamented, "turn aside from thy path to breathe my name in Timbuctu. Bear thither the greeting of an exile who sighs for the soil on which his friends and family reside. Console my near and dear ones for the deaths of their lords who have been entombed."

After he was imprisoned a year, the important marabouts of the city succeeded in freeing Ahmed Baba and persuaded him to serve as professor of rhetoric, law and theology in the principal mosque.

While Ahmed ei Mansour lived, the distinguished Songhoi captive was forbidden to leave the city. When Ahmed's son Zaidan succeeded in 1603, the scholars who loved and revered their black colleague managed to restore his freedom. After his return to Timbuctu, Ahmed Baba lived until 1627, and was buried beside his father at the north of the city beside his beloved Sankoré Mosque-University.

The Timbuctu that Ahmed Baba returned to was a tragic contrast to the city that he had left. It was no longer the city of which Leo Africanus could say that, of all ways of making a fortune there, the greatest lay in the selling of books. Ahmed Baba himself had lamented, in earlier years, that among his book-loving friends he himself, owning only six hundred manuscripts, was considered poor.

For twenty years the Moorish Pashas took their orders from Morocco and collected and delivered the annual tribute. After that, in the long anarchy that followed El Mansour's death, they were on their own but finally were crushed and at the mercy of marauding tribes—especially the desert Touaregs. So terrifying was Touareg rule and robbery, until the coming of the French in 1894, that the imperious blows of their iron spears against the brass-studded doors of Timbuctu houses was a signal to hide treasures, dress in rags and pray to Allah, usually in vain, for the safety of the women.

Under French rule, the Touaregs lost their insolence. Their Bellah slaves were theoretically set free. Two French forts and a garrison guarded the desert approaches. Another language was added to the Songhoi, Bambara, Peuhl, Mossi, Tamachek and Arabic heard in the market place and at the river port. Roads as well as caravan trails and the myriad lakes, branches and *marigots* of the Niger connected Timbuctu to the outside world. Today that era is also finished. The Timbuctu of the independent Republic of Mali is no longer the colonial Timbuctu of the French Soudan. Ahmed Baba would be glad to see it free again as it was in the days of Kankan Mousa and the Askias.

The modern Ibn Batuta would arrive today by plane instead of by

A Timbuktu street, changeless as ever. / *Author*

camel—in a Russian Ilyushin two-engine plane flying once a week from the capital, Bamako, with a Russian or Czech pilot. He would find a simple new hotel with a view of sand dunes and sunset from the terrace that would make him understand Ahmed Baba's longing to return. There would be electric light from six in the morning until ten at night, generated by the hotel, running water from the hotel's wells, a telephone, a portable radio on the terrace or in the restaurant-bar, picking up news and music from

143

savanna and jungle. Beyond the broad avenue of soft sand east of the hotel, he would find the town compact, flat-roofed, silvery grey against the blue sky, not unlike an Indian village of the American southwest. Only the size, not the appearance, has changed since the Moorish conquest. The Great Mosque, the Djingerebar, once the heart of the town, is now on the edge. At the northern end, the Sankoré still stands, but the reactivated medersa, once so famous, has been moved into unimaginative modern buildings with an acacia-shaded campus on the broad avenue near the hotel.

Like the houses, the mosques are built of the same silvery grey adobe. Only their size, the crenellations of the roof, the long unpierced walls and their extraordinary minarets distinguish them from the two-story houses. From the cone-shaped minarets and towers, split palm trunks stick out irregularly to give the mason a footing for slapping on mud. Ahmed Baba during his exile undoubtedly would have exchanged with joy every shimmering turquoise tile and golden ball of the Koutoubia Tower for the sight of one of these bristling Soudanese minarets of grey mud and split palm logs. Though the "sights," in the guide-book sense of the word, are limited to three mosques, the market place, the houses of the explorers—the French Caillié, the German Barth, the English Laing, and the house still owned by the family of the "White Monk of Timbuctu"—there is endless pleasure in watching the life of street and market place, in the ease of making friends among young and old, in the rich color of the ankle-length *gondourahs* and billowing *grand boubous* worn by men and women of regal carriage, but above all in the way Timbuctu seems to be handling its new freedom. When the astute politician, Mahamane Haidera, president of the General Assembly, makes a plea in the public square for the national loan, he urges his people to make sacrifices to provide the needed funds themselves. "When we take money from others," he warns the enormous crowd, "there will be strings attached."

This is the wisdom and ideal that we hope to find in these young African republics. The fulfillment of the ideal will take time, but the awareness of its importance promises well for the future of Mali and its caravan city of Timbuctu.

Crossing the Sahara northward again, and plunging back into the sixteenth century, we find that El Mansour's enjoyment of stolen Songhoi gold was short-lived. For the first half of the last decade, it raised his prestige among the European powers to dazzling heights. Philip of Spain, jealous of the gold, schemed to channel some of it off into his own treasury by seizing Cape Arguin, south of Porte Etienne in the present Mauritania. At the news of this planned robbery, El Mansour quickly prevented it by entering into an alliance of offense and defense with Elizabeth of England and Henry of France. A year later, Philip died and Elizabeth turned her attentions to the West Indies.

As El Mansour's European troubles ended, his domestic ones began. En Nasir, his nephew, a brother of the "Flayed" Mohammed, who had taken refuge at the Spanish court, stirred the discontented to serious revolt. No sooner was En Nasir's head hung from the gates of the capital than El Mansour's own son and heir, El Mamoun, despicable, dissolute, and perverted, attempted to seize the throne. When he was finally defeated and captured, the council recommended death as a punishment; the father, however, loved the vicious creature too much to agree, and compromised on prison.

The next tragedy, showing how little man—king or beggar, pious or profane, with or without gold—controls his own fate, was a seven-year scourge of the plague. As powerless against its death and famine as the Songhois had been against the gunpowder of his muskets, El Mansour watched it devastate his land, turning all the gilded hopes and ambitions of his youth to grey dust. Finally, its pains shot through his own body, glazed his eyes and numbed his tongue and took his life. In that same year, 1603, Elizabeth of England also died. In the city of London, the plague took 38,000 victims.

Now for the last time the old story occurs of a dynasty fizzling like a spent firecracker because its most brilliant ruler engendered mice instead of men. Three sons were left ready to poison, strangle or behead each other for the sake of the throne. One of them, El Mamoun, was, as we know, in prison. The people of Fez chose Zidan; the people of Marrakesh, Abou Faris. This division of the country into two kingdoms lasted until the next dynasty came into power.

El Mamoun soon managed to regain his freedom, and the three brothers chased each other around from capital to capital until El Mamoun's son strangled Abou Faris and somebody else murdered El Mamoun, the worst of the three. Zidan, the least objectionable, lasted the longest, although, if he were not being driven out of one capital or another by his brothers, the marabouts, again high in the saddle, made life unhappy for him.

Zidan, thrown out of Marrakesh three times during his rule, is not entirely unworthy of our sympathy. He enabled Ahmed Baba to return to Timbuctu; he built the magnificent west portion of the Saadian tombs where his father's gravestone lies surrounded by twelve marble columns; and, in one of his flights from Marrakesh, he made every effort to save his highly treasured library of 3,000 volumes, consigning it to a French vessel bound for a friendly port. Unfortunately, Spanish pirates seized the ship. In the Escorial of Madrid, many of the stolen volumes perished in the fire of 1671—among them, it is believed, a manuscript by St. Augustine.

Following Zidan, there were two drunkards of which there is nothing of interest to be said except that one was "exceedingly fond of music and very vicious." The next ruler, Mohammed ech Cheik el Seghir, was the

145

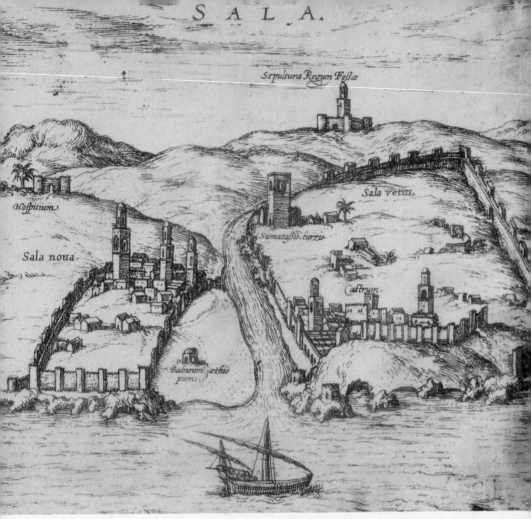

Sepultura Regum Feßæ

Sala vetus.

Hoſpitium

Sala noua.

Sumatassis turris

Castrum.

Balneum æthiopum.

Salé and Rabat, showing the Almohad wall, from an old engraving. /
Ladreit de Lacharrière

first Moroccan prince to assume the title of "Sultan." The title lasted from his own day to the present, when the late Mohammed V changed it to "King" in the second year of Morocco's independence—1957.

In the southern Kingdom of Marrakesh, though the marabouts exerted power more often than did the princes, a nominal thread of Saadian rule lasted until Er Rashid, the first Alaouite Sultan of the next dynasty, proclaimed at Fez in 1666, gave it its death blow.

In the north in the Kingdom of Fez, the ineffectual Saadian princes had more than marabouts to contend with. A small independent pirate republic of Andalusian exiles had developed on the right bank of the mouth of the Bou Regreg River under the walls of the Rabat Kasba, in alliance, between quarrels, with the older pirate nest of Salé on the opposite shore.

146

European governments protested the nuisance of their piracy and, at times, blockaded the river mouth. On the other hand, European merchants— especially the British and the Dutch—unscrupulous and greedy, furnished pirates, marabouts and Saadian princes alike the contraband weapons and supplies, rigging, cannons and gunpowder, with which to fight each other. For the Dutch black-marketeers, there was another motive besides money. A hundred years of Spanish tyranny had made the Dutch hate the country of Philip II and the Duke of Alba as fiercely as Morocco did. Every charge of gunpowder, every cannon ball they put into pirate hands, they hoped would blast some Spanish galleon to the bottom of the sea.

First of the marabouts to spread discord from the mouth of the Bou Regreg to the walls of Fez was the holy man of Salé, the clever and crafty El Ayachi, known to the Christians—for whom he had the usual fierce marabout abhorrence—as "Santo." The word "Santo" in the case of this terrible marabout had diabolical rather than saintly connotations, especially as he boasted of having been responsible for 3,600 Christian deaths. During Zidan's rule he had led an unsuccessful jihad against Mazagan, which was still held by the Portuguese. After a quarrel with Zidan, he first encouraged the Rabat-Salé Republic in its independence and defiance of Saadian tribute, then, as he was immensely powerful throughout the north, tried to take it himself. Between the years 1618 and 1626, this Republic, in conjunction with the Andalusian exile city of Tetuán, claimed a record of 6,000 Christian captives and booty valued at six million pounds.

When Sultan Mohammed, afraid of El Ayachi's power, rushed up from his Marrakesh capital to foil El Ayachi's plans, El Ayachi called on the powerful Dila marabouts of the Middle Atlas for help. The defeated Sultan, chased back to the south, was ordered never to cross the Oum er Rebia River again. El Ayachi, with the Dilas' consent, took over the pirate republic. Vengefully he began a fearful massacre of the Rabat Andalusians who had resisted him when he first began the siege. In deep disapproval and full of regret for putting him in power, the Dila marabouts quickly turned against him, with the result that his head was exhibited through the streets of Rabat, to the immense joy of the Andalusians as well as the Spaniards and Portuguese. Those who still defended his piety claimed that the sacred head continued to recite the Koran.

Now the Dilaites held Fez and the north. Though they seemed to have none of the bloodthirsty viciousness of El Ayachi, the people of Fez had no use for them. After ten years under their rule, the city sent an invitation to their rivals, the Cherifs of the Tafilalet oasis, under the leadership of Moulay Mohammed.

These Tafilalet Cherifs, originally from Yenbo on the Red Sea, were the second of those holy Arabian families who had been invited to settle in the oases at the edge of the Moroccan desert in the hope that their *baraka,* the miracle-working property of their sacred blood, would increase the fertility of the date-gardens. In the eyes of the haughty Tafilalet Cherifs, the Saadians were not true descendants of the Prophet but merely descendants of the wet nurse who had suckled him in the desert and who belonged to the tribe of the Beni Saad.

In his attempt to seize Fez from the Dilaites, Moulay Mohammed was at first successful, but failed in his attempt to hold it. He had, however, succeeded in chasing the Dilaites out of Tafilalet and in rescuing his imprisoned father from the fortress of a powerful marabout in the Sous. He also held territory as far east as the Algerian-Turkish border. Where this Alaouite Cherif failed in safeguarding his future was in not destroying, in the fashion of the day, his younger brother, Er Rashid. If he had managed to take care of this, Er Rashid would not have been able to escape into the Rif, murder a rich Jew for his tremendous treasure, raise an army, and meet and kill his brother on the plain of Angad.

Two years later, in 1666, Er Rashid was proclaimed Sultan of Fez and, after two more years and a bloody massacre of the usurping Chabana tribe at Marrakesh, both capitals were in his possession. The present ruling dynasty of Morocco was now at last firmly established on the throne.

The year 1662, four years before Er Rashid began his rule, marks the first conflict of interest on Moroccan soil between England and France. It was the beginning of the great give-away by colonial powers of what was not theirs to give. When Catherine of Braganza, sister of King Alfonso VI of Portugal, married Charles II of England in 1663, the dowry had consisted of the city of Tangier along with Bombay and 300,000 pounds. By this substantial offering, English protection of Portugal against her enemy, Spain, was assured. Though France had had a hand in engineering this marriage of convenience, she was far from pleased to find England established so solidly in a country she herself was beginning to find interesting.

Moroccan opposition to the arrival of the English came not from the Tafilalet Mohammed but from a picturesque figure of Andalusian descent named Ghailan, who had seized power in the north and was ruling the pirate cities of Tetuán and Salé. Though he set out to harass the Christian intruders in the beginning by seizing and enslaving four hundred of their soldiers, by 1664 he had aligned himself with the Redcoats of Tangier against their common enemy, Er Rashid, now recognized as Sultan at Fez.

Ghailan was a great blond giant, with a cultivated mind, dynamic energy and magnificent courage. After his false start, he had begun to get along splendidly with the British until a Colonel Norwood began to meddle with the affairs of his harem. Ghailan, who had been defeated in battle and besieged in Asilah by Er Rashid, had escaped to Tangier with the help of a British ship—and not alone! The full entourage of a lusty Arab's four

Ghailan, the ferocious. / *O. N. M. T.*

wives and numerous concubines pricked the interest of every monogamous Britisher in whose veins the blood reputedly ran at a cooler temperature.*

   * S. P. Scott in his *History of Moorish Empire in Europe* claims that "The passions of Orientals are far stronger than those of Western nations bearing to each other a ratio approximating to that of the warm blooded mammalia to the sluggish reptilia."

The passions of Ghailan had been particularly aroused by a beautiful young Portuguese girl whom he had forced to renounce her religion on entering his harem. When Colonel Norwood aided her escape, witnessed her repudiation of Islam, and sent her back to her parents in Lisbon, the raging Ghailan would gladly have exhibited every British head, severed and bleeding, above the gates of the city. Unable to accomplish that, he escaped to Algiers, returned to collect a new army, and took on both Tangier and the Cherifian Sultan as enemies. Er Rashid, known to the British as the "Great Tafiletta," opposed him unsuccessfully, but his brother, Moulay Ismail, in the year after his accession to the throne, met him in battle. Though Ghailan fought with his usual fury, and though four horses were killed beneath him, in the end his giant body was no match for musket fire, and his great blond head was carried in triumph on the tip of a lance to the tent of the new Sultan.

CHAPTER XIII

THE TERRIBLE LION
(Moulay Ismail, 1672–1727)

Drunken riding ended the life of the first Alaouite sultan, Er Rashid, in the year 1672. Galloping through a Marrakesh orange orchard after drinking too much brandy, he caught his head in the forked limb of a tree and fell to the ground with a broken neck. But the vigorous and cruel rule of the "Great Tafiletta" was only a curtain raiser for the drama to follow. During the fifty-five-year rule of his brother Ismail, Morocco was under the iron heel of a religious despot as bloodthirsty and fanatical as history has ever recorded. Every act and every scene, every entrance and every exit was branded by psychopathic sadism.

If an unnatural ecstasy in the spilling of human blood, delight in causing pain, a fiend's cunning in the invention of new tortures were all that the great Ismail stood for, we could dismiss him with a few contemptuous lines, toss him off as a Moorish Caligula, Nero or Heliogabalus. But not one of those decadent Roman monsters had the force, the genius and the iron will to bring leadership and order, prosperity and fame to a country received in a state of chaos, famine and decay. Not one of the

151

The terrible emperor, Moulay Ismael. /
Ladreit de Lacharrière

three Romans knew how to create a personal army unswerving in its loyalty for more than half a century. Caligula and Heliogabalus, when less than thirty, were murdered by their Praetorian Guards; Nero at thirty-one committed suicide at the news of his death sentence from the Senate; but Moulay Ismail died peacefully in his bed at the age of eighty-one. The great men of the court reverently washed his body and said the last prayers, and the poets wrote: "In the days of peace you surpassed the moon in beauty and in the day of battle you have proved yourself a terrible Lion."

As for "surpassing the moon in beauty," that is not the way he appeared to his two thousand English slaves. "As to his person," one of them wrote, "he is a Mulatto of a dark complexion, and of a very lean and thin body exceeding amorous and as eminent for the Sports of Venus as for Martial Exploits." And from the impressions of a French slave: "His face is of a bright chestnut complexion, longish, and the features are not amiss; he wears a beard a little forked."

Ismail was twenty-six and governor of Meknès, when a swift camel messenger brought from Marrakesh the news of his brother's death. Of Er Rashid's eighty living brothers, Ismail was nearest to Fez, the capital, and most easily able to seize it. If we believe the Arab historians, his father and mother both were of Arab and Cherifian descent. If, however, we follow the majority of the French historians and Europeans who visited his court, his mother was a black Soudanese slave given to his father while the latter was a prisoner in the Sous. Where records are at variance, the Arab historians naturally choose to keep the dynastic lineage pure. The French often yield to the temptation of emphasizing the barbaric background of the people they undertook to civilize.

Not his eighty brothers, but a nephew, Ahmed ben Mahrez, beloved as governor of Marrakesh, became the first and most serious threat to Ismail's rule. The two were enemies, friends and again enemies. The threat ended only with Ahmed's death fifteen years after he had first defied his uncle. In their earliest encounter, Ismail drove him out of Marrakesh and divided 10,000 enemy heads for display on the walls of that city and of the capital, Fez. In the next great battle, the Sultan made clever use of a blinding dust-filled wind to achieve victory.

From the outset of Ismail's rule, the grisly sadistic incidents occurred. The display of 10,000 heads on city walls was nothing new; but no one before Ismail, in marching an army across a stream, had interwoven the bodies of prisoners with giant rushes to form a bridge. Such a horror and those to come are not pleasant to write about. They are, nevertheless, part of the true picture; the records of reputable European eyewitnesses are too numerous to ignore.

Religious fanaticism cloaking psychopathic cruelty; a human stud-farm of his Negro subjects for the creation of a personal army as black as his black mother; a harem of 2,000 wives and concubines; sons to the number of 528; a palace aping the grandeur of Versailles, built by Christian slaves; a marriage offer to a daughter of Louis XIV; and an orderly centralized government—these are the things that have stamped Ismail's name on the pages of history.

One of Moulay Ismael's Negro guard, which still exists
today. / *Relation de l'Empire de Maroc, Paris 1695*

Nothing in the famous picked bodyguards of vulnerable monarchs— the "Immortals" of Xerxes, the Praetorians of the Roman Emperors, the Mamelukes of the Fatimite Caliphs, the Janissaries of the Ottoman Turks— can be compared to the ingenious creation of Ismail's black "Abid Bokhari" or "Slaves of the Book." Where the others were chosen, these were *bred!*

This breeding, one of Ismail's first undertakings, began with a forced assembly of every Negro, male and female, throughout the land—10,000 in all.

"That take that," he ordered, lining them up, the two sexes opposite each other, and pairing them off, then settling them near his capital. Ten years later he collected the first crop. "And thus," wrote the English visitor John Windus, "he lays foundation for his tawny nurseries." For the boys, he organized five years of carefully planned training—during the first year, a trade such as masonry or carpentering; next a year of handling mules; in the third year, the making of bricks and concrete; in the fourth, horsemanship, bareback and bridleless; and in the fifth, horsemanship again, this time with emphasis on shooting from the saddle. At the end of the five years he had an army of sixteen-year-olds formed by his own hand. There was more to the plan than mere physical skills. He sealed the boys to him with the strong emotional bond of Islam.

"You and I," he said, "are Slaves of the Book."

The "Book," *Hadith el Bokhari,* a huge ninth-century collection of traditions concerning Mohammed, was surpassed in sacredness only by the Koran itself. The Blacks took their oath of allegiance upon it, and carried it with them into battle. Their Sultan made them feel that they and he were leagued together against all that was hostile, Arab or Berber, Christian or Jew. He gave them power and pride. He gave them wives, also trained at his command not only in the domestic arts but also in music to delight them between bouts of warfare. Willingly they brought him their own ten-year-olds down through the many generations of his long rule. They built and garrisoned his seventy fortresses among the hostile tribes of the Atlas. They fought his battles. They became the keystones of his own strength. At his death they numbered 150,000.

In Morocco today, their descendants are part of the superb weekly pageant, in Rabat, between palace and mosque as King Hassan II, like his father and grandfather before him, shows himself and his court on the way to the Friday prayer. Though reduced in numbers and activities, they are still the King's "Black Guard," very grand in their red uniforms and still as splendidly black as their brothers on the distant banks of the Niger.

Five hundred and twenty-eight sons who lived to mount horses, an even greater number of daughters who escaped strangling at the hands of the midwives; four legal wives and a constantly replenished harem of 2,000 with a thirty-year age limit; a woman visited every night, but rarely the same one twice unless she had borne her lord a son: this was the "amorous" life that staggered Christian witnesses. On the face of it, such a record has the ring of alcoholic excitement, depraved debauchery, satyriasis; yet, on closer examination, that is not the picture. In his piety Ismail prided himself on a meticulous observance of Koranic law. His legal wives never exceeded four (Mohammed left no numerical restriction on concubines). He drank no wine, no spirits, and indulged in no bacchanalian revels. His favorite and daily food was the simple North African *couscous* of tent and hut—a dish of steamed grain with vegetables and meat. Though he greedily accepted presents of splendid brocades and jewels for his treasure chests, his own burnous was of homespun wool. Like the Prophet, he refrained from wearing silk. During his rule, drunkenness and sodomy were punishable crimes.

His own people found nothing strange or improper in the huge number of his progeny and the size of his harem. On the contrary, the pious among them welcomed the five hundred new-born cherifs with the blood of the Prophet in their veins. In their eyes, Ismail's extraordinary and long-lived virility added to his prestige. It was only the monogamous Christian Europeans who noted the statistics with astonishment and fascinated horror— the ambassadors, the consuls, the renegades and, especially, the captured slaves and the celibate Catholic Fathers who came in the hope of ransoming them.

Again, in the eyes of his own True Believers, much of the bloodthirsty taking of human lives seemed less monstrous than it did to the foreign infidel. No one explained more carefully than Ismail how happy he would be to embrace any Christian slave who would turn Moslem. Every slave had his or her chance. Those that refused forfeited, if not their lives, at least their freedom. His religious duty, Ismail declared, gave him no choice. The very piracy itself that furnished him with these Christian slaves by the thousands was only an extension at sea of the meritorious Holy War against the infidel. (It must not be forgotten that Christians themselves during those supposedly enlightened centuries were not above torturing and killing their fellow human beings: the Revocation of the Edict of Nantes by Louis XIV in 1685 led to torture and the gallows for unnumbered Huguenots; Salem's most famous witch hunt took place in 1692; and the Spanish Inquisition was not abolished until 1820.)

This is not an attempt to whitewash Ismail's bloodthirsty killings of both Christians and Moslems. (His own excuse for the impulsive killing of Moslems was that he enabled them to taste the joys of Paradise earlier than by waiting for a natural death!) He was without question a twisted human being. It is only an effort to show that the terrible religious fanaticism that motivated and justified in his own mind so much of his butchering was not uncommon in his day, and that, if he stood out as a mountain of human cruelty, the surrounding foothills were not far below.

156

Though the Saadian palace of Ahmed the Gilded still glittered in Marrakesh, and the Merinids had built magnificently in nearby Fez, neither of these two royal capitals found favor with Ismail. The city of Meknès, in its setting beneath the olive-covered slopes of the Zerhoun Mountains, which he had governed under his brother Er Rashid, was Ismail's choice. With slaves enough to drag the marble and transport the mosaics and other treasures of the Saadian palace, El Bedi, 280 miles across the country, and even more easily the Roman marbles of Volubilis only 20 miles to the north, he soon began the palace he hoped would rival or, better still, surpass the one Louis XIV was building at Versailles.

The first step was to set the slaves, housed in the beginning in gloomy, vermin-infested underground silos, to building their own high-walled compound. With this accomplished, work on the royal grounds and palaces began. Here, too, the walls were high. Inmates of the huge harem were often as eager to escape as Christian slaves were. Sometimes, in spite of high walls and the close guard of 1,000 black eunuchs, moonlight meetings were achieved, but hardly often enough to make life sweeter for either miserable group of captives. Moreover, discovery led to torture or death —usually both.

When darkness ended the long day's work of hollowing out lakes and sunken gardens, digging foundations, mixing quicklime and gravel, climbing scaffolds, the slaves were herded back to their dungeons. During their misery, the threat of the overseer's whip was bad enough. In addition, Ismail himself supervised the work—running the lazy, the idle, the stupid through with his iron lance, removing heads, or ordering someone to be buried alive in a vat of quicklime.

"If I have a bag of rats," he said, "and keep shaking the bag, they cannot gnaw their way out."

Out of this grueling labor the wonders of the palace took shape. Not a mock Versailles, not a Moorish copy of the inspired creation of Le Vau and Mansart—that was not Ismail's dream. Rather, a showplace in the glorious tradition of Islam that would make the world talk, envy and admire, and of which Ismail himself would be the architect.

The grandeur that impressed the Englishman John Windus in 1720 consisted of the vastness of the royal grounds, an area of four square miles, and of the endless scattering of palaces and pavilions, patios and sunken gardens, fountains, pools and pleasure lakes shut off from the city below it by triple walls. Windus admired the long marble arcades, with their columns looted from Volubilis, and the deep sunken garden, half a mile long, spanned with a bridge from which one looked down on the tops of seventy-foot cypress trees; but above all he admired the "plaster fretwork," the shimmering mosaic of multi-colored tiles covering patio courts, fountains and the bases of pillars, and the sea-green glaze of the tiles on pavilion roofs.

157

Twelve hundred horses stood in the royal stables. Like the palaces, the stables were a thing of wonder—two arcaded galleries more than two miles long, of marble and tiles. Six hundred of the horses who had made the pilgrimage to Mecca, the "noble" ones, were visited by Ismail every day. If he venerated them too much to mount them, they returned his esteem by bowing their heads at his approach. Criminals able to take refuge between the legs of these horses could consider their necks safe from his scimitar. Two slaves for each ten horses kept the olive wood shavings of their bedding neat and pure by catching all droppings before they reached the ground. In a land of eunuchs, not one of these splendid animals was gelded. Sacred verses from the Koran hung in red leather amulets around their necks.

European visitors were impressed—and well they might be—by the quality and beauty of these Barbary horses. In England during Ismail's reign, two famous Arabians and one Barb were creating the great Thoroughbred of the English races. Of the trio, the Godolphin Barb was no less important than the Byerly Turk and the Darley Arabian. He was foaled in Morocco probably about three years before Ismail's death. Ismail's 1,200 pedigreed Barbs would have resembled the Godolphin in beauty of fine bones, arched neck and fiery spirit.

Horses were not the only animals Ismail loved. He knew each of his thirty cats by name. Despite his affection for them, his zeal for stamping out thievery among his subjects caused him to have one of them beheaded in a public ceremony, for stealing a small fish. Fights between his lions and his huge dogs gave him great pleasure. If the dog was getting the worst of it, a slave, usually at the cost of his life, was sent into the pit to rescue him.

For slaves who tried to escape, and many did though few with success, the huge number of lions between Meknès and the Christian ports of the coast was one of the dangers, especially when the fierce beasts chose the springs and sparse waterholes for their hunting grounds. (The Moroccan lion is only recently extinct. In the late twenties of this century a postcard was on sale in Moroccan cities photographed from an airplane showing a lion silhouetted against the winter snows of an Atlas pass.) Other dangers for escaping slaves were the soldiers of the Black Guard, the bloodhounds sent out to track them down, the rewards placed on their heads, and hunger and thirst. If the lives of recaptured escapees were spared, the flogging they received left their backs raw, and the weight of their chains was doubled.

From France, England and Spain came ambassadors and Redemptionist Fathers to try to buy back the wretched prisoners. Ransom prices were enormous. Presents of great value—jewels, watches, rich brocades and broadcloths—were expected as extra offerings. The Sultan's greedy eyes glittered like those of a child as the presents were unwrapped before him. His acceptance of them was no guarantee that the slaves would be redeemed.

The English were the most successful. Abdallah ben Aissa, Grand Admiral of Ismail's fleet (pirate of course), when captured and held at the English court, had been entertained with the utmost courtesy. When the embassy that included John Windus returned to London, it had succeeded in buying back every one of the three hundred English slaves in Meknès at the time. Safely home, the three hundred marched through the cheering street crowds to Saint Paul's to give thanks for their miraculous escape.

Second in favor at the court were the Spaniards. They had the privilege of supporting a convent in Meknès to care for sick slaves. Strong slaves were of more use to Ismail than feeble ones.

Of all the Christians who led lives of torment as Ismail's property, the French stood the smallest chance of being redeemed. The reason for this did little credit to their King. Louis XIV would come to no agreement to exchange the Moorish captives he himself held for the French at Meknès. He insisted on keeping his Moors, and redeeming the others with money.* The strong Moorish arms at the oars of his galleys suited him better than the inferior performance of his own subjects. The Redemptionist Father Dominique Busnot leaves a pitiful account of his frustrating missions, reaching Meknès on foot through the lion-infested forests, to return the first time with no slaves at all, the second time with a few of the ones nearest death from brutal treatment. After pocketing the ransom money and watching the humble priests take their final leave, Ismail scowled fiercely. "Ya Allah," he exclaimed, "we are rid of a nuisance."

There was also the affair of the Princesse de Conti to sour Ismail against the French. But before touching on that fantastic incident, let us consider the rebellious tribes that were to be subdued in the Atlas, the Christians to be driven from Atlantic ports, and the Negro kings (defaulting in their taxes at the Saharan salt mines) to be brought to heel.

Though the entire western Sahara, from the Anti-Atlas to Timbuctu and the Niger, was still nominally a possession of the Sultan, no tribute had been offered or enforced since the death of the conqueror, El Mansour, in 1605. Almost a hundred years had passed since the Saadian conquest. Not only were the routes better known than in Saadian days, but also the advantage of Moorish over Negro arms had become even greater than in the day when El Mansour's General Djouder had, with the noise and fire of his muskets, wiped out the terror-stricken archers and javelin-throwers of the Niger King.

* Two hundred and thirty-three Moors were to be found in Louis' Navy during the invasion of England in support of James II against William II in 1689.

Ismail, at peace for a brief moment with his rebellious nephew Ahmed, entrusted him with an expedition to re-establish tribute from the Thagazza salt mines half way between the Atlas and the Niger. If the routes were better, the dangers still existed—dangers of thirst, hunger, heat and hostile oases. Fifteen hundred dead from the expedition were left behind for the hyenas to scratch out of their shallow graves. On approaching a settlement, in order to give the illusion of four instead of many, the horsemen, with the camels hidden, would form into four single files with the foot soldiers similarly aligned behind them—a ruse of the modern Touaregs up to the recent end of their raiding days, to hide their numbers. When the Moors arrived at the Thagazza mines, arrows and javelins showered them; but in the end the black inhabitants met the same fate as their countrymen of the Niger a century before. The triumphant Moorish army returned with gold dust, slaves and eunuchs, bounty levied upon the rich princes, and the assurance that the annual salt tax would be paid.

In his domestic conquests, the Sultan made sure of keeping the subdued tribes powerless against him. When he conquered a rebel tribe in the *Bled es Siba,* the "Land of Insolence," he not only took away the horses and the arms but often uprooted the people from their own mountain pastures, from which they drew joy, strength and the will to fight, and settled them in a different part of the country. In the case of the Beni Idrassen, after confiscating their horses and arms he gave them 80,000 sheep, demanding only wool and cheese as tax. Perhaps the most important contribution to his success was the chain of seventy mountain strongholds built and garrisoned by his faithful Blacks.

When the country was at last in order, when every proud and defiant chieftain had been stripped of his independence, and every thief of a hand and a foot, when it could be said again as in the days of the Almohads that a woman, a child or a Jew could walk alone in safety from the River Moulaya to the River Noun, the Sultan began to intensify his efforts to dislodge the Christians from the coastal ports.

Neither Charles II of England nor his government, least of all the besieged garrison struggling to defend it, took any satisfaction in the possession of Tangier. The Stuart king, though a collector of fewer women than Ismail, let women's extravagant demands interfere more with the efficient management of his country. He could spare no money to bolster the fortifications of, or furnish provisions for, his African city. In the House of Lords the members were all for abandoning it. The House of Commons, on the other hand, anti-Catholic and anti-French, afraid it might go to France, objected. In the end the Commons lost. Too many outposts had fallen to the Moors. Too many renegade Greeks and Turks, all skillful miners and sappers, were leading their tunnels and trenches dangerously close to the very walls.

In the course of Ismail's twelve-year siege, one of the British Governors, a Colonel Kirke,* and the Sultan struck up a friendship.

"O Emperor of the Moors," Kirke addressed Ismail respectfully to the latter's delight. When Kirke wrote to his friend Sackville, he said: "Morocco is the most civilized country in the world. I would send my son here for his education rather than to France."

On his part, Ismail said: "While you are here there shall be peace."

We have a letter from Ismail to Kirke. "I hear," the Sultan writes, "that there are very few lions in England. I am sending two young little ones to your master. He sent me recently three coach horses. Everyone knows a coach wants four horses. Oblige us in this by all means. By all means. Farewell. We depend upon it."

No other governor duplicated Kirke's pleasure in Morocco. When the orders to abandon the city arrived in 1683, inner fortifications and everything of value were as completely demolished as they had been by the Portuguese on their own indignant withdrawal. Samuel Pepys of the coded *Diary*, also Secretary of the Admiralty, organized the orderly evacuation, and, in his uncoded *Memoirs*, describes the historic incident of the Redcoats marching down through the shattered walls to the waiting ships.

Ismail gave thanks to Allah, moved an army of Riffians into the empty city, and turned his attention to Spanish Asilah and Larâche. When these two cities fell to his army, the Atlantic seaboard, except for Portuguese Mazagan, was free of Christian "stains." To celebrate the victory of Larâche in 1689, he ordered the color of his subjects' slippers changed from black to yellow. In the siege of Spanish Ceuta, luck was against him. The Sun King's vigorous Bourbon grandson, Philip V, succeeded the ineffective Charles II, last of the Spanish Hapsburgs, and broke up the Moorish siege. Ceuta and Melilla still remain Spanish, despite Morocco's independence in 1956.

East of the Moulaya River, Ismail had enemies of his own religion in the Deys of Algiers. By 1659 a revolution in that city had destroyed the original Turkish domination established in 1518 under beylerbeys and then pashas. Though nominally part of the Ottoman Empire until the coming of the French in 1830, the pirate stronghold had now become an independent state under deys of its own choosing. The four great beylerbeys, admirals in the Sultan's Navy, Kheir ed Din or Barbarossa, his son Hassan, Euldj Ali and Salah Reis, had ruled with deference to the Porte. With the death of Salah Reis in 1587, pashas (one horsetail on their standard instead of two) were sent out triennially from the East. A steady decline in their power in the face of corsairs and janissaries ended in complete

---

* The commander of "Kirke's Lambs," the Tangier Regiment, is still loathed in Somerset for the bloody aftermath of Monmouth's rebellion. They had the Paschal Lamb on the regiment flag.

Ambassadors of Morocco to France. / *B. N., Rabat*

impotence. After the revolution of 1659 they were not even allowed to land.

From the beginning of Ismail's reign, Turkish influence had fomented Berber rebellion. He himself, aided by his sons and his nephews, undertook to punish this interference. In one campaign, Ismail, wounded, barely escaped capture. Three thousand Moroccan heads were sent in triumph to Algiers.

It is not quite clear why, after several successes and the establishment of garrisons well inside the Algerian border, he suddenly gave up and recognized a former treaty agreed to by his oldest brother, Mohammed, designating the River Tafna as border. By this agreement the essentially Moroccan city of Tlemcen, with its lovely Merinid mosques and medersas, became forever Algerian. Some historians say it was because Ismail at this period, having deliberately caused the death of his two favorite sons, was threatened with danger from the others. Another theory is that in his great piety he bowed to a request delivered by an ambassador from the Ottoman Sultan at Constantinople, Selim ben Ibrahim, "to conclude a peace with the Algerians." Since their conquest of Egypt, each Ottoman Sultan had assumed the title of "Caliph of Islam." No Moslem who prided himself on his piety could defy their wishes.

In 1688, Ismail sent Abdallah ben Aissa of Salé, Grand Admiral of his fleet (the same Aissa who had been held a prisoner at the court of the Stuarts), to Paris with the assignment of ratifying a treaty of peace drawn up in 1682 but never signed. Aissa with his suite of twenty landed in Brest. Before he left for his overland journey to the capital, France took good care to parade her naval power before his eyes. Paris awaited him eagerly. The dandies, the wits, the satirists, the clever ladies, the whole mocking court, brittle and brilliant, was ready for delicious laughter at the barbarous African. Never had these worldlings been so wrong in their anticipations. They had forgotten, if they ever knew, how many African Moors, especially the Andalusian exiles of Salé, had their roots in a century-old civilization that had lighted many of the lamps for their own.

In Morocco's Grand Admiral they found to their surprise a polished diplomat, a man of wit and learning, a man who met and sometimes exceeded the highest standards of their own critical demands. As master of the flowery compliment, he soon had the ladies in the hollow of his hand. Asked by one of them to explain the polygamy of Islam, he replied: "It assures us of finding in several women that which in France is found abundantly in each individual."

As the perfect appreciative guest, he exclaimed during his ten-week visit: "If these waters (the Seine) were ink, they would not be sufficient to describe the wonders I see every day and that only proclaim the grandeur and magnificence of his Majesty."

163

In a meeting with James II, ex-king of England, a refugee at this Catholic court, he shed tears at his old friend's cruel exile and devotedly pronounced himself "your affranchised slave." Paris saw him leave, with regret.

"Nothing," murmured a great beauty of the day, "detracts from his glory, his departure will detract from ours."

In spite of his *succès fou* at the Court of the Sun King, Ben Aissa returned to Meknès without signatures on the peace treaty. Louis still stubbornly insisted on keeping his Moorish captives at the oars of his galleys. Ismail, despite his anger, listened with eager interest to the marvels of his rival's court. Though he examined with dutiful interest such documents as the plan of the Hôtel des Invalides and the description of the burning mirror begged from the Observatory for the astronomers of Fez and Marrakesh, what really fascinated him were Louis's women, not only their shameless bare faces but, even more shocking, their bare shoulders and, of course, their beauty and their charm. The greatest beauty of them all, the Princesse de Conti, bastard daughter of the King, roused his interest to its highest pitch. A plan for a treaty of peace better than any scrap of paper began to take shape in his mind. He himself would marry this Princesse de Conti. She could keep her religion, and live at Meknès as she was accustomed to live at Versailles.

When the offer reached Pontchartrain, Minister for Foreign Affairs, and became public, all the esteem Paris had felt for Morocco in the person of Aissa burst in a bubble of scorn, outrage and unpleasant laughter. Scurrilous verses poured out of the printing presses. Ismail was told to renounce his religion before daring even to think of such an offer.

Ismail smarted with fury. For once he could not express his rage by spilling blood and slashing off heads. At Versailles, no one dreamed at the time that French lack of diplomacy and manners would injure the future welfare of their country. Ismail had revenge when, five years later, in a struggle between France and England for Gibraltar, his consent and help enabled the British to take the "Rock."

Of all the cold-blooded marriages of history arranged to enhance the power or security of a state, it is hard to imagine one that would have been more fantastic than that of Ismail and the French princess, if Louis had found the offer to his advantage. Voltaire would have had a pungent addition to his *Siècle de Louis XIV*.

In the shifting harem population of two thousand filling the Meknès palace, only three stand out: the first, the anonymous "English Queen," a captive converted to Islam by the torture of boiling oil; the second, a Georgian of great beauty, also a Christian captive forced to acknowledge Allah by threats and torture, and the mother of Ismail's firstborn and favorite son Mohammed; and the third and most important of them all,

Abdallah ben Aischa, the admiral who became a diplomat in Paris. /
B. N., Rabat

called the "Black Sultana," Zidana, Soudanese sorceress, harem bully, and
worthy mate for the sadistic Ismail.

The "English Queen" enters the picture only here and there as she
used her influence to help free English captives, or sent delicious dishes
from the palace kitchens with her compliments to visiting ambassadors
from her native land. The Georgian, a favorite because of her beauty, was
strangled at Ismail's orders on a charge of adultery with a Christian slave,
trumped up and spread by the jealous Zidana.

165

From first to last, the "Black Sultana" holds the center of the stage. She was the mother of Zidan, second in Ismail's affection to Mohammed, the Georgian's son. Curiously enough, her love and loyalty to Ismail transcended her love and ambitions for this son when he defied his father. Together she and Ismail planned his murder; earlier, however, it was she alone who was at the root of Mohammed's death.

From the beginning, Mohammed, born to Ismail before the seizure of the throne, was his father's darling. The people of Meknès cheered at the sight of their young governor, the baby in one arm, a lance in the other, galloping at full speed through their streets. As soon as the child was old enough to walk, Ismail himself began his education as horseman and warrior; to train his son's mind he called in the most learned among his priests and scholars, while the increasing horde of the favorite's brothers were left to wallow in ignorance. Zidana watched this partiality with growing fury. Her own son, brutal and ignorant, matched his father in sadistic cruelty.

For a lifetime of more than thirty years, Mohammed lived without resistance under the Sultana's venomous hatred. When, however, in Ismail's absence, she stole the royal seal to forge a command ordering him to kill the revered and honorable Cheik Bou Chafra, and was not punished by his father when her guilt for the Cheik's death was discovered, he no longer felt safe. It was then clear to him that it would be impossible to expect justice from his father while Zidana wove her diabolical plots against him. His only safety lay in open rebellion. By seizing a caravan of gold dust from Guinea destined for Meknès, and raising an army of 45,000, Mohammed took Marrakesh. Zidan, sent to capture him, succeeded (through bribery and betrayal) in sending him back in chains to his father.

Though Ismail had promised forgiveness, he met his rebellious son outside the city with his butchers and a cauldron of boiling tar. The butcher's order was to cut off a hand and a foot.

"I would rather lose my own head," answered the butcher. His head rolled at Ismail's feet. The second butcher obeyed with reluctant horror. He too lost his head for spilling Cherifian blood. Mohammed's bleeding stumps were thrust into the boiling tar. Throughout the city, of all the people who loved Mohammed, only one daughter was allowed to scream in grief. Thirteen days later Mohammed died. From gangrene or from Zidana's last lethal poison? Allah alone knows. In front of the house where his son lay dead, Ismail touched his forehead to the ground and wet the dust with his tears.

Now Zidan was lord of the south—of Marrakesh, the Tafilalet and the Sous—a powerful kingdom in the hands of a fiercely proud and power-thirsty ruler. With the idea of cutting down his arrogance and demoting him to a lesser command, the Sultan summoned to Meknès this only capable son among the many incompetent weaklings. Who can blame Zidan for refusing to obey? The road to Meknès led to death by mutilation—witness his brother Mohammed; to death by being strapped to a board and sawed in half—fate of the Cheik Bou Chafra. Father and son knew each other too well for any such thing as trust to exist between them.

"I am needed here to keep the rebels in order," was the excuse stubbornly adhered to as the insistence of the commands increased. The crafty Zidana, forced to make a bitter choice, stood loyally by her mate.

"Come to Meknès," she wrote. "Your father is ill."

Zidan sent his regret and repeated his excuses.

"Your father is dying," was the next message.

Even "Your father is dead" could not bring him.

For fifty-two days Ismail hid in Zidana's quarters, while Zidana herself, armed like a sultan, prepared to rule as did her contemporary, Queen Anne of England.

The game was up when the people resented rule by a woman, and a younger son of Ismail's marched into Meknès, claiming the throne. Ismail came out of hiding, and Zidan congratulated himself on not falling into the trap, while Zidana turned her ghoulish mind toward planning a better one.

Brandy baited the second trap. Zidan was not only a drunkard, he was also addicted to murderous cruelty during his debauches. There was no difficulty in bribing a Genoese merchant to supply Zidan with a brandy of extra high potency, and his seven favorite concubines to strangle him as soon as he had swilled himself into a stupor. The losers were the merchant and the seven favorites, brought in chains to Meknès, where Zidana devised a fiendish death in punishment for killing her son.

For twenty years after the death of the two sons to whom he had hoped to leave his throne, Ismail lived on. He was an old man. His teeth had decayed and broken off. His face had sunk into wrinkles. He chose his food carefully for its heat-giving quality, "needing," in the words of a contemporary, "the greatest incentives to provide his Lust."

Other sons held the cities where Mohammed and Zidan had defied their indomitable father—weaklings all of them in contrast to the two lions who had tried to shake the throne. The order that Ismail had established throughout the land was too firmly rooted to be injured by either their petty warfare or their incompetence. The conquests he had made remained, but there were no new ones. The Spaniards still held Ceuta and Melilla, and small ports along the Riffian shore. A bitter blow fell at the news that one of his sons, brought up like the rest to acknowledge no God but Allah, had fled as a Christian to France under the name of Don Pedro de Jesus.

When he could no longer mount horses and slice off heads, Ismail spent the long sad hours of old age surrounded by the learned men of his court. Because the screams of the tortured and the dying often troubled his dreams, he needed the assurance, and needless to say received it, that every action of his long life, every drop of the spilled blood—the two murdered sons, the strangled Georgian, the tortured captives, the heads on city walls and those that had fallen at his own sword—had all been for the glorification of Allah and his Prophet.

"Allah has rewarded our Sultan for his piety with eternal life," the people began to whisper as they watched his years increase. "He will never die."

Ismail died on the 28th day of the month of Redjeb in the year 1139 of the Hegira or, according to the calendar of the Christians, April 4th, 1727.

He was buried in the shrine of the holy Cheik Elmoudjoub. Austere and simple as his piety, his tomb still stands. Two marble pillars on either side of the arched entrance rise clear-cut against the crumbling tabby of the walls. Except for the sea-green tiles of the pyramidal roof, you would not notice it as you looked down the long colorless corridor between the triple walls of what was once the "Moroccan Versailles" of the "Terrible Lion," Moulay Ismail.

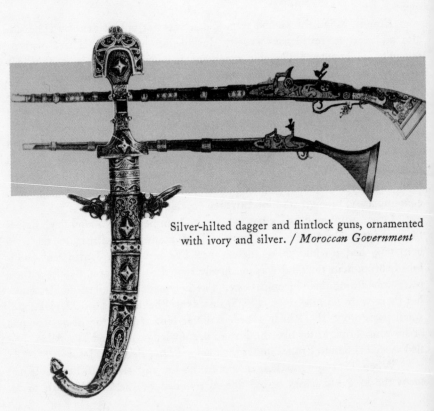

Silver-hilted dagger and flintlock guns, ornamented with ivory and silver. / *Moroccan Government*

168

꧁꧂꧁꧂꧁꧂

CHAPTER XIV

A BRIG NAMED "BETSEY"
AND THE "SKIMMERS OF THE SEA"
(Piracy and Moroccan Recognition of the
United States, 1727–1822)

꧁꧂꧁꧂꧁꧂

There must have been a sudden wonderful feeling of heads safely and solidly attached to bodies at the news of Ismail's death; and a cessation of dreams from which one awoke clammy with terror at the imagined touch of the scimitar's edge, the lance's point, the rope tightening about the throat, the bite of the whip, the gory vision of blood spurting, drying, stinking, wherever the monster put in his appearance.

Imagine the joy of the Christian slaves! Along the mountain road from the Volubilis ruins to Meknès the slaves dropped the great marble blocks that they had been dragging behind their bent backs. A century and a half later Budgett Meakin was able to trace their route by the discarded burdens of massive stone.

A son, another Ahmed el Dehbi, the Gilded, reached his father's deathbed three days before the end. Even if he had been more colorful than he appears to have been, he would have been helpless against the power of the Black Guards. With the Sultan who had put them in power now dead, Morocco lay in the hollow of their dark-skinned hands. Neither Arab nor Berber had the discipline, the arms, the solidarity to oppose them. For the next twenty years the Black Guards pulled the strings of seven puppet sons, dropped them onto the throne and jerked them off, cutting off their heads, throwing them into prison, or exiling them to the desert for possible future recall. In the meanwhile, the Berbers retrieved their confiscated horses and arms, and hurled their strength against the fine order of the country imposed by Ismail's strong and bloody hand.

Only one of the seven candidates developed in time enough of his father's strength to get the better of the Black Guards. In a period of twenty years, Abdallah ascended the throne and lost it three times. Because his sadistic cruelty equaled that of his father, the people were always as eager to get rid of him as the Black Guards were.

It is probable that Abdallah owed his first reign of six years not to his own ability but to the talent of his grand vizir and general, a Dutch adventurer of great wealth, noble birth and ignoble cunning, the Duke of Ripperda. Ripperda, ex-prime minister of Philip V of Spain, arrived at Abdallah's court as an escapee from a Segovian prison. Crimes such as the betrayal of state secrets and appropriation of state funds had ended his Spanish career. At Abdallah's court, where he won the lasting friendship of the Sultan's mother and of the Sultan himself, his lost fortune returned quickly. He commanded a successful siege of Fez; he showed Abdallah how to debase coinage to increase his own private riches; he turned Mohammedan to please the Moslems, was courteous to the Jews, and forbade the plundering of the countryside during the sieges of Ceuta and Oran. All in all, he seems to have been a very engaging scoundrel.

Though Abdallah profited from Ripperda's guidance for several years, he paid for it in the end. The people, rebelling at the state of their worthless money, overthrew both sultan and vizir. It must be admitted that historians disagree about Ripperda's distinguished career at Abdallah's court. Budgett Meakin and Coissac de Chavrebière both take the Ripperda *Memoirs* at their face value. His biographer in the *Encyclopaedia Britannica* considers them highly embroidered.

During the thirty years between his father's death in 1727 and his own in 1757, Abdallah ruled intermittently for about twenty. His father tore down the Saadian palace, "El Bedi," in Marrakesh; Abdallah tore down the Meknès "Versailles," designed and built with such pride by Ismail. Only the ruins, the walls and Ismail's tomb stand today.

For the last seven years of his life, Abdallah held the throne for the third time, thanks only to his extraordinary son Mohammed, viceroy of Marrakesh. This phenomenon among royal Moroccan offspring honored his undeserving father enough to refuse the throne offered him by the people of Fez; instead he used his own popularity to reconcile the Fassi with his father, to check the latter's hated cruelty, and to keep him recognized as sultan. In the meanwhile, to the great benefit of the country, he himself took over much of the rule.

Mohammed ben Abdallah, except for his piety, was not a grandson Ismail would have been proud of. He was both peaceful and just. Bloodshed gave him no pleasure. Scholarly study of history and poetry and the prosperity of his country through commerce rather than war were the interests and delight of his long reign (1757–1790). He founded schools and distributed his father's collection of manuscripts among the libraries of the university-mosques. He appointed as governor of the south the famous historian Ez Zaiani, after the latter returned from his post as ambassador to the Porte.

This of course does not mean that no blood was shed during Mohammed's reign. The Rabat-Salé republic lost the independence it had regained after Ismail's death. Rebellious defiance, wherever it cropped up, was punished with the traditional lopping off of heads and, for lesser crimes, the loss of a hand and a foot. However, coinage was restored to its former value; foreign merchants and consuls were encouraged to settle in the ports; the Portuguese were forced to evacuate Mazagan, which they themselves had built in 1506, and had held ever since; and the prosperous new southern port of Mogador was Mohammed's creation.

In Moslem eyes, from its earliest days, piracy was an honorable propagation of the Faith, the *jihad* or Holy War, carried out to sea. If piracy brought with it riches in the form of slaves, tribute squeezed out of the supine European powers, and vengeance against the old enemy, Spain, that was all to the glory of Allah.

Mohammed built the town of Mogador to provide his corsairs with an all-weather port without a high sand bar such as the one that restricted tonnage in and out of Salé. Mogador was to be a spider's web where the "skimmers of the sea" could wait and pounce on the treasure-laden galleons returning from the Indies of both east and west. Because Mohammed hired a Frenchman for his city planning, it is no surprise to find the streets straight unlike those of other Moroccan towns, meeting at right angles instead of wriggling and writhing from wall to wall like a brood of newly-hatched snakes.

Moroccan piracy was at its height during the second half of the eighteenth century. It had begun with the vengeful Moorish exiles of Granada in 1492, and continued with the great wave of banished Moriscos a century later. The Moors, not inventive themselves, had renegade Europeans—especially the Dutch and the British—to thank for enabling them to keep pace with the Western world in the production of larger vessels, more sail and an armament of guns. Over the years, their fleet grew from low, slave-propelled galleys with as many as sixty banks of oars to the

171

great high three-masted Salleemans or Sallee Rovers bristling with guns on their two lower decks.

To describe Mohammed's navy, Budgett Meakin uses, among other contemporary sources, the French consul, Louis Sauveur de Chénier, father of the poet, and a London surgeon of the Gibraltar garrison, Dr. William Lemprière, who visited the Sous in 1789 to attend a son of the Sultan. The fleet consisted of the usual miscellaneous pirate vessels and about a dozen frigates, plus xebecs, galliots and galleys. They all carried guns. Most of them depended on oars for swift pursuit of the helpless merchantmen, as well as sail, which included lateen and square rigging and a combination of the two. With one exception, the vessels were held down to 200 tons in order to cross the high sand bar of the Rabat-Salé river mouth. Even at high tide the depth of the water was only ten to twelve feet. For the overweight exception, which carried 350 men and 45 guns, the guns had to be taken over the bar in barges and delivered in deeper water. The low draw of these Moorish "skimmers of the sea" made them able to slip to safety like foxes into their holes, leaving the pursuing enemy helpless outside the bar at the mercy of the fortress guns.

SAL

Views of houses in Salé. / *Moroccan Government*

In *Our Navy and the Barbary Corsairs*, Gardner W. Allen quotes a description by William Eaton, the first United States consul at Tunis, of a corsair attack in 1799:

> Their long lateen yards drop on board the enemy and afford a safe and easy conveyance for the men who man them for this purpose; but being always crowded with men they throw them in from all points of the rigging and from all quarters of the decks, having their sabres grasped between their teeth and their loaded pistols in their belts, that they may have the free use of their hands in scaling the gunnels or netting of their enemy. In this mode of attack they are very active and very desperate. . . .

Today Morocco's most enchanting Moorish café, carved out of the thick walls of the Rabat fortress, looks down on river and sand bar at the base of the steep cliff. Beyond the river, white Salé, washed of its wickedness, lies tinged with pink in the early sunset. Forget time as you sit there sipping mint tea and listening to a native orchestra of flute, rebec and hand drums. Imagine yourself the spectator of a scene two centuries or so ago, perhaps the day when Paul Revere on the far side of the Atlantic rode to Lexington, or the day Cornwallis surrendered his sword at Yorktown . . .

In a fever of excitement, the people of Rabat swarm like hornets along the crenellations of the sea and river walls. From the gates of Salé on the opposite bank, the people pour out onto the sandy beach. Word has gone out from the lookout tower topping the pilot school of the fortress that a Sallee Rover is dashing for safety with Christian frigates in pursuit. The dull and distant sound of gunfire grows nearer, drowns the shouting of the crowd, the quavering cries of the women.

The rakish line of a lateen sail slanting across a mast appears against the sky; then come the sharp prow, the sweep of half a hundred oars and, in the distance, the square-rigged frigates of the pursuers, the wind swelling their sails, and gunfire bursting from their portholes. The Christians gain on the galley.* The crowd roars as the whips fall on the barebacked slaves at the oars. The slaves double their efforts. The galley skims across the bar to safety. *"Hamdullah,* praise be to Allah!" the crowd exclaims. The backs of the slaves are scarlet with blood as the oars drop out of their hands. In the offing, the Christian frigates veer into the wind and disappear on the horizon. From the fortress walls the crowds hurry down the cliff side to the port, to inspect the loot and, especially, to see the Christian cap-

---

* Budgett Meakin quotes the French consul Louis Sauveur de Chénier on Morocco's naval force in 1788: ". . . six or eight frigates of 200 tons burden with portholes for from 14 to 18 six pounders with perhaps a dozen galleys." Also on the same subject Dr. William Lemprière, a surgeon of the Gibraltar garrison, in 1793: ". . . 15 small frigates, a few xebecks, 20 to 30 row gallies."

tives huddled between the benches, before the latter appear at public auction or are set apart for ransom.

During the second year following the Declaration of Independence, the United States signed a Treaty of Amity and Commerce with France (February 6th, 1778). Article VIII provided that the most Christian King (Louis XVI) would employ "his good offices and interposition with the King or Emperor of Morocco or Fez, the regencies of Algiers, Tunis and Tripoli . . . to provide as fully and as efficaciously as possible for the benefit and safety of the said United States against all violence, insults, attacks or depredations on the part of the said Princes and States of Barbary or their subjects."

Soon after the signing of the Treaty, the peace commissioners, Benjamin Franklin, Arthur Lee and John Adams, had occasion to appeal to the King for help, not against Morocco, but against the eastern Barbary States threatening American trading vessels in Italy. They were advised by Louis's foreign ministers to apply to Congress for authority to treat with the Barbary powers, and for funds for presents. Congress took no steps.

In the meanwhile, the Moroccan Sultan Mohammed was friendly and opened his ports to American vessels. (His claim to have been the first foreign sovereign to recognize the new United States is paraded with flowery compliments on both sides at every top-level meeting between the two countries since Morocco's independence.) Twice Mohammed made overtures to Franklin via foreign agents in Salé. Again Congress made no move.

In 1783 we signed our peace with England. In most British eyes we were still the enemy. When the liberal Pitt introduced a bill proposing free trade between the two countries, Lord Sheffield (friend and editor of the historian Gibbon) countered with the opinion that for the great maritime powers to facilitate American commerce would be disadvantageous, and that it would not be to their interests to protect the Americans from the Barbary States. "If they (the maritime powers) know their interests, they will not encourage the Americans to be carriers—that the Barbary States are advantageous to the maritime powers is obvious."

In July of that same year Franklin, still in Paris, wrote to the Secretary of Foreign Affairs saying he thought it was not improbable that the English were encouraging the Rovers "to fall upon us and keep us out of the carrying trade," and that among London merchants he had heard the maxim, *"If there were no Algiers, it would be worth England's while to build one."*

In October, 1774, the brig "Betsey" bound for Tenerife was captured by Moorish pirates and taken to Tangier. Six months later, when both the vessel and the crew, which had suffered no hardship, were released through Spanish help, the Sultan gave orders to respect the American flag until

174

Lateen-rigged Barbary rover, pursuing a merchant brig (about 1790). / *From a painting by F. Perrot, B. N., Paris*

peace could be arranged. In the meanwhile, Congress had moved at last, and peace negotiations were under way in Paris. Thomas Barclay, consul-general in the French capital, appointed by the commissioners as agent, arrived in Morocco in June, 1786. Within a month, a Treaty of Peace and Friendship was drawn up. A year later, July 18, 1787, it was ratified by Congress at a cost of $10,000 in presents but *no tribute.* In every way the terms were more liberal than those granted to any other foreign power. Most important of all, Article VI stipulated that "American citizens or goods seized by a Moor shall be released."

Tribute was expected from many nations more powerful than the young United States. In 1751, Denmark had set an evil precedent for small countries by consenting to a tribute clause in her treaty with Morocco. The final abolition of all tribute from all people to the four Barbary States was not achieved until the completed conquest of Algeria by France in 1847. Actually, the honor goes to the United States which, in its wars with Algiers and Tripoli earlier in the century, was the first nation to defy the ugly imposition. (It might be mentioned here that the familiar slogan "Millions for defense but not one cent for tribute," so often associated with our tangles with the Barbary States, had nothing to do with any of them. It originated in Paris with the United States Commissioner Charles Cotesworth Pinckney during the famous "XYZ Affair," an attempt of the corrupt French Directory to extort money from the United States.)

Considering the astonishingly generous terms of our 1787 Treaty with Morocco, it is not surprising that George Washington addressed a letter dated New York, December 1st, 1789, to Mohammed ben Abdallah as

175

"Great and Magnanimous Friend" and continued in the following grateful vein:

Since the date of the letter which the late Congress, by their president, addressed to your Imperial Majesty, the United States of America have thought proper to change their government and to institute a new one, agreeable to the Constitution, of which I have the honor of herewith enclosing a copy. The time necessarily employed in the arduous task, and the derangement occasioned by so great, though peaceable a revolution, will apologize, and account for your Majesty's not having received those regular advices and marks of attention from the United States which the friendship and magnanimity of your conduct toward them afforded reason to expect.

The United States, having unanimously appointed me to the supreme executive authority in this nation, your Majesty's letter of the 17th of August 1788, which by reason of the dissolution of the late government remains unanswered, has been delivered to me. I have also received the letter which your Imperial Majesty has been so kind as to write, in favor of the United States, to the Bashaws of Tunis and Tripoli, and I present to you the sincere acknowledgements and thanks of the United States for this important mark of your friendship for them.

We greatly regret that the hostile disposition of those regencies toward this nation, who have never injured them, is not to be removed, on terms in our power to comply with. Within our territories there are no mines, either of gold or silver, and this young nation, just recovering from the waste and desolation of a long war, have not, as yet, had time to acquire riches by agriculture and commerce. But our soil is bountiful and our people industrious, and we have reason to flatter ourselves that we shall gradually become useful to our friends.

The encouragement which your Majesty has been pleased, generously, to give to our commerce with your dominions, the punctuality with which you have caused the Treaty with us to be observed, and the just and generous measures taken in the case of Captain Proctor, make a deep impression on the United States and confirm their respect for, and attachment to, your Imperial Majesty.

It gives me pleasure to have this opportunity of assuring your Majesty that, while I remain at the head of this nation, I shall not cease to promote every measure that may conduce to the friendship and harmony which so happily subsist between your Empire and them, and shall esteem myself happy in every occasion of convincing your Majesty of the high sense (which in common with the whole Nation) I entertain of the magnanimity, wisdom and benevolence of your Majesty. In the course of the approaching winter, the national legislature, which is called by the former name of Congress, will assemble, and I shall take care that nothing be omitted that may be necessary to cause the correspondence to be maintained and conducted in a manner agreeable to your Majesty and giving satisfaction to all parties concerned in it.

May the Almighty bless your Imperial Highness, our Great and Magnanimous friend with his constant guidance and protection.

George Washington

When Mohammed died in 1791 on the way to punish his rebellious son El Yazid, the United States government took steps to have the Treaty of 1787 ratified by his successor. Again Thomas Barclay left Paris for Morocco. Barclay never got beyond Lisbon. Mohammed's son El Yazid was fighting a different brother at each point of the compass for possession of the throne. The lurid account of such blood-spilling fratricide from the Morocco-hating Portuguese was doubtless enough to stop any prudent consul in his tracks until one of the contestants came out on top. The worst of the chaos lasted for five years. Two years before it ended, Barclay died.

No decent father deserved a son like Moulay el Yazid, especially not Mohammed, who had shown such rare loyalty to his own vicious parent. In his early youth the young prince, son of an Irish concubine, an excellent horseman, brilliant soldier, and passionate student of artillery, seemed the perfect heir to the throne. Unfortunately, popularity went to his head. Sent by his father to put down a rebellion of the Black Guards at Meknès, he let them proclaim him instead. At the news that his father was marching north to punish him, he took refuge in the sanctuary of a *zaouia* until he was assured of forgiveness. Incorrigible, he repeated his threats until his father, despairing of all reform of character, sent him on the annual pilgrimage to Mecca, both to get him out of the country and to keep him out of mischief.

If Mohammed had thrown his odious offspring into prison, or, better still, cut off his head, he might have been spared the most original and outrageous disgrace inflicted by any sultan's son on a pious father. Beyond the Red Sea, El Yazid organized a successful bandit gang to rob the caravan of the valuable presents sent by his father to the Cherif of the Holy City.

Unfortunately for Morocco, El Yazid became his father's successor for a ghoulish rule of twenty-two months. The rule can be briefly described: he more than lived up to his principle that to impress his people a sultan should see to it that blood flowed in a steady stream from the palace gate to the city.

The three years following El Yazid's death were a period of such chaos and multiple rule in different parts of the country that some chronologers list Hicham as sultan from 1792 to 1795; others begin his brother Soleiman's long and stormy rule in 1792. By 1795, all pretenders and their supporters were finally disposed of. For Soleiman, however, the struggle between the freedom-loving Berbers and the Maghzen went on without cease.

Though Soleiman had all the virtues of his father Mohammed— piety, intelligence, appreciation of the arts and love of justice—he lacked the necessary genius to mold Berber and Arab into a cohesive whole. Force was not enough; diplomacy was not enough, and never had been. A nobler policy than anything tried before was needed. Down through the centuries

177

not even the bond of Islam had been sufficiently strong to unite two such disparate peoples. But, in Morocco today, in its first decade of independence, it seems as if the new freedom might be the long-sought mortar to unite the two races.

In 1795 Soleiman, visited by James Simpson, United States Consul at Gibraltar, ratified the Treaty of 1787 with the United States adding the comment: "The Americans, I find, are the Christian nation my father most esteemed. I am the same with them as my father was and I trust they will be with me."

This time the cost was $20,000 in presents—a cost somewhat mitigated fifteen years later by a gift of a palace in Tangier to house our consulate. This became the first U.S. property on foreign soil.

During the last decade of the century, Tangier began its curious role of being partly run, if not ruled, by its consular corps. This led eventually to an international status that lasted until the end of French rule. Unlike his father, Mohammed, Soleiman took no interest in foreigners. European consuls were not invited to the courts at Fez or Marrakesh, but were restricted to the city at the entrance to the Straits. The consuls were probably happier there, almost in sight of clean and civilized Gibraltar, limiting their excursions outside the walls largely to wild boar hunts in the surrounding hills. Though from all accounts the foreign consuls seem to have been a jealous, competitive, dog-eat-dog lot, they were drawn closely together in one respect—the horror of native indifference to public sanitation. Open sewage, polluted water, contaminated meat, plague introduced by pilgrims returning from Mecca revolted their senses and threatened their lives.

As early as 1792, the consular corps created the Sanitary Council of Tangier. In 1797, France and the United States were included. By persistent appeals to the Sultan, the germ-conscious Westerners were able eventually to establish a quarantine against Algeria where the plague was raging. In 1818, the Governor of Tangier, defying the Council's order, permitted a pilgrim steamer from Alexandria to dock; as a result plague spread through the land.

From this beginning, the achievements of the Westerners increased decade by decade. By 1840 the representatives of the Christian Powers were charged by the Sultan "with the honorable Mission of maintaining the public health upon the coast of the Empire, to make all rules and to take all measures to reach this end." As special agents, the Council engaged a captain of the port, a doctor and sanitary guards. An outbreak of cholera in 1865 led them to establish Mogador as a quarantine port for all incoming pilgrim ships. Toward the end of the century they were sprinkling the streets, paving the roads, improving the sewage system, and building a sanitary slaughterhouse where Arabs, Christians and Jews could have their meat butchered according to their particular rites.

178

Another area in which the Tangier Christian colony made demand for special privileges and protection from the Sultan's government in the late eighteenth century was in the matter of settling legal controversies. Islamic law, essentially religious, and limited to the True Believer, was unequipped to deal with legal disputes between Christian and Christian, and between Christian and native. This problem was solved in the form of extraterritorial jurisdiction that lasted until after World War II. Not only were the Christians permitted to be judged for their offenses in the consular courts, but the privilege was extended to the natives—Arabs, Berbers and Jews—employed in legations and consulates as interpreters and domestic servants. As each of the Powers had native vice-consuls in the numerous ports, and as natives were eager to pay an unscrupulous consular official for the privilege of calling themselves servants (thereby becoming exempt from Imperial jurisdiction and taxes), the protégé population increased in numbers to such an extent that its existence became a flagrant abuse. For example, when one of our consuls was accused of extending his protection to more than a hundred Moorish subjects, he not only denied the charge but pointed out that the British representative protected not only whole villages but his camel drivers and 200 beaters for his boar hunts.

In the present century under French rule and misrule, American protection was most eagerly sought in both city and bled. When the unscrupulous *colon*,* in league with unscrupulous courts, asked the illiterate Arab or Berber to put his mark against a "lease" for his land, which turned out instead to be a deed of sale, the wretched victim had no redress. As an American protégé he would have been safe from such trickery. In my own visits to Morocco during Protectorate days, in the business of importing Moroccan rugs and handicrafts, Moroccans (not only those whom I came to know well but also casual acquaintances) eagerly offered services or rewards in return for my legal protection. The most tempting offer consisted of three acres of fertile farmland in the lovely Riffian foothills north of Fez.

In spite of Soleiman's amiable promises at the time of ratifying our Treaty of 1787, events during the second year of the War with Tripoli (1801–1805), while our navy was blocking the port, caused a short break in our friendly relations.

In May, 1802, Commodore Richard V. Morris and his Mediterranean squadron arrived at Gibraltar to find that the United States Consul at Tangier, the same James Simpson formerly at Gibraltar, was having trouble with the Sultan of Morocco. In the first place, Soleiman had been demanding a passport for one of his ships loaded with wheat for Tripoli; in the second place, he had been pressing for the release of the "Meshuda," a

_____
* French settler.

179

Tripolitanian cruiser being held by the Americans at Gibraltar. When neither Morris nor Simpson agreed to his demands, he declared war. Simpson retreated to Gibraltar.

At the sight of the squadron's flagship, the "Chesapeake," sailing in Tangier waters, Soleiman, impressed by the splendor of the frigate, invited Simpson to return. No sooner had the squadron sailed for Tripoli, leaving the "Adams" to guard the "Meshuda," than Soleiman's boldness returned. He not only demanded the "Meshuda" as his own property but sent thirty Moors from Tetuán to take possession of her. They were, of course, helpless against both the twenty-eight guns of the "Adams" and the firm stand of the captain, who refused to release her without a passport from Simpson. In the meanwhile, Soleiman was also attempting to extort presents from Simpson, falsely claiming that they had been agreed on. By October, things took a turn for the better, when Commodore Morris reversed his decision in the matter of granting a passport for the Sultan's wheat ship —partly out of fear of war with Morocco, partly because he understood that in Tripoli there was no great need of the extra food.

There was nothing cowardly about fear of war with Morocco. In fact, the very daring of our infant navy in entering the Mediterranean bottle-neck at the mercy of the four Barbary States—Morocco, Algiers, Tunis and Tripoli, steeped in 300 years of piracy and in fear of no one— took extraordinary courage. From Morocco, the United States had a promise, and there was a chance of peaceful relations; with the deys, beys and pashas of the other pirate powers, she had none. She was wise to make whatever concessions lay within her honor to appease the Sultan Soleiman.

In the end, peace between the two countries was restored; not, however, before a Moroccan cruiser out of Tangier with a captured American seaman aboard was discovered and taken prisoner by Captain William Bainbridge of the frigate "Philadelphia." One of our policies must have been to set the pirates an example of superior Christian conduct, because members of the Moroccan crew, to their surprise, were treated with great kindness, and the "Philadelphia's" ship's corporal was flogged in their presence for having struck one of them.

In mid-September of 1803, Commodore Edward Preble on the flagship "Constitution" (the famous "Old Ironsides") arrived with his squadron at Gibraltar. Unwilling to leave a hostile Morocco in his rear while he sailed east to Tripoli, he assembled and paraded his squadron in all its force and glory in the waters between Gibraltar and Tangier. Two frigates —one with forty-four guns, the other with thirty-six—three brigs with sixteen guns each, three schooners with twelve, a ketch with four, two bomb vessels and nine gunboats spread their sails for the benefit of the Sultan who had arrived in Tangier with his army.

At the imposing display, Soleiman decided to return to his original stand of esteeming the Americans and cultivating their friendship. Salutes were given and returned. A present of bullocks, sheep and fowl was sent out to the ships, and peace negotiations were soon under way.

Exactly a month after Preble's arrival in the Straits, the Treaty of 1787 was again ratified and confirmed; again no tribute, and this time no presents. And, ever since, there have been friendly relations with the rulers of the Moghreb el Aksa.

Plague and Berber rebellions disturbed the last ten years of Soleiman's reign. In 1817 he set out to suppress piracy in his empire by disarming his ships. During the plague he contributed generously from his private treasury for the relief of famine and misery. There seems to be no record of such generosity to the credit of former sultans.

From his father Mohammed, Soleiman had inherited not only his piety but also his conversion to the teachings of the Arabian reformer, El Wahabi. El Wahabi, first a student of law, which of course meant Koranic, and then a teacher in Central Arabia, had become deeply shocked at the enormous gulf between the simple life preached and practiced by the Prophet and the luxury and sensual indulgence of eighteenth-century Arabia. In addition to the pleasures of silk, music, the dance, and, of course, drinking of wine, he stormed against the forbidden saints and pilgrimages to their shrines. Though El Wahabi was by no means the first reformer to preach austerity (we have seen Ibn Toumert smashing musical instruments and wine jars and pushing unveiled princesses into the gutter), he became the most powerful. By converting the most important war lord of Central Arabia, Mohammed Ibn Saud, and marrying his daughter to him, he was able to spread his movement throughout the country by force, and to become the ancestor of the present ruling dynasty.

Wahabism played much the same role for Arabia as sixteenth-century Calvinism did for Europe with its threat of hell fire for all sins and pleasures of the senses, and its attempt to root out pagan rites and the worship of saints and their relics from the Church of Rome. Any member of the Arabian American Oil Company will be well aware that Wahabism is still the official religion of the Saudi Arabian kingdom. When "Aramco" first established its colonies at Dahran and Ras Tamura, Americans were strictly forbidden to take into their clubs or houses not only liquor but also phonographs.

Wahabism sifted into Morocco by way of pilgrims returning from Mecca. A practising Wahabi himself, Soleiman tried without success to establish it among his subjects. He forbade the importation of European luxuries, setting the example by doing without luxuries of any kind. He closed the door to Christians, and forbade his own subjects to leave the country. He tried in vain to abolish pilgrimages to the shrines of marabouts and discouraged the semi-pagan *mouss*ems* or harvest festivals so dear to the Berbers.

Despite his failure, Malikite Morocco and Wahabi Arabia retired

181

into the same shell of isolation and shared the same hostility to Christians during the course of the nineteenth century. Charles Doughty of the *Arabia Deserta* almost lost his life before the end of the journey. William Gifford Palgrave, brother of Francis Turner Palgrave, author of the *Golden Treasury*, taking advantage of his Jewish grandfather, disguised himself as a full-blooded Jew for his famous *Year's Journey through Central and Eastern Arabia* (1865). In forbidden Morocco, Charles de Foucauld also disguised himself as a Jew for his mid-century travels across the Atlas; and René Caillié, after his discovery of Timbuctu, returning across the Sahara and the Atlas to Tangier, in the role of an Egyptian, came nearer to detection and death on the doorstep of the French Consul at Tangier than anywhere else during his year-long dangerous journey through Moslem countries. Saudi Arabia still has its forbidden Mecca and Morocco its holy city of Moulay Idris, which no Christian may enter after sunset, as well as the mosques that are always closed to Christians.

Soleiman died in 1822, so deeply discouraged at his inability to control his rebellious subjects that, toward the end, he seriously considered abdicating. His successor, a nephew by the name of Moulay Mohammed, inherited a storm-torn country unimproved by his uncle's virtuous and conscientious but ineffectual reign.

AN UNWELCOME NEIGHBOR TO THE EAST

(Three Reigns: Abderrahman, Mohammed XVII
and Moulay Hassan, 1822–1894)

For the new sultan, Abderrahman, the tremendous event dominating his reign began in 1827 on the far side of Morocco's eastern border when Hossein, Dey of Algiers, during an argument struck the French consul in the face with his fly whisk. On the surface, the fly whisk incident, drifting back over the caravan trails to Moroccan souks and palaces, must have seemed to Abderrahman nothing more than a pleasant humiliation to an unbelieving Nazarene, and of no more importance than a fly itself. Three years later, when the Turkish Regency of Algiers fell to the French, he found himself embroiled with an enemy of more potential danger than either Spain or Portugal had been since the fatal fall of Ceuta.

Since the days of the Barbarossa brothers, no ruler of Algiers had ever restrained his insolence or his temper in the presence of the Christian dogs whose sovereigns paid him tribute. Now, despite orders from the Sublime Porte, Hossein refused to humble himself and apologize. In 1829 a French vessel carrying a flag of truce was bombarded by Algerian batteries as it entered the harbor. On the strength of this added insolence, Charles X declared war in January, 1830.

183

At the decisive battle of Staoueli in July, Charles's landing force was victorious and Hossein capitulated. (The excellent Algerian Staoueli wine is said to owe its superior quality to the blood-soaked soil of its battlefield vineyards.) Three weeks later Charles, who had counted on regaining his vanished popularity by his Algerian conquest, lost his throne in the July Revolution. For Abderrahman the repercussion of this conquest was the arrival of a delegation from the frightened city of Tlemcen begging for his protection.

With Metternich saying in Vienna, "It is not for a slap of a fan that a hundred million are spent and forty thousand men endangered," the citizens of Tlemcen were well justified in fearing that the conquest would not stop with the city of Algiers.

The law-abiding Abderrahman, no high-handed despot like his ancestor Ismail, consulted the *oulema* (jurist-theologians) of Fez before yielding to the temptation to retrieve Tlemcen from nominal Turkish rule. Without the consent of all the people of Tlemcen—Turks, Moors, and the half-Turk, half-Moor Kouloughlis—the oulema forbade the seizure of Ottoman territory. When Tlemcen's answer came back declaring that in its eyes the Dey was a usurper and Turkey too distant to be of any use, Abderrahman promised help and declared the *jihad* against the Christian invaders.

Native tribes supported the royal forces. While the French were taking the port of Oran and were threatening Tlemcen, caids of the Sultan's choosing governed the important inland towns. When the French sent an envoy to protest, Abderrahman had him arrested in Tangier. After twenty months of fighting, with the advantage to the invaders, the French sent the Comte de Morny, half brother of the future Napoleon III, and later Duke as envoy extraordinary to Tangier. This time the mission, backed by a French squadron in the harbor and the threat of bombardment, was successful. Moroccan agents were withdrawn, and Algeria left to defend itself.

In March of 1832, when the Comte de Morny's mission arrived in Tangier, the Sultan Abderrahman was holding court in his Meknès palace. Meknès lies about one hundred and fifty miles south of Tangier, and inland from the slanting coast. For the Count and his entourage it was a ten-day ride across the spring carpet of Moroccan wild flowers with the Sultan's safe conduct to pass them through the territories of hostile tribes. Furnished also by the Sultan was a caid as guide, as well as soldiers, servants, luxurious tents and, in a land destitute of inns, the privilege of calling on the local communities for *mouna* or food.

In the journal of a young artist friend whom the Count had invited to join his mission, the jottings expressed excited enthusiasm. "Crossed a beautiful and fertile country. . . . Flowers without number of a thousand kinds forming the most variegated carpet . . . Morny is as much impressed as I by the beauty of nature here."

The artist was Eugène Delacroix at the age of thirty-four, ardent rebel against the classical restraint of line and color. For this first Romanticist, who already thought, felt and expressed himself by means of color and fluid lines, the piercing African sun, the Oriental richness of architectural ornament, the moving drapery of djellaba and burnous, the gold and velvet of saddles and bridles, and the fiery action of the Arab horse became something he was to dream of and paint for the rest of his life.

De Morny's mission had its lifelong influence not only on Delacroix himself but on the entire nineteenth-century Romantic School of his followers. For some, this influence was merely a liberation from classical standards; for others it became a passion for the Moslem East—Morocco, Algeria, Egypt, Syria, Turkey. For Regnault, the passion was for Moorish Spain. In his "Execution without Judgement under the Moorish Kings," a head severed from its body rolls down marble steps at the foot of the turbaned executioner who might be the bloody Ismail himself. Gerôme's dramatic "Grief of the Pasha" catches all the lost medieval Moorish grandeur. In a marble court of honeycombed Alhambraesque arches, a tiger in a dazzling pattern of gold and black lies dead on a Persian rug strewn with rose petals. In the corner, a turbaned Pasha in silk and jewels broods as though the light had gone out of his life. During ten years in Morocco Benjamin Constant, famous for his portrait of Queen Victoria, filled his sketchbooks with ideas and material that influenced much of his future work. Algeria, its *sahel* and its Sahara, laid its spell over Fromentin. In his "Falcon Hunt," "The Arab and his Dying Horse" and many other paintings, Fromentin was the first of a long line to show France the new country that she had conquered.

But the pioneer was Delacroix, the first to see the Moghreb through the eyes of a great painter, the first to absorb its color, its human interest, its magic blend of Africa and the East.

Thursday, March 10th, of Delacroix's Journal is headed "Audience with the Emperor." When he had recreated the scene on canvas many years later, calling it "The Reception of the Emperor Abderrahman," it was exhibited in the Salon of 1845. Today the painting hangs in the Museum of Toulouse. In Delacroix's eyes Abderrahman bore "great resemblance to Louis Philippe." The notes continue: ". . . younger, thick beard, fairly dark complexion. Burnous of fine dark cloth closed in front. A haik underneath on the upper part of his chest and almost completely covering his thighs and legs. . . . silver stirrups, yellow slippers which hang loose in back. Harness and saddle of pinkish color and gold. Grey horse with cropped mane. . . ."

If the young Sultan Abderrahman thought that his submission to the French would end all trouble on his eastern border, he underestimated the fierce resistance of the Algerians. And if the French thought, as they did in the beginning, that the capitulation of Algiers assured a swift and bloodless conquest of the entire Regency, they, too, were tragically mistaken. Arab and Berber tribes in all their proud and fanatic hatred of the Christian massed for a Holy War to defend their native land. As leader they chose not only a great Algerian but a great human being.

A hater of bloodshed, lover of the life of the mind and the spirit, Abd el Kader, the twenty-four-year-old Emir of the Arab Hachem tribe, reluctantly accepted the call to war. To his admirer and ultimate conqueror, the French Marshal Bugeaud, he looked like a painting of "Christ or a saint." At four he had learned to read; at fourteen he knew the Koran by heart. Shortly before the fall of Algiers, he had returned with his pious and learned father from the pilgrimage to Mecca. Two years later, in flying scarlet cloak, he rode his black stallion at the head of the *jihad* to begin a war of fifteen long and bloody years—a war lost in the end not through any lack of his own determination and courage but through abandonment by Morocco, and desertion by the Kabyle Berbers of his own country.

From the year 1832, when Abderrahman pledged his neutrality to the French, to the year 1839, when Abd el Kader had won control over two-thirds of Algeria, Morocco remained an onlooker during her neighbor's struggle for freedom. Nothing in the records seems to indicate that Abderrahman possessed the qualities to honor patriotism, courage and chivalry in the Emir of the Hachem. It is even probable that he resented the Emir's successes. Western Algeria and the Sahara south of it had often been under Moroccan rule. The oases of the Touat still paid their taxes to the Alaouite Sultans. The ancient Treaty of the Tafna (1648) between the first Alaouites and the Algerian Turks had fixed a twenty-five mile boundary inland to the town of Oudjda from the mouth of the Tafna River. So far from the sea, coastal control was only nominal. Abderrahman, pushed back by the French, took no pleasure in seeing Abd el Kader carving out for himself an independent state in the region south of Oran. And yet, by opposing the Emir, he would only bring upon himself the disapproval of his deeply pious subjects, who were emotionally behind the Holy War and its leader.

By 1837, Abd el Kader had fought two short and successful wars against the French for control of the Algerian hinterland, and signed two treaties. In the first, the French appointed him Dey of the inland town of Mascara. According to the conditions of the second, he became master of two-thirds of Algeria, with the French holding the coastal ports and a narrow inland strip. In 1839, when a French army marched illegally through his territory, he thanked Allah for the excuse of declaring war for the third time.

For three years things still went his way. Then, at last, the French discovered the secret of waging war with the slippery, volatile Arabs; then at last, cutting down the weight of clumsy uniforms and heavy packs, they turned defense into offense. Marshal Bugeaud, Governor of Algeria, succeeded in pushing his enemy westward across the Moroccan border.

Again Morocco was fighting the French—the Sultan unwillingly, the people with enthusiasm. In public, Abderrahman was the pious patriot. "Rise up, O Moslems, listen to the voice of Allah and of his Prophet and follow our beloved son Sidi Mohammed who will fight for the glory of Allah at the head of a powerful army of holy warriors and may the wind of victory wave the standards of Islam. . . ."

But writing secretly to Mohammed, his tone changes. "If you are marching west, stop at Taza. Peace is more profitable for us than war for the Moslems of Morocco are feeble. We must accept the peace offers of the French, may Allah curse them. . . ." And again a disturbed note of warning to Mohammed. "Remember that the French, enemies of Allah, have occupied this country for several years; that they are accustomed to all fatigue and all danger; the lightning of battle has flashed before their eyes a thousand times and their ears are accustomed to its thunder. . . ."

A Moroccan attack on the French camp across the border and French reprisals brought matters to a climax. The Prince de Joinville bombarded first Tangier and then Mogador and, on the banks of the River Isly, Mohammed's army of 50,000 Moroccan horsemen fought for two hours against 8,000 French, until the Moorish camp was overrun and the Sultan's son acknowledged defeat.

Isly stands out as one of the great decisive battles in the French conquest of North Africa. In their exultant pride and unfortunate lack of tact, the victors gave its name to streets, boulevards and squares of Algerian cities.

For Morocco, the defeat meant the end of help and asylum to Abd el Kader. The order to seize the Emir and intern him or expel him by force was among the conditions of the peace. It also meant a narrow escape from a march on Fez. Thanks to English pressure on the French prime minister Guizot, Marshal Bugeaud was forbidden to follow up his victory with an invasion across the border. The situation must have been analogous to the twentieth-century outrage in certain quarters when MacArthur was forbidden to invade North Korea. England's motives, of course, sprang from a determination to keep a power as strong as France from facing her across the Straits.

For Abd el Kader, the valiant struggle continued for another two and a half years. The end came after the tribes of Kabylia, lukewarm acceptors of Islam, withdrew their support; and when the fainthearted Moroccan

The Emperor Moulay Abderrahman, from a sketch
by Eugène Delacroix. / *B. N., Rabat*

government expelled him by force, he again fled across the border in search of safety. In 1847 he gave himself up voluntarily to the French, on condition that he might retire to a Mohammedan country of his own choice in the Middle East. The promise was made. Trustingly he surrendered his sword and his horse—and spent the next five years as a prisoner in *France!* In a belated effort to redeem French honor, Napoleon III took him to Paris as the hero of a great celebration, then at last gave him the exile, first at Brusa, then Damascus, that had been solemnly promised.

It was far from comfortable for Abderrahman to find his subjects rising in fury at their Sultan's betrayal of the Algerian patriot. Afraid for both his treasure and his life, he moved himself and the numberless chests of coins and jewels to a desert fortress of the Tafilalet until the fury subsided. After his return, the usual tribal rebellions filled the last years of his unpopular reign. Perhaps the most admirable thing to be recorded in his favor was his realization of the backwardness of Moroccan education, and his unsuccessful attempt to introduce geometry into the curriculum of the country's medersas or colleges. Bigoted tradition, narrowing education to such subjects as theology, law and rhetoric, frustrated his attempts.

With the British bulldog carefully watching every step, France, except for a brief attack upon Salé, drew back for the time being to the borderline east of Oudjda established by the 1847 Convention of Tangier. In the impossible problem of passing fair judgment on the justification of wars and conquests, with their hideous subjugation of man by man, it must be said in all justice to the French that, in destroying the Turkish Regency of Algiers, they wiped out the century-long scourge of piracy. Their subsequent sin lay in the failure to observe their ideal of *"Liberté, égalité et fraternité"* in ruling the people whom they had conquered.

In 1858 Abderrahman sent an embassy to London, which returned with fifteen cannons and military provisions to repair the fortifications of Salé bombarded by the French. The Anglo-French rivalry that was to mount in increasing intensity until its sudden shift into the Egyptian-Moroccan deal of 1904 was now on in full swing. The ominous shadow of future colonialism began to blacken across the land.

Abderrahman's son, Sidi Mohammed, vanquished at the Battle of Isly, succeeded his father in 1859. Under the pretext of attacks by the surrounding tribesmen of Ceuta, and other minor grievances, the old enemy, Spain, seized the critical moment of the enthronement of a new sultan to declare war. In a slow and dangerous campaign, the Spanish army, under three of Spain's most famous generals—O'Donnell, Rios and Prim— battled its way twenty-three miles south from Ceuta, through fierce mountaineers and winter rains, to Tetuán. For the taking of the deserted city, O'Donnell, a statesman as well as general, whose family had left Ireland after the Battle of the Boyne, was created Duke of Tetuán. The painter Regnault increased General Prim's fame by the portrait hanging in the

Salvador Dali's famous painting, *The Battle of Tetuán.* / *The Huntington Hartford Collection, Gallery of Modern Art, N.Y.*

Louvre of the General on his fiery black horse, reined back and ready to charge against the Moorish infidels.

In our own day, Salvador Dali draws the eyes of the world to this Moorish-Spanish conflict. In his recent gigantic historical masterpiece, "The Battle of Tetuán," acquired by the Gallery of Modern Art, New York, the Moorish Army, superimposed on symbols that could be spawned only by the mind of a Dali, gallops across twelve and a half feet of canvas. Advance or retreat? In the explanation of the work, the artist refuses to say. For Dali, Tetuán is as important a "vision of history" as Guernica is for Picasso. Instead, however, of being a bitter invective against the horrors of war, it represents a great milestone in the age-old symbiosis of Spaniards and Moors. Most important of the hidden symbols is the molecular structure of DNA (deoxyribonucleic acid) considered the basic determinant for hereditary traits. Writing of himself, the artist says, "Dali, fascinated by modern biology, considers the persistence of memory is localized in DNA,

190

whose two spirals are the Christian world and the Moslem world inter-twined, history being only the genetic persistence of the two memories." And again Dali, "Just as Moslem action in Spain provoked feelings of patriotism and gave direction to Spanish life, so did the Spanish action in North Africa beginning with the Battle of Tetuán, become a stimulus to feelings of nationhood in the Moroccan people."

The battle of Tetuán was a victory for Spain, with peace made on Spanish terms—the exaction of an indemnity of four million pounds, with Tetuán under Spanish control as pledge for the payment. To avoid a second Spanish town beside Ceuta, so near to the Straits, Britain came to the rescue by paying off much of the immense debt herself through a loan raised in London and a lien on the Moorish customs receipts. As a result of British supervision, the receipts between 1861 and 1873 rose from a third of a million pounds to a million and two-thirds.

Powerless, Sidi Mohammed sat thinking black thoughts as he watched the cunning Europeans produce order and profit out of confusion and small returns. As he watched, members of the diplomatic corps representing the foreign powers were becoming more and more demanding, asserting more and more pointedly in their arrogant Christian way—that he and his people were incapable of keeping their own country clean and healthy. First it had been a Sanitary Corps that they wanted, then Quarantine rules, then markets protected from flies! Now they were complaining about the dangers of the unsheltered coasts, the shipwrecks on moonless nights where the currents were strong and rocks forbidding. They wanted a lighthouse! A lighthouse to twist the ways of Allah to suit their own profane and imperious purposes! And yet, there was no denying it, they were the clever, the powerful ones. He dreamed that, through learning to follow in their footsteps, Morocco might become as strong as they were; and as long as their rivalry lasted he seemed to be safe from their cupidity. When it stopped, his kingdom would go the way of his Algerian neighbor. For the present at any rate—praise be to Allah!—the three snarling lions kept chasing each other away the moment any one of them reached out for the Moroccan prize.

Sidi Mohammed let them have their lighthouse, building it himself but stipulating that the cost of its support was their responsibility. In a treaty of 1865, the European powers bound themselves to respect its neutrality and pay $285 apiece for its upkeep. They built it on Cape Spartel, eight miles west of Tangier, where Straits and ocean meet. In the beginning, it threw its light for thirty-six miles out to sea. Over the years they increased its power. In 1892, they added a semaphore by Lloyds; and in 1905, a fog signal.

In 1871, two years before he died, the fears of European aggression haunted the Moroccan Sultan to such an extent that he turned in desperation to the United States. During a visit to Fez of a United States Consul, Felix A. Mathews, Mohammed discussed his awareness of the cupidity of, and the existent rivalry among England, France and Spain. In case of danger from any one of them, he begged the United States to act as arbiter. So great was his apprehension that he even suggested placing his country under United States protection. As the United States was singularly without colonial ambitions, the offer was tactfully refused.

Though the establishment of the first Moroccan printing press in Tangier did not take place until a decade after Mohammed's death, news of the outside world sifted into the country constantly with every boat, every pilgrim, every traveler crossing the indeterminate Algerian border, and every caravan plodding up from the Senegal and Niger River lands.

From the north, the news was splendid for Moroccan ears. France, the travelers reported, had been forced down to her knees by her new enemy Germany; her armies had been beaten, her emperor deposed, part of her territory seized and enormous indemnity demanded worse than that exacted by Spain after their own recent defeat at Tetuán. But from the south the news was ominous. In Senegal the French Governor Faidherbe had begun boasting five years after Abd el Kader's surrender that he would expand French territory from the Atlantic to the Red Sea. Now he was pushing his armies toward the Niger and Timbuctu. From that direction the danger seemed as great for Morocco as for the black tribal kings—Bambara, Toucouleur and Mandingo—who had been forced into surrender. No Moroccan ever forgot (or forgets today when King Hassan refuses to go to the Conference of African Nations at Addis Ababa because independent Mauritania is represented) that under the eleventh-century Almoravids and again with the conquest of Timbuctu by the Saadians, the southern Morocco boundary was the Senegal and the Middle Niger.

When Sidi Mohammed died in 1873, his son and appointed heir, Hassan, was leading an army against the turbulent tribes of the south with their insolent claims to independence. Though Marrakesh acknowledged the new sultan with enthusiasm, it took two months of hard fighting on his way back to the capital for him to gain the recognition of the northern cities.

Nothing harsher has been said about this last independent Moroccan sultan, Moulay el Hassan, than that he lacked the force to stand up against the bigoted conservatism of the oulema and vizirs, and put through the reforms and modernization that he knew his country needed; and that he did not cut off enough heads.

The Italian novelist Edmondo De Amicis, like the painter Delacroix guest of his country's ambassador in Tangier on a visit to the Moorish court, leaves us his vivid impression of the young Sultan in the early years of his reign.

We were fascinated. This Sultan whom we had visualized in the guise of a savage and cruel despot was the most beautiful and appealing youth ever to fill the dreams of an odalisque. He was tall and slender with large and tender eyes. A short black beard defined the perfect oval of his tawny face—a face of a most noble expression and full of sweet gentleness. His cloak, white as snow, fell from head to foot. Yellow slippers covered his stockingless feet. Of purest white, also, was his magnificent horse in green harness and with stirrups of gold. . . . All this whiteness and the long full cloak gave him a priestly appearance, the grace of a queen, a simple and loveable majesty matching perfectly the gentle expression of his face. In short, his whole person and manner had something so solemn that it inspired an irresistible sympathy, a profound respect.

This was the young Hassan before the grueling and unending campaigns against dissident tribes had sapped his vitality, before the terrible year of famine and pestilence, before he had fallen so ill three times that Europe's men-of-war had gathered in the ports to protect their nationals during the chaos sure to follow a sultan's death. It was before he had seen France add Tunis to her Algerian conquests. It was before he knew, as he must have known, that his frustrated efforts to fit his country into the modern world were not enough to save it, that the Scottish Caid Sir Harry Maclean drilling his infantry and the French lieutenant Erckmann training his artillery were no more than two showers of rain in a year of drought. France, England, Spain, hovering like falcons, and now another bird of prey waiting to dive. Germany was sending a fleet of steamboats down the Atlantic coast and, with Spanish connivance, smuggling Krupp cannon and Mauser rifles into the Rif.

It is no wonder that the French writer Pierre Loti, visiting Fez a decade later than De Amicis, added the lines of strain and weariness to the Italian's impression; but the same fundamental qualities of character surprised and fascinated both Europeans.

And now at last he stopped close to us. The last son of Mohammed crossed with Soudanese blood. His costume of sheerest wool, fine as a cloud, is of immaculate whiteness. His horse, too, is purest white. The large stirrups are of gold, the silken harness of palest green delicately enriched with an even paler greenish gold. . . . His half hidden face, the color of parchment, framed in white muslin, has noble and pious features, the expression one of great melancholy and lassitude. He has an air of gentleness, a quality which, according to those who surround him, he really possesses . . . No, certainly he is not cruel. With that sadly sweet expression he could not be. . . . He is someone whom we in our time can no longer understand or judge but he is certainly someone great and imposing. And there, before us, a being from another world, close to us for a few minutes, he has something indefinably shy, almost timid which endows him with a singular unexpected charm. *

* From *Morocco* by Pierre Loti. Quoted by permission of Calmann-Levy, Publisher.

Something of the same appealing quality reappeared in our own day in the late King Mohammed V—a family magnetism known as the "Alaouite charm."

When Hassan was interrupted by his father's death in his task of subjugating the Sous, he threatened to return and punish that insolent region. Nine years of zigzagging across the land north of the Atlas to extinguish dangerous conflagrations passed before his army of 40,000 men marched south again. This time he was successful in stamping out independence. Perhaps the success was due to his innovation of sending supplies down the coast in foreign steamers to meet him; perhaps to the terror inspired by his thundering artillery; or to his warning against the Christians in the seaports.

"Acknowledge my sovereignty and I will protect you from them [the Christians]," he promised the assembled tribal chiefs. When the chiefs yielded to his offer, he proved his sincerity by transforming the village of Tiznit, near the Spanish enclave of Ifni, into a strongly fortified and garrisoned town, and by forbidding Christians to settle in the south of his empire.

Perhaps he sensed that his end was near when he decided in the year 1893 to visit the Tafilalet, the cradle of his Cherifian ancestors. The army went with him of course, the 40,000 again, to hew a way through the hostile tribes of the cedar forests of the Middle Atlas, to cross the high passes of the Great Atlas in order to punish more insurrections on the desert's edge before moving eastward to the oases of the Tafilalet.

There, fifty *ksour* or walled villages and their palm groves lined the banks of the River Ziz. There the dates, long as a woman's finger and as full of juice as a grape, were the finest in the Moghreb. The Filalian Cherifs from Arabia had indeed benefited the palms with their baraka. At El Aam, southernmost of the *ksour,* the trans-Saharan caravans ended the long four-month journey from Timbuctu.

Almost two centuries had passed since Hassan's ancestor, Moulay Ismail, had sent his superfluous wives, concubines and children to the old Tafilalet capital of Sidjilmassa, and seventy years since the wild desert nomads of the Ait Atta had reduced Ismail's kasba and palaces to rubble. Hassan himself had chosen the nearby oasis of Tigmahrt for his own great brood of sons born of a harem numbering 300, and had given it walls, palaces and mosques.

In a Saharan oasis the flow of water from garden to garden is scrupulously alloted and measured in minutes; the population finds its own level in relation to the dates, fruits, vegetables, grain and pasturage each oasis is able to produce. No sultan valuing the loyalty of his subjects could expect an army of 40,000 to exact provisions in a land of such limited fertility. Though delayed by his desert campaigns, Hassan left the home of his an-

194

cestors in late October to return to Marrakesh across the Glaoua Pass of the High Atlas.

It may be strange to think of African Morocco in terms of snow and bitter cold, but the mountains of the High Atlas tower into peaks of perpetual whiteness, and the Glaoua Pass, cut by an ancient glacier, crosses the majestic range at an altitude of 8,000 feet. By the time Hassan and his army started the ascent from the scorching desert, winter rains had turned to sleet and snow. Clinging to precipices in the rugged defiles, threading beneath beetling cliffs, zigzagging across brawling rivers, deep in snow, slippery with ice, slimey with mud, the men, horses and pack animals, slithered, slipped, and sometimes died. When Hassan reached Marrakesh with what remained of his army, he was a feeble old man. A third of his baggage animals lay frozen on the trail behind him.

While he tried to regain his strength under the welcome winter sun of his southern capital, new troubles disturbed his rest. In the north, Spain was threatening punishment because the war indemnity of 1861 was not being paid in prompt installments. To the northwest, the Tadla tribes were staging their usual uprisings. On the Algerian border, the French were expecting the shifting nomad tribes of his empire to keep themselves and their flocks back of an imaginary line in shifting sands. And by caravan from the south, on the far side of the Sahara, came piteous appeals for help from the black notables of Timbuctu. The French, they said, marching inland from Dakar, had reached Ségu less than 400 miles above them on the Niger, and they begged Hassan's advice and protection.

Bedeviled on all sides, Hassan followed the only course open to him in answer to Timbuctu—an evasive stalling for time. He wrote:

> Praise be unto the one God. May blessings and salutations be upon our Lord Mohammed, upon his family and upon his companions.
>
> Greeting to the chief of the town and the notables.
>
> I have paid great attention to the help and protection you ask of me. I am greatly disturbed. I should have responded to your appeal and given you good support but the great distance between us compels me to be cautious. Your neighbors must come to your assistance.
>
> I will march upon the French and drive them away for you but you must first send me proofs of your dependence on my high government and my kingdom. . . .
>
> Salutation
>
> Moulay el Hassan

By the time the letter returned by caravan to Timbuctu the French were firmly installed. A fort commanded the desert approach from the north, and a second guarded the river approach from the south. The pillaging Touaregs had finally met their master, and the people of Timbuctu, who described themselves as "women who do not fight," could now enjoy their riches and their women without fear of Touareg spears denting their massive doors. In 1894 his Moroccan Majesty's letter was handed to the French Commandant who, as recorded by Felix Dubois, author of *Timbuctu the Mysterious*, "delicately placed it in the archives."

Perhaps Moulay el Hassan had already died by the time the letter reached Timbuctu. Frail and exhausted, he had set out again on the warpath to put down rebellion in that age-old hotbed of defiance, the Tadla region of the Middle Atlas. Practicing to the end his creed that "a sultan's throne should be his saddle," he died as he had always lived, "a riding sultan."

To avoid chaos and to ensure his own rise to power, Ba Ahmed, the Sultan's iron-handed chamberlain, concealed the death on the homeward journey. Because the law said no corpses might enter the city of Rabat, he had a hole secretly cut in the wall by night. As soon as the dead body of the Sultan lay beside his noble ancestor, Mohammed ben Abdallah, the crafty Ba Ahmed, deservedly titled "Bismarck of Morocco," proceeded to appoint a new sultan of his own choosing.

Women clothed in costumes native to different regions of Morocco. / *Moroccan Government*

CHAPTER XVI

THE FRENCH MOVE IN

(The Reigns of Abd el Aziz, 1894–1908,
and Moulay Hafid, 1908–1912)

Three of Moulay Hassan's sons became sultans. The first, Abd el Aziz, a boy of fourteen and his father's choice, was proclaimed through the authority of the chamberlain Ba Ahmed; the second, Moulay Hafid, seized the throne through his own strength; the third, Moulay Youssef, became the puppet sultan of the French in 1912 when they moved in to "protect" the country.

The boy Abd el Aziz, placed by force on the back of his father's great white horse, rode for the first time through the streets of Rabat under the Cherifian umbrella, with tears filling his eyes. The tears were for the father whom he had adored and suddenly lost. They might also have been tears of evil omen for the tragedy of his coming reign.

During the six years of his minority, his educated Circassian mother and the powerful Ba Ahmed acted as regents. In 1900, Ba Ahmed died. Abd el Aziz at twenty showed no stiffening of the gentle childish character into the stuff of a "riding sultan." Of an age to rule, he lacked the might, the maturity and the majesty to impose his command.

No sultan since the bloodthirsty Yazid of 1791, with his passion for the study of artillery, had shown such a curiosity in the mechanical wonders of the Western World as did young Abd el Aziz. As a result, power-hungry viziers and foreign adventurers filled the palace with model railroads, motorboats, diving bells, grand pianos, gramophones and balloons—every gadget from the useful to the ridiculous. By such premeditated cunning, the viziers diverted the sultan from the business of government; the foreigners played upon his extravagance, and forced him into dependence on their proffered loans. On the advice of his Circassian mother, Abd el Aziz made the British his favorites, and among the British especially the jolly Scottish bagpiper, the "Caid," Sir Harry Maclean, who had trained and commanded his father's army, and Walter Harris, correspondent of the London *Times*, who became the authority *par excellence* on the Morocco of his day.

English friendships, French bank loans to reorganize the army, a new land tax to end exemptions for foreigners and their protégés, the suggestion of building a railroad—all combined to turn the young Sultan's country against him from the Atlantic to the Algerian border. Tribes revolted, pretenders arose, bandits seized foreigners for spectacular and costly ransoms.

French historians write with injured bitterness of Caid Maclean and favoritism for the British during the first half of the young Sultan's rule. A strange point of view, when their columns were seizing Moroccan territory to both the west and south! First, in 1900, the French seized the fertile "Road of Palms"—that long line of oases on the most direct caravan trail to their most recent conquest, Timbuctu; then, moving north from the lower Senegal in the capture of Mauritania, they laid their lion's paw on the entire Western Sahara—all, that is, except the Spanish Sahara, an empty coastal strip from the River Dra to Cape Blanco, and the minute Ifni, both tenaciously held by Spain. With this control of the desert, and the organization of a native camel corps with French officers, they succeeded in putting an end to the lawless raids of those blue-veiled pirates of the sands—the Touaregs.

The eastern border traced by the French in the Moroccan Treaty of 1844, after a jog east, from the small Mediterranean port of Saidia, dropped almost due south across the coastal foothills, and over the forested Atlas to the mournful region of the High Plateaus. There, through the bleak pasturage of Alfa * grass and wormwood, it moved on in hazy uncertainty to meet the red-gold sand dunes of the desert.

To the tribes whose "houses of black hair" moved with their camels and their flocks, the line was for the most part as non-existent as a line

---

* The esparto or Spanish Grass (*Stipa tenacissima*) common to Spain and Algeria, valuable for the making of rope, sandals, mats and especially fine paper.

drawn across air or water. Where, however, it took concrete form in a scattering of outposts, it became a challenge to attack convoys, cut telegraph lines and wipe out garrisons. These nomad tribes and their cheiks had made no pact with the Christian dogs, not even with the despicable Christian-loving Sultan at Fez. If they paid allegiance to anyone, it would be to pious Moslems, to the two heroes, Bou Amama and Bou Hamara, who promised to lead them against both French and Sultan.

Even before the coming of the French, this was *bled el baroud* ("powder country"), with tribe against tribe, with plunder, pillage and camel-lifting the essential drama of life. In the summer of 1903 a force of four thousand tribesmen, crossing the *hammada,* or stony desert, from the Moroccan Tafilalet, besieged the French outpost of Toghit, south of the railroad end at Colomb Béchar. Three weeks later, a convoy of supplies lost thirty-six men by death and filled the nearest hospital at the military post of Ain Sefra with its wounded.

Into this powder keg, this seething lawless *Sud Oranais,* the terrified War Ministry in Paris sent a colonel of Hussars from Alençon, to throw the fear of Allah into the marauders—not that it concerned them that he was eating his heart out in idle boredom in France, but because they respected his achievements in the previous danger zones on the Chinese border of Tonkin and in the Hova Province of Central Madagascar.

Colonel Louis Hubert Gonzalvo Lyautey was fifty-one when he arrived as Commandant of the Subdivision of Ain Sefra, to enforce law and order along the Algerian-Moroccan border. Behind him lay his seven years of distinguished service in Indo-China and Madagascar, and, most important of all, apprenticeships under the revolutionary governor-general Jean-Marie Antoine de Lanessan, and the great colonial general, Galliéni. Throughout his active life Lyautey was to put into practice Lanessan's principal maxim: "Govern *with* the mandarin, not *against* him," and to follow the pattern of Galliéni's passion for creating Western order and prosperity in the wake of pacification. Because he was an aristocrat himself, sympathetic to the highborn of all races, amateur of arts and letters as sensitive to the exotic as to the familiar, respecter of all religions, advocate of diplomacy rather than force, the methods of Lanessan and Galliéni became for Lyautey also the ideal methods for spreading the *pax romana* in its modern dress of French civilization across ancient *Mauretania Tingitana.*

As the new Commandant of Ain Sefra had sought the friendship and cooperation of the Mandarins in Tonkin jungles, he now set himself to win over the tribal chiefs of desert and mountain.

Over the uniform of France he wore the flowing burnous of the enemy he had come to subdue; the tiger-skin trimmings of his saddles vied in splendor with the native trappings of red leather and velvet; his fine horses showed their ancestry of desert blood. As he had bestowed enchantment on his Tonkinese army quarters by means of carved teakwood and ivory, handwoven silks and incense-burners of chased silver, he soon dispelled the bleakness of desert quarters. When he received the great chiefs, they were both surprised and captivated to find the same richly colored tribal rugs and cushions of Moroccan leather, the same shimmer of brass and copper that decorated their own proud tents. When he failed to win them over as friends, he won their respect as an enemy.

In the meanwhile, the government of Algeria and the Foreign Ministry represented at both Tangier and Fez were pulling in opposite directions in their Moroccan policy. The game at Fez was to move with velvet-gloved diplomacy toward French control of Moroccan affairs, to persuade the Sultan, sunk in debt and frightened by both his mouldering army and hostile subjects, to accept French help gratefully.

Algiers, on the other hand, had no use for such artful maneuvering. Moroccan tribes were wiping out her border garrisons, and she demanded action. The Treaty of 1894 gave her the right of pursuit but not of seizing territory. With the mobile enemy melting into the interior, the right of pursuit became an empty privilege. Lyautey's old and tried system was to encircle rebellious spots, then come to terms with the ruler. As the ruler at Fez was a ruler in name only, the Frenchman could see no solution for a peaceful Algeria other than military invasion and control of eastern Morocco.

Two rebels defied him from the Moroccan side of the border. One, an aspirant to the Moroccan throne, Bou Hamara, the Rogui (Pretender), the other, the formidable Algerian rebel, Bou Amama. When Lyautey established a base within striking distance of this enemy, Paris ordered him back across the frontier. Lyautey, furious, threatened to resign, until his loyal and admiring chief, Jonnard, Governor of Algeria, succeeded in extinguishing the fireworks. In the resulting compromise, Moroccan and French troops together—Lyautey's idea—policed the disputed region. Lyautey had triumphed in the first step of what he called his "discreet penetration of Morocco secretly begun."

In this same year of 1904, an important change for Morocco took place in the alignment of the European Powers through a new Anglo-French treaty. Since 1882, when France had enraged Italy by taking Tunis, the Triple Alliance against her consisted of Italy, Germany and Austro-Hungary. Though France and England, barely sidestepping war in 1898 in upper Egypt (the Fashoda Incident), had come to an agreement on zones of influence in Northeast Africa, they still eyed each other with ill will on the question of both Moroccan and Egyptian hegemony. In the following six years the ominous establishment of Germany in the commerce of the Moroccan Sous, and her interest in such Atlantic ports as Agadir, threw France and England into an even more "cordial" agreement. For a free hand in Egypt as set forth in Article II of this new treaty, "His Britannic Majesty's Government recognize that it appertains to France whose dominions are coterminous for a great distance with those of Morocco to preserve order in that country, to provide assistance for the purpose of all administrative, economic, financial and military reforms which it may require. . . ." In Article VIII, "The two Governments inspired by their feeling of sincere friendship for Spain take into special consideration the interest which that country derives from her territorial possessions on the Moorish coast of the Mediterranean. In regard to these interests the French Government will come to an understanding with the Spanish Government. . . ."

The agreement was signed May 4th, 1904.

Not everyone in England was happy about this high-handed deal. Robert Cunninghame-Grahame, lover of freedom, of social justice, and of the Argentine Pampas and the Moroccan Atlas, sprang to the defense of a country he knew and prized even as the one-time prisoner of an Atlas chief. In his foreword to M. Aflalo's bitter indictment of British foreign policy, *The Truth About Morocco*, he says: "England has given up to France that which was never hers to give and France as gratefully received it as a 'fence' received the swag from the swell mobsman's hand when all the police are down the areas or are drunk."

Wilfred Scawen Blunt, the poet and, with his wife, Lady Anne, the great breeder of Arab horses at Crabbet Park in Sussex, left an equally severe verdict in his diaries. As quoted by H. G. Wells, Blunt regarded the continued stay of the English in Egypt, when they had pledged themselves to go, as the greatest cause of the troubles that culminated in 1914. To pacify the French over Egypt, he charged England had connived at the French occupation of Morocco, which Germany had looked upon as her share of North Africa. Hence Germany's bristling attitude to France and the revival in France of the *revanche* idea, which had died down. Said the former Prime Minister, Lord Rosebery, Liberal Imperialist preceding the Conservatives, the Marquis of Salisbury and Arthur Balfour: ". . . I hope and trust rather than believe that the power which holds Gibraltar may never have cause to regret having handed Morocco over to a great military Power." In Berlin, Chancellor von Bülow assured the Reichstag that he saw no threat in the new Anglo-French Treaty, and that it would not interfere or affect Germany and her commerce south of the Atlas.

Confidently, France approached the Sultan with the reforms that now, with England behind her, she could order instead of suggest. Her respite from German jealousy was short-lived. Within less than a year, Emperor William II dropped anchor in the harbor of Tangier and assured Morocco, in the person of the Sultan's uncle, of Germany's friendship and support against French interference. World War I very nearly began in the spring of 1905, instead of in the summer of 1914. A meeting known as the Algeciras Conference in the shadow of Gibraltar postponed it. Suggested by the Kaiser, summoned by the Sultan, angrily and reluctantly attended by France and England, the meeting presented the Moroccan problem to twelve European nations.

Only United States assurance against unreasonable German demands had persuaded France to agree to the conference. As things turned out, she gained rather than lost by its decision. Of all the powers, only Austria sided with Germany against her. The conference, begun in January 1906, produced the Act of Algeciras, ratified by the Powers at the end of the year. The Act reaffirmed the independence and integrity of Morocco, with equal commercial rights for all nations. France was entrusted with the policing of Lyautey's Algerian-Moroccan frontier. For the rest of the country, a Franco-Spanish police force was decided on. In the establishment of a state bank, France again was granted majority control.

In March of the following year, the French Doctor Emile Mauchamps was stabbed to death in Marrakesh. Most historians pass over the poor doctor with one line about his murder as they move on to French revenge, which consisted of the occupation of the Moroccan town of Oudjda on the Algerian (!) frontier by Lyautey. To the English anthropologist Nina Epton as indicated in her *Saints and Sorcerers: A Moroccan Journey*, Dr. Mauchamps is known as the author of one of the best documented books on Moroccan magic, apart from Westermarck's well-known *Ritual and Belief in Morocco*, since Edmond Doutté's classic on the subject. Nina Epton's story of Dr. Mauchamps' murder is an interesting elaboration of the meagre account given by the average historian. This disapproving doctor found no charm in the actions of djinns and their magic, upon which he was such an authority, even less in the tricks and charlatanism of the clever marabouts. His aim was to substitute modern medicine for ancient superstition. Naturally, the most powerful of all marabout-magicians became his enemy and planned his death.

Dr. Mauchamps' enemy was the Cheik Ma el Ainin, known as the "Blue Sorcerer" of the south—"Blue" because he belonged to those "Blue Men" of the western Sahara who were enveloped from head to foot in somber indigo cotton, their dark skins stained by its unfixed dye. Ma el Ainin was another Mahdi, a Deliverer, another reformer determined to purge the religion of Islam of its corruption, and to chase the Christians out of the country.

Throughout the western desert, his influence was enormous. From 1906 to 1909 he harassed the French in their efforts to push north from Senegal and add Mauritania to their colonial empire. At Tidjika, only three hundred miles north of the Senegal River, he had besieged their new post. When the French moved north to the iron mountain and salt works of Idjil, their future Fort Gouraud, he massed Moroccans and "Blue

A *ksar*, or fortified village, in the Moroccan Sahara. / *Th. Schmied,*
National Library, Rabat

Men" in the north to stem their advance. In the meanwhile, supported by
his son, "El Hiba," he fomented trouble for them north of the Atlas—
trouble such as the murder of Dr. Mauchamps in Marrakesh and, in the
same summer, 1907, an attack by Chaouia tribesmen on Casablanca.

The "Blue Sorcerer's" Casablanca mischief consisted of engineering
the murder of nine European laborers at work on the new harbor. They
were murdered by neighboring Chaouia tribesmen on the charge of having
desecrated a native cemetery. Again there were French reprisals. Lyautey's
eastern military wedge gained a western counterpart. Casablanca and the
surrounding Chaouia were brought under military control.

Lyautey, promoted to Division Commander at Oran, returned from a
discussion with the Sultan, established at Rabat, to find that Paris had withdrawn some of his troops for the Casablanca front, at the very time that
the war-like Moroccan tribesmen, the Beni Snassen, were about to stage an
attack across his Algerian border. In a passionate rage, Lyautey included

his opinion of the Paris imbeciles in his report to Algiers. Unluckily for him, the communication missed Governor Jonnard, who usually expurgated and toned down such outbursts before they left Africa. This time Paris received the full impact of Lyautey's rage. In vain, Jonnard, in Paris himself, tried to calm the furious Clemenceau.

"What do you expect?" Jonnard asked. "He is a blooded horse. Sometimes he kicks the shafts."

"Maybe," snorted the minister, "but I refuse to allow him to send his *'crottin'* ('dung') to the Government."

When Lyautey received the letter ordering him out of Moroccan Oudjda and back to Oran, he left at once for Algiers, this time to smash the galling shafts and resign his command. On the heels of his arrival, the news of the bloody and fiery invasion of the Beni Snassen filled Algeria and Paris with terror. A telegram from Clemenceau cancelled the demotion and rushed Lyautey back to the border to handle the dangerous tribesmen. In two weeks the General had the raiders back in their wild mountains, stripped of their arms and flocks, and ready to ask for *amam* (peace). In the following year at a meeting with Lyautey, Clemenceau also made his peace and joined the admirers of the blooded horse, the *cheval de sang*.

When Lyautey paid his visit to the Sultan, who had fled from hostile Fez to Rabat, he had had to make the journey by sea, so great was the chaos and lawlessness on the trails connecting city to city. Not even the fifty-seven miles between Casablanca and Rabat or the one hundred and fifty from Rabat to Tangier would have been possible by horseback, for Abd el Aziz was not only unable to impose any authority on the hostile tribes of the surrounding Gharb but was a prisoner in his own palace with a crescent of enemies at his back.

To the north, the bandit Raisuli, ruling the Tangier region, had kidnapped three important foreigners worth fat ransoms. The first, Walter Harris, correspondent for the London *Times*, described his own capture in his *France, Spain and the Rif*. In his case, perhaps because of his friendship with the Moors, he was released without ransom after three weeks, on Raisuli's condition that the Sultan's army, marching into the bandit's territory, be recalled and the captured prisoners released.

The second victim made Raisuli's name a household word in the United States. Theodore Roosevelt's famous "Perdicaris alive or Raisuli dead" referred to a rich Greek of dubious United States citizenship who, with his British stepson, spent seven weeks in Raisuli's mountain lair until a ramson of 14,000 pounds, plus other privileges forced out of the Sultan, procured their release.

When Caid Maclean was sent by the Sultan to discuss terms with the lawless bandit, he found himself the third important prisoner. After a captivity of seven months, Maclean's freedom was bought for 20,000 pounds.

204

Tough and cruel, wily and ambitious, Raisuli reappears a few years later, baiting the French with German arms during World War I, and again in the early twenties selling his services to Spain in the war with Abd el Krim.

In the west, the foxy Arabized Berber, Bou Hamara, was gaining power by posing as Moulay Mohammed ben Hassan, the former Sultan's eldest son who had mysteriously disappeared. To his enemies he was known as the *Rogui* ("Pretender"). With immense armed strength, he threatened the French in the region of Oudjda and the Sultan on the Atlantic region of the Gharb. Like the "Blue Sorcerer" in the south, he too owed his prestige to his skill in tricks that passed for magic. Abd el Aziz was helpless against him.

In the south the most dangerous enemy of the three was Moulay Hafid, no pretender like Bou Hamara, the Rogui, but true son of the late Sultan and elder brother of Abd el Aziz. In Marrakesh he ruled as the Sultan's *khalifa* or representative.

By the summer of 1908 Morocco had two sultans: the pathetic Abd el Aziz in Rabat, the fanatic Christian-hating Moulay Hafid, proclaimed in the southern capital, Marrakesh, and soon afterward in the northern capital, Fez. Between the two, France stepped delicately. In his role as diplomat, Lyautey advised against taking sides. Abd el Aziz, with his gentle charm and submission to French guidance, was by far the more desirable of the two to deal with. Hafid, who would have cut French throats with pleasure, was the strong one who would probably win the struggle. It would be well not to slam the door in his face. Without French help, Abd el Aziz led an army south to Marrakesh in the hope of winning back his southern capital. Betrayed and deserted outside the city, he managed to escape with his harem to the safety of French lines near Casablanca. There his fourteen sad years on the Moroccan throne ended with abdication in favor of his brother, the acceptance of a lifelong pension, and retirement to a villa in Tangier, where he died during World War II.

The new sultan made himself acceptable to the foreign powers by agreeing to accept the Act of Algeciras. Of the two remaining rebels, the scoundrel Raisuli not only promised Hafid his allegiance but presented to him the 20,000 pounds of ransom money he had squeezed out of Abd el Aziz for freeing Caid Maclean. The Rogui, on the other hand, made the mistake of holding out tooth and nail against him. First, after a long-drawn-out struggle, Hafid succeeded in crushing the Rogui's army; soon after he burned him out of a supposedly inviolable sanctuary where he had fled for refuge.

The diplomatic corps assigned to Morocco in Tangier had from the beginning hardened their sensibilities to the blood-thirsty cruelties of this country where time seemed to have stopped somewhere in the Middle

Ages. They had become used to seeing enemy heads shriveling on city walls and the empty stumps at wrist and ankle marking a thief. Nothing that they had experienced, however, equaled the sadistic tortures inflicted upon the prisoners of the Rogui's army by Sultan Hafid. The governments of Europe drafted a letter of protest to be read to the Sultan at Fez. In defiant response, he inflicted the terrible "salt treatment" on all Rogui's prisoners still alive. The "salt treatment" involved cutting four slits in the palm of the hand, filling them with salt, and sewing down the fingers to grow inward into the flesh. The Moroccan excuse for this fiendish punishment was that death itself was not a sufficient deterrent to crime.

As for the Rogui himself, he was exhibited, cramped in a wooden cage, throughout the country for a year. He then died in Fez either in Hafid's lion pit or by gunshot: the accounts vary. In Protectorate days the cage was the center of interest in the beautiful Dar Batha Palace-museum of Fez. Today, under independence, it has significantly disappeared.

Hafid came to the throne with an empty treasury, no source of income except direct taxation from war-torn tribes, and a bill for 163 million francs from France for such items as the cost of the French conquest of Casablanca and the neighboring Chaouia. To enable him to meet the debt, France offered a loan with forty per cent of the customs rights as security. The new Sultan found his position no more auspicious or secure than that of the brother whom he had pushed off the throne.

At this point on the eve of the Protectorate, the path of Moroccan history divides sharply three ways, two of them in bitter opposition represented by *colons* versus nationalists with a third middle road laid down in the beginning by the first Resident-General, Lyautey, and followed by other French men of good will. In proof of this threefold path, the next important event in Moroccan history, which again all but started World War I, has two conflicting versions.

For the typical French version, with its parallel in the "white man's burden" attitude of the British, here is the condensed account of Coissac de Chavrebière:

> In the year 1911 a dangerous ferment exploded in Fez and among the neighboring tribes. The besieged Sultan and his desperate Maghzen asked for and received the aid of French troops. Ten thousand men under General Moinier from the conquered Chaouia marched to the rescue with strict instructions to observe all treaties and refrain from interfering with the Sultan's independence and prestige. With his task completed Moinier returned to the coast leaving, at the Sultan's request, fortified posts along the way.

Now to the more sinister account presented by Rom Landau in his *Moroccan Drama 1900–1955* from Edmund Morel's *Morocco in Diplomacy*. In this version, the blood-thirsty tribes swarming down from the hills to murder the helpless European colony existed only in the newspapers of Paris. The object of this fabrication of false news was to terrify the public and frighten the government into sending Moinier and his troops—30,000 in this version—to occupy the capital and scatter fortifications from Rabat to Fez. The threat of this non-existent uprising was planted in the venal Paris press by a powerful group of bankers and industrialists organized as the *Comité du Maroc,* with the sordid object of exploiting the fertile lands, mineral resources and cheap labor of Morocco for their own benefit. To implement this exploitation, military control and French rule were essential.

The fact that this group, this *Comité du Maroc,* this *colon bloc* reappears with its Bidaults and Soustelles defying the decrees of its own government, even plotting against it, during both the Moroccan and the Algerian struggles for independence, strongly suggests that the Fez uprising of April, 1911, was indeed a staged affair.

In 1909, soon after European recognition of Moulay Hafid, Germany entered into a new agreement with France, reaffirming German commercial rights and acknowledging the privileged position of France, but taking a firm stand that this position did not imply the establishment of a protectorate. Now, with the French troops in the capital representing a flagrant violation of the Act of Algeciras, Germany demanded concessions. The entire French Congo was the unexpressed price. As no satisfactory offer had been made during June talks with the French Ambassador in Berlin, German threats took concrete form. The "Panther," a German gunboat, appeared in July in the harbor of Agadir on Morocco's southern coast, very menacing in the small trading port. At the same time, the Mannesmann brothers, German agents from the north, tried to buy over the local tribal chiefs of the Sous. These same brothers, according to Walter Harris, were in league with the rebel bandit Raisuli in the north, both before and during World War I; later they became backers of the Riffian Abd el Krim.

With the appearance of the "Panther," known to history as the "Agadir Incident" and interpreted rightly by France as a threat of war, Ambassador Cambon was quickly authorized to make an offer of Congo territory, a strip of land that would give Germany trade communications between her own colony of Cameroon and the Congo River. To Germany this paltry offer was nothing more than an insult. In the end, peace and a free hand in Morocco brought a far greater price costing France the Corridor to the Congo River, plus 275,000 square miles—a region larger than Texas and almost twice the size of Morocco to the north and northwest of the French Congo. France received in exchange 12,000 square miles, about the size of the state of Maryland, in the Lake Chad region. The Congo concession was returned to her at the end of World War I.

In the meanwhile England, angry at Germany for being ignored and unconsulted during the move against France, and as fearful of war as France herself, had begun preparing for the long-dreaded explosion.

By November 4th, 1911, with the signing of the French-German Convention, an uneasy peace reigned again. Now France could afford to be outspoken about her Moroccan ambitions. Addressing the Senate on February 10th, 1912, Poincaré, as Prime Minister, was frank.

"For a long time," he said, "France has wanted to establish herself in Morocco as a vital requisite for governing her Algerian colony. In order to obtain this result France has struggled against men and events; she has consented to sacrifices of time, troops and money. Little by little she has surmounted the obstacles and today Morocco is in her hands."

The Protectorate Treaty, also known as the Act of Fez, imposed upon and signed by Moulay Hafid on March 31, 1912, provided, among its agreements, for the introduction of "a series of reforms, administrative, judiciary, economic, educational, financial and military, judged useful by the French Government." Though the initiative of the measures belonged to the protecting government, the right of enacting them belonged to the Sultan. *Nothing* in the terms of the Protectorate Treaty reduced Morocco to a colony. *Nothing* robbed her of her status as a sovereign state. Lyautey, as we shall see, adhered staunchly and honorably to these agreements. His successors, with rare exceptions, flouted them with highhanded tyranny.

Hafid had signed the Treaty under protest. Regnault, former French Minister, now first Governor, had given him no choice, not even that of abdicating. It could come as no surprise to the miserable Sultan to find himself despised and hated for selling his country to the Christians. He had seized the throne as the bold champion of Islam, the leader of the Holy War, the sworn enemy of the French. Four years later he found himself as helpless against them as the brother whom he had destroyed. The old Rogui, he must have thought, was an honest Moslem friend in comparison to these Christian dogs. Ya Allah, if he could only lock all these Frenchmen into wooden cages half the size of the Rogui's, and inflict the salt treatment on all their greedy hands!

On April 15th, Governor Regnault gave a great banquet to honor the Sultan and establish friendly relations between the two countries. Two nights later, revolt broke out in the barracks of Fez, culminating in the massacre by the Sultan's troops of their eighty French officers. Joining the soldiers in rioting and violence, the rabble poured into the mellah to rob, rape and murder. By the thousands, the panic-stricken Jews forced their way to the safety of the Palace grounds, into the Palace itself, even climbing into the empty cages of the menagerie next to the lions.

Most frightened of all was the Sultan Moulay Hafid, pleading frantically for French troops from Meknès. The troops arrived, planning to restore peace by bombarding the city. Fortunately, Regnault objected. Confusion and terror spread from wall to wall.

Two conflicting explanations for the trouble were offered to Paris: one that the military had blundered by deducting the cost of the soldiers' mess from their pay instead of letting their wives cook for them; the other that the country at large was seething with fury at the conditions of the Treaty and that Hafid himself was behind the massacres. Disagreements between the military commander and Governor Regnault increased the gravity of the situation.

As a result, it was decided in Paris that a civil governor was inadequate; the explosive possibilities called for military authority. General Lyautey, commander of an army corps in Rennes since 1910, was the choice of President Fallières and his ministers.

Lyautey, arriving in Morocco at the end of May, must have visualized the roads he would build as he made the slow twelve-day journey on horseback from Casablanca to Fez. Entering Rabat through the twelfth-century city walls of the Almohads, he flew into one of his splendid rages at sight of half-built French barracks. Such barracks were hideous enough in France, but doubly hideous here where every mellow line of the great horseshoe gates and crenellated walls, every sea-green minaret delighted the eye. Before moving on to Fez, Lyautey gave the order to his future Director of *Beaux Arts* to redesign the barracks in keeping with the character of Moslem architecture.

In Fez Lyautey found his officers desperate. André Maurois in his life of Lyautey describes the first terrible night and day. With tears in his eyes, General Brulard told the new Resident-General that he was too late to save the city, that tribesmen in uncounted numbers were pouring down out of the hills to surround it, that there was no hope for the 4,000 Europeans among 90,000 fanatical Fassi.

That very night the attack began. To acknowledge that a situation was hopeless was not in Lyautey's character. "Govern with the mandarin, not against him," remained his maxim. But where was the mandarin? The Sultan Hafid, neurotic, cowardly, out to save his own skin, was threatening to abdicate, to escape from the city. If he left, he could find safety only with the rebel tribes. Also, if he left, the European powers who had not as yet recognized the Protectorate Treaty would accuse the French of deliberately ousting him.

The Sultan was no "mandarin." But Fez held men who made and unmade Sultans, the oulema (the faculty of the Kairouiine Mosque-University) and the equally proud and powerful *Chorfa* or Cherifians—the direct descendants of the Prophet through such dynasties as the Idrisids and the Alaouites. Lyautey summoned them. During the morning, with the battle visible from the rooftops, there was nothing immediate that they could do. However, they were with him. They and he understood one another. He was the first Frenchman who had not made them feel the "corporal's boot," not classed them and their age-old heritage of learning with water carriers, street cleaners, muleteers and other illiterate riffraff. They, too, had no desire to have the blood-thirsty Berber tribesmen swarm through the streets, looting their rich stores of merchandise and raping their women. They would let it be known throughout the mosques and souks that the welfare of Fez lay in siding with the French.

By afternoon, the situation as seen from the rooftops appeared hopeless. At the most strategic point, a company of Legionnaires was retreating. Lyautey decided to make a last stand, if necessary, at the hospital in the heart of the city. That morning in summoning the oulema and the Chorfa he had turned for guidance to his old chief, Lanessan. After dinner he remembered Galliéni, who read Stuart Mill on the evening before the battle. Among the officers at his mess he had a poet. Lyautey asked the man for his last sonnet, then for poems by Alfred de Vigny. Later he asked to be waked after an hour's sleep.

When he woke after ten hours instead of one, it was daylight. The city was saved. The retreat of the Legionnaires, instead of causing disaster, had enabled the artillery to scatter and turn the advancing tribes. Before the latter could collect to attack again, reinforcements arrived from Meknès.

A neurotic, hysterical woman could not have been more impossible to advise and protect than Moulay Hafid. First he insisted on leaving Fez for Rabat, then on leaving Morocco by the end of August. Nothing could have suited Lyautey better. With relief, the Resident-General looked over the Alaouite House for a successor. Hafid's choice was one of his own infant sons. Lyautey had no desire to work with a temporary regent. Though the deposed Abd el Aziz still lived in his Tangier exile, the four years of his brother's rule had neither improved nor strengthened his feeble character. A third son of the old Moulay Hassan, Moulay Youssef, ruled as Hafid's khalifa at Fez. In the words of Walter Harris who knew him, this Prince was "young, of sufficient intelligence, of pleasant manners and of a thoughtful and serious disposition." At Lyautey's prompting, Hafid designated this brother as his successor, and the oulema duly proclaimed him their choice.

Throughout the fifteen years during which Moulay Youssef dutifully signed and affixed his seal to the decisions presented to him by his French protectors, Lyautey and, after him his successor, Steeg, had no cause to regret the choice.

CHAPTER XVII

§O§€O§€O§€

LYAUTEY AFRICANUS AND THE "WOLF OF THE RIF"

(The Reign of Moulay Youssef, 1912–1927)

§O§€O§€O§€

On his first day, Lyautey had won over the oulema and the Chorfa of Fez by sharing his problems with them while the Berber bullets whined down from the hills. His next two steps won over the Fassi themselves. First he countermanded a huge fine imposed by his predecessor on the innocent population for the massacre by the Moorish soldiers of their French officers. More surprising still to a people with Moulay Hafid's vengeful torturing and killing of the Rogui fresh in their minds, he reprieved the death sentence for the soldiers themselves.

First acts, then promises. Promises to respect Morocco's religion, customs and mosques, her traditions and her way of life; promises to keep the word "protect" from being twisted into the word "exploit"; promises to govern through the Sultan and the Vizirs.* Naturally this soldier of vision

* In the same year the great British administrator Sir Frederick John Dealtry Lugard (later Lord Lugard) was appointed governor of Northern and Southern Nigeria where he ruled with the same high minded, humanitarian principles making the welfare and progress of the people under his protection his main concern.

had a blueprint of reforms ready for them: above all things peace, stability and order from the Straits to the Sahara and from the Atlantic to the Algerian border; then roads, railroads, harbors, power plants, sanitation, schools and hospitals, and the rescue and restoration of their own splendid but neglected monuments.

For the rich, well-fed merchants of Fez in their enchanting "palaces," for the scholars of the mosques, for the artisans of souks stamping slippers with gold or hammering trays of brass and copper—city men all of them since the days of Idris—the prospect of peace was anticipated with rejoicing. But for the Berbers of the black tents, of the mud villages, of the great ochre kasbas of mountain and desert edge, with fight in their blood, with their rifles and their freedom dearer to them than their moneybags and their security, Lyautey's threat of peace was a call to arms, a challenge to harass, ambush and destroy every invading Christian column, every Sultan's *harka* as they had sought to destroy every would-be conqueror since Roman days.

Three "zones of insolence"—*bled es siba*—demanded Lyautey's attention by the time he had brought order to Fez and moved his headquarters to Rabat, his future capital. In the Sous, the "Blue Sultan" El Hiba, son of the "Blue Sorcerer," Ma el Ainin, was championing the cause of Islam and threatening Marrakesh. In the east, the turbulent tribes of the "Taza Corridor" sealed off the only natural land passage to the Algerian border. And from the raiding Zaian tribe of the Middle Atlas the fertile and already pacified plain and peneplain of the Chaouia were gravely endangered.

In Paris the *colon bloc* cried out for immediate military action, for strafing columns hurled against the *sales indigènes*. Lyautey's timetable ran on a different schedule. He wanted roads and railroads to accompany his advances. He wanted blockhouses built to protect them. Always he had played to win with the minimum loss of life on the enemy's side as well as on his own. The kind of peace brought about by his own deliberate strategy would be, he knew from experience, a more lasting one than the wanton raking of machine guns to teach the proud Berbers who their masters were.

Marching north from the Sous, El Hiba gave his enemy no chance to move slowly. In Marrakesh the people proclaimed him Sultan. There he made the mistake of taking prisoner eight Frenchmen who had not fled with the rest to the coast at the news of his approach.

Because of El Hiba's eight prisoners, French prestige was at stake. A column under Colonel Mangin attacked the city. Frightened by the cannon balls that curved threateningly but harmlessly over the walls, El Hiba fled south to his Taroudant stronghold. Colonel Mangin had received support and a warm welcome into the southern capital from one of the three Great Caids of the Atlas, Si el Madani Glaoui, head of the Glaoua tribe and the most important tribal chief in the country.

Here at last, in these Berber Caids of the great Atlas, Lyautey found his "mandarins." To the East, Si el Madani Glaoui and his younger brother, El Hadj el Thami, lorded it over the Telouet Pass. This strategic gorge led down into the fertile oases of the upper reaches of the river Dra and, by way of the Tafilalet caravan head, to the land of slaves and gold. Westward along the snow-capped crest, El Goundafi ruled the pass to Taroudant, capital of the Sous. This was the same El Goundafi who in 1898 had held the writer Robert Cunninghame-Grahame a prisoner in his kasba, Thalaat el Yakoub, thereby supplying George Bernard Shaw with the material for "Captain Brassbound's Conversion." On the last of the western passes, the caravans paid tribute to El Mtougi; below, on the plain between Marrakesh and Mogador, the tribes supplied men for his harkas and claimed his protection.

During the mounting feebleness of the central government after Moulay Hassan's death, these robber barons of the Atlas were steadily increasing their power and the extent of their domains. They were the medieval lords of the castle, with partisans and slaves in the roles of serfs, and thick-walled kasbas in place of moated towers. Not even the anachronisms of their automobiles, electric lights, telephones in their town palaces, or visits to Paris spoiled the picture of their medieval despotism. Their shrewd seizure of power, their autocratic rule, their ability to enforce order were all qualities that won Lyautey's admiration and understanding. At the same time their proud bearing, their princely manners, the exquisite luxury of their kasbas and palaces appealed to all that was sensuous and, if not feudal, at least monarchical in his anti-republican nature.

These, then, were the "mandarins" through whose help the "Blue Sultan" was finally driven back across the border into the Spanish Sahara, to die and be buried in the ancestral *zaouia*. These were the allies through whose help and loyalty Lyautey, in August, 1914, could send the backbone of his troops to the western front and still, after the armistice of November, 1918, present a Moroccan empire to France. When Paris demanded Lyautey's divisions, and ordered him to withdraw all garrisons and civilians to the coastal ports, they informed him that the fate of Morocco would be decided in Lorraine. His answering telegram might well have told them that it would be decided in the Glaoua Kasba of Telouet.

The Glaouis were the favorites. Old Si el Madami died in 1918 after six years of collaboration with Lyautey and France. El Hadj Thami, tall, dark and sinister as a graveyard cypress, succeeded him as lord of Telouet and Pasha of Marrakesh. He, too, found his powers and his riches increasing by bolstering the rule of France. There was a saying in the souks: "Morocco is a cow. France holds her by the tail and El Glaoui milks her." Lyautey depended upon the Great Caids throughout the thirteen years of his Moroccan rule.

In the contemporary analysis of Lyautey's magnificent achievements, this collaboration has been held against him. Those who find so much to admire in all he accomplished, at the same time regret that he was too much the *grand seigneur* to ally himself to the young bourgeois intellectuals. In them he would have found Moroccans more devoted to the welfare of their country than, like El Glaoui, to personal power. That, of course, is historical hindsight. For how could Lyautey have foreseen the villain's part played by El Glaoui in the dethronement of Mohammed V, or have imagined the caid as the world saw him on its newsreel screens in November, 1955, crawling across the floor on his knees to kiss the feet of his former enemy, the restored Sultan, and beg forgiveness!

When France drew up her Protectorate Treaty in March, 1912, no mention was made of Spanish interests. And yet, in the Anglo-French Treaty of 1904, Article VIII had stipulated that France would take into consideration Spain's interests in Morocco and come to an understanding with the Spanish government in regard to them. It may seem strange that in the final agreement of November, 1912, the line marking the Spanish Protectorate was clearly defined only at each end: the Lower Moulaya River in the east, and the River Loukkos and latitude 35° in the west. In between, there was nothing definite, just general phrasing such as "the heights dominating the Ouergha River."

Ten years later much tragedy for Spain, for France and for the tribesmen of the Rif and the Djebala mountains, grew out of this ill-defined frontier in Abd el Krim's struggle for independence. It must be remembered: first, that a modern land survey in these hostile unsubdued mountains would have been out of the question; second, that such vague definitions as "heights dominating the Ouergha River" cut through tribal territories, assigning part to one country, part to another; and third, and most important of all, that there was at no time the slightest gesture of consulting the Riffians themselves in this arbitrary cutting up of their coastal mountains. Abd el Krim himself pointed out in a letter to Walter Harris that he had been "no party to the Treaty of 1912"; that any arrangement the French and the Spaniards might have come to on the subject of a frontier in a country which they had never visited and where they had no subjects or moral interests was "a preposterous act of totally unjustified and unjustifiable imperialism." His fight for the freedom of the Rif was a natural protest against losing it to the old hereditary enemy by the stroke of a pen.

In respect to Tangier, the Treaty called for a separate agreement to be decided on later. World War I postponed that settlement until 1923.

Though Lyautey had never had such a free hand as here in his African empire, he was still bedeviled by the restrictions that cramped the furious ardor of his progress. By the Act of Algeciras, France had agreed to accept bids from the twelve signatory powers in Tangier for all materiel bought for the Moroccan Government. He could be very sure that German consuls were watching eagerly for any violations of the agreement. Purchase and delivery of dredges for his ports, rolling stock for his narrow-gauge military railroads, machinery for building his roads all met with infuriating delay.

Yet the work progressed. The railroads moved inland. By May, 1914, armies moved from east to west for the first overland meeting in the dangerous "Taza Corridor." Though this progress by no means represented the final crushing of the menacing Tsoul and Branès tribes in their perpendicular mountains to the north, or of the spirited Ghiata and Beni Ouarain to the south, it did mean the taking of the stubborn town of Taza and an important step in uniting east and west.

Another major military success, in the early summer of 1914 (before the outbreak of World War I suddenly drained the Resident-General of his best troops), was the capture of the Middle Atlas stronghold of Khenifra in the region of the headwaters of the Oum er Rebia. Now at last the Chaouia plain could be made safe from the raids of the Beni Zaian at the very time when the grain of its rich alluvial soil and the flocks that fattened on its pasturage would be desperately needed in war-torn France.

There were other campaigns of course, generals and colonels leading their columns into the wild mountains, where the winter snows lay heavy on the cedar branches, where the headwaters of rivers rose and tumbled through narrow gorges, where every rock and tree hid a Berber and his musket.

Though these campaigns were classed as "pacification," from the first years to the end in 1934, when the last tribes gave up under attacks from the air, that term was far from honest. Freedom-loving Berbers dropped from the machine-gun fire of the French, and patriotic young Frenchmen and Foreign Legionnaires dropped from sniping by the Berber muskets. When it was all over, General Guillaume, later one of the arch-foes of Moroccan independence, wrote in his *Les Berbères et la pacification de l'Atlas Central:* "Not a single tribe submitted to us without having first exhausted to the bitter end its means of resistance."

From the beginning, Lyautey, the colonizer, introduced an important measure to mitigate the slaughter of Lyautey, the conqueror. He organized a mobile sanitary corps. Side by side with each military outpost, an infirmary welcomed the natives of the region. Dr. Paul Chatinières of the Mobile Sanitary Group of Marrakesh left a vivid account of accomplishments in his *Dans le Grand Atlas Marocain;* and Lyautey in his introduction to the book and his tribute to Chatinières explains his reasons for this form of colonization:

You know my ideas on the importance of the role of the doctor in the colonies and the help he can bring to the pacification of a country. Many misunderstandings end when people know each other. Now, what is pacification mainly, if not the end of misunderstanding? But, since, at first, explanations are difficult, someone who inspires preliminary confidence is necessary. No one fills this role better than the *toubib*. From the day that a notable, a caid, any poor wretch who suffers decides to see the French doctor and leaves comforted, the ice is broken, the first step is taken and relationship is established.

Somewhere else he words his feelings in even stronger terms: "The role of the doctor is the only excuse for colonization."

Lyautey decided in July of 1914 to defy Paris and hold the hinterland of Morocco as well as the coast, a difficult decision to make. In a meeting, his four loyal regional chiefs—General Gouraud of Fez, General Henry of Khenifra (the Middle Atlas), General Brulard of Marrakesh, and Colonel Peltier of the Taza region—assured him that they could spare the troops Paris demanded and still keep order in their territories with a skeleton force and the help of the tribes that had already submitted. By substituting reserves from France for his experienced divisions, and by training Senegalese from West Africa, Lyautey deceived the Moroccans with numbers. As he himself neatly put it, he had emptied the lobster but kept the shell. With psychological astuteness he ruled out any discussion of the war. France, he let it be known, would win not only without fail but easily.

In the meanwhile, he entertained and impressed the country with fairs in Casablanca, Rabat and Fez. With a mock unconcern for the long home front, fighting for its life from Dunkirk to Belfort, he proceeded to enlarge harbors, multiply roads and railroads, and build schools and hospitals. By the end of 1915, Morocco, which had been without a single mile of road in 1912, had 270 miles, leading from city to city. Despite the agony and the tragedy of the war, felt by no one more keenly than the deeply-patriotic Lyautey, he was emperor of his country as he had never been before. In Paris, the government, far too involved and desperate to concern itself with his imperious ways and keep track of his infringements of established colonial practices, gave him free rein, especially since he was soon sending trained native Moroccan troops to strengthen government forces. In the purchase of materiel for his economic improvements, he was now free of the formal red tape, imposed by the Act of Algeciras, that had hampered his progress. Now he could buy whatever was needed where it was most cheaply available. To his particular relief, he was no longer confined to the narrow-gauge railroads formerly insisted on by the Germans.

In every other respect, however, Germany was a constant and dangerous menace throughout the long four years of the war. From the neutral Spanish zone to the Sous, her agents fomented rebellion with gold, contraband arms and promises. In the Tangier region, the bandit Raisuli was easily bought. In the region to the east and in and around Taza, Abd el Malek, an unworthy grandson of the great Algerian patriot Abd el Kader, worked in Germany's pay to cut the vital railroad and telegraph lines along the Fez-Taza-Oudjda corridor. In the Middle Atlas, though the stronghold of Khenifra was in French hands, the Zaian tribe as a whole was spreading trouble. In the Sous, the "Blue Sultan," El Hiba, furnished with German arms, still defied the Maghzen.

At the end of December, 1916, after a year of inconclusive fighting for both sides along the Western Front, Lyautey received a telegram from Prime Minister Briand asking him to be Minister of War in his new cabinet. Lyautey's old chief Galliéni had filled the post until his death the previous spring. On its way to Paris was the Resident-General's last report, describing his fear of German landings in the Sous to join forces with the "Blue Sultan," and his fear of bombardments of Casablanca and Rabat by German submarines sighted along the Atlantic coast. In his refusal of the Prime Minister's offer, he explained that he had no one on his staff capable, in his opinion, of filling his place. On receiving this news, Briand proposed to transfer from the Western Front the very man who would have been Lyautey's own choice, General Henri Joseph Gouraud.

"If Gouraud replaces me, I accept," Lyautey agreed. He could feel assured that Morocco would be in the best of hands. Gouraud, prior to his brilliant work for Lyautey as Regional Chief of Fez, had won fame by defeating and subduing the fierce "Blue Men" of Central Mauritania. Ma el Ainin, the "Blue Sorcerer" of the Spanish Sahara, was an old enemy. Gouraud, as commissioner of Mauritania, had been the first European to reach the salt mines of Idjil where the future stronghold, Fort Gouraud, was to be named after him. (In June, 1963, Fort Gouraud made news as the end of the first Mauritanian railway to transport to the coast the valuable iron ore from the deposits of the Idjil hills. In this ore, the iron content is so high that pilots flying the mail between Morocco and Dakar notice its effect on their magnetic needles.)

No general of Gouraud's calibre would have willingly left his army during a war for an administrative post like that of Resident-General of Morocco. Briand tricked him into accepting. When Gouraud begged to stay with his men on the battle line, Briand said slyly, "I am hoping to make Lyautey my Minister of War. How does that choice strike you?"

Gouraud agreed that Lyautey was the perfect choice, that the war needed a man of Lyautey's great vision, who could see and direct it as a whole and end the disrupting quarrels of opposing factions.

"But," said Briand, "he refuses to accept unless you replace him!"

217

In his new post, from the very beginning until he resigned in March after a stormy and unpleasant scene in the Chamber of Deputies, Lyautey was unhappy and frustrated. The very unity that he thought he had been asked to give, and which he felt himself capable of giving to the war effort, became in his mind an impossibility under a new cabinet change. The change created separate ministries for transport and war materiel and included the appointment of Joffre as Commander-in-Chief and Technical Advisor to the Armed Forces. Lyautey was Minister of War, but General Headquarters planned offenses. Nivelle's plan, for instance, for the offensive between Soissons and Aulurive, was adopted without Lyautey's approval, even despite his objection. Jealous quarrels of prestige between the staffs of different armies injured the common good. Was the victory of the Marne due to Joffre and his command of the north and northeast army, or to Galliéni who had so brilliantly commandeered the taxicabs of Paris to rush up the necessary reinforcements?

With disunity in the French command, disunity in the Allied command, interference by Parliament, Lyautey was up against everything he despised most. He could see, simply by looking at the perfect discipline and clockwork precision of the German Army, the reforms needed to oppose it successfully; yet he lacked the power to enforce them. Only his patriotism, only his awareness that his resignation would increase the dangerous confusion kept him from abandoning his hopeless role.

The climax came on March 14th in the Chamber of Deputies. Lyautey had taken the podium to explain that, to a body as large as Parliament, the presentation for debate of certain technical information risked endangering the national defense. At the mention of Parliament, he was suddenly, rudely and belligerently heckled by members of the Left. With a rising fury, which neither the Right nor the President of the Assembly himself was able to quell, the attacks came like machine gun fire. What did the Minister of War mean? He wants to destroy Parliament! He disowns Parliament! Parliament has saved the country! Parliament cannot be insulted! Long live the Republic!

In desperation, President Deschanel dismissed the sitting. Lyautey resigned. Briand's cabinet fell. By the end of May, the ex-Minister of War was back in Morocco.

In the year and a half before the Armistice, Lyautey threw himself back with relief into his role of absolute monarch. Again he was free to exercise his military and administrative talents unhampered. Again he worked miracles in Morocco as he led it into the modern world.

In October of 1918, the American novelist Edith Wharton arrived at Lyautey's invitation to produce in book form a picture of Morocco under the Protectorate. These two, with the sensitive vision of artists, foresaw the attraction that this displaced fragment of the Arab East would have for tourists as soon as the war was over. A French *Guide Bleu* was in preparation, but Edith Wharton's enthusiastic and intelligent tribute, *In Morocco*, was the first comprehensive account of the country's astonishing economic progress, its physical beauty, and all that was, in her own words, "exquisite and venerable in Arabic art." She drove by car over Lyautey's first roads, from Rabat east to Fez and from Rabat south to Marrakesh. German prisoners had helped build them. She was among the first Europeans and probably the first American to see the Saadian tombs at the time the government had begun the repair of the mosque containing them.

"It is not only the novelty of its plan," she writes, "that makes this Saadian mausoleum singular among Moroccan monuments. The details of its ornament are of the most intricate refinement. . . . And the slant of sunlight on lustrous columns, the depth of fretted gold, the dusky ivory of the walls and the pure white of the cenotaphs so classic in spareness of ornament and simplicity of design. This subtle harmony of form and color gives to the dim rich chapel an air of dreamlike unreality."

In her tribute to Lyautey's miraculous accomplishments during two years of initial chaos and four years of European war, she explains it in his own words: "It was easy to do because I loved the people."

The Armistice of November, 1918, and the Treaty of Versailles in the following June brought about a certain easing of tension. Articles 141 to 146 of the Treaty concerned the Cherifian Empire and the liquidation of all German rights (mining rights especially), privileges and claims. But peace on the widespread fronts of Europe and the Middle East failed to bring peace along the rebellious fronts of Morocco's mountains and desert inlets. Lyautey's columns were active from the Djebala region of Ouezzan and the Rif region of the Ouergha River near the northern Spanish border to the southern oases of the Tafilalet and the Dadès and Dra Rivers.

The authority to keep German trouble-makers out of the Protectorate did not, unfortunately for France, extend to the Spanish Zone. There the short-sighted Spaniards made no attempt to check German activity— a mistake paid for tragically by the rocket-like rise to power of the Riffian leader Abd el Krim.

Mohammed ben Abd el Krim el Khatabi, born in 1882, was the son of the Caid of the Beni Ouarighel, a Riffian tribe of the mountainous territory between Alhucemas Bay and the Franco-Spanish frontier north of Taza. The father, a former agent of the German Mannesmann brothers in contraband weapon trade and holder of an interest in their mining activities, had given both his sons an unusual and modern education. The elder, the future independence leader, was graduated from the University of Kairouiine at Fez; the younger, who became his brother's commander-in-chief, studied mining engineering for three years in Madrid.

Until 1920, father and sons lived on good terms with Spain. The future "Wolf of the Rif" worked in the Bureau of Native Affairs in Melilla, taught Berber dialects to Spanish officers, and edited Arabic columns for the Spanish newspaper. In 1920 the wind changed. Spain ordered her army to push westward from Melilla to subdue the Zone that France had presented to her. Abd el Krim found himself in prison, perhaps because of seditious propaganda, perhaps because of a quarrel with a Spanish officer. Even Walter Harris, who knew him well, was not sure of the reason. Soon after his escape, the Spanish at Melilla established a military post as far west as Anual. From there they were advancing still farther into independent tribal territory. The Beni Ouarighel had declared a Holy War. The old Caid had been killed fighting the invader, and Abd el Krim, who had succeeded him, was proclaimed leader.

The seizure of and massacre at Anual, the fall of post after post, the panic of the Spanish retreat, the abandonment of endless supplies of military materiel, above all the total defeat of an army of twenty thousand European soldiers by two or three thousand mountain tribesmen turned the leader of the Beni Ouarighel into the hero of the Rif. Spain, in her humiliation, and with the hope of concealing the disgrace from England and the rest of Europe, clamped a rigid censorship on all news of the disaster. In a subsequent report to the Spanish parliament from a commission of inquiry, an incredible sink of corruption was revealed. Officers had grown rich on funds for feeding and outfitting their men; they had shirked their military posts for the cafés of Melilla; they had left lines of communication unguarded; they had raped Moorish women; they had sold their arms and ammunition to anyone who would pay for it. In short, through their greed, negligence and cowardice, their soldiers had been ill-fed, ill-clothed, untrained, unprotected, and uncared-for when sick and wounded.

And yet, even taking into consideration the miserable calibre of the Spanish army, Abd el Krim's achievement was tremendous. Nothing proved this more forcibly than the almost similar and astonishing destruction of the well-organized and incorruptible French line of outposts four years later.

On the subject of the French campaign, Walter Harris refers to letters from Abd el Krim, who wrote to his English friend saying that he had no desire to attack the French, that Spain was the enemy he wanted to drive out of Africa, and that all he demanded was the independence of the Rif. Harris thinks that if Abd el Krim had tried to talk peace with Lyautey (who desired it most eagerly) at Rabat, instead of with the military at the front, French bloodshed might have been avoided.

The trouble began in 1924 when the French moved across the Ouergha River sixty miles north of Fez to pacify and fortify the band of territory below the Rif Mountains. This ran parallel to their important Taza Corridor, with its east-west railroad and telegraph and telephone lines. Within its borders were tribes who furnished both men and taxes to Abd el Krim, counting in return on his protection.

In the spring of 1923 a dangerous gall bladder inflammation had brought Lyautey close to the point of death in Fez. The oulema and the imams of the mosques recited the prayer known as the *ia el atif*—uttered only at a time of great danger to Islam. He went to Paris for one operation, and had to return for a second one in the spring of 1924.

Lyautey was then seventy. Old age, illness and surgery had blunted the dynamic physical drive that had made him summon staff meetings at 3 A.M. and had taken him by car and horseback over every unmapped mountain ridge, into every tongue of desert sand dunes and rock-strewn hammada. He had created a country on the road to peace; he had interwoven the charm of medieval Islam with the wonders of modern progress. He was ready to hand over his beloved Morocco to his successor.

Ill health was not the only reason for Lyautey's decision not to return to Morocco. The May elections of 1924 had swept his old conservative friends out of the government. The *Cartel des Gauches*, a combination of Radicals and Socialists led by Herriot and Painlevé, had forced President Millerand's resignation. Lyautey's friendship with Millerand went back to 1912, when the latter, as Minister of War in Poincaré's cabinet, had chosen him for the Moroccan post. Of the new men in power, the sensitive scholar Herriot was a man Lyautey had been able to get on with, despite their opposing politics; he knew only too well that not only were the rest not his kind but that they felt he was not theirs.

Radicals and Socialists were not Lyautey's only enemies with power in Paris. From the very beginning, that combination of bankers, industrialists and colonials, the formidable *Comité du Moroc*, and their colleagues had resented this first Resident-General, because he fiercely protected his wards from their colonial greed. They resented among his policies his keeping the French as much as possible out of the administration and preventing them from exploiting for their own private interests a valuable phosphate find. They had thwarted him, however, in the business of seizing rich agricultural land. By 1924 they had begun to be well established in their flourishing orange orchards, vineyards and grainfields. Now they were looking for a new Resident-General who would put their interests before those of *"les sales indigènes."*

On his arrival in Rabat, to pack his possessions and return to France for a well earned and restful old age, Lyautey found a situation threatening to destroy all the peace and order for which he had worked so long and so hard. Abd el Krim had suddenly become as dangerous a menace to France as he had been to Spain. In Spain, the new dictator, Primo de

Rivera, had abandoned all defense of the interior and had withdrawn his troops to the coastal ports. For Spain this was a wise move. For France it was disastrous. Excited by their triumphs, the Riffians appeared, poised to strike along the southern edge of their mountains. When Lyautey reported the danger of the situation to Paris by wire, he was again, in the eyes of both friend and enemy, the indispensable man of the hour. Paris begged him to save the situation by staying.

As usual, the patriotic soldier put the welfare of his country and Morocco before his own desires. He might have been saved much of the fighting and many of the losses of the following spring, if France had sent him the reinforcements he had so urgently requested in December. On a two-hundred-mile front, exalted by Abd el Krim's promise of independence, by the joy of fighting for its own sake, by the age-old zeal of repelling the Christian invaders, the Riffians struck within ten and twenty miles of Rabat, Fez, and Taza. As the advance French posts above the Ouergha either fell or were blown up by heroic garrisons, only a few remained to defend the cities.

Abd el Krim had all the advantages of modern mechanized warfare, plus the skillful guerilla skirmishing of mountain tribesmen. Telephone lines connected his headquarters at Targuist near the Mediterranean to his front lines fifty miles to the south. Cannon, machine guns, modern rifles and hand grenades—mostly Spanish loot, partly German contraband— were handled more skillfully by Abd el Krim's army of tribesmen than by the untrained Spanish soldiers who died at their hands. Perhaps part of the blame attaching to the Paris government in failing to send the reinforcements requested by Lyautey lay in its natural inability to conceive of Riffian tribesmen, no matter how enormous their numbers, as a menace to the great tried armies of France.

In the end the belated reinforcements turned the day, but only with the help of another Western power. Spain alone had been no match for the "Wolf of the Rif." France alone was no match for him. Only after the two European countries combined their forces of three marshals, forty generals and armies of almost half a million men, and then thanks only to ultra-modern weapons of destruction which the Riffian leader lacked— the tank and the airplane—were they able to bring about his surrender.

The day on which Abd el Krim had agreed to give himself up to the French was May 27th, 1926. Preliminary negotiations had ensured protection for himself and his family. When he rode into the French camp at sunrise, he found a regiment of infantry drawn up to pay him military honor. The trumpets sounded and the tricolor dipped its salute. Toward the end of the summer he began an exile of thirty-seven years to the tropical island of Réunion, off the East African coast.

A reader interested in Morocco owes a great debt to Walter Harris for

222

his account of the country from the reign of Moulay Hassan through the pseudo-reign of Moulay Youssef. However, Harris's summation of Abd el Krim's crusade for freedom, even without the hindsight of history, seems extraordinarily undiscerning, not only in its analysis of Moorish character but in its failure to perceive the stirrings of nationalism born of World War I, and the awakening of the Arab world.

"His departure," Harris wrote, "left the Moors indifferent. In a country where everything is considered as directly ordained by God a fall from power means a fall from memory. The man whose, name had only a few months before been well known, who had played so important a part in the recent history of Morocco, passed into exile and oblivion."

On the contrary! Abd el Krim, Sultan of the Rif, became the flame that kindled the Istiqlal, the Islah, and every splinter group that met exile, prison and death in the struggle for Moroccan independence. Shortly before he died in Cairo in 1963 at the age of eighty-one, Abd el Krim spoke of returning to his native land to work for a federation of the North African countries. Abd el Krim did *not* "pass into oblivion," and he never will in the future history of the Moghreb.

In the final surrender of Abd el Krim, Lyautey had played no part. He had resigned for the last time in September of 1925, when the Riffian war, though not ended, was safely under control. He had expected the worst from the Painlevé government and, according to his outraged admirers, received it. In the previous summer when the situation was critical, with the enemy burning villages only twenty miles from Fez, Painlevé had visited the front. On his return to Paris, he had relieved Lyautey of the military operations through the appointment of General Naulin as commander-in-chief.

As the situation grew worse, Marshal Pétain had been sent to inspect the front. Pétain's report gave France the first frank admission of the power of the enemy and the blows that it had inflicted. On August 18th, without preliminary explanation, Lyautey received the brusque order to hand over the supreme command to Marshal Pétain. For a month Lyautey endured this humiliation with the self-control of the disciplined soldier. On September 24th he handed in his resignation. A month of subservience to a stranger, in the empire he himself had created and saved for France during the war years, was not a happy ending to the thirteen years of absolute rule. Like all men of character and greatness, Lyautey had enemies; but he did not deserve to return to France with no official reception committee on the pier at Marseilles and nothing to welcome him in Paris except a notice to settle a small unpaid tax.

CHAPTER XVIII

ΕΛΣΕΛΣΕΛΣΕ
ΕΛΣΕΛΣΕΛΣΕ

DREAMS OF INDEPENDENCE
(Mohammed V, 1927–1943)

ΕΛΣΕΛΣΕΛΣΕ
ΕΛΣΕΛΣΕΛΣΕ

The Morocco of the late twenties and the thirties became the tourists' paradise, a dream given reality by its first and greatest Resident-General. Travelers who crossed the Atlantic on the French Line in those days will remember how they were cunningly lured to Morocco and points east by the enchanting watercolor sketches of Jules Sandoz decorating the menus at every meal. Sea-green minarets, black tents against yellow dunes, red walls, horseshoe gates, snake charmers and biblical figures in hooded cloaks were irresistible in their appeal.

When the travelers reached Paris, the pressure grew. There were huge posters, advertisements of North African tours, and free motion pictures in the French Line office. And because this was before the day when the airplane could take one to Baghdad or Timbuctu as easily as to Paris or Rome, it seemed wonderful to be able to reach such a glamorous corner of the Arab world in less than twenty-four hours by boat from Marseilles or in only three from Algeciras.

In Morocco the tourists learned to call the French Line the "Transat" (the abbreviation for *Compagnie Générale Transatlantique*) as they rolled across Lyautey's roads in luxurious "Transat" buses and stayed at unforgettable "Transat" hotels—the Palais Jamai in Fez, the Mamounia in Marrakesh, and all the others, smaller perhaps but each with its own charm, wrapping the Westerner in a luxury that isolated him from every thing but the romance and picturesqueness of this "Forbidden Land." They saw Morocco as a magnificent barbaric spectacle staged, act by act, by the clever French for their delight: the Sultan in Rabat in his golden coach driving to the Friday prayer and returning on a stallion under the green umbrella; the story-tellers and the snake charmers of the Djemaa el Fna in Marrakesh; the galloping powder play of the Berber tribesmen; the frenzied blood-stained Aissoua, devouring crushed glass and cactus thorns at the Meknès gathering of their Brotherhood. They saw Morocco as a world unrelated in either time or space to their own and looked at the people through the viewers of their cameras as if a gulf as deep as the Straits of Gibraltar separated them and this Berber-Arab branch of humanity.

It would undoubtedly have surprised the tourists to learn that in these cities that seemed to them pure "Arabian Nights" there were educated young Moroccans touched indirectly by all the post-war stirrings of a nationalism inspired in great part by Woodrow Wilson's "Fourteen Points." By 1926, a handpicked few in a new generation of students had profited by the first of Lyautey's secondary schools. When Lyautey arrived in 1912, boys aged six began their education, as in the past, in their own Koranic schools, where they learned to read, to write and to memorize endless pages of the Prophet's revelations—sometimes the entire 114 *Sura,* or chapters. For the Arab, with his unusually retentive memory, both inherited and trained, this was not so difficult as it may sound. (Arab universities offer courses in the science of mnemonics.)

The clever students, the sons of notables, and others who could afford it moved on from their primitive classrooms of teacher, switch and blackboard into Protectorate schools founded to instill the French language and civilization into a small group of potential civil servants. In this atmosphere they were introduced to the great evolutionary and revolutionary history of France, the enlightened philosophic thought of the eighteenth century, and the Declaration of Human Rights. They met the words *"Liberté, Égalité et Fraternité."* Their keen and receptive minds stored the ideas of the West side by side with the traditions of Islam. Some of them moved on from this French schooling to the universities of Paris—young eighteen-year-old Ahmed Balafrej to the Sorbonne, Ben Hassan Ouazzani to the École Libre des Sciences Politiques. There they and their friends took part in forming an "association of North African Moslem Students." For them Paris became a treasured and second spiritual home.

When Abd el Krim surrendered to the French in May, 1926, the two most important of the young Moroccans who first started their country on the road to freedom and independence were eighteen years old—Ahmed Balafrej, founder of a group in Rabat, and Allal el Fassi, founder of a similar student group in Fez. During the five years of the Riffian War, the Moroccan air had been electric with the hope of freedom from foreign rule. Thanks to the close bond between Islamic countries, every struggle of the Middle East from Egypt to Turkey was being watched with avid interest along North African shores. The overthrow of the Ottoman Empire would be worth very little in Arab eyes if it meant only the substitution of rule by European powers.

Saad Zaghlul, founder of the Egyptian *Wafd* (Freedom Movement), with his success in 1923 became a hero in Moroccan eyes only second to Abd el Krim. His speeches, recited from memory by Moroccan disciples, were revered by Rabat listeners. A frequent visitor from his Geneva exile to the northern Spanish Zone was Chekib Arslan, the Syrian Druse converted to Islam, and leader of the Pan-Arab Movement with an influence that lasted until his Axis support in 1936. In Turkey, the sweeping reforms of Kemal Ataturk brought about mixed reactions in a country as profoundly pious as the Cherifian Empire. Later the young Moroccans would be sharply divided among their own ranks on the issue of discarding so much that was basic to Islam—the veiling of women, the brimless fez in which the forehead could meet the ground in prayer, the Arab characters in which the Koran had been preserved for posterity, and the Sultan as the spiritual head of Islam and Caliph of the Prophet.

Though not the exact wording, the spirit of Wilson's "Fourteen Points" swept like a sweet rush of fresh air through the oppressed colonial world. Almost twenty-five years later, the Roosevelt-Churchill Atlantic Charter raised the same hopes. Point Five of the Fourteen stated: "A free, open-minded and absolutely impartial adjustment of all colonial claims, based upon a strict observance of the principle that in determining all such questions of sovereignty *the interests of the populations concerned must have equal weight* with the equitable claims of the Government whose title is to be determined."

Point Twelve: ". . . Nationalities now under Turkish rule should be assured an undoubted security of life and *an absolutely unmolested opportunity of autonomous development.*"

And Point Fourteen—the one that especially gave birth to high hopes —"A general association of nations must be formed under specific covenants for the purpose of affording mutual guarantees of political independence and territorial integrity to great and small states alike."

When Lyautey left Morocco in October, 1925, he was succeeded by Theodore Steeg. The actions of Steeg, a former member of the Algerian administration, swept all the Lyautey ideals under the carpet. The friendly rapport between the Resident-General and the Moroccans ceased to exist. Sultan and viziers were brusquely informed of legislation and decisions. Lyautey had started to train Moroccans to administer their country. Steeg's officials were French from the highest to the lowest ranks. The word "colony" buried the word "protectorate."

Meanwhile the crushing of dissident tribes continued in localized warfare for another eight years—warfare as tragic for its victims as a larger-scale conflict.

The small student group, both pious and patriotic, under the leadership of Ahmed Balafrej, was stirred to dreams not only of a Morocco as independent as Egypt but of a Morocco dedicated to a return to the pure source of Islam cleansed of all defilement. It dated its beginning in Rabat during August of 1926, the same month in which its hero, Abd el Krim, began his thirty-nine-year exile. Its members called themselves the "Supporters of Truth." A second name with patriotic overtones, to be kept secret from the French, was the "Moroccan League."

There had always been, as we have seen, through a thousand years of Moroccan history, a gulf of antagonism between the Arab Moslem of the orthodox Malikite rite with its literal interpretation of the Koran and the Berbers of the Brotherhoods to whom the worship of saints, the mysticism of the Persian Sufists and, especially, their own ancient animistic beliefs in trees and stones and springs were more appealing than the rigid monotheism of Islam.

These heresies alone were bad enough in the eyes of the young reformers, but when certain leaders of the Brotherhoods took it upon themselves to support the French rulers in their "pacification" and became informers to French police, the impulse to opposition grew into action.

Abd el Hai el Kittani, an *alim* ("professor"—singular of the word *oulema*) at Kairouiine University and head of the Kittaniya, one of the politically most important Brotherhoods, became the principal target of the young patriots. Among his students was a well-born young poet and scholar by the name of Allal el Fassi. Jean Lacouture describes him as having eyes as "blue as a Fez sky." These eyes blazed with outrage at El Kittani's double role of infamy—perverter of the orthodox faith and accomplice of the French police. In Fez, El Fassi became the *zaim* or leader of a group named the "Students' Union," out to destroy the power and influence of the crafty old Kittani. Down through the long struggle for independence, whether in jail or in exile, and afterward during the first years of freedom, only the King himself had more baraka, more magic, over the people than El Fassi.

English has, as noted earlier, no equivalent for the elusive Arabic word *baraka*. Douglas Ashford, in his scholarly analysis of Moroccan independence through the eyes of a political scientist, comes as near to it as possible with the theological expression "charismatic." Χαρισμα is the Greek word for gift—in this sense a special divine or spiritual gift, a grace. "In Morocco," Ashford says, "charismatic relationships are found between the King, and to a lesser extent, the leader of the Istiqlal, Allal el Fassi, and the populace. Such a relationship enables one of the actors in a situation to establish moral imperatives for some part of the behaviour of another actor or other actors."

In the spring following Abd el Krim's exile, the two groups, learning of each other's existence and finding that they shared the same zeal for religious and political reform, merged into "The Moroccan League." Soon afterward, a northern group was established at Tetuán in the Spanish Zone. In French Morocco the magnetic El Fassi kept the distinction of zaim; the brilliant but reserved Balafrej played a less flamboyant but equally powerful role. (In 1961 King Hassan II appointed Allal el Fassi to head the committee for drawing up the eagerly awaited constitution; as of March, 1964, Ahmed Balafrej holds the post of representative of the King, with rank of minister.)

In the beginning, the meetings of the Moroccan League, except when their offices were raided and closed down by Residency orders, were held alternately in Rabat and Fez. During the first decade and a half after their merger, the political reforms that the young nationalists considered themselves justified in claiming fell well within the provisions of the Protectorate Treaty—provisions as familiar to them as the Bill of Rights and its amendments are to our American Negroes. In 1943, however, after the Allied Forces had landed on the Moroccan coast, after Franklin D. Roosevelt had invited their young Sultan and his thirteen-year-old son to dinner during the Casablanca Conference, they enlarged their demands and changed their name. From January, 1944, on they were *El Hisb el Istiqlal*, the Party of Independence.

Two years after Lyautey's resignation, the gentle and submissive Sultan whom he had chosen so wisely for his purposes died. It was up to Theodore Steeg to choose a successor—or rather to announce his choice to the oulema of Fez, who in their turn would announce it with all due pomp to the people as if it had been their own.

Steeg must have thought he was choosing as wisely as, if not more so than Lyautey had done, when he decided on a boy of only eighteen, Moulay Mohammed, third son of Moulay Youssef. How easy it would be to carry out the farce of advisor to the Sultan when the Sultan was such a timid, fragile-looking youth. How easy to fashion him into the decorative but harmless figurehead as Mohammed V, to parade before the Moroccans who honored any and all Cherifian blood, as well as before the spellbound tourists.

The young nationalists saw him in a different light. This young Sidi Mohammed, not an "Old Turban" but a boy close to their own age, son of a pious father, educated by his wise old palace tutor, Si Mammeri, now both Sultan of the Cherifian Empire and spiritual head of its religion, might some day share their dreams for a new Morocco and acquire the power to make the dreams come true.

A year after the young Sultan's accession to the throne, a school for members of the Royal Family was founded in Fez. From brothers and cousins, news of student life and activities gave the lonely young Sultan his first knowledge of the force that later shaped his life.

In 1930, when Sidi Mohammed was barely twenty, he innocently affixed the royal seal to a *dahir* ("decree") presented to him by the new Resident-General, Lucien Saint. This decree not only outraged the orthodox Moslems but also focused the eyes of the Arab world on French interference with Islamic traditions in Morocco.

To understand why the historic "Berber Dahir," as it came to be called, made such a stir both at home and abroad, one must remember that the *chraa*, or Islamic law, is based on the Koran and the Hadith, or Traditions of the Prophet, and administered in the name of the Sultan by his representatives—pashas in the cities and caids in the bled. Side by side with the chraa, there was also among the Berber tribes a so-called "customary law" of native pagan origin and secondary importance, dealt out by the djemaas, or village councils.

By the "Berber Dahir," the French transferred the judicial powers of caids and pashas to the village councils, and for criminal cases established their own courts. The geographical region, no longer administered by Koranic law and now under the "Berber Dahir," ran south of Fez and Meknès to the Sahara, and from Rabat east to the Algerian border. The curtailment of the Sultan's prerogatives and the splitting of the country into sections—Arab and Berber—with different legal systems, was immediately recognized by the nationalists and others as the insidious policy of the "Berber Bloc." This was the ancient policy of "divide and rule": a policy singling out the Berber for special favoritism and building him in power to neutralize the Arab. Without doubt the Berber, with his Mediterranean background and thin veneer of Islam, was far more sympathetic to the French than the Semitic Arab with his Eastern blood and rigid faith. There were even fears among the Arab Moslems that the French had plans for converting the Berbers to Christianity.

Thanks to the propaganda of Chekib Arslan, the exiled Syrian Pan-Arabic leader in Geneva, with his review *La nation arabe* and his Middle Eastern disciples, news of this affront to Koranic law spread to every land of the Middle and Far East, where the words of the Prophet were the laws men lived by. Rom Landau says that, when he talked twenty years later to Moslem delegates to the United Nations from Eastern countries, they told him that it was through the reports of the "Berber Dahir" that they were first aware of a "Moroccan problem."

In addition to gaining the sympathy of the Moslem East, this decree brought French Socialist support to the Moroccan nationalists and encouragement for their national review, *El Moghreb,* published in Paris and smuggled into their own country.

Before 1933 the worst interference the nationalists had met at French hands was the arrest of one of their members for founding and conducting a free nationalist school. That arrest resulted from information fed to the French by the enemy of the nationalists, the head of the Kittani Brotherhood. By 1933, however, the French had themselves become aware of nationalist activity and of Chekib Arslan's effective propaganda throughout the Arab countries of the Middle East. When the association of Moslem students, founded in Paris with the help of Ahmed Balafrej, planned to have its third congress take place in Rabat, the French forbade the meeting. Their hands were full enough with the last bitter struggles of dissident tribes in the Tafilalet and south of the Atlas, without risking defiance from hot-headed young patriots who had the impudence to object to their alliance with the Berber Brotherhoods and otherwise criticize their administration. In this same year they also forbade meetings of the student alumni of the colleges of Rabat, Fez, Marrakesh and Casablanca, and removed Allal el Fassi as a lecturer from the University of Kairouiine.

In 1934, twenty-seven years after Lyautey crossed the Algerian border to occupy Oudjda in revenge for the murder of Dr. Mauchamps in Marrakesh, and General d'Amade had taken over the Chaouia region after the port murders at Casablanca, the French could at last say that Morocco was "pacified." The last regions to hold out were the Saharan fringes below the Anti-Atlas. When the final resistance died away and all was peaceful south of the river Dra, Spain promptly claimed her enclave of Ifni, which she had considered hers since the Treaty of 1860, but had never been daring enough to attempt to seize from the fierce Requibat and Ait ou Amran tribesmen.

Lacouture suggests that the word "order" is more just and fitting than the word "peace." Order there was indeed. The central government or *Maghzen* under French administration had perfect control over city and bled. The economy flourished. Tourism was at its height. The rate of crime in comparison to that of many countries north of the Mediterranean was low.*

Order, instead of peace, then, was what French arms and administration had brought to Morocco by the end of 1934. Peace, Lacouture justly

* For the security of the streets at night, I can vouch personally. During the summer of 1931 I had rented a house between the walls of "Old Fez." As a result of the hospitality of my Arab friends, I returned to it late many nights after feasts and other entertainments. The only time I was ever uneasy was on one black moonless night when an Arab with a candle turned into the *cul de sac* where I was trying to unlock my door. When I discovered his only object was to help me find the keyhole by the light of his candle—I was deeply ashamed of my sudden unjustified terror.

claims, implies respect for civil liberties and equal treatment for all citizens, and does not include arbitrary subjection to imprisonment and exile and a lack of freedom to circulate throughout the country.

In the same year that the last dissident chief laid down his arms, Marshal Lyautey died in France at the age of eighty. At his own request, he lies buried in Rabat, the Moroccan capital that was his own creation. His tomb stands close to the *Chella,* the mausoleum of the Merinid Sultans. The inscription cut there is in his own words:

HERE LIES
LOUIS HUBERT GONZALVE LYAUTEY
WHO WAS THE FIRST RESIDENT-GENERAL OF FRANCE IN MOROCCO
1912–1925
HE DIED IN THE CATHOLIC RELIGION
WITH FAITH
PROFOUNDLY RESPECTFUL OF THE ANCIENT TRADITIONS
AND OF THE MOSLEM RELIGION
PRESERVED AND PRACTICED BY THE PEOPLE OF THE MOGHREB
AMONGST WHOM HE HAS DESIRED TO REST IN THIS LAND
WHICH HE LOVED SO WELL
MAY GOD KEEP HIS SOUL IN ETERNAL PEACE

The young Sultan Mohammed ben Youssef—son of the Youssef whom Lyautey had chosen to "protect"—had, during rare visits to France, become his friend, with their last meeting a few months before the Marshal's death. One wonders whether they discussed the subject of nationalism. As far back as 1920, when El Fassi and Balafrej were still boys of twelve and the Sultan was nine, Lyautey wrote:

> It would be an absolute illusion to believe that the Moroccans are not aware of the exclusion from public affairs in which they are kept. They discuss it and suffer from it. A youthful element is developing among them which feels alive and eager for action, which has a zest for education and public affairs. For want of outlets so sparingly provided by our administration and of such inferior quality, it will find its path elsewhere . . .

By the age of twenty-four, the quiet boy chosen as window dressing by General Steeg had aroused the affections of his people. On a visit to Fez he received such huge ovations from the crowd that the worried French canceled his ceremonial Friday visit to the mosque and hurried him back to Rabat. To the displeasure of both the nationalists and the French, the disappointed crowd showed its resentment by rioting. From the very beginning, the nationalist leaders had held themselves averse to violence and bloodshed.

In their hope of gaining less interference in their country's affairs by reasonable and peaceful action, the leaders drew up a Plan of Reforms, which they presented as a petition to the Sultan, the Resident-General and

French Premier Laval. Nothing in the Plan of Reforms made demands on France incompatible with her role of protector and advisor. Among the complaints were the exclusion of Moroccans from the administration, the appointment of tribal caids and city pashas to carry out French policies, and unjust fiscal measures. Their demands included Moslems as state employees, more and better schools, protection for peasants against the unfair appropriation of land, liberty of the press, abolition of travel restriction, and protection of native artisans from an influx of European machine-made goods.

The Resident-General tossed the petition to the winds as "a good thesis for a Ph.D.," but the angry young men submitted a second one, two years later. By this time there was another grievance. French *colons* were demanding representation in the municipal councils as if they had never read or heard of the Protectorate Treaty guaranteeing Morocco's status as a sovereign state. A bitter discussion on the subject between El Fassi and the unpopular Resident-General Peyrouton would have led to trouble for the nationalists had it not been for the sudden coming into power of the Popular Front in Paris.

Leon Blum's ministry, with its Socialist, Radical Socialist and Communist support and its spirit of anti-colonialism and social reform, brought hope to the Moroccan nationalists for their own Plan of Reforms. Through the friendly interest in their problem and in their *Paris Revue* shown since the Berber Dahir by Paul Vienot, Under Secretary of State for Foreign Affairs, and others, they expected help, only to meet disappointment in the Popular Front's choice of their next Resident-General.

Though General Charles Noguès had served with admiration under Lyautey and from the beginning showed a warm personal friendship for the young Sultan, which the present King Hassan still remembers gratefully, his relations with the nationalists inaugurated the long series of imprisonments and exiles aimed to crush the movement.

The clever French, sons of their own revolution, were not so clever as one would have expected them to be in crushing a movement such as Moroccan nationalism. Whenever their repressive measures—the curtailment of a Sultan's visit to Fez, the outlawing of a student congress or a scheduled nationalist meeting—brought about demonstrations from the public, they seemed to think that throwing nationalist leaders into jail or exiling them to Gabon near the Equator would end the menace. But for every head that was lopped off, their monster grew a hundred new ones. In little more than two decades from the time of their first demands, its power and size and the offspring it had spawned had forced them out of the country.

The first punishments of General Noguès were mild—a month in jail for El Fassi and two other leaders. These were followed by a sudden

policy of apparent conciliation—permission to republish nationalist newspapers provided *French* editors censored the contents, permission for Europeans to organize Moroccan trade unions, which Moroccans were permitted to join though not permitted to organize on their own.

Among the most fertile regions of Morocco is the region surrounding Meknès, watered by the Bou Ferkane River and other tributaries of
the great Sebou. The colonials spread out their giant farms over what had
been the small holdings of the native tribesmen. Behind modern tractors,
ploughs cut deep into the fertile soil, and harrows smoothed out the clods.
When the vineyards, citrus orchards, almond groves and vegetable gardens
started bearing, the pioneering owners made fine profits, especially because
the land had come into *colon* hands through the administration at token
cost, and because abundant labor was available at a price that no self-
respecting peasant north of the Mediterranean would have considered.

In the wet winters the cultivated soil stayed moist; but in the sum-
mers, without irrigation, much of it would have blown away as dust.
Trouble came in the summer of 1937 when a small group of high-handed
French *colons* persuaded French officials to direct water from the Bou
Ferkane River to increase the irrigation of their farms. A stormy protest arose from the Moroccan losers. Five hundred angry objectors stormed
into Rabat. The crowds sympathized, closed their shops and went to the
mosques to pray for them.

When five of the five hundred were arrested, demonstration spread
throughout the countryside—thought by the French to have been fomented
by the Istiqlal. No one punished the French officials who had illegally rear-
ranged the waters of the river, or the French *colons* who had instigated
the theft. General Noguès sent Allal el Fassi to Gabon in Equatorial Africa,
where he remained for nine years; Balafrej to Corsica; and a third idol
of the masses, Mohammed ben Hassan Ouezzani, founder of the Democratic party, also out of the country for nine years. Later, in 1943, when
Morocco was cleared of the Vichy French, even de Gaulle felt easier keeping El Fassi in his distant exile.

The arbitrary line between French and Spanish Morocco, dividing
a homogeneous people ruled by two different European powers, brought
with all its disadvantages one definite benefit to Morocco during her struggle for independence. With the beginning of the Spanish Civil War in 1936,
Franco had two reasons for making concessions and holding out promises
of future benefits to the nationalists of the northern zone. In the first place,
before the war ended in March, 1939, he had 135,000 Moorish troops
fighting for him; in the second place, he was only too happy to hinder
and irritate his enemy, the Popular Front Socialist government of France.
As a result, the Spanish Zone with its capital, Tetuán, became a refuge
for French Zone nationalists threatened with prison, as well as head-

quarters for two northern nationalist groups with permission to print their Arab newspapers. It is, therefore, not surprising to find a nationalist leader like Abdel Halq Torres (the Allal el Fassi of the north) installed as Minister of Education in the administration of the Spanish Zone. During the disturbance following the Berber Dahir, the Pan-Arab leader Chekib el Arslan had visited the capital. Safe from the French who would never have let him cross their border, he had made contacts with El Fassi and other leaders of the southern zone.

Despite the age-old enmity between Spaniard and Moor, or perhaps because of it, if Dali's "Love equals hate" theory of their relationship is right, the association of Moroccans and resident Spaniards in the north was a much pleasanter one than that existing between Moroccans and French in the south. In the French Zone, the French were the prosperous top dogs, and for the most part looked down their noses upon the *sales indigènes*. In the rugged unproductive North, the resident Spaniards were largely of simple background and often as poor as the poor Moroccans around them. The difference between the two religions was not enough to keep the two peoples, whose blood had mixed throughout so many centuries, from sitting together in cafés. As the Moroccan struggle for independence grew steadily in intensity until it finally burst out into organized war, the Spanish Zone became more and more valuable as refuge, headquarters and training center for the future Army of the Liberation.

How to drape the *ksa*, shown in steps from the left: one end is fixed in the girdle and the *ksa* is thrown over the left shoulder, drawn down front, then draped over the head, forming a large loop. The loop is folded back on the left shoulder. The material remaining is brought over the left shoulder in the same way. The garment's front flap has been carefully rolled waist-high. The flap hanging right, the top of which is held under the chin, has been fittingly pleated, placed on the right arm and then thrown back over the left shoulder. The last picture shows the pleated flap, with the whole of the draping slung over the shoulder. / *Moroccan Government*

From the time of El Fassi's Gabon exile in the fall of 1937 to the declaration of World War II on September 3, 1939, nationalist figures of the French Zone who had escaped the prolonged exile of the zaim moved in and out of prison and in and out of the country. Offices were opened and forcibly closed, newspapers published and outlawed.

With the declaration of war, the Sultan promised his loyalty and offered the resources of his country to General Noguès and France. These are the Sultan's words as quoted by Rom Landau: "From today and until such time as the efforts of France and the Allies are crowned with victory we must render her every help without reserve. We will not stint any of our resources and will not hesitate before any sacrifice." Rom Landau adds, "France was thereby immediately at liberty to send twenty thousand Moroccan troops into battle." Following the Sultan's example, the nationalists pledged their own loyalty and that of the youth of Morocco. Even when France fell in 1940, neither Sultan nor nationalists took advantage of her weakness.

Among six resident-generals, Noguès was the first to show Mohammed ben Youssef such attentions as daily visits to the hospital when, at one time, the Sultan lay ill for ten weeks; yet the first Cherifian defiance was recorded on the occasion when General Noguès commanded the Sultan to enforce the Nuremberg anti-Jewish regulations upon the Jews of Morocco.

"My Jewish subjects are as much under my protection as the Moslems," the Sultan answered as he refused to obey. Furthermore, because Morocco had declared war on Germany and had taken no part in the Vichy armistice, the Sultan refused all contacts with the German Commission established in his country.

November 7, 1942. The last glimmer of sunset along the Atlantic coast of Morocco. Then winter darkness. With it a senseless command over the air from the London B.B.C.

"Roger arrive. Roger arrive."

To the listening Germans and the Vichy French it might have been some *avant garde* poem of the B.B.C.'s Third Programme; but to a small excited group of Americans in Morocco and to the French in their confidence it was as significant as the number of lanterns hung in Boston's North Church tower "on the eighteenth of April, in Seventy-five." It meant that the colossal Anglo-American invasion forces with 850 ships under General Dwight D. Eisenhower were standing off the Moroccan and Algerian shores in the blackness of night to disembark troops at 0400 before the sunrise of D-Day.

At three chosen points along Morocco's Atlantic coast, three task forces of "Operation Torch" under General Patton began their forced and dangerous landings under cover of darkness. In the meanwhile, two

Vice-Consuls from the United States Consulate at Casablanca drove to Rabat with identical letters from President Roosevelt for the Sultan and the Resident-General. Without hesitation, Mohammed ben Youssef promised his support to the Allies, while his master, General Noguès, loyal to Pétain's Vichy government, ordered French guns turned on the landing Americans.

Of the three landing points, Safi, Fedhala, fifteen miles northeast of Casablanca, and Port Lyautey near Rabat, Safi with its medieval Portuguese fort fell most easily to the invaders. At Safi it was planned to land medium tanks to help in taking the invaluable port of Casablanca. Heavy resistance at both Casablanca and Port Lyautey continued until late into the night of November 10, but by afternoon of that day the seventy-six P-40s from the carrier "Chenango" were using Port Lyautey's battle-scarred airfield.

Then, at last, the Vichy government, finding that Allied strength was too great, ordered an end to the resistance.

On November 11, General Patton received General Noguès and Admiral Michelier with a guard of honor at his headquarters in the Hotel Miramar at Fedhala. With a welcome of great dignity and compliments to General Noguès on his defenses, he read the terms of the preliminary armistice.

"One more requirement," he demanded after its acceptance by an informal gentleman's agreement. Their sudden anxiety was quickly dispelled. "A toast to the liberation of France by the joint defeat of the common enemy!"

Through the success of the Moroccan landings in Casablanca, the Allies had won a magnificent port for unloading supplies for the eastern campaign, and in Port Lyautey both an air base for their P-40s and a sea base to control German submarines.

It was a bitter disappointment to the Moroccans and all anti-Vichyites to learn that General Noguès and his colleagues were not to be instantly removed. In the opinion of General Patton, because General Noguès was experienced in the rule and control of Morocco, it would be better to keep him on as resident-general, despite his first resistance, than to turn the country over to some pro-Ally novice. As a result, though Morocco continued to send her troops to fight and be killed for Free France and her Allies, she received no reward or recognition for her sacrifices.

Two months after the French were congratulating themselves on their successful prevention of contacts between the Moroccans and the American forces stationed in the coastal cities (thereby avoiding the spread of any such highly contagious ideas as freedom, anti-colonialism and democracy), they received a nasty shock. On January 22, President Roosevelt, in Morocco for the famous Casablanca Conference with Churchill and the Allied High Command, invited the Moroccan Sultan and his thirteen-

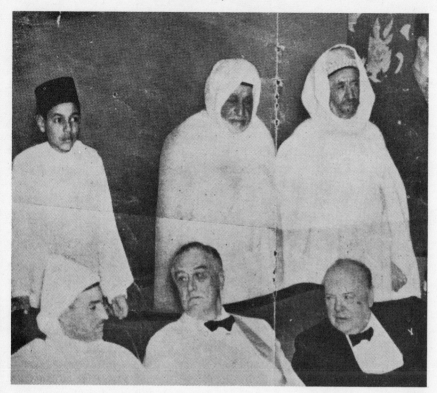

The fateful meeting at Casablanca of Mohammed V, Roosevelt and Churchill./
Moroccan Government

year-old son Hassan to dinner. Such an event had never been permitted
before, and would not then have been permitted if the Residency had
dared to antagonize the President of the United States by forbidding it.

Sidi Mohammed accepted with delight. The other guests were Churchill,
Harry Hopkins, Elliott Roosevelt, and the Sultan's Grand Vizir and Chief
of Protocol—the two last, like their sovereign, in flowing white silk robes—
and General Noguès. In deference to Moslem law, no cocktails, no wine,
no brandy accompanied the dinner. Churchill sulked. Elliott Roosevelt in
his *As He Saw It* gives a vivid and amusing account of the Prime Minister, annoyed not only at the lack of liquor and at the use of French,
which was not his strongest language, but also and above all at the anti-
colonial tenor of the conversation—paraphrased and condensed as follows:

In discussing the natural resources of Morocco, the President ad-
vises keeping the wealth within the country.

The P.M. grunts.

"Don't let outside interests obtain concessions," the President warns.

The P.M. tries to change the subject.

237

The Sultan asks for advice in dealing with the French government. The President assures him that the post-war colonial question will differ sharply from its pre-war state.

The P.M. tries to change the subject.

The President makes uncomplimentary remarks about French and British financiers' combining into syndicates to dredge riches out of colonies.

When the P.M. coughs, shifts in his chair, finally tries not to listen, the President continues with his subversive suggestions. "Train scientists and engineers in American universities. Engage United States firms on a fee or percentage basis to develop your country's mineral wealth, thereby keeping control over it and eventually taking it over."

For the Sultan, the dinner became a landmark. From it he drew a stiffening of resistance to all that he knew was unjust and illegal in the distortion of the Protectorate Treaty.

Later, commenting on the colonial question, the President told his son Elliott that de Gaulle expected the Allies to return all colonies after the War. "But," the President said to his son, "I am by no means sure that we'd be right to give back France her colonies at all, ever, without first obtaining in the case of each individual colony some sort of pledge, some sort of statement of just what was planned."

And still on the same subject: "When we've won this war I will work with all my might to see to it that the United States is not wheedled into the position of accepting any plan that will further France's imperialisic ambitions or that will aid and abet the British Empire in its imperialistic ambitions."

Is it any wonder that the French tried to keep Moroccans from talking with Americans!

 క0§కి0§కి0§కి

RESISTANCE AND SACRIFICE
(Mohammed V, 1944–1955)

క0§కి0§కి0§కి

Gabriel Puaux, the new resident-general replacing General Noguès in March, 1943, was, in the words of Edmund Stevens, "high-handed and pig-headed." Stevens, Rome correspondent for the *Christian Science Monitor* at the time he wrote *North African Powder Keg,* paints the black roles played by Puaux as high commissioner in Syria and Lebanon, where he dissolved parliaments and suppressed constitutions, and in Tunisia as resident-general, where he removed the Bey. Few French officials from Damascus to Tangier were more thoroughly hated by the Moslem world.

For the Moroccans, all the high hopes of 1943 had faded as the year reached its end—hopes of help from President Roosevelt and the United States, hopes based on the promises of the Atlantic Charter, hopes that the Free French might share their freedom with the country that was helping them win it. But de Gaulle, ruling from London, sent them Puaux; and, again, they saw their sanctioned sovereign state going the way of a colony, this time even more rapidly than before.

By now the nationalist leaders were familiar with the inside of jails. El Fassi was still an exile in Gabon. They were all aware of Puaux's

239

abhorrence for their nationalist aspirations and his methods of exterminating them, yet nothing now could check their course. Nothing now could hold them back to the restraints of 1934 and 1936. They were no longer a Committee of Action requesting reasonable reforms. They were, without fear of jail, exile or death, without compromise, recession or surrender, The Party of Independence—*El Hisb el Istiqlal.*

In early January, 1944, a small group of nationalists met in Fez at the house of M'Hammed Zeghari. These leaders who had met as eighteen-year-olds in Balafrej's garden in 1926, who had rejoiced at the appointment of a youth their own age as Sultan, leaders of the organization that General Noguès had tried to crush in 1937, were now men. To a younger group who had joined the *Comité d'Action,* they were *les anciens,* "the ancients." Before the fight ended, members of this younger group, led by Mehdi ben Barka, Abderrahman Bouabid and Abdallah Ibrahim, were to become *les demi-jeunes,* "the half-young," in contrast to the hot-headed young militants of the Resistance, *les vrais jeunes,* "the truly young."

Les anciens were in general well-to-do *bourgeois,* who could comfortably afford their Paris educations; the *demi-jeunes* were of simpler background who had made their own way into the intellectual world. Ben Barka had been one of Prince Hassan's mathematics teachers. The group had met at Zeghari's house to put the final touches on momentous demands. On January 11, 1944, they were ready to explode their verbal bomb. Through their friends in the palace, the Vizir of Justice and the Vizir of Education, the Manifesto of the new party of independence went to Resident-General Puaux and to the representatives of the Allied governments. From the sponsors of the Atlantic Treaty there was no help; from Puaux and de Gaulle, the same scornful unyielding attitude that had met their requests in the thirites.

Outright independence was the essence of the new demands, because, as their declaration asserted: "A country which does not enjoy the different attributes of its sovereignty is inevitably destined to remain the slave of the one who withholds them." Specifically the Manifesto demanded unification of French, Spanish and International zones, a constitutional monarchy, participation in signing the Atlantic Charter, respect for national traditions and, again, Arabic as the official language.

In scanning the fifty-eight signatures, Puaux, representing the Free French government, found new elements in rebellion against French "protection." Added to the original rich bourgeois group of Rabat and Fez were the poor young intellectuals from the new proletariat of the growing cities (Casablanca in particular), the educated Berbers who resented the policy of playing the Arabs off against them, merchants of the artisan class who found their prosperity diminished by the cheap imports of Europe, and nouveau riche middlemen (again of Casablanca in particular), who sought political power as well as fortunes. Backing the new party in spirit, though not in name, the Sultan Mohammed ben Youssef gave it the incalculable prestige of his tacit approval.

Alarmed at the growing menace, the French moved in the same familiar pattern: jail for Balafrej and Mohammed Lyazidi, the two master minds among *les anciens*, on fabricated charges that they had collaborated with the Germans; and removal of the Vizirs of Justice and Education from the palace. At the news of the arrests, the people countered with the same familiar demonstrations, riots and bloodshed—even the seizure of Fez. Before the restoration of order by French troops, several thousand Moroccans were in concentration camps.

When the United Nations Conference met in San Francisco in the spring of 1945, though Balafrej had merely been moved from prison to a Corsican exile, Mohammed Lyazidi had been released. As acting head of the Istiqlal, Lyazidi sent a formal message to San Francisco requesting the admittance of Morocco into the new organization. As a Protectorate, Morocco had, of course, no chance to join a union of free countries. What the request amounted to was a protest addressed to a group of world powers against the galling unjustified rule of France.

Turning to the East, Morocco, in the company of her neighbors Algeria and Tunisia, watched with interest and approval the birth of the Arab League in Cairo. As they themselves were without friends among the Western nations, it comforted the three countries of Northwest Africa to see the free Arab states of the Middle East consolidating their strength.

With the end of the European war, General Franco, who had taken over Tangier in 1940, withdrew his troops. Again the ancient Tingis of Hercules became an international island in the Spanish Zone, under a committee of control made up of the consuls of the eight signatory powers of the Act of Algeciras, with the United States and Russia replacing Germany and Austria. For the foreign colony, this open port with its lack of income tax—a flat twelve and a half per cent ad valorem duty on all imports, except gold, silk and precious stones at seven and a half per cent—made it a pleasant spot in which to live well and grow rich through business affairs. Not so pleasant, however, for the needy Moroccan populace, for the lack of income tax exacted from the rich deprived the administration of funds for the general welfare.

To the Moroccan nationalists in the south, International Tangier became even more valuable than Franco's friendly Spanish Zone. Though the *mendoub*, the Sultan's representative, was no more than a French puppet, and though the lion's share of control went to France, there was still enough authority left in the hands of the Western Powers to protect a Balafrej or an El Fassi when the French would have preferred him in jail.

While the high-handed Resident-General Puaux pursued his oppressive efforts to stamp out nationalism by means of jail and concentration camps, a group of French friends assailed the Paris government on Morocco's behalf. Fourteen scholars (several of them Arabists of the highest distinction) signed a letter presenting saner and more honorable ways of handling the Morocco problem. Such names as Lévi-Provençal, Julien, Massignon, Brunschvig belonged to that great Arabist branch of Orientalists following in the footsteps of Baron de Slane, the mid-nineteenth-century translator of such Arab celebrities as the noted historian-philosopher Ibn Khaldoun.

Under the spell of the romance and color of the Moghreb, men of learning had turned their minds to its past. Like Lévi-Provençal, they had learned Arabic in order to read and translate the old chroniclers of the dynastic histories. Others, also masters of Arabic, had become archaeologists, like Stéphane St. Gsell, or anthropologists like Edmund Doutté; authorities on art and architecture—Prosper Ricard; historians of North Africa from pre-historic days to the present—Charles-André Julien. The list is endless. In North Africa they were professors at the University of Algiers, at the École des Hautes Etudes Marocaines in Rabat, where over the years the archives became rich in records of the past, and in Paris at the Sorbonne and the School of Oriental Languages. With Lyautey they shared a love and admiration not only of the Moorish past but of the contemporary people. As dedicated scholars and humanists, the fourteen men who signed the letter to the French government abhorred the materialistic greed of the *colons* and the shameful distortion of the Protectorate Treaty. No concrete reforms resulted from their letter; however, in March 1946, the government recalled the detested Puaux.

In Eric Labonne, Morocco had a resident-general of great ability and great good will. No one since Lyautey had showed such genuine concern for the material welfare of the Moroccan people, or worked out such practical plans to achieve it. The reason for his failure was that he faced two raging conflagrations already too overpowering in their intensity to be extinquished by any one man: one, the increasing success of the *colons* in acquiring complete control of the administration; the other, the increasing determination of the nationalists to achieve independence.

In the beginning things went in favor of the nationalists. El Fassi was released from his nine-year exile in Equatorial Africa, and Balafrej from two years in Corsica. El Fassi, still not permitted to return to Fez and his professorship at Kairouiine University, settled in Tangier. Jails and concentration camps opened their doors for great numbers of prisoners. No restraint from the Residency barred the Istiqlal from the rapid expansion of its cells in city and *bled*. In London and Paris, Damascus, Cairo and Madrid, Istiqlal information bureaus were run by Moroccan students. Istiqlal free schools not only educated Moroccan children but indoctrinated them with nationalist ideas. Boy Scout and sports groups played the same roles.

Within a few months after his appointment, Labonne proposed his platform of reforms to the three divisions of the Council of Government. Nothing in his proposals gave new advantages to the *colons*, the merchants, or the industrialists who, he naturally thought, were doing very well for themselves without his help. The reforms he envisaged for the welfare of the Moroccans included better education—more money from the budget to be allotted to schools; training of Moroccans to take more part in their government; more and better housing for the sub-proletariat in the cities; freedom to form unions; improvement and modernization of native agricultural methods, to bring up the productivity of the impoverished peasants to equal that of the *colons*; and a limitation of thirty per cent of private capital in the investment of state enterprises involving exploration for coal, lead and oil.

In the Council of Government, Labonne's reforms, supported only by the professional group, were defeated by *colons*, merchants and industrialists. From the point of view of *colon* profits, any educational and economic prosperity for the Moroccan masses, either urban or rural, which would lift them out of the class of cheap labor was a definite injury.

On the other side of the fence, the Istiqlal also rejected the Labonne program. What the party demanded now was the right for Morocco as a sovereign state to put through her own reforms. To have them handed out on a platter as a favor was not enough. To have the administration change from greedy oppressive colonial rule to benevolent, paternalistic colonial rule was not enough. Istiqlal—independence—or nothing. Labonne with all his hopes for a contented Morocco had no intention of granting anything as radical as that. Nor would he have been permitted to do so by his Home Office. In a post-independence interview, Jean Lacouture, co-author with his wife Simone of *Le Maroc à l'Épreuve*, asked the prominent Istiqlal leader Omar ben Abdel Jalil, then Minister of Agriculture, why his party had shown such antagonism to the offers of reform.

"Men in jail," Abdel Jalil answered, "are not inclined to applaud the jailor!"

When Sultan Mohammed ben Youssef decided to pay a visit to Tangier, an integral part of his empire in spite of its international status, he played into the hands of the French or so it seemed to them when they gave permission. In their eyes such a visit from their well-behaved puppet represented a splendid opportunity to irritate their Fascist opponents, for in Tetuán, capital of the Spanish Zone, the Sultan's Khalifa was by no means the docile rubber stamp that they considered their protégé to be. This was not exactly how it worked out.

Things might have gone smoothly if, shortly before the Sultan left for his April visit, bloody riots had not broken out in Casablanca. Two Senegalese soldiers had attacked a native woman outside a French Army barracks. In the ensuing melee between natives who came to her help and the armed soldiers who opposed them, close to a hundred Moroccan men, women and children were killed and several hundred wounded. No police appeared in time to prevent the bloodshed. Because this was by no means the first occasion in which the French police had failed to protect natives attacked by French citizens or troops, and because it was even suspected that the massacre was purposefully fomented to create trouble, the Sultan left for his northern city in an angry mood.

In Tangier, the warm welcome of the Moroccan citizens, coupled with his outrage at the lost lives of his subjects, gave him a new courage. For twenty years he had let France and Spain bend him to their will. Today, as he began the delivery of his speech, he had surprises for them. To the horror of both French and Spanish officials they heard such phrases as "the legitimate rights of the Moroccan people" and talk of strengthening bonds with the Arab League. In final defiance, the peroration of the speech supplied by the Residency in praise of Protectorate rule was bluntly omitted.

In the furor that followed the "Tangier Speech," a milestone in Protectorate history, no one was surprised when the liberal Labonne tendered his resignation. In Paris, Bidault, friend of the colonial bloc and of the Army clique that had engineered Lyautey's resignation in 1925, was Minister of Foreign Affairs. He was quite willing to remove a man who let Sultans and nationalists get out of hand, and replace him with a Resident-General capable of sterner discipline.

With the appointment of General Alphonse Juin in May, 1947, the curtain rose on the bitter, unvarnished conflict between the Residency and the defender of Moroccan independence.

Juin and Mohammed ben Youssef hated each other from the beginning. Each knew what the other was after. Each in his own singular way used every power at his command to thwart the other.

General Juin was a man of humble origin who ended his brilliant Army career as Marshal of France. His father had been a French policeman in Bône, Algeria. His mother was of Corsican descent. During the Vichy period of the war, Pétain had appointed Juin as his successor. Like the *colon* group to which he belonged by marriage and by inclination, the General felt that every Frenchman, no matter how humbly born or how deficient in education, was innately superior to all natives. Had Averroës, Ibn Batuta or Ibn Khaldoun lived in an age to cross his path, their giant minds and their contributions to Western thought would have left him unimpressed.

One of the first incidents to create tension between the Residency and the Palace was Juin's attempted creation of municipal councils composed of Moroccans *and* French in equal numbers. This not only would have given the French an illegal participation in Moroccan affairs but a representation out of all proportion to their numbers. Without the Sultan's signature and seal, this dahir had no validity. It became the first of sixty-eight dahirs presented by General Juin and repudiated by Sidi Mohammed during the six years of their cold war.

In the same month that the French had discovered a new rebel or, as John Gunther put it, "a scorpion" in their Moroccan Sultan, an old rebel slipped between their fingers to freedom. For twenty-one years they had kept their former enemy, Abd el Krim, in exile on the Island of Réunion. By 1947 they had evidently decided that their power was strongly enough established to let him return from the steaming Indian Ocean and settle in France. While his ship stopped at Cairo, the old Riffian slipped into the city. There, under the protection of a fellow Moslem, King Farouk, he found a safe refuge.

To give the French even more cause for concern, Allal el Fassi, the nationalist leader, had succeeded in slipping out of Tangier, where he had been supposed to remain after his release from Gabon. In Cairo, with the Spanish Zone leader El Torres and the Moroccan students of Cairo's University el Ashar, he was waiting to welcome the idol of his youth. There is no tangible measure of the influence the old "Wolf of the Rif" exerted during the next six years before independence was won. That it existed there can be no doubt. When he died at Cairo in 1963, at the age of eighty-one, he was making plans to return to Morocco and work there for a federation of North African states.

In 1950 the United States again entered the Moroccan scene, this time unfortunately in a way that undid much of the good will created by the Roosevelt dinner during the Casablanca Conference of 1943. The United States bypassed the Moroccan Sultan and his Maghzen on the matter of air bases on Moroccan soil. Technically, the action was justified. Article 5 of the Protectorate Treaty stated that the resident-general should "be the sole intermediary between Sultan and foreign representatives." However, tact, diplomacy and, above all, courtesy could have avoided wounded pride and bitter resentment. The Sultan's first news that five great slices of his country were to be handed over by the French to the United States and that ten thousand Air Force personnel were to be stationed there came to him after the preliminary permission had been arranged.

Of course it was General Juin who accompanied the French Prime Minister to Washington for the final discussion unaccompanied by any member of the Sultan's cabinet. General Juin had already boasted that the "co-sovereignty of France and Morocco" was his aim in the Sultan's empire.

The crises began rolling in and breaking like great waves in an angry sea. In the Moroccan section of the Government Council presided over by General Juin, fifty of the members were pro-French appointees of the Residency; the remaining ten—all members of the Istiqlal—were elected

Mohammed V, patriot and King. / *Moroccan Government*

by Moroccans. During the first of the December meetings in 1950, Ahmed Lyazidi, who had directed the party during the Corsican exile of Balafrej, boldly accused the Protectorate of slanting its financial policy to the benefit of the colonials. Juin sharply requested him to refrain from expressing such views in the Council. Unintimidated, the Council members continued to defend the rights of their constituents. In the third meeting, arguments and accusations boiled up into an ugly scene. Ahmed Lagzhaoui, a rich and clever businessman who had organized a fleet of buses in successful competition with the original French company, was angrily ordered to leave the Council Chamber. Voluntarily sharing his dismissal, his nine fellow party delegates followed him out of the door. At the palace a few hours later, Mohammed ben Youssef shared their indignation.

246

Before the end of the month, General Juin was ready with his next move, a pre-arranged visit of El Glaoui to his enemy the Sultan. To further his purpose of crushing Sultan and Istiqlal, Juin had leaned even more heavily than his predecessors on the help of the Sultan's two arch enemies, the tall, sinister Pasha of Marrakesh, El Hadj Thami el Glaoui, swarthy as an Othello, and Abd el Hai el Kittani, fair-skinned and benignly evil in appearance, head of the Kittaniya Brotherhood. Since the "Tangier Speech," Mohammed ben Youssef had come out openly and fearlessly on the side of the nationalists. To the nationalists, especially *les anciens* with their enlightened French education, nothing was more repugnant than the dark feudal cruelties and superstitions, added to the love of French money, of El Glaoui and El Kittani. To El Glaoui and El Kittani nothing was a greater threat to their power and their riches than the growing strength of the Istiqlal and the growing popularity of the Sultan and his splendidly educated oldest son, Prince Hassan.

Some years before there had been, if not friendship, at least truce between Sultan and Pasha. From the Glaoui, Sidi Mohammed had received as a present a Berber girl of such fascination that he had made her the second of his two wives. (During the enforced Madagascar exile of 1953–1955 she became the mother of his sixth and last child.) But on this visit of December 21st, instigated by the Resident-General, El Glaoui's only gift for the Sultan was malice.

Assuming the role of spokesman for both orthodox Arabs and Berbers, the old "Fox of the Atlas" began to upbraid the Sultan for his unorthodox way of life. Specifically, the charge referred to a French education for the Sultan's five children. In the case of his first wife's first pregnancy, it meant a trip to Paris to bring back a crib, diapers, sterilized bottles, baby scales and a French midwife, declaring that he wanted his son's umbilical cord cut in the twentieth-century manner. It meant tutors for the two sons, governesses for the three daughters. It meant the appearance of the two oldest daughters unveiled in public, in bikinis on the beaches and, in the case of the oldest, Princess Ayesha, at the wheel of her own car and behind the microphone of Radio-Maroc, urging women to discard their veils and enter the modern world.

On the subject of the nationalists, the old conspirator was equally abusive. With El Glaoui's final affront, "You are not the Sultan of Morocco but the Sultan of the Istiqlal and you are leading the Empire to disaster," Mohammed ben Youssef had had enough.

"Go, dog," he ordered angrily, showing his enemy out of the palace forever.

This, of course, was precisely the way General Juin and El Glaoui had planned it.

With this open breach, El Glaoui threw off any pretended allegiance.

On a tour of the tribal regions, he extorted signatures from local caids, to be appended to a document denouncing the Sultan. Few of the caids could read the abusive diatribe against their *imam* to which they had given their mark. In the meanwhile, General Juin paid a visit to the palace. This time he minced no words.

"Sign the sixty-eight unsigned dahirs and denounce the Istiqlal, or abdicate. You have two weeks while I am in Washington to make your choice."

The Sultan had no intention either of signing the dahirs and denouncing the Istiqlal or of abdicating. On his return from Washington to Rabat, Juin repeated his ultimatum with rising temper.

Vizirs and oulema, all standing solidly behind the Sultan, were drawn into the crisis. At Juin's orders, the French civil authorities of the bled had commanded the tribal horsemen to converge on the cities of Fez and Rabat. The reasons given for the command differed. Some tribes were enticed with the promise of extra rations of sugar and tea. Some were ordered to report for vaccination. As the Berber horsemen never moved without their rifles, they were a menacing and formidable sight as they began to circle the outskirts of the two cities.

To the country at large and to the Paris newspapers, the arrival of the Berbers was explained as pious outrage at the behavior of the Sultan, his daughters and the Istiqlal. To "protect" the Sultan and Prince Hassan from tribal attack, both the Palace and the Prince's suburban villa were surrounded by French troops and cannon.

Now the terms of the ultimatum had become even more bitter.

"Sign the dahirs. Denounce the Istiqlal or the tribesmen will begin their attack!"

To avoid the bloodshed of his subjects, Mohammed ben Youssef signed, with the reservation that, since the signature was forced upon him, it carried no legal value.

For General Juin, the ultimatum to the Moroccan Sultan had unexpected and disturbing results. When the Berbers found out that they had been tricked and that their Sultan had been threatened, the majority of them came over to their sovereign's side. When the news reached the Arab League, its delegates turned the spotlight on this Moroccan event before the entire world during the sixth session of United Nations. Among the nationalists, three splinter groups made their peace with the Istiqlal. The Democratic party in the French Zone and the Union party and the Islah in the North formed a Nationalist Front, pledging themselves to work together for complete independence and the avoidance of Communist entanglements.

Jailing all *les anciens* among the party leaders and many of the *demi-jeunes* was another of Juin's mistakes. *Les anciens*, as we have seen, never at any time advocated force. On the contrary, they held the young militants, resentful of their elders' ineffective efforts, on a tight leash hoping to gain their ends without bloodshed. Now the young ones, trained in the hard school of Morocco's new proletariat, closer to the *bidonvilles* * or shantytowns of Casablanca than to the "palaces" of Fez, wise in the ways of Communist cells and trade union tactics, had other ideas on the subject of handling the French.

When General Juin was recalled to France in the late summer to take charge of SHAFE, there might have been great rejoicing among the Moroccans if his successor, General Guillaume, had not walked in the same footsteps. Moreover, General Juin, soon to become Marshal Juin, found that with the help of Foreign Minister George Bidault it was as easy to control Morocco from Paris as from the Residency of Rabat.

The end of 1952 brought another explosive December crises. In Tunisia, too, national independence had become the burning desire of every Moslem. There, too, the *colon* faction exploited the fertile breadbasket of the Romans for its own profit. Ferhat Hached was both an influential nationalist leader and an internationally known union organizer. His murder in Tunis shook the three Moslem countries of France's African empire. Because his murderers were never found and because the Tunisian police formed a venal organization, subservient to the worst element of the *colons* and known as the "Red Hand," it was thought that the "Red Hand" was responsible for his assassination.

Ferhat Hached had been invited to an international labor meeting in the United States. The Red Hand hated both Ferhat Hached and the United States. One of the Red Hand manifestoes was:

> Against the enslavement of Tunisia
> by the imperialist American grocers,
> the exterminators of the Red (Indian) race,
> the assassins of the Puerto Ricans,
> the maintainers of black slavery,
> the hangmen of the Philippines
>   Rally to the RED HAND
> Against Ferhat Hached the American
>   Rally to the RED HAND

Fifteen hundred miles away, in Casablanca, a sympathy strike as a tribute to the murdered Tunisian leader had been planned for December 8, 1952. When the Casablanca police went through the squalid slums the day before, forbidding the strike, the populace rose in angry demonstration against the decree. It was a dismal four-mile region of dismal, half-starved,

---

* Bidonville takes its name from *bidon* or "gasoline tin." Flattened out, the tins form the roofs and walls of the miserable slums of Moroccan cities, especially of the vast one outside Casablanca.

under-employed and unemployed. Most of these slum-dwellers were un-
skilled country people who were forced to look for work in the cities as a
result of losing their land to the *colons*. They became Morocco's first
proletariat.

The immediate action of the police, as the would-be strikers rose
against them, was machine-gun fire into the mob of men, women and
children. The next, on the following day, became known as "Operation
Mousetrap." Permission was given for a giant union rally in one of the
workers' halls, so that police could surround the building and cart the Moroccans off to jail as they emerged. From these Casablanca riots, rebellion
against the French spread sporadically throughout the country. The French
labeled it a combined conspiracy of the Istiqlal and the Communist party,
outlawed both, and doubled the prisoners in the concentration camps.

Though the Residency belittled the affair and played down the number
of Moroccan victims in reports to Paris, a more realistic account reached
the outside world both through foreign correspondents and through the
French element in Morocco that bravely opposed the Gestapo methods of
the *colon* group and the corrupt police.

In Paris, men of honor and Christian ideals, led by François Mauriac
of the Circle of Catholic Intellectuals, concerned themselves deeply with
the flagrant violations of the Protectorate Treaty and the use of police
clubs and machine guns. Though they succeeded in spreading the truth
about what was going on, they were powerless to stop it. By now the colonial
bloc was too strong for them. The wheels were rolling too fast toward the
deposition of the Sultan. Even Robert Schuman, sincerely wishing to improve conditions during his tenure of office as Foreign Minister, found himself helpless against the powerful lobby of the French settlers.

For Morocco, 1953 opened in an atmosphere of terror. Evacuation
plans for immediate execution in case of need were drawn up for the
personnel of the United States air bases.

Increasing terror, bloodshed and disorder all furthered the plot against
the Sultan. Without permission from Paris, the *colons* and their Resident-
General had no authority to remove him. Their scheme was to make it appear that it was the Berbers, led by El Glaoui and Abd el Hai el Kittani,
who were demanding the dethronement.

Again El Glaoui extorted petitions from caids to present in person
to the Paris government. From Paris he moved on to London to the corona-
tion of Queen Elizabeth, to which his friendship with Winston Churchill
had won him an invitation. There the splendid crown of gold and emeralds
he had brought as a present was politely refused.

August 13th brought another ultimatum from General Guillaume.
Again the command was to sign the dahirs or abdicate. Outside the palace,
tanks and troops formed an ugly circle. Mohammed ben Youssef signed.

Two days later in Marrakesh, El Glaoui and his followers proclaimed the Sultan's aged and colorless uncle, Moulay Mohammed ben Arafa as Imam, or spiritual head of the Cherifian Empire. Legally this could be done only by the oulema of Fez. Actually, El Glaoui, backed by the French, was too powerful to be crossed. In Paris, the government, harassed by ominous strikes, had no time for the Moroccan problem. On one side, Guillaume and his followers were declaring that the Sultan must be dethroned and exiled for his own safety before the Berbers attacked him; on the other side, Frenchmen like the Sultan's friend, the ex-ace and war-time hero Pierre Closterman, and the Academician and Nobel Peace-prize winner François Mauriac were working desperately to save France from such a blot on her reputation.

In the crucial decision, Guillaume triumphed. While Paris concentrated on avoiding a revolution of organized labor, Guillaume returned to Morocco with a free hand to play the dictator. By the time he reached Rabat, El Glaoui's tribesmen were again circling the city. In the medina (the walled native section), ever since Ben Arafa's appointment as *imam*, the desperate people had been chanting the *ia el latif*—the prayer for help when danger threatened the empire—the prayer that had been intoned beneath Lyautey's window in Fez when he lay dangerously ill.

During the siesta hour on August 20th, a telephone call from General Guillaume announced his immediate arrival at the palace. Rom Landau, friend and biographer of the Sultan, describes the meeting. As soon as an advanced force of French motorized troops had deprived the Black Guard of their unloaded rifles and ordered them to face the wall, the General followed with his security chief. The curt order to abdicate came as no surprise to Mohammed ben Youssef. When he explained that his religion forbade abdication, the General threatened angrily that in that case the Sultan and his sons would be taken away. The only choice left to the Sultan was agreement.

Even so, Mohammed ben Youssef was taken as far away as a third of the distance around the world, his sons with him. From the palace, with nothing but djellabas thrown over their siesta pajamas, the Sultan, Prince Hassan and Prince Moulay Abdallah were driven in separate cars to a nearby military airport to a waiting plane. No seats, straw on the floor, no heat, no food, no water. The first lap of the exile, where the Sultan's two wives, his three daughters and a small number of members of his harem were permitted to join him, was Corsica. Early in 1954, the royal household was moved to Madagascar. During the twenty-nine-month exile, all expenses were confiscated from the Sultan's personal assets.

In Morocco the pious belief in miracles saved the people from despair. The second night after the sun had set over the grief-stricken land, an excited villager discovered the beloved and familiar face of their Sultan

Mohammed V and his two sons leave for exile, allowed no baggage. /
Moroccan Government

Mohammed ben Youssef looking down on his people from the bright surface of the moon. Like wildfire the great news spread from mountain village to walled city. Every night Moroccans saw the "Sultan in the Moon." They knew that, with the help of their Sultan's *baraka* and their own resistance and sacrifices, they could bring him back.

There was nothing strange in this acceptance of the miraculous, when one remembers that as Moslems the Moroccans were devout believers in the miraculous life of their Prophet Mohammed. There was nothing more miraculous in this appearance on the moon of a true lineal descendant of the Prophet than in the Prophet's own ascent to Heaven on his winged mare "Al Borak"; nothing more miraculous to the followers of a revealed religion than in the "Voices" of Jeanne d'Arc at Domremy or the modern miracles of Lourdes.

When a small country fights for its freedom on its own soil, it has advantages over a more powerful but alien resident enemy. With inspired ingenuity, the Moroccans launched their campaign. They gave up smoking—tobacco was a government monopoly. They avoided the French imports of tea and sugar. They boycotted French cinemas, cafés and stores. They blew up factories, warehouses and railroad lines; they burned wheat fields and farmhouses. They shot those of their own countrymen who were in enemy pay. All the fine edifice of Moroccan prosperity collapsed in terrorism. Since men still gave the date of their birth not by year and day but by the reign of Sultan So-and-So, Lysistratas by the thousands avoided the risk of bearing sons during the illicit reign of the hated Ben Arafa. Because the khotba, the Friday prayer in the mosques, was said in Ben Arafa's name, the mosques stood empty.

Only in the Spanish Zone where Francisco Franco, furious at France's unilateral action, refused to acknowledge Ben Arafa, the people could still hear the khotba recited in the name of their exiled Sultan. And there, behind the shelter of the Spanish Zone frontier, militant nationalists of the French Zone resistance movement collected arms, trained men and built up their Army of Liberation.

From New York, Ahmed Balafrej, as secretary in exile of the Istiqlal, laid down clear-cut terms to the French for calling off the terror. Balafrej and El Fassi had fortunately left Morocco before the Casablanca riots of 1952 to attend the seventh session of the United Nations. The Istiqlal terms were: return the Sultan from exile, bring to trial the prisoners taken after the Casablanca riots, and remove the new laws agreed to by Ben Arafa.

By the summer of 1955, Prime Minister Faure realized that nothing but concessions to the Moroccan people could stop the bloodshed and restore order. Yet every move he made was blocked by the *Présence Française* group of *colons* in Morocco, and the *Comité de Maroc* lobby in Paris. With the added counter-terrorism of the *colons*, Morocco had become an inferno. No liberal Frenchman was safe from his own countrymen's organized murder.

As day after bloody day followed each other, the impotency of the legitimate government of France and the diabolical defiance of its opposing junto began to attract the shocked attention of the outside world.

In the end, with bloodshed between hard-won steps, Prime Minister Faure won his battle. In a conference with a nationalist delegation at Aix-les-Bains in August, he promised the immediate dismissal of Ben Arafa, the return of the Sultan from exile, and a Throne Council.

The *colons* managed to hang on to Ben Arafa until October 1st; the Throne Council of four had three members of *colon* choice; and the Sultan was kept in Madagascar until the end of October.

In late October the *colons* lost their staunchest supporter. In a curious reversal, El Glaoui came out publicly for the return of his old enemy. The reason? Perhaps he had expected greater rewards from the French for the

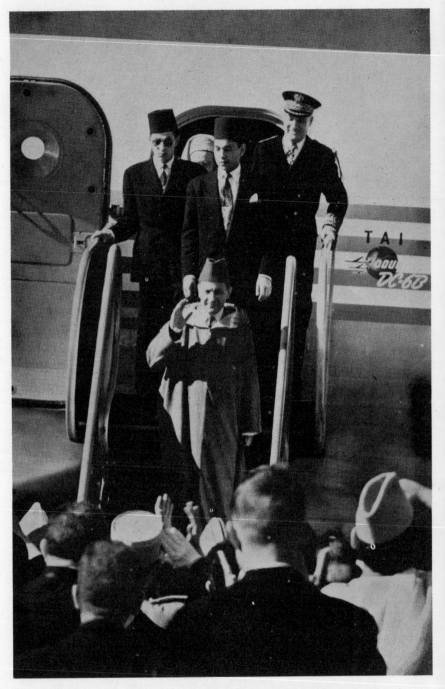

The return of the King and princes in triumph, November 16, 1955. /
Moroccan Government

support he had given them. Perhaps he wanted to jump onto the bandwagon of an independent Morocco and assure his own future and that of his sons.

On October 31st, Mohammed ben Youssef and his retinue arrived by plane in Nice. The following day, the restored Sultan was the honored guest of the French government in Paris. On November 6th a declaration, taking its name from the Chateau de la Celle St. Cloud where the agreements were worked out, guaranteed independence for Morocco.

The nobility and the dignity with which Mohammed ben Youssef disregarded the barbarous iniquities he had received at the hands of the French are not surprising to anyone familiar with his photographs. His smile is one of great gentleness and sweetness. The whole expression is one probably achieved only by a lifetime devoted to the welfare of others, with no time or desire to dwell on personal injuries. His photographs remind one of the descriptions of his grandfather, Moulay Hassan, by Edmondo De Amicis—"A face of most noble expression and full of sweet gentleness . . ."; and Pierre Loti—"His face framed in white muslin has noble and pious features. He has an air of gentleness, a quality which, according to those who surround him, he really possesses."

On November 16, 1955, the plane returning Mohammed ben Youssef to his land and his people circled over the Rabat airport. To the thousands waiting below, their Sultan was returning at last, bringing with him the independence of Morocco.

CHAPTER XX

~~~~~~~~~~~~~~~~~

INDEPENDENCE
(The Triumph of a King, 1955–1961)

~~~~~~~~~~~~~~~~~

Independence burst over Morocco. With celebrations, rejoicings, violence, bloodshed and solemn ceremonies, it took on as many hues as a Roman candle.

In front of the palace on November 18, 1955, the traditional Throne Day, fifty thousand Moroccans listened with feverish excitement and, for many, little understanding, to their Sultan's clear and realistic appraisal of the task ahead. For a population kept largely illiterate throughout the Protectorate era, problems of establishing a constitutional monarchy, training administrators, modernizing agriculture, meeting governmental costs, raising the standards of living and education and, above all, procuring technical and financial help from the former enemy, France, were beyond comprehension.

For the submissive people of the bled, who had smarted under French bureaucracy and tax collection, independence stood for uncontrolled liberty. For the organized fighters of the resistance—both the secret branches of the cities and the Army of Liberation of the north—it meant increasing license to attack French and Spanish troops and to loot foreign property. It also meant fighting to keep the new government from becoming a monopoly of the original Istiqlal party. For the industrial proletariat, it meant a chance to organize openly into unions and also to join in the struggle for power. For the urban sub-proletariat, thrown out of work by the flight of French citizens and capital, independence meant the right to seize the necessities of life no matter how lawless the means. For the many women who had played a heroic part in aiding terrorists and smuggling arms, independence meant a new life with the right of exchanging veils for votes, in spite of orthodox disapproval.

For the Istiqlal leaders, back as *les éloignés* from their prisons and exiles, independence meant the achievement of their life's work. *Les anciens* remembered that summer night in 1926 when Abd el Krim's struggle in the Rif and freedom movements in the Moslem Middle East had fired their young blood with the goal of Morocco's sovereignty. Within the party, however, the progressive *demi-jeunes*, who had resorted to violence when words failed, saw the victory as their own triumph. With *les anciens* they were in perfect accord that the Istiqlal deserved control of the government; but they had no intention of handing back exclusive party leadership to these grey-haired conservatives. Young and old were also in perfect agreement that no other party, Independent or Democratic, should share Istiqlal authority when the Sultan chose his first Council.

In this last they were overruled by the Sultan himself. Mohammed ben Youssef had his own ideas of what independence meant to the country. During the two long years of his Madagascar exile, he had had endless hours to think about it. From the beginning, his profound faith in Allah's rewarding of a just cause had convinced him of the final triumph. The immense distance between Morocco and the Indian Ocean, combined with his own calm and balanced mind, gave him a perspective unshared by any of his subjects. Independence, as he saw it, signified a constitutional monarchy with the monarch above any and all parties. As father of all his subjects, he was aware of everyone's role in the bitter struggle; aware, too, that the struggle that lay ahead differed in kind but not in intensity from the struggle that lay behind.

Neither Allal el Fassi, the Istiqlal zaim, grumbling in Cairo because the word "interdependence" had joined "independence" in the French negotiations, nor Ahmed Balafrej, secretary-general of the party, was the Sultan's choice to head his government. His choice for President of the Council fell upon the independent M'Barek Bekkai, a personal and loyal friend who belonged to no party. M'Barek Bekkai was a Berber of the Beni Snassen, the tribe whose fierce attacks had once given Lyautey trouble near the northern Algerian border. He had been a lieutenant colonel in the French Cavalry, had lost a leg in World War II, and had been ap-

257

pointed Pasha of Sefrou but had resigned his post in protest to the Sultan's exile. Between him and the Istiqlal members there was to be constant friction during his two successive governments, lasting for the next two and a half years.

Ten out of twenty-one ministerial posts went to the Istiqlal, with the polished and cosmopolitan Balafrej holding the portfolio for Foreign Affairs. Five went to the Istiqlal's rival and hated Democratic party. From the beginning to the end of his life, the Sultan kept the important Ministry of Defense in tight control by giving it to a close friend of his own and of Prince Hassan's, Ahmed Reda Guedira. (Today Guedira serves as King Hassan's Minister of Foreign Affairs.) Despite the proverbial uneasiness of crowned heads, a king who has control of his defense, his army and his police force has come as near as possible to securing his own authority and safety. This Mohammed ben Youssef succeeded in doing.

When it came to selecting the chief of the *Sûreté Nationale,* or state police, the Sultan sent a cable to Mohammed Laghzaoui in New York, inviting him to dinner in Paris. Laghzaoui was the highly successful Moroccan businessman thrown out of the Protectorate Government Council by General Juin in a fit of rage in 1952. He had managed to leave Morocco as a voluntary exile before the French added him to their many prisoners. Laghzaoui had planned to return to New York after his dinner with the Sultan; instead, he accepted the appointment of heading the *Sûreté,* a position he held for the next four years, making his police force into an organization of efficiency and prestige excelled only by the Royal Army itself.

The promise of independence and sovereignty in the La Celle St. Cloud Declaration had been made during the Sultan's fortnight in France in early November. This was before his return from exile to Rabat. The next step was an intricate series of negotiations. Though delayed by one of France's habitual collapses of government, the negotiations began in Paris in mid-February of 1956, with Mollet replacing Faure as Premier, and Pineau succeeding Pinay as Minister for Foreign Affairs. The red carpet was rolled out at Orly Airport for the Sultan and his wives.

In addition to the La Celle St. Cloud promises, the violence of unsatisfied urban terrorists and the uncontrolled activites of the Army of Liberation in the north, directed against French and Spanish forces in scourging guerrilla warfare, proved excellent bargaining cards in the hands of the Sultan and his ministerial negotiating commission.

On March 2, 1956, the historic Franco-Moorish declaration sanctioning national independence was signed with great ceremony in the *Salon de l'Horloge* of the *Quai d'Orsay,* by M'Barek Bekkai in the name of His Majesty the Sultan, and by Christian Pineau for the French Republic. In essence, the declaration scrapped the detested Treaty of Fez of 1912 and recognized independence, implying especially the right of diplomacy, an army and the integrity of Moroccan territory. In addition, it stated that the two countries as equal and sovereign states would conclude new accords defining their interdependence in fields of common interest, and guaranteeing the rights of French citizens in Morocco and of Moroccans in France.

During a visit to Madrid in April, the Sultan received a similar guarantee of independence for the northern zone, though the *presidios* or garrison towns of Ceuta and Melilla remained part of Spain. On the Atlantic coast opposite the Canary Islands, Spain also withheld the small enclave of Ifni and the Spanish Sahara composed of Seguia el Hamra and the Rio d'Oro. A third strip of Saharan territory, known as Tarfaya or Spanish Morocco, was designated to be turned over to Morocco in April, 1958. These sandy territories of the "Blue Men" kept by Spain, which may very possibly cover rich oil and mineral deposits, are still in dispute. And Morocco was and is, of course, equally eager to pry Spain out of the Mediterranean ports of Ceuta and Melilla. The first Christian seizure of Moroccan soil, in 1415, was Ceuta, and the loss still rankles.

The ink was scarcely dry on the Spanish agreement of April 7th before Prince Hassan hurried to Paris to ask for French help in acquiring trained men and weapons for a Moroccan army. After forty years of being ground under the heels of foreign armed forces, this new sovereign state was eager to parade an army of her own before the world. France cooperated with the Prince's requests by relinquishing contingents of Moroccans serving in her own army, and by providing officers and weapons. On May 13th, the Prince, as General-in-Chief, was able to parade the Royal Armed Forces of Morocco (consisting of 1,500 armed men) before his father and Commander-in-Chief, the Sultan. Soon the numbers were increased through the integration of 5,000 of the fiery guerrilla warriors of the Army of Liberation.

Not all the fighters of the Army of Liberation were willing to forego their irregular and lawless warfare against French and Spanish troops, still firmly established in the new sovereign state, in exchange for the modern discipline of Prince Hassan's Army. About twelve thousand drifted to the south where they formed a loose but effective band known as the Army of Liberation for the Sahara, which continued to harass the French on the indeterminate Algerian border, and the Spanish in their Saharan territories. Though the existence of this Army was disowned by the palace, they received unofficial support from the Istiqlal, and especially from the party leader, Allal el Fassi, passionate champion of his country's dominion over the western Sahara under the name of "Greater Morocco."

Whenever and wherever the clear-minded Sultan addressed his subjects, he pleaded with them for the order, the unity and the selflessness that would create a prosperous, modern and progressive state.

"Independence," he warned them, "by no means signifies the rule of license and anarchy; nor the indulgence of selfish interests; nor does it signify insubordination and the refusal to pay taxes upon which the state and its activities depend. . . . We are preparing further negotiations with the French Government. Take care not to commit acts of vengeance and reprisal. Has the law of Islam ever authorized the individual under a legitimate government to usurp the place of competent authority by taking justice into his own hands?"

And yet the disorder and the lawlessness continued. Inside the Istiqlal, between opposing factions, there was bloodshed and assassination; between party and party—Istiqlal and Democratic—also bloodshed and murder.

From among the furious French *colons* and a French Army clique, which together refused to recognize their government's decrees, there were underhand attempts to stir up Berber rebellion against Arab domination. In reprisal, a group of ringleaders were rounded up by the Moroccan police at midnight for instant expulsion by air. Only an angry call from the French Ambassador to the Palace delayed the forced departure until afternoon, giving the victims a few hours to settle their affairs. After that day, no Frenchman was permitted for some time to enter Morocco without a visa.

Against this background of sporadic disorder, the pattern of the new order began to take shape. With enthusiastic dedication to the ideals of the United Nations, Morocco entered that organization in July, 1956. Ambassadors were exchanged with great and small countries. The charm and attraction of Abderrahim Bouabid as first Ambassador to France won him a popularity reminiscent of that of his seventeenth-century countryman, Abdallah ben Aissa, at the court of Louis XIV. As a step toward future elections, the King appointed a National Consultative Assembly, a composite body of seventy-six members, representing all groups from labor unions to university professors, inaugurated under the presidency of Mehdi ben Barka.

The gigantic task of training officials for government positions, technicians for industry, officers for the Army, teachers to wipe out illiteracy, professors for technical schools and universities was looked upon as one of the two most immediate problems. Irrigation was the other. Education and irrigation—schools and water—appeared as the two basic needs. For their fulfillment, the new friendly relations with France were of vital importance.

In October of 1956, in the second year of the Algerian War of Independence, Mohammed ben Youssef hoped to bring about an understanding between his Moslem neighbor and his former enemy. With the permission of Prime Minister Mollet, he invited the five top Algerian leaders, en route from their Cairo refuge to independent Tunis, to visit him in Rabat for a discussion of their problems.

To two French Air Force intelligence officers in Algeria this seemed a superb opportunity to seize the hated Ben Bella and his associates. Approached for his permission for this dishonorable act, Mollet sternly refused it. The two Army plotters, however, in the true spirit of the later O.A.S. (*Organization de l'Armée Secrète*) took matters into their own hands, forced the French pilots of the Air Maroc plane, in which the Algerians were traveling as the Sultan's guests over international waters, to come down in Algiers instead of proceeding to Tunis. At the Algiers airport, gendarmes with tommy-guns boarded the plane, seized the five leaders and carried them off to prison.

Stunned at the violation of his agreement with France and the violation of his hospitality, the Sultan exclaimed, "This is morally worse than my exile!" Though all his demands for the release of the prisoners were in vain, he nevertheless gave strict commands to his country to refrain from revenge and bloodshed. In Paris the honorable Mollet was as powerless against the Army clique and *colon bloc* of Algeria as his predecessors had been against the *colon bloc* of Morocco.

Morocco, deeply involved emotionally with Algeria's struggle for independence, buzzed like an angry rattlesnake at the kidnapping of her guests. Despite the Sultan's orders, innocent Frenchmen in the Meknès area paid with their lives and the loss of their farms by fire, in revenge for the treachery of their countrymen. Ambassador Bouabid was recalled from Paris, and the Sultan's youngest son was withdrawn from a French school. Many terrified French fled the country. Capital was withdrawn. French investment stopped. Half-finished buildings remained skeletons. Unemployment shot up. Bekkai's government fell. All the friendly relationship so painstakingly built up on both sides collapsed like a house of cards as a result of the "Algerian incident" and the "Meknès massacres."

Though Mohammed ben Youssef, himself a man of honor, still remained convinced that the men at the top in France were also men of honor, he must have asked himself bitterly how far France could be trusted, when the Army clique and its *colon* affiliates could still defy their own government. He had stood up for France against the disapproval of his own people. He had relied on her help to lead Morocco into the modern world. Following step by step the magnificent education of his oldest son Hassan from the earliest tutors to the final law degree from the University of Bordeaux, he had exulted in the knowledge that his son represented both the cherished traditions of Islam and the enlightenment of France. And now—now he would have to start from the beginning again to win back the confidence on both sides, for he still saw Morocco in need of France. He still saw the bulk of his people in the backward state forced on them by his predecessors—the pleasure-loving Abd el Aziz, and the bigoted xenophobe Hafid—and continued through the Protectorate era by the Juins and the Guillaumes of the Residency. In spite of all he had suffered at the hands of France, he was still determined that the two countries could and should work together under the new status of sovereign states.

For his second government, the Sultan again persuaded the Istiqlal to accept Bekkai as President of the Council. This time they consented only on condition that the party should hold a larger number of important ministerial posts. In this way they succeeded in elbowing out their enemy, the Democratic party.

This second Bekkai government lasted for close to a year and a half until it fell in May, 1958. It was for the most part a turbulent, unhappy period, marked by tribal rebellion, party friction, unemployment, scarcity of skilled personnel, inadequate budget, housing shortage, dire poverty in the ex-Spanish zone in the north, trouble with Spain over Ifni and the Spanish Sahara in the south, a hostile France, and, most tragic of all, the worst drought since 1945.

Like much of southwestern United States, Morocco depends on two types of agriculture. In the first, crops and animals reach maturity through the benefit of seasonal rains from November through spring, aided by the so-called *petit hydraulique* or primitive irrigation. This precarious semi-dry farming is characteristic of the desert fringes to the east and south of the infertile mountains of the Rif, and of plains such as the Haouz between Marrakesh and the Oum er Rebia River. In the second kind, modern dams and large-scale irrigation furnished by everflowing rivers and streams provide year-round cultivation on the grand scale practiced by the prosperous French *colons;* and, on a smaller scale, winter snow and streams of the High and Middle Atlas provide moisture for the pasturage and cereal crops of the mountain tribes.

When drought strikes, it is the people of the pre-Saharan region and the arid plains who suffer most, whose lambs die at birth, whose barley fails to sprout, whose date palms no longer stand with their feet in water. In the rainless winter of 1956–1957, while the new government was as yet too disorganized and short of funds to meet the crisis, wheat from the United States and the Argentine saved uncounted Moroccan lives.

In the meanwhile, Mohammed ben Youssef and his statesmen called on every resource at their command to work out a five-year master plan for 1960–1964—to conquer the problems of agriculture, education, industry, commerce and social welfare. With their Western educations and their urban backgrounds, the government leaders realized that their first necessary step, as unpopular as it was important, must be detribalization. This meant the breaking-up of the six hundred tribes that made up the country's rural population, or four-fifths of the country's twelve million inhabitants, and the transfer of tribal loyalties to a national patriotism.

For the tribesmen, detribalization meant those thorns in the flesh for all hide-bound peasants fiercely attached to minute plots of ancestral lands—

agrarian reform and cooperatives. It meant the smooth city Arab lording it over the proud illiterate Berber. It was sure to produce trouble and friction. And yet how else could land be arranged in large enough areas for deep or contour ploughing, for harrowing, seeding, cultivating and harvesting with tractor-drawn implements? How else could the land be made to yield more? How else could the people not only be fed but produce a surplus for the marketplace, which would bring them buying power for the durable goods of industry as well as their daily tea and sugar? So the plan was to make the government commune the basic unit of the country, replacing the old tribal *djemaa* or village council. Each commune would have its school, its primitive court, its market place and its cooperatively owned farm machinery.

Wherever it could, the government went into action as well as into paper plans for the future. At the beginning of the year, a battalion of engineers from the Royal Army came to the aid of the Tafilalet region. In this Saharan birthplace of the Alaouite dynasty, the famine-stricken inhabitants lacked the strength, the skill and the money to rebuild the sand-banks and irrigation systems for their date gardens. In order to relieve near starvation in the ex-Spanish Zone, where the fighting between the Liberation Army and French and Spanish troops had been heaviest, the King and his government launched a relief fund to be raised through private subscription. Also to help the pitiful economy of the north and to heal the old division between the two zones, a road link was built by twelve thousand young Moroccan workers as a voluntary project during their summer vacation. Under the name of "Unity Road," it ran from the Ouergha River north of Fez through the wildest goat tracks of the Rif to the only east-west road of the ousted Spaniards. From the United States the workers received contributions worth a hundred thousand dollars in the form of blankets, mess-kits and clothing.

In July of this same summer of 1957, the Sultan officially appointed his oldest son, Hassan, as heir to the throne. A month later he exchanged his own title of "Sultan" for the more western one of "King."

After twelve centuries of Moroccan dynastic history, with the prevailing father and son relationship one of a murderous struggle for power, it is most pleasant to end the present record with a deep bond of mutual love, pride and respect between the late King Mohammed V and his chosen heir, Crown Prince Hassan, now Hassan II.

Born in 1929, with his "umbilical cord cut in the twentieth-century manner" by a French midwife, and with his brilliant and acquisitive mind shaped both by the scholars of Islamic law and by French tutors, schools and universities, he had become his father's link to both modern and Western worlds. Indulged in some respects, rigidly disciplined in others (Palace servants were ordered to beat him when he fell below the standards set for

263

him by his father), he grew up knowing both gaiety and responsibility. He shared his father's love of fast cars and splendid horses. In his student days, he had brought his freedom-loving young countrymen and liberal French friends to the Palace. A short-lived reputation as a spoiled and handsome playboy faded in the grim two years before the August exile. During that time he made friends with intellectual Americans attached to Radio-Maroc, among them Marvine Howe, recently Morocco correspondent for *The New York Times*, whom he taught to ride and who in her book, *The Prince and I*, with penetrating sensitivity describes the young Hassan and his friends of those two critical years. During the brief period between his matriculation as a Bachelor of Law and the family exile, only the brilliant young mathematics professor, Mehdi ben Barka, of the *demi-jeunes* faction of the Istiqlal was hated more by the *colons* and the Residency than was the Sultan's eldest son.

By the summer of 1957, as creator and general-in-chief of the Royal Armed Forces, Hassan had proved his ability to play an effective role in Morocco's new status as a sovereign state. Though both father and son inherited a generous share of the Alaouite charm, their mutual admiration was not due to seeing in each other their own images. In his son, Mohammed ben Youssef saw a keen rational mind tempered by a modern education to the fineness of a Toledo blade. In his father, Hassan saw an intuitive and a spiritual quality, a faith in the prevalence of right without force, a magical hold over the people more effective in calming disorder and violence than all his bright new army with its tanks and guns—in short, a *baraka* of unusual potency.

Before the end of 1957, the break in the relations with France over the "Algerian incident" and the "Meknès massacres" had been partly mended. A cultural convention was signed, in which France recognized Moroccan schools, thereby entitling children of the French population (which now numbered 160,000) to enter French universities and the Civil Service.

Relations with Spain, on the other hand, flared into the worst fighting in the Sahara region since 1934. In 1934, the French had "pacified" it and driven Merebbi Rebbu, brother of El Hiba, the "Blue Sultan," to take refuge in his family stronghold of Samara, in the northern province of the Spanish Sahara. In early 1957, France and Spain together defeated the Moroccan Army of the Sahara. With a stubborn unwillingness to call an end to the struggle, King Mohammed paid a visit to the Saharan oasis of M'Hamid on the river Dra, at this time with the purpose of giving his official sanction to the claim of "Greater Morocco."

For the boundaries of "Greater Morocco," drop a line from Colomb Béchar on the Moroccan-Algerian border, carry it southeast through the oases of the Touat to Insalah, an oasis due south of Algiers, then west again north of the Mali border and across western Mauritania through Oualata—

Mohammed V greets Mrs. Eleanor Roosevelt, 1957. / *Moroccan Government*

the city whose women shocked Ibn Batuta six hundred years ago—to the Senegal River. By April, an uneasy peace had been established with the prearranged transfer from Spain to Morocco of Tarfaya, the coastal region between the river Dra and 27° 40′.

In May of 1958 the second Bekkai government fell. The friction that had existed from the beginning between the President and the Istiqlal reached a climax when a newly formed political party, the Popular Movement, composed of rural Berbers and headed by ex-resistance leaders, received sympathetic support by the Berber President of the Council. On the grounds that Bekkai, by endorsing one of the movement's petitions to the King, had failed in his promise to maintain a neutral position, the Istiqlal ministers resigned in a body.

The King, still above all parties, and loyal in his gratitude to all men of the resistance, took no sides against any group, but consented to an all-Istiqlal Council with Ahmed Balafrej as president, in hope that harmony within the administration would speed the putting of Morocco on her feet.

An important landmark during the short Balafrej government was a brave step forward by the King in behalf of Moroccan women. The Prophet had come to the rescue of women by forbidding his followers to bury their infant daughters alive. The Moroccan King, in a new dahir, summarily abolished three age-old man-made evils of Islamic custom. No father could now force his daughter into a marriage against her will; no father could marry off a daughter under fifteen; and to repeat "I divorce thee" three times no longer enabled a husband to cast off his wife for no justifiable reason. In accordance with the King's new law, a woman had the right to bring her case to court. For such men as those who married the legal limit of four wives during the sardine-canning season at Agadir, when women drew steady wages, and divorced them at the close of the season, this new law must have been regarded as most unpleasant.

The year of 1958 ended as it had begun—with violence, this time internal. In Casablanca a dissident faction of the Moroccan Labor Movement, the U.M.T., hostile to the conservative policies of the Balafrej government, instigated a series of strikes. In the north the Rif tribesmen, desperate from poverty and hunger, and smarting under the impression that their troubles were being ignored by Rabat, rose in fury. When the humane and moderate Balafrej refused to use the state police and the army to crush both the urban and the rural rebels who had helped achieve independence, his enemies accused him of weakness and brought about the downfall of his government.

Outspoken opposition to Balafrej and the other *anciens* of the Istiqlal had begun soon after the forming of the third government. Throughout the summer the younger and more radical element of the party had increased its bitter attacks upon what it termed the reactionary, feudal and pro-French policies of the movement. These rebels had as their leaders the young Mehdi ben Barka—General Juin's *"l'adversaire, c'est lui"*—now President of the National Assembly; Abderrahim Bouabid, first ambassador to France, now both Vice-President of the Council and Minister of National Economy; Abdallah Ibrahim with a Sorbonne education known as the "Red Cherif," by birth a descendant of the Prophet and thereby worthy of the title of "Moulay," but by political inclination more concerned with the welfare of the masses than with his Cherifian descent and the pomp of monarch and palace; and Mahjoub ben Seddiq, who had risen from railroad worker to head of the Moroccan Labor Union.

Many in this group, though still loyal to the person of the King, had become critical of his autocratic government and had begun to oppose the young Crown Prince Hassan, in whom they saw a potential dictator. This opposition was heartily returned, as Hassan naturally became more and more hostile to their radical and anti-monarchical outlook. They were a group waiting impatiently for a government with both an elected representative assembly and a constitution, and passionately eager to play their own part in it; a group eager to see French and Spanish armies pulling out their last men from Moroccan soil, and the United States closing down her air bases. They wanted more economy in government spending: less splash in entertaining, in travel and in foreign cars; a faster "Moroccanization" of all public and private organizations; the stamping out of all that smacked of feudalism and rule by viziers; and, above all, rigid avoidance of that *bête noire* of all newly independent peoples—neo-colonialism.

By neo-colonialism they meant economic control of the country's industrial and natural resources by foreign powers.

At first the two party groups became known as the right and left wing of the Istiqlal. By early 1959 the split was complete. Mehdi ben Barka formed what became known as the National Union of Popular Forces. Today, in 1964, it still functions as an opposition party.

Out of this group, King Mohammed, still deeply anxious to represent all his people, chose as his next Council President Abdallah Ibrahim, the "Red Cherif," who took office in December, 1958. The King must have made his choice with some reluctance and distrust of the party, because he not only increased the proportion of independents in the Council but sidestepped the strong Istiqlal leaders in favor of men technically competent in their posts. Moreover, he made it very clear that the Council would be of a limited duration and chiefly concerned with the task of arranging municipal and communal elections.

By the end of 1959 the new movement, labeled communistic, atheistic and anti-monarchical by its enemies, cost Ben Barka his position as President of the Assembly. When the Istiqlal accused him of involvement in a plot to assassinate Crown Prince Hassan, he prudently left the country for a Paris exile. Though he was now limited to vitriolic attacks upon the King and his government, with nothing more dangerous than pen and ink, his National Union took solid root in the urban proletariat of the coastal cities. There it received warm support from the progressive wing of the Moroccan Labor Movement and the politically-minded and organized student group.

During the Ibrahim government, no corner of the Cherifian Empire felt the leftist impact more than did the former international glamor spot of Tangier. In the second year of independence, the King had granted it a Royal Charter permitting it to keep its special status as a free port and free money market. Ibrahim and his National Union supporters, with touches of nineteenth-century xenophobia and Marxist class prejudice,

267

decided that nothing could be gained by encouraging a rich foreign colony, not even through the lavish spending of a Barbara Hutton. In April, 1960, therefore, Tangier became no longer the haven of the smuggler, the tricky financier, the wily Indian merchant, no longer the big money exchange of more than 300 banks, but just another Moroccan city wholly integrated into the national economy. It is thought that the unlovely Casablanca, with its population of a million, and with two-and-half miles of piers, jealous of Tangier's special privileges and resort charms, may have had a hand in attempting to reduce her rival to her own mediocrity.

Like all cities of Morocco—and those of the world in general where the age of handicrafts gives way to the machine age—Tangier has lost much of its old visual charm. The skyscrapers march in, hiding low roofs; streets the width of a loaded donkey and as devious as the path of a maggot give way to thoroughfares for cars and buses, and the homespun djellaba bows to the ungraceful attire of Western man. But the curved waterfront is still there; the ancient kasba with its shafts of minarets still sits high on the hill; and the white city, as it comes into view to the European approaching from Tarik's mountain, still prompts a curious excitement and an impatience to cross the threshold into the Moroccan world.

Ironically enough, the eleven-hundredth anniversary of the founding of the Mosque-University of Kairouiine fell during the regime of the "Red Cherif," Abdallah Ibrahim. To the Istiqlal leader, Allal el Fassi, who wore the white turban of an *alim* or professor, and to the other *anciens,* Kairouiine stood as a symbol of the free and illustrious Moroccan past—the Almohad days of Averroës, the Merinid days of Ibn Batuta and Ibn Khaldoun. To Ibrahim and his National Union colleagues, however, it stood as an archaic, theology-ridden institution of learning obstructing modern progress. The architectural triumphs and the cultural traditions of the Moorish past were not precious to this realistic social reformer. He had shocked Morocco's friend, Rom Landau, by declaring that the magnificent twelfth-century Almohad walls encircling Rabat's medina or native city, should come down to let fresh air and modern development sweep through the congestion of medieval decay. An event of eleven hundred years ago left him unimpressed. He would have agreed with Voltaire that the early Middle Ages were no more deserving of study than wolves or bears.

Kairouiine was founded in 859 by a woman, a rich and pious young refugee from Sidi Okba's Kairouan to the Fez of the Idrisids. Proudly enlarged and enriched by succeeding dynasties, it became Morocco's greatest mosque and foremost seat of learning—in fact *the* foremost seat of learning and center of culture for all Northwest Africa. In the twelfth century, the well-traveled Jewish philosopher Maimonides of Cordova, who lived in Fez from 1160 to 1165, said that never in Damascus, in Arabia or in Egypt had he seen its equal for learned men.

268

It never has been, and never will be, easy to strike the ideal balance between a reverence for the traditions and monuments of the past and a concern for the economic needs of the present and future. To the detached onlooker, both the Allal el Fassis and the Abdallah Ibrahims appear necessary to the new Morocco. The magnificent ocher walls of the Almohads should stand, in order to "give pleasure to the eyes" of their own people and the world in general; the Mosque-University of the Kairouiine should look back as proudly to its medieval past as do the Universities of Paris, Cambridge and Oxford. But at the same time the bidonvilles must go; modern science must be taught at all levels of education; and, if cooperative ownership of land and farm machinery is one of the answers to an improved standard of living, then the Ibrahims must have a free hand to carry out such reforms.

From the beginning, Ibrahim's government had been an uneasy coalition. As the second year began, friction between Palace and President of the Council increased. While the King felt that Ibrahim was fostering a dangerous left-wing influence, Ibrahim felt that Prince Hassan was assuming undue powers and going over the heads of ministers. In February, many of Ibrahim's friends were arrested on grounds of plotting against the Prince. Ibrahim himself was accused by the superstitious of having caused the Agadir earthquake through possession of the evil eye.

The Agadir earthquake was a cruel disaster for a newly-independent country struggling to its feet through financial troubles, illiteracy, underdevelopment and internal friction. Earthquake, tidal wave and fire. Seventy per cent of the city demolished. Out of a population of 48,000, an estimated 20,000 dead. The earth moved four feet under the city, then four feet back. The tidal wave swept inland for 300 yards. Bulldozers from the United States air bases scraped trenches ten feet wide to bury the dead. When the King and Prince Hassan visited the ruins, the King pledged his personal fortune toward funds for rebuilding the grisly desolation.

On May 20, 1960, Ibrahim was abruptly dismissed as President of the Council. Behind the story was a friendship between Prince Hassan and a gay and dynamic young Texan named Leo Blair, public relations officer at the United States Naval Base at Kenitra. Among Blair's presents flown from Texas to the royal family were a cow-girl suit for Princess Ayesha and four prairie dogs for the Royal Zoo. At the end of Blair's Kenitra assignment, Hassan asked to have him appointed liaison officer at the Palace. When Ibrahim refused his approval, the King dismissed his Council President for meddling in Palace affairs.

Perhaps the King was discouraged when he looked about for a successor to Ibrahim. He had tried his trusted and politically-independent friend Bekkai, and the jealous Istiqlal had forced the latter's resignation.

He had then turned to the Istiqlal and appointed the wise and moderate Balafrej, only to have the new left wing obstruct the progress of the government by the venom of its attacks. He had next chosen the "Red Cherif" Ibrahim; and the latter, besides meddling in the affairs of the royal family, had seemingly preferred Moscow and China to France. The political parties had been given their chance to submerge their differences and pull together for the good of the country. Instead they had worked selfishly for party interests. On May 23, 1960, the King announced that he himself was taking over the government and appointing the Crown Prince as Deputy Vice-President.

As the King addressed himself first to the people, then to his new Council, he repeated his intention of making the Moroccan government a constitutional monarchy.

"A constitution before the end of 1962," he promised, "that will allow all the members of the nation to take part through their representatives in handling the affairs of the country and in controlling the actions of the government . . ."

To the twentieth-century Westerner this promise may not seem anything out of the ordinary. For Morocco it was a giant step forward into the modern world, especially when one remembers that it was the King's uncle Hafid who not only punished by means of the "salt treatment" but exhibited his arch enemy the Rogui up and down the country in a cage for more than a year before he threw him, in the manner of the ancient Romans, *ad bestias*.

Municipal and communal elections took place a few days after the King took over the government. In the big cities, in Casablanca particularly, the leftists gained the majority of the seats.

In contrast to the many difficulties in the path of progress, there were also bright flashes of hope and promise. In early June the King laid the cornerstone for the great Mechra Klila dam south of the northwestern coastal town of Nador and first and most important in a series to harness the force of the Moulaya River, the country's second greatest watercourse. With water for irrigation and power for industrial use, the rich soil of the valleys and the iron ore of the mountains could bring prosperity to the poverty-stricken eastern provinces of Nador and Oudjda.

Later in the same month, at Fedhala on the Atlantic, another cornerstone laid by the King pointed to progress in the industrial field.

The port of Fedhala chose this occasion of the King's visit to change its name to Mohammedia in his honor. Like Fedhala, several other cities changed their names with the coming of independence. Near Rabat the town of the former United States naval base, Port Lyautey, reverted to its old Arabic name, Kenitra. Southwest of Fedhala, Mazagan threw off its hated Portuguese name for El Jadida; and Mogador became Es Saouira.

Within the cities, names of streets and squares that had honored the memory of the generals who had "pacified" the country—Avenue du Général Moinier, Avenue du Général d'Amade—now glorified Mohammed V, Ibn Khaldoun, Avicenna, even Lumumba.

The cornerstone laid by the King in Mohammedia in June, 1960, was for the first oil refinery, not only in Morocco but in Northwest Africa. Financial backing came from Italy's *Ente Hydrocarburi* headed by the financial giant Enrico Mattei. Georg Gerster speaks of Mattei as having the reputation of being the most powerful Italian since Augustus. In a subsidiary Moroccan-Italian company known as SAMIR, Mattei became the power behind Morocco's first petro-chemical center. He had already been given prospecting rights in the ex-Spanish Tarfaya, when Spain released it to Morocco in 1958. This, of course, was an example of the foreign entanglement feared and hated by the National Union and by all other socialistic groups who looked on it as the devil's own combination of imperialism and neo-colonialism. In the king's eyes, however, this was an agreement freely entered into by the government on its own terms as a sovereign state.

Like all African countries, both those who had thrown off their own colonial rule and those who hoped to, Morocco was deeply concerned with the independence of the Belgian Congo on June 30, 1960. In the first fearful days of anarchy when the army mutinied against its Belgian officers, and Belgian troops were rushed to protect Europeans, President Kasavubu and Prime Minister Lumumba, prior to their bitter enmity, together appealed to the United Nations for help against the Belgians. In response to the United Nations' answer to the request, Morocco supplied 3,000 men, the largest single contingent of troops.

By the end of the year, however, the King had angrily withdrawn this force. Government sympathies, like those of the Soviet bloc, were with Lumumba and, after his arrest and murder, with his successor, Gizenga. Lumumba, dismissed by Kasavubu but upheld by the Assembly, had stood for the territorial integrity of the Congo and was in bitter opposition to the secession of the Katanga and Kasai provinces. In the eyes of anti-colonial Africa, the secession of Katanga was staged by Belgium and the West to keep a neo-colonial control of the immensely rich and powerful *Union Minière,* source of the uranium for America's first atomic bombs.

On January 4, 1961, King Mohammed invited a group of the African states that shared his disillusion with the policies of the United Nations to a conference at Casablanca. There, as host to Ghana, Guinea, Mali, Libya, the United Arab Republic and Algeria's government-in-exile, he stressed his desire for a free and independent Africa. The summary of his aims expressed what all his guests desired for their countries and their continent.

"This meeting," he began in his inaugural address of welcome, "marks a historical and decisive point in the history of Africa. The peoples of this continent, for long periods divided and forced to live under colonial regimes, were unable to have free and direct contact with each other. . . ."

The points he laid down were: African unity; African independence and neutrality; the end of foreign military occupation; the avoidance of neo-colonialism such as foreign control of strategic raw materials by Katanga's *Union Minière;* the end of interference with elected governments by such actions as Lumumba's arrest; an end to the partitioning of national territories in order to weaken them, as exemplified by Katanga's secession and French control of Mauritania; and an end to the use of Africa as testing grounds for nuclear experiments, as represented by France's explosions at Reggan in the Central Sahara.

This Casablanca Conference of January, 1961, turned out to be the final effort by a ruler who had dedicated his life to independence. He had achieved it for his own country. Now his hope was to help Black Africa. A short-lived hope. A month later, on February 26th, he died suddenly and unexpectedly of a heart attack during a minor nasal operation.

In a great surge of love and grief, the country was immediately pulled together by its King's death. Emotional forces outside the experience of the modern Westerner intensified the agony of the loss.

This direct descendant of the Prophet, this Commander of the Faithful, this revered *imam* of his country's religion, this man of magic, whose image had appeared in the moon and whose *baraka* had furthered their freedom in both his offices and his person, had won the devotion of his pious subjects. On the day of his funeral, party strife vanished. Among the critics and opponents, all, with the exception of the arch-rebel Mehdi ben Barka, paid their respects. Thousands filled the immense parade ground in front of the Palace for a last look at the shrouded coffin on its way to burial in the Hassan Mosque.

A description of the scene comes from Charles Gallagher, the Moroccan expert for the American Universities Field Staff, who was there to witness it. Women tore their faces, worked themselves up into trances, fainted. Both men and women—the simple masses and their sophisticated leaders—moaned and sobbed.

"Who that was there can ever forget the low hoarse moan of the people at that moment (the appearance of the shrouded coffin) welling up into one great communal cry of bereavement from thousands of throats, as if finally, disbelievingly, the crowd understood for the first time what had really happened. And there was nothing to do, for everyone, but to shed tears."

CHAPTER XXI

ᏬᏬᏬᏬᏬᏬᏬ

A KING OF TWO WORLDS
(Hassan II, 1961–   )

ᏬᏬᏬᏬᏬᏬᏬ

Mohammed ben Youssef had been dead five hours, from 1 P.M. to 6 P.M., before the Moroccan public or even the royal family was notified. According to one account, Moulay Hassan acted with much of the same sort of dramatic precaution that the Chamberlain Ba Ahmed had employed in secretly returning the body of his great-grandfather, Hassan I, through a hole in the walls of Rabat. With both doctors and nurses locked by his own hand into the Palace clinic, he telephoned to the chiefs of the Army and state police and to the governors of the provinces, commanding the strictest secrecy and a guard on all public buildings. Next, as Deputy Vice-President of the Council, he summoned his ministers, to declare him King. At six in the evening he announced his father's death over the radio.

Outside the Palace, the growing crowd, hysterical, uncontrolled, full of anger, accused foreign doctors of killing their king. It took courage for the new young ruler to appear before them. His experienced advisors warned against it. But courage is a quality Moulay Hassan has never lacked. His reward was a swift shift of emotion.

"*Yahia el Malik Hassan*—Long live King Hassan!" they shouted. He was accepted.

He had conquered the first hurdle—first of all those that lay before him—many of which were more difficult, more dangerous, more unpredictable than this. Through many critical years he had been steeling himself to meet them when the time came. Added to the courage was a hard core of determination to rule well, wisely and with authority.

The new king, born in 1929, was thirty-one on March 5th, the day of his enthronement. Deliberately absent from the ceremonies were his enemies, the representatives of the National Union.

In physical appearance, as seen in photographs, King Hassan shows no resemblance to his father. He is shorter and slimmer, and his skin is much darker. His mother is said to be a Berber. ("Said to be" because information is not given out to the public concerning the wives and concubines in the Cherifian Palace.) This Berber heritage shows in the rounded contour of the King's face and the small straight nose. In contrast, his father had a cleft chin and an imposing nose, high-bridged and pointed like that of a desert Arab. Hassan's mouth is short, the lips full and the eyebrows thick and black. Both father and son have the same high intellectual forehead. They are the first Moroccan rulers to appear clean-shaven. Mohammed V was known disparagingly as the *Djellabat el Malik*, "King who wears a djellaba." Over Western shirt and tie he wore the graceful sleeved garment of his country, hooded and flowing, in soft pastel shades of grey or blue broadcloth. King Hassan prefers well-cut Western clothes from his Italian tailor. On the Friday day of Prayer, however, he drives from palace to mosque in his gilded coach, returning on a velvet-saddled stallion, his body enveloped in the traditional cream-colored, finely-woven sleeveless burnous of his ancestors.

This man of two worlds, of the burnous and the tweed suit, of the Arabic language and the French, of the laws of the seventh-century Koran and twentieth-century organized labor, this descendant of despots and ruler of a people clamoring for democracy and a constitution, was well aware that he would have to watch every move forward as warily as a lion stalking its prey. There were people ready to shout "Long live King Hassan!" There were also people ready to assassinate him. There was a country still rife with hunger, unemployment and illiteracy; a people dissatisfied and disillusioned with what five years of independence had brought them. The bidonvilles still spread their festering sores at the city's edge; the children of the bled were still without classrooms. Foreign military units—French and American—still made themselves at home in this sovereign state. Foreign capital was lacking for the development of mineral resources; and the winter of 1961 had been another year of drought.

In June, the King chose his first council. As the National Union refused

His Majesty, Hassan II, King of Morocco. / *Pottecher*

his invitation to take part, it was a rightest coalition government of independents, Istiqlal, Democratic Party and Popular Movement. Balafrej, absent since his own government leadership in 1958, was back as Minister of Foreign Affairs. Allal el Fassi served as Minister of Islamic Affairs. The two leaders and organizers of the resistance and its outgrowth, the Popular Movement—Dr. Abd el Krim Khatib and Mahjoub Aherdane—both Berbers, became respectively Minister of African Affairs (a new portfolio) and Minister of Defense. Abd el Kader Benjalloun represented the Democratic Party. The independent, Ahmed Reda Guedira, closest of all Ministers of the Council to both Kings since the beginning of independence, became an official of far greater importance than was indicated by his title, Minister of the Interior and of Agriculture.

On the day when the King inaugurated his new Council, he officially proclaimed the new Fundamental Law of the Kingdom. As a forerunner of the Constitution promised by his father for the end of 1962, this law proclaimed that the Moroccan state was Moslem by religion and Arabic by language and culture. It guaranteed liberty and justice for all its citizens, and committed itself to the anti-colonial and independence principles of the Afro-Asian Bandoeng Conference (1955), as well as to loyalty to the Arab League, the United Nations, and the Charter of the Conference of Casablanca.

To relieve the suffering of the bled, the young King moved fast. During the early summer he set up a system of public works for the benefit of the rural unemployed and the illiterate. For many Moroccan farmers, the working period was limited to the short growing season of their cereals. By using this idle manpower under skilled government direction for building schoolhouses, bridges, hospitals, for reforesting eroded hillsides and improving irrigation, the undeveloped land benefited, and 70,000 destitute farmers staved off starvation by a government wage of four *dirhams* (eighty cents) a day—two in currency, and two in grain. In Western eyes this may seem like pitiful payment. For a Moroccan, where the average per capita income is about $150 a year, or forty cents a day, it was welcome money. Government agencies in Rabat and the provincial governments were called on to offer their technical skills and organizational facilities. By October a thousand classrooms were ready to make a small dent in the schooling of rural children.

For a massive attack against adult illiteracy, the Middle Atlas province of Beni Mellal was chosen. For this wild and rugged region, where the new communes are separated by heavy snow in winter, a crash program was set up to wipe out illiteracy between January and April.

Thanks to radio broadcasts originating in the capital town of Beni Mellal and sent out to every local classroom, each step of the project was synchronized. In the preceding November, the provincial teachers were drilled in their roles. On January 3rd, at 6.30 P.M., the mosques and the 1,087 new schoolrooms were filled with tribesmen whose beards varied in color from deepest black to the white of the snow outside. With slates and crayons, their gnarled fingers traced the willowy letter *alif*, to which the poet compares the grace and slenderness of his beloved, and which begins the name of their Lord, Allah.

For an hour and a quarter each evening they worked at the letter of the day, at numbers, at simple arithmetic, at lessons of history, geography and hygiene. Then the radio took over, reviewing the lessons of the preceding three days. Conspicuous in the heart of the commune, an outdoor blackboard held the letters and figures of the previous lesson. Fascinated, the enthusiastic new alphabetarians gathered about it during the day, helping each other, then moving off to practice on empty walls.

The lesson of each day was important to the tribesmen in more ways than one. It became the password for their daily activities. Without mastering it, no postage stamp could be bought, no legal document transferred, no case pleaded in court. For any student who failed, postmaster, district supervisor, judge and local sheriff turned teacher until the test was passed.

It would be a pleasure to be able to report that the Beni Mellal literacy achievement spread from province to province, that today all Morocco is able to read the praises of Allah woven into the arabesques of their mosques and medersas, and that the professional village scribe has been put out of business. Unfortunately, despite such government efforts, the problem of illiteracy in this underdeveloped country is still a major one, instead of a minor one as in the United States. In our "developed" land "functional" illiterates—those who have not completed fourth grade—number 8.3 million, while the illiterates unable to read or write are estimated at 2.8 million.

Toward the end of his first year on the throne, the King laid the cornerstone for an ambitious new industrial enterprise of great importance to Morocco's future—a chemical complex at the port of Safi south of Casablanca. Its purpose was to process the phosphate rock of the country's rich deposits into commercial fertilizers for both domestic consumption and export. As an underdeveloped country, Morocco had been mining and exporting phosphate rock since its discovery in 1921, until she had become the world's largest exporter and second largest producer.

Now, as a country striving for industrial development, she aimed at higher profits by setting up, on a far larger scale than before, facilities for reducing and refining the bulky ground mineral rock. To produce the finished product of triple superphosphates, factories for the necessary sulphuric acid and phosphoric acid were planned as part of the complex. For sulphuric acid—one of the discoveries of Morocco's Arabian ancestors— mines at Kettara north of Marrakesh held immense deposits of pyrites or iron sulfides that would furnish not only the necessary sulphur but also profitable residues of iron and copper. It is the treatment of rock phosphates with sulphuric acid that makes the chemical element phosphorus soluble and available to the roots of plants.

The building of these factories and the railroads to the Kettara mines, and the enlargement of the Safi docks would employ an estimated 10,000 men during a period of three years, and 1,400 permanent workers when the complex was in full swing. Yearly production was planned for 200,000 tons of the triple superphosphate, 300,000 tons of phosphoric acid, and 400,000 tons of sulphuric acid. The complex was to be completed by the beginning of 1964, and the cost was to be $3.5 million. In October, 1962, French and West German firms had made investment loans of $2.5 million. The Moroccan phosphate industry is a state monopoly managed by the Royal Cherifian Office of Phosphates.

Among Moroccan minerals phosphates make the greatest contribution. In 1963 the annual production reached eight million tons. There are in addition other riches waiting beneath the soil for intensive cultivation. Iron ore in the Rif, cobalt and manganese south of Ouarzazate, oil on the banks of the Sebou River and between Agadir and Tarfaya, and coal near the northeastern border.

The mining of many of these ores goes back for centuries. The Sous has long been famous for its copper. Copper alloyed with zinc is the material of the traditional Moroccan brass trays. Traces of ancient iron mines abound in the Rif and elsewhere. Rock salt from the region of Fez, and common salt from the brine marshes near Safi were once exported as far as central Africa. Veins of unusually pure antimony furnished much of the *kohl*, the fine black powder with which Moslem women and Touareg warriors stain their eyelids to make their eyes lustrous. (The word *kohl* comes from the Arabic verb *kahala*, "to stain." In the words *al kohl*—to become our "alcohol"—the concept of the fineness of the powder was transferred to the fineness or distillation of a liquid.)

During Protectorate days, the mineral riches had been exploited by both French and Spanish private interests. Recently the world-wide demand for many of them has increased. Manganese as an alloy has become more and more important; so has cobalt, of which Morocco is the third largest producer, not only as an alloy but as a radioactive isotope in the form of cobalt-60 for cancer therapy.

For development of these mineral resources, as for Morocco's light industries, foreign investments were badly needed. Expanding factories for such products as textiles, detergents, plastics, cellulose (from great plantings of eucalyptus trees), paper, dyes, matches and pharmaceuticals could provide more work for the unemployed. The King and his appointed ministers saw this clearly. The opposition shouted neo-colonialism.

Reversing Abdullah Ibrahim's leftist reluctance to allow Tangier her old special privileges so alluring to rich foreigners, the King proclaimed the former international city again a free port, as of January, 1963. Fast train service now connects Tangier with Casablanca.

Algerian independence, finally granted on July 2, 1962, after seven years of bloody warfare, produced a radical change in the relationship between France and Morocco. Earlier, while de Gaulle was still defying not only the rebels but also his treacherous army in order to achieve it, he made offers of friendship to the late King Mohammed. These were warmly returned. The bitterness resulting from the "Algerian incident" and the "Meknès massacres" dissolved. Vanished also was Morocco's anger at seeing a Moslem neighbor refused its freedom, and France's anger at the passage of Russian and Chinese arms across the Moroccan border.

On the day of Algeria's independence, the new Morocco, though cherishing both her own independence and traditions, proudly showed herself to be a country of two cultures. In the old Roman city of Volubilis, against a background of Caracalla's Arch of Triumph, the half-fallen marble of the basilica and the fluted columns of third-century villas, Morocco inaugurated a new Mediterranean Festival of Music and Drama with a performance of Corneille's *Le Cid*.

Curiously enough, the French language, so bitterly resented when forced upon the people during Protectorate days, has since then become as important in the schools as Arabic. In secondary education and at the university level, it is the language used for the teaching of mathematics and the sciences. French school teachers are eagerly sought. The school year of 1962–1963 opened with, for the first time, half the children from six to fourteen in school. A third of their teachers were French. Instruction by the other two-thirds, many of them very young and products of a crash program of education, was of a dubious quality but far better than none at all.

The King himself, to whom French has been a second language since childhood, speaks it with perfection—better, it is said, than most of the 160,000 Frenchmen living in his country. His favorite author is Proust.

The October revolution of the Yemen, which transformed that country from an ancient feudal monarchy under the Imam el Badr to a republic under Colonel Sallal, was the cause of the break between King Hassan and President Nasser of the Arab Republic. At the start, the weekly edition of the Istiqlal newspaper, dated October 27, 1962, swung its sympathies to the side of Colonel Sallal.

"The despotism of the Imams," the paper stated, "their feudal tyranny was able to keep the people in a prehistoric state. . . . The revolution at least has the purpose of waking up sleeping minds to the world that surrounds them. It will not be the work of a day, but if the first step has been taken, it is already a success."

This of course was also the attitude of President Nasser, his Arab

Republic, and of Algeria's Ben Bella. King Hassan, however, was anything but in favor of overthrowing monarchies and turning them into republics. The memory of the assassination of King Feisal II of Iraq in 1958 was still fresh in his mind. The result there had been the establishment of a republic with General Karim, leader of the revolt, as premier.

Among the Arab states, the number of monarchs had been reduced to only two besides the King of Morocco—King Hussein of Jordan and King Saud of Saudi Arabia. Now the three sided with the deposed Yemeni Imam. Nasser scorned each one of them—Hussein for seeking British protection, which he claimed was given in the hope of Jordanian oil; King Saud for caring more about American oil royalties than for advancing Arab socialism and unity, and Hassan for his friendly relations with the very country which had ruled his own with such arrogant imperialism.

Nothing in King Hassan's long-awaited draft constitution, promulgated in December, helped to soften Nasser's contempt. The document was equally objectionable to the left-wing opposition, who boycotted the national referendum three weeks later on the grounds that it was feudal and provided for a one-man government by the King. The National Union, fundamentally anti-monarchic, naturally objected to the statement that the monarchic and Islamic nature of the state could not be modified, that the Moroccan crown would be passed on to the oldest male descendant in direct line. In the old difficult days of sultans, they claimed that the oulemas of Fez at least had had the honor of nominally choosing the ruler.

The document called for a bi-cameral parliamentary system, to be set up in from five to ten months, consisting of a lower House of Representatives, to be elected by national suffrage, and an upper House of Councilors, elected through indirect suffrage and chosen from such organizations as Chambers of Commerce, Industry and Agriculture. Bitterly resented by its opponents was the fact that nothing defined the parliament's powers and participation in the government. On the contrary, government powers were clearly stated to be in the hands of the monarch, who would name his own council president and ministers. By submitting a referendum to the people, the monarch would also be empowered to dissolve the Chamber of Representatives and bypass the Chamber of Councilors, at any time that his measures were vetoed.

The bill of rights as it appeared in the draft constitution was more or less a repetition of the one guaranteed in the Fundamental Law of June 1961—rights denied during the Protectorate but already taken for granted, especially by the progressive urban proletariat, during almost six years of independence. These included: freedom of movement, religion, expression, assembly, association, the right to strike, and the equality before the law of all Moroccans—men, women and Jews.

In spite of the opposition's boycott, and demonstrations by the leftist

Students' Union, the King won overwhelming support for his constitution. About ninety-five per cent of the country's four and a half million voters cast their ballots. Warm sunshine, a paid holiday and the threat of prison and fines for disturbing the peace helped the King's cause. For the most part, order prevailed, though the National Union claimed that a thousand of its members had been arrested. Later they accused the government of swinging the vote by a distribution of United States wheat, and filed an unsuccessful petition with the Supreme Court, demanding a cancellation of the referendum.

Now not only the National Union but also the Istiqlal expressed its disappointment in the monarchial aspects of the new constitution. It, too, joined the opposition. In early January of 1963, in a reshuffle of the Council, three Istiqlal ministers were dismissed. They were Allal el Fassi, the founder and leader, who held the post of Islamic Affairs; M'Hammed Douiri, Minister of the National Economy, a brilliant mining engineer, educated through scholarships given by Mohammed V; and M'Hammed Boucetta, Minister of Justice. Of the old-timers, *les anciens,* only Ahmed Balafrej stayed on. However, as a result of a disagreement with Allal el Fassi, he no longer belonged to the party that the two together had founded in the early days of 1926.

As *Emir el Mouminin,* Prince of True Believers, King Moulay Hassan, descendant of the Prophet, takes his role seriously. No one is more impressively pious than he as he appears in his gilded coach, draped in fine white wool, on his solemn passage from palace to mosque to conduct the Friday prayer. It is probable that such progressives as Abdullah Ibrahim and Mehdi ben Barka, and many of their colleagues among the trade unions and student groups are no more impressed by the pomp and ceremony of this gorgeous pageant of scarlet uniforms, noble horses and white-robed ministers than they are by the splendid twelfth-century walls of Rabat's medina. But the crowd still gathers, deeply stirred.

The constitution has proclaimed Morocco an Islamic state. The powerful hold of Islam over 430,000,000 people throughout the world is a force not fully realized by Westerners unfamiliar with Moslem lands. To question the King's religious sincerity as incompatible with his modern education would be as unjustifiable as to doubt the sincerity of Western rulers attached to the Catholic Church or to the Church of England. At the same time, this Prince of True Believers realizes the value of his country's religion as a source of unity, and recognizes, too, the advantages of stimulating religious fervor.

For the holy month of Ramadan in February, 1963, the customary obligations of daytime fasting and religious observances were strengthened and emphasized. Under King Hassan, the Prophet's curious commands to abstain from all food, drink and pleasures of the senses between sunset and sunrise reverse the activities of night and day with more rigor than in the socialist Arab republics to the East. If the hungry, thirsty, cigarette-starved workers loaf on the job, their lapses are forgiven. Cabinet meetings are held at night. When cannon and air raid sirens announce the critical moment when a white thread can no longer be distinguished from a black one, "breakfast" in the literal sense of the word begins the night. The breakfast includes a cigarette, coffee, the special Ramadan "soup of a hundred spices," dates and honey cakes. After that comes prayer. From the Palace, religious talks in the presence of the King, his ministers and ambassadors from Moslem lands are televised and broadcast to the public. For the rest of the night, women cook, men play cards, children set off firecrackers until the pre-dawn repast and the sunrise ushers in another day of fasting and celebration of the month in which the Angel Gabriel delivered the words of Allah to his messenger, Mohammed.

Second only to the King in power at this time was Ahmed Reda Guedira, the Director of the Royal Council and Minister of the Interior and of Agriculture. The two had been friends from boyhood, with Guedira only six years older than Moulay Hassan. As a political independent, Guedira had been with the goverment since the return of the royal family from Madagascar, first as spokesman for the negotiating committee in Paris in 1956, then as a member of the two Bekkai Councils. It was Guedira who, by the edge of the swimming pool at the royal suburban villa, had first begun to brief Hassan as student prince on the events of the day. Now, with all his official posts, to which was added that of National Economy after Douiri's dismissal, he became the all-powerful agent of the King's autocratic rule.

In March, at the King's request, Guedira formed a new party of which he himself became the head. From the initials of its ponderous French name, translated as "Front for the Defense of Constitutional Institutions," it became known as *Fudeek*. It was the King's party, and still is, remaining essentially a manifestation of loyalty to the monarch, to monarchy itself, and to the new constitution.

Algeria's Ben Bella was far from pleased when King Hassan insisted on paying him a visit in early March. Ben Bella, expecting President Nasser in May, was planning to honor the latter, his esteemed fellow socialist, as the first foreign ruler to visit his country since its independence in July, 1962. Any friendly relationship that might have existed between the two North African neighbors before Ben Bella took control and exhibited his leftist leaning had been rapidly sliding down hill since the birth of the Moroccan constitution. Rumors that King Hassan was arranging a match between his twenty-two-year-old sister, Princess Noszha, and Ben Bella had come to a halt.

The King was an unwelcome guest in spite of his alluring gifts to war-ravaged Algeria—armored cars mounting 75 mm. cannons, jeeps, mor-

Hassan II and the late President Kennedy, on the King's American tour. /
Moroccan Government

tars and motorcycles—and his willingness to pay his own expenses for his
delegation of eighty. His reception was lukewarm though civil. As for
encouragement to Hassan's proposals to run a Saharan pipeline of Algerian
oil through Morocco, or ship iron ore from the Tindouf region through
Moroccan parts, there was none whatever.

Two weeks after being cold-shouldered in Algeria, King Hassan was
receiving a twenty-one gun salute from the United States destroyers "Corry"
and "Cecil" and an escort into New York harbor. Above his ship, the

"Constitution," the Navy's "Blue Angels" put on their show of precision flying. In the harbor, a welcoming committee boarded the ship, and on the pier Hassan was greeted by an honor guard of the United States Marines and a Navy band. In Washington a red carpet was rolled out in Union Station, and President and Mrs. Kennedy were waiting as his train pulled in.

For the eleven days of his state visit, the country honored the young Moroccan King, his brother, Prince Moulay Abdallah, and his sister, Princess Nozsha. Conferences, public appearances before the United Nations, the press and television cameras, lunches, dinners and receptions filled his short visit. The public saw King Hassan on "Meet the Press" and the "Today" show. With the President and the Secretary of State, he discussed the subjects of air bases and economic assistance. On a visit to Casablanca in December, 1959, President Eisenhower had promised to evacuate the five-million-dollar establishment by the end of 1963. President Kennedy confirmed the promise.

Since 1957, when Morocco first requested help, the United States has provided between forty and fifty million dollars a year in various forms of grants, loans and technical cooperation. The United States officially proclaims: "her deep interest in the country and its future" and that "it is of great importance to her that the strategically located North African land remain a sovereign and independent member of the community of nations and that this can be achieved if Morocco's democratic institutions are able to meet the economic and social needs of her people."

From 1957 on, there has already been help for agriculture, with its problems of soil erosion, droughts and floods, help for the Agadir earthquake, the building of the Moulaya dam system, for housing, education and the training of technicians and administrators. The need for future help was, and still is, great. In requesting it, King Hassan could feel that he was dealing with sympathetic friends.

As a devoted horseman, the King must have been disappointed to have his present of a grey Arab pony for Caroline Kennedy politely turned down on the grounds that the White House could accept no more horses. In his gift to the United Nations he was more fortunate. A great mosaic panel in the twelfth-century Andalusian style, executed by an old artist of Fez, with inscriptions from the Koran and the United Nations Charter in Arabic, was accepted. For the public, in general, it will stand as a sample of the charm of Moroccan decorative art. For those fortunate enough to know Morocco, it will be a happy reminder of mosques, medersas and palaces.

On his return to Morocco, the King found himself again at odds with Algeria. A meeting of the Casablanca Conference composed of six of Africa's neutralist nations (his father's last creation) had been scheduled for the previous October. After a postponement by Nasser because of his involvement in the Yemeni revolution, it was now planned for May 8th. The original object of a heads-of-states meeting had been to reach an agreement of opinion before they met again later in May as part of a group of thirty-one independent African nations in the Ethiopian capital of Addis Ababa. In December, Nasser, again giving the Yemeni disorder as an excuse, had demanded a second postponement. In reality his reason was a mounting resentment against Hassan for not recognizing Colonel Sallal's revolutionary Yemen regime. This time, Algerian Ben Bella backed out a week before the appointed day. Like Nasser, he felt that not only was there no common bond between him and his royal neighbor, there were also causes for antagonism and distrust. For one thing, he had no intention of letting Morocco add to her Saharan territory by claiming Mauritania. Of the other four members of the Conference, King Idris of Libya had lost interest soon after the first meeting, and the three members from black Africa—Touré of Guinea, N'Krumah of Ghana and Keita of Mali—found the lands north of the Sahara too Arab and alien to hold their interest and cooperation.

So King Mohammed ben Youssef's dream of leading Africa to unity dissolved in a little more than two years, and Morocco now stood alone in the African world with only middle-of-the-road bourgeois Tunisia as a possible future friend.

One hundred and forty-four seats were contended for by 500 candidates from the Royal Front and the two opposition parties—the Istiqlal and the National Union—plus a handful of independents. As Minister of the Interior, the party leader, Reda Guedira, had the usual advantages of the party in power—in this case the apportionment of the voting districts, control of radio and television, appointment of provincial officials, and distribution of United States wheat in the "Food for Peace" program. By the opposition he was vehemently accused of abusing every one of his powers in order to rig the elections. And yet the government party lost a majority vote. Only sixty-nine seats went to the Royal Front, forty-one to the Istiqlal, twenty-eight to the National Union, and six to independents.

On election day itself, foreign observers expressed surprise at the comparative order, honesty and fair play during the country's first nationwide experience at the polls. But four Istiqlal deputies, no more afraid of jail now than in the days of their youth, lodged a protest with the United States Embassy against the misuse of American grain to sway votes. Their punishment was jail for the next two months.

In the following July, those who followed Moroccan news with special interest read in *The New York Times* an account of wholesale arrests among members of the National Union. A few days before communal elections, the police, forcing their way into the Secretariat building of the party, arrested 130 members of the Union's National Council. Included in the arrests were three foreign journalists covering the meeting—among them John Cooley of the *Christian Science Monitor*, who was released the next day upon the intervention of the United States Ambassador. In addition to the closing of the Algerian-Moroccan border, telephone links with France and Algeria were also cut off.

The official explanation accused those arrested of involvement in a plot to overthrow the government and assassinate the King, and of planning to acquire weapons from the United States navy base at Kenitra, with the connivance of venal American personnel. Rumor indicated that six Americans had been implicated and punished.

No one can say with certainty whether there was or was not a plot. History abounds with governments overthrown by revolution and rulers assassinated; history also records absolute and near-absolute rulers maintaining their goverments by jailing their opponents. Members of the National Union had died or gone to jail before, for what they believed was the welfare of their country. The King, steeped in the century-old tradition of monarchy, believed, as his father had done before him, that the reins of power, for the present at any rate, must be kept in his own hands.

Hostility between the National Union with its proletarian origins and the Palace with its privileged royalty is easy to understand. Such class antagonism exists even in liberal England. What is not so easy to understand is the deterioration in relationship between the Palace and the Istiqlal, for it was the young Hassan who as a liberal and freedom-loving prince had smuggled many of the independence leaders through the back door of the Palace to present their ideas to his father. It was as much with the help of the Istiqlal as with the help of the younger independence groups that his father had been able to regain his throne. Now the Istiqlal was accusing their former champion of praising but not practicing democracy and turning Morocco into a one-party state.

Hassan is, of course, not alone among the heads of new African countries in preferring the one-party system. Few of the new leaders encourage opposition. Perhaps they are still too near in their history to the omnipotence of sultan, king and paramount chief. Perhaps, on the other hand, they are better able than even the most interested, informed and sympathetic observer to size up the ability of their own politically illiterate masses to handle the freedoms of democracy.

H. G. Wells, in explaining the fall of the illustrious medieval Arab civilization, says: "From first to last the Arabs never grappled with the problem, still unsolved, of the stable progressive state; everywhere their form of goverment was absolutist and subject to convulsions, changes, intrigue and murder, that have always characterized the extremer forms of monarchy."

286

Though Wells may have been right concerning the past, there is no reason to think that Arab government is doomed for the future. In ninth- and tenth-century Cordova polished scholars and courtiers undoubtedly took an equally dim view of progress in Western Europe with its illiteracy and brutish squalor. There is no reason to think that the Arab, being part of the human family, heir of a magnificent past and now in intimate contact with the modern world, which has its own grave cruelties, will not in time solve the problem of the stable progressive state.

Ideological conflict, prestige and minerals caused the border dispute between Morocco and Algeria that broke out in October, 1963, into three weeks of undeclared war. Most of the stubborn fighting centered around two miserable little water-holes—Hassi Beida (White Well), a small grove of dusty palm trees; and Tinjoub, a few caved-in adobe huts, south of the region where the Dra River makes a sharp bend to the west on its way to the Atlantic.

A second scene of fighting involved Figuig and Ich near Colomb Béchar on the border of Algeria's Oran Province—a region rich in manganese; and a third, the strategic town of Tindouf on the trans-Saharan caravan trail leading from Agadir through Mauritania to Senegal. Eighty miles southeast of Tindouf, at Gara Djebilet, lies the most important iron deposit in the Sahara, and one of the five or six richest in the world.

Morocco claimed not only that Algeria's provisional government in exile had promised her territorial concessions as a reward for help during the seven-year war of independence, but also that this Saharan territory had been hers over the centuries until unlawfully annexed by France. Ben Bella, denying that there had been any promise to reward Morocco for military aid, upheld the former French boundary. So the insults and the bullets flew across the sands, men were killed, and both countries wasted huge sums of money. For Morocco the cost was $14,000,000, which she could have used far better for education, a new dam or a sugar refinery. Finally, the mediation of Emperor Haile Selassie of Ethiopia and President Modibo Keita of Mali brought about a meeting at Bamako, Mali's capital, and a cease-fire was agreed upon.

The truce came as a relief to the Western powers—to France and the United States especially. Egypt had been helping Algeria with troops, and Cuba had landed at least three freighters in Oran with cargoes of what Algeria called "sugar" but what appeared to observers on the scene to be Russian fighter planes and other military supplies. Though neutrality was the aim of both France and the United States, it would have been clearly against their interests to sit by and watch Algeria crush the Moroccan monarchy.

In mid-November at Addis Ababa, during a meeting of the Organization for African Unity, the Ethiopian emperor called on the two countries to settle their differences. "Enough blood has been shed," he declared,

287

"and misunderstandings among the thirty-one signatories of the Charter should be considered a family affair." As a result, an Ethiopian-Malian boundary commission was appointed to propitiate the two truculent opponents.

Two and a half months later, the efforts at arbitration had proved unsuccessful. Both countries were still snarling over the bones buried beneath Saharan sands. On January 27, 1964, the border commission in Bamako adjourned until March.

When the Moroccan House of Representatives met for the first time in November of 1963, its chief function lay in examining the budget and planning the economy. There had been changes again in the Council. As a concession to public opinion, Reda Guedira had been transferred from the Ministry of the Interior to the Ministry of Foreign Affairs—a post held until then by Ahmed Balafrej. Balafrej, in turn, received the title of Special Representative of the King, with rank of minister.

After eight years of independence, neither budget nor economy showed signs of health. The economy had stagnated, but the population had moved forward by about two per cent a year. The $551,000,000 budget of 1963, unmatched by revenues and foreign aid, in spite of a phosphate output increasing to eight million tons, had a deficit of $70,000,000. To make matters worse, the budget estimate for 1964 would have to be even greater, because of an enlarged army, the engagement of new teachers and social workers, and a huge subsidy to protect an infant beet sugar industry.

In addition to an austerity program, which included more trade schools and less higher education, the new government limited its goals to far fewer grandiose projects than those included in the defunct Five Year Plan of 1960–1964. It now laid out a Three Year Plan for 1964–1967, with emphasis on six realistic undertakings. Heading the list was the quick-money-producing tourist trade. In succeeding order of priority came: the Safi Chemical Complex for transforming raw phosphates into fertilizer, an increase in the hydro-electric power output, more dams on the five major river systems, development of food and textile industries (including more acreage in long staple cotton), decentralization of industries from the coastal cities, and more protective tariffs to expand the home market. Indifferent to the scorn of their socialist neighbors and their Arab brothers to the East, the Moroccans made no secret of their desire for foreign aid —from France, from the United States, from Russia, from any country that would offer it without endangering their sovereignty and their independence.

It is not impossible that the advantages of economic cooperation in handling the riches of the Sahara, especially oil and natural gas, will soon be more effective in settling the October border dispute than the Malian-Ethiopian arbitration commission. After a similar period of angry conflict, Algeria and Tunisia have reached peaceful accords concerning

288

the passage of Algerian oil by pipeline across southern Tunisia to the Mediterranean. In 1964, in a race to beat the development of recent natural gas discoveries in Holland, an international consortium, with the support of the French government, is proposing a pipeline to carry Algerian gas across Morocco to Gibraltar and from there via Spain to northern Europe. The two budget-troubled African countries would do well to bury the hatchet and take advantage of this half-billion dollar investment.

In December of 1963, Premier Chou En-lai began his grand tour of ten Western countries, which ended with the capture of French recognition of Red China. Morocco had recognized Red China in 1957. During the government of the "Red Cherif," Moulay Abdallah Ibrahim, active trade relations had begun, built primarily around Morocco's need for green tea. In Moslem lands where alcohol is forbidden, a milder stimulant usually takes its place—coffee in the North African lands once under the Turks; in Morocco, the ubiquitous mint tea. The green tea for this sticky tea, sugar and mint concoction is imported from China at a cost (in 1962) of $9,000,000. In exchange, at a cost to China of $4,000,000, Morocco sends phosphates, sardines and trucks.

For Morocco, Algeria, and Mali, Chou En-lai had in 1963 an even more interesting proposition than new trade accords. This was an offer to Mali to help finance a network of Saharan highways linking North and West Africa. For this project he is reported to have pledged $24,000,000. Mali's capital is Bamako, but the city best known to the Western world is the once-fabulous Timbuctu.

The mere suggestion of this Red Chinese proposal sends those who are under the spell of the "Great Desert" and the "Golden Age of Caravans," with its give and take between the Niger and the Atlas, hurrying to maps to speculate upon the possible results. A network implies much more than mere improvement of the three main north and south *pistes*, or trails, where the motorized vehicle now can, hedged in with harsh rules and warnings, and at some risk, displace the camel.

Of the three routes the one farthest to the west, known as the "Mauritanian Trail," would lie entirely within Moroccan territory if that country's claim to "Greater Morocco" is ever realized. Starting at Agadir, it crosses the present Algerian border at the Dra and, shortly beyond Tindouf of the great Western Saharan camel market, enters Mauritania. Skirting the eastern edge of the Spanish Sahara, it passes through Fort Gouraud, with its spectacular new iron mines and ancient salt mines, then past the copper mines of Akjoujt, reaching the Atlantic town of Nouakchott about 170 miles north of the Senegal River. In 1936, a convoy of three cars crossed the desert and returned by this old caravan trail, taking twelve days from Casablanca to Dakar (2,000 miles) each way. The new railroad opened in June, 1963, to transport the iron ore of Fort Gouraud to an Atlantic port, also new, takes a shorter cut to the Atlantic, near the capital, St. Etienne. The revolutionary effects on this primitive land of *Miferma* (*Mines de Fer de Mauritanie* financed by French, German and Italian capital) will undoubtedly make this "Trail" and any connecting links through the land of the "Blue Men" the most important of the three, whether or not Chou En-lai pours road money and Chinese labor into Saharan highways.

In the northern half of the Algerian Sahara, a network of passable roads already skirts the Great Eastern *Erg* or Region of Dunes, to connect the many oases strung along the underground water supply that is known to geologists as the Albian "sea." Many tourists know Colomb Béchar on the Moroccan-Algerian border, Ghardaia, south of Algiers, now a booming oil town on the verge of acquiring traffic lights, and Biskra, the setting for Robert Hichens' famous novel *The Garden of Allah*. In 1927, the first regular fortnightly public *camion* or bus service took travelers from Oran on the Mediterranean to Gao on the Niger—a trip of 1,700 miles.

Below the Touat oases, the Colomb Béchar and Ghardaia roads meet to enter the terrible 500-mile emptiness and desolation of the Tanezrouft. "Tanezrouft" is the Berber word for "thirst," and this is the country of thirst and hunger. To the Saharan nomad, "pasturage" means a water-hole every 125 or 150 miles. The Tanezrouft is *not* pasturage! But motor vehicles with special equipment adapted to desert travel get through with the aid of beacons six feet high spaced at distances of about a mile.

A third highway, the dramatic "Hoggar Road," dropping south from Biskra, links Arab Africa to the Negro countries of the south by avoiding the Tanezrouft and, instead, crossing that wild and black immensity of mountain and plateau known as the Hoggar. These are the mountains of the northern confederation of Touareg (once the veiled pirates of the desert), the mountains where Père de Foucauld was murdered, where Pierre Benoit set his haunting novel, *L'Atlantide,* where giant rock carvings of the elephant and the giraffe and the extinct North African ox cover the walls of rock shelters and caves, and where today the prospectors comb the savage landscape for platinum, diamonds and uranium. South of the Hoggar Plateau—Tassili Oua-N-Ahaggar—the road leaves Algeria to enter the Republic of the Niger. By the time it reaches the ancient capital of Zinder, skins are black.

These, then, are the highways the map designates with a solid line as possible roads for the combustion engine. Between them, spun out like the irregular threads in the web of a black widow spider, the dotted lines of the caravan trails skirt the empty regions of the waterless dunes as they connect waterholes and oases. Until the French in 1901 occupied the oases of the Touat on the Tanezrouft Trail, and the oases of the Tidikelt with its principal ksar Insalah on the Hoggar Road, these fertile palm gardens, with their age-old artesian wells and unsuspected subterranean fields of natural

290

gas, were under the rule of the Moroccan sultan. Like Mauritania, they are wishfully included in "Greater Morocco."

It is curious that Chou En-lai is concerning himself with highways for Africa's Sahara, and a rebirth of the days when the Libyans galloped their chariots across the "green desert." Surely he must have more important problems of his own, nearer home. However, if this strange form of foreign aid comes to North Africa from Red China via Mali, Morocco will welcome it. Good roads and easy transportation lie at the heart of all economic expansion and prosperity.

By the end of December, 1963, Morocco had the satisfaction of seeing the United States withdraw her forces, as promised, from the last of the air and navy bases. As the American personnel moved out, native thieves stripped the immense self-contained communities of every movable object left behind, from electric motors to latrines. From the American point of view, it seemed that Morocco, for the sake of stiff-necked pride, had relinquished a useful source of income and employment. On the other hand, if one examines the issue through the eyes of the Moroccans, one realizes: first, the bases were forced upon Moroccans by the French without consent; second, the Moroccans are still smarting under the memory of fifty years of control by the arrogant armies of France and Spain; and third (perhaps the only valid reason for removal), the presence of bases would make Moroccan neutrality impossible in the case of war among the great powers.

One form of foreign aid that has reached Morocco, not only without interest, without condition and without condescension, but freely and generously, is the late President Kennedy's unique creation, the United States Peace Corps. For the year 1964 the Moroccan government asked for volunteers in three special fields—community development, reforestation and irrigation. The community development project required women trained in child care and hygiene and men skilled in agriculture, economics, cooperative movements and construction of low-cost housing. There was also a request for teachers of art, music and drama. The new Peace Corps volunteers, who trained throughout the summer and arrived in Morocco in September, joined the group already at work there since February, 1963. During the three-month training period, new volunteers for Morocco acquired, in addition in some cases to the needed skill for the job, a working knowledge of French, a smattering of Arabic, and an intensive survey of the history, economics, politics and culture of the country.

A daring and admirable innovation, in the dispensing of foreign aid by a well-to-do country to one in need of help, is the Peace Corps arrangement for living conditions. Allowances provided restrict the volunteers to food and board at a level *comparable to that of their fellow workers.* This novel limitation may in itself be the volunteers' most valuable con-

291

tribution to international understanding. In a common sharing of the same frugal standard of living, barriers vanish. The young people of the two countries learn to meet on common ground; through them the countries themselves will draw closer together. No young American who has planted pine saplings on the eroded slope of a Moroccan mountain side by side with a Mohammed, an Ahmed and an Abdallah, or dug irrigation ditches at the edge of the Sahara, or introduced modern hygiene to Berber mothers, will see Morocco through the myopic eyes of a tourist. In his turn, he will never be remembered as that alien creature, the foreign tourist, by his Moroccan friends.

The tourist, however, plays his own special role of importance in the Moroccan economy. The goal of the Ministry of Tourism in 1963 was to attract a million of these valuable budget-balancing props during 1964. With 60,000 tourists recorded in 1963, this was not an impossible aim, provided there was hotel room to take care of them. Tangier already has trailer camps and camp sites with Danish-modern bungalows. The extraordinary influx into Spain in 1962 of eight million middle-class Europeans, the majority of them motorized, has already poured its overflow into Morocco. A hundred new hotels are planned during the next five years. A new Hilton hotel is going up in Rabat, a new vacation area at El Jadida, a Polynesian village of grass huts on the Riffian beach of El Hoceima. Charles Gallagher, writing of Morocco in the summer of 1962, describes the people of Europe "perched on the northern shore of the Strait of Gibraltar, and like lemmings blindly pushing their way across to seek new and uncluttered vacation sites." Though the majority of the tourists are European, Pan American Airways has inaugurated a new direct flight from New York to Rabat, and Morocco has opened a new office and arts and crafts showroom in midtown Manhattan.

The Morocco explored by car, motorcycle and bus by this new generation of tourists will not be the old Morocco of the haik and the burnous, the de luxe "Transat" hotels, and the honest and enchanting handicrafts fashioned for the most part without an eye on the tourist trade. The new tourist will not care. What he is missing is something that he has never seen. For him the discovery of this Moorish land will still be as much of an excitement and delight as it was to those who first explored Lyautey's new roads and drank mint tea with the burnous-draped merchants of the souks. For today's tourist the same wild flowers that delighted Delacroix still cover the fields in early spring; the same medieval walls surround the four imperial cities; the same storks nest between the crenels of the Rabat pirate fortress. Camels still wind up over the Atlas trails from the South, and black cobras sway to the sound of flute and hand-drum in the great Djmaa el Fna square in Marrakesh. The tourist will find all this and much more unchanged. In addition to the old delights he will ski at Ifrane, drive the new Rif Corniche edging the Mediterranean, swim on the beaches of

Morocco today: the modern city of Casablanca. / *M. Lacroix*

both sea and ocean, dance in the night clubs, and, happily unaware of financial crises, economic turmoil and political antagonism, make friends with the progressive young Moroccans, the *evolués* of the cafés and coffee bars.

In the meanwhile, behind the scenes in the offices of the Royal Palace, in the buildings housing the ministries—Education, Finance, Agriculture, Public Works and all the others—in the secretariats of the trade unions and the meeting places of politically conscious students, Moroccans worry about the future stability of their country. Though they are at odds with each other, they are all sincerely zealous in their hunger for the welfare of the land for whose independence they and their fathers have sacrificed so much. They are no longer the type of Moslem who shrugs off the future with a fatalistic "*Mektoub*—It is written."

Like so much of human history, the story of Morocco has, at present, a beginning but no predictable end. The future is a small and fascinating question mark among the many that make up the great cosmic question mark of the human race and human civilization. The friends of Morocco, and they are many—those who live there because they love the country, those who have once lived there and long to return—wish this ancient land with its new independence all prosperity, happiness and peace; above all, peace—*es salaam*. Those who have lived there in close friendship with the Moroccan people know in their hearts as well as in their minds what is meant by Arab hospitality. They understand Lyautey perfectly in his answer that his task "was easy" because he "loved the people." They understand why he wanted to be buried by the carved marble tombs of the Merinid Sultans.

293

BIBLIOGRAPHY

ALFALO, M. (1904) *The Truth About Morocco*. London: John Lane.

ALLEN, GARDNER W. (1905) *Our Navy and the Barbary Corsairs*. New York: Houghton Mifflin.

AMICIS, EDMONDO DE (1889) *Marocco*. Milano: Fratelli Treves, Editori.

ARBERRY, A. J. (1950) *Sufism. An Account of the Mystics of Islam*. New York: Macmillan.

ASHFORD, DOUGLAS (1961) *Political Change in Morocco*. Princeton: Princeton University Press.

Les Auteurs Arabes (*Pages Choisies des Grands Ecrivains*) (1924) Paris: Librairie Armand Colin.

L'Avant Garde (October 27, 1962) (Weekly). Casablanca.

BAEDEKER, KARL (1911) *The Mediterranean*. London: T. Fisher and Unwin.

IBN BATUTA. *Travels in Asia and in Africa 1325–1354*. Translated by H. A. R. Gibb (1929). London: Routledge and Kegan Paul.

EL BEKRI. *Description de l'Afrique Septentrionale*. Traduite par MacGuckin de Slane (M.G.) Paris: Imprimerie Imperiale, 1859.

BLUNT, WILFRID SCAWEN (1947) *Desert Hawk Abd el Kader and the French Conquest of Algeria*. London: Methuen.

BODLEY, R. V. C. (1946) *The Messenger. The Life of Mohammed*. New York: Doubleday.

294

Bougie et la Petite Kabylie (1914) Syndicat d'Initiative de Bougie.

BOULTON, LAURA (1941) "Timbuctu and Beyond," *National Geographic Magazine*, Vol. LXXIX, No. 5.

BOWLES, PAUL (1959) "The Moslems," *Holiday*, Vol. 25, No. 4.

BRIGGS, LLOYD CABOT (1960) *Tribes of the Sahara.* Cambridge: Harvard University Press.

BUSNOT, PERE DOMINIQUE (1714) *Histoire du Règne de Mouay Ismael.* Rouen: G. Behourt.

The Cambridge Modern History, Vol. XII, The Latest Age (1910) New York: Macmillan.

CAMOES, LUIS DE (1950) *The Lusiads.* Translated by Leonard Bacon. New York: The Hispanic Society of America.

CASTRIES, HENRI DE. *Sources inédites de l'histoire du Maroc (arch. des bibl. de France et des Pays Bas)*, 8 vol.; *Moulay Ismael et Jacques II* (Paris, *l'Islam, impressions et études 1896:* Leroux, 1903).

CELARIÉ, HENRIETTE (1923) *Un Mois au Maroc.* Paris: Hachette.

CHAMPION, PIERRE (1924) *Tanger, Fes, Meknès.* Paris: Laurens.

CHATINIERES, PAUL (1919) *Dans le Grand Atlas Marocain.* Paris: Librairie Plon.

CHAVREBIERE, COISSAC DE (1931) *Histoire du Maroc.* Paris: Payot.

CHENIER, LOUIS (1787) *Récherches Historiques sur les Maures et l'Histoire de l'Empire de Maroc.* Paris.

CHEVRILLON, ANDRÉ (1926) *Marrakech dans les palmes.* Paris: Calmann-Levy, Editeurs.

COOLEY, JOHN (1962) "King Hassan's Unbound Morocco," *Reporter*, Oct. 11.

COON, CARLETON (1951) *Caravan: The Story of the Middle East.* Rev. ed. 1958. New York: Holt, Rinehart & Winston.

COUR, AUGUSTE (1904–1906) *L'Etablissement des Dynasties des Cherifs au Maroc et leur Rivalité avec les Turcs de la Régence d'Alger.* Paris: Leroux.

CUNNINGHAME-GRAHAME, ROBERT BONTINE (1930) *Moghreb-El Acksa. A Journey into Morocco, 1898.* Introduction by Edward Garnett. New York: Viking.

DAN, LE R-P PIERRE (1649) *Histoire de Barbarie et de ses Corsaires* (2nd ed.). Paris: Rocolet.

DAVIDSON, BASIL (1959) *Lost Cities of Africa.* Boston: Atlantic–Little Brown.

DEFONTIN-MAXANGE (1929) *Le Grand Ismail, Empereur du Maroc.* Paris: Marpon et Cie.

DELACROIX, EUGENE (1937) *The Journal of Eugène Delacroix.* Translated from the French by Walter Pach. New York: Covici.

DELATTRE, LE R-P (1897) *Le Nécropole Punique de Carthage.* Extrait des Memoires de la Societé des Antiquaires de France, t. LVI. Paris.

DIEULAFOY, MARCEL (1913) *Espagne et Portugal.* Histoire Generale de l'Art. Paris: Hachette.

DOUGLAS, NORMAN (1926) *Fountains in the Sand.* London: Martin Secker.

DUBOIS, FELIX (1897) *Timbuctu the Mysterious.* Translated from the French by Diana White. New York: Longmans, Green.

EBERHARDT, ISABELLE (1914) *Notes de Route. Maroc–Algerie–Tunisie.* Paris: Librairie Charpentier et Fasquelle.

——— (1922) *Pages d'Islam.* Paris: Librairie Charpentier et Fasquelle.

ELGEY, GEORGETTE (1962) "The Conscience of a King," *Réalités*, January.

Encyclopaedia Britannica (13th ed.) (1926).

——— Britannica Book of the Year, 1958–1962.

EPTON, NINA (1958) *Saints and Sorcerers. A Moroccan Journey.* London: Cassell.

ERCKMANN, J. (1885) *Le Maroc Moderne.* Paris: Challamel.

295

FAURE, ELI (1921) *History of Art*. Vol. I, *Ancient Art*. Translated from the French by Walter Pach. New York: Harper.

—— *Histoire de l'Art*. Vol. II, *L'Art Medieval*. Paris: Les Editions G. Cres et Cie.

GALLAGHER, CHARLES F. (1961a) "North African Crossroads." Part I, "The Reign of Mohammed V." *American Universities Field Staff Reports Service*. North Africa Series, Vol. VII, No. 2. Morocco.

—— "North African Crossroads." Part II, "The Reign of Hassan II." *American Universities Field Staff Reports Service*. North Africa Series, Vol. VII, No. 3. Morocco.

—— (1962) "France in Morocco. A former colony lives amicably with the French." *American Universities Field Staff Reports Service*. North Africa Series, Vol. VIII, No. 1. Morocco.

—— (1963a) "The Death of a Group. Members of the Casablanca Pact Fall Out." *American Universities Field Staff Reports Service*. North Africa Series, Vol. IX, No. 4. Algeria and Morocco.

—— (1963b) "The Meanings of the Moroccan Elections. The Nation Elects Its First Parliament." *American Universities Field Staff Reports Service*. North Africa Series, Vol. IX, No. 5. Morocco.

—— (1963c) "The Discovery of Morocco. Mass Tourism Comes to the Moghreb." *American Universities Field Staff Reports Service*. North Africa Series, Vol. IX, No. 9. Morocco.

GAUTHIER, E.-F. (1931) *Moeurs et Coutumes des Musulmans*. Paris: Payot.

—— (1935) *Sahara, The Great Desert*. Translated by Dorothy Ford Mayhew. New York: Columbia University Press.

GERSTER, GEORG (1961) *Sahara, Desert of Destiny*. Translated by Stewart Thomson. New York: Coward-McCann.

GIBBON, EDWARD (1845) *The History of the Decline and Fall of the Roman Empire*. Philadelphia: John D. Morris & Co.

GODARD, M. L. (1860) *Description du Maroc*. Paris: C. Tanera.

GORCE, PAUL MARIE DE LA (1963) *The French Army*. Translated by Kenneth Douglas. New York: George Braziller.

GRAVES, ROBERT (1934) *I, Claudius*. New York: Harrison Smith and Robert Haas.

—— (1935) *Claudius, the God*. New York: Harrison Smith and Robert Haas.

—— (1938) *Count Belisarius*. New York: Random House.

GREEN, JOHN RICHARD (1894) *A Short History of the English People*. New York: Harper.

GUBB, ALFRED S. (1909) *The Flora of Algeria*. London: Baillere, Tyndall and Cox.

Les Guides Bleus (1958–1962) *Afrique de l'Ouest*. Paris: Hachette.

—— (1923) *Algerie et Tunisie*. Paris: Hachette.

—— (1927) *Espagne*. Paris: Hachette.

—— (1925) *Maroc*. Paris: Hachette.

Guide Dunlop (1923) *Tourisme Automobile en Algerie-Tunisie* (Jean de Taillis).

GUIFFREY, J. (1913) *Le Voyage de Eugène Delacroix*. Facsimile de l'Album du Chateau de Chantilly. 2 vol.

GUNTHER, JOHN (1953) *Inside Africa*. New York: Harper.

HALL, LELAND (1927) *Timbuctoo*. New York: Harper.

HARRIS, WALTER B. (1927) *France, Spain and the Riff*. New York: Longmans Green.

HOFFMANN, ELEANOR (1932) "The Terrible Lion," *Asia*, May, June, July.

HOLT, GEORGE EDMOND (1914) *Morocco, the Piquant, 1907–1911*. London: William Heineman.

HOURTICQ, LOUIS (1911) *France* (Histoire Générale de l'Art). Paris: Hachette.

HOWE, GEORGE F. (1957) *Northwest Africa. Seizing the Initiative in the West*. United States Army in World War II. The Mediterranean Theatre of Operation. Washington, D.C.: Office of the Chief of Military History, Department of the Army.

HOWE, MARVINE (1955) *The Prince and I*. New York: John Day.

HUXLEY, JULIAN (1954) *From an Antique Land*. New York: Crown.

Istiqlal, Al, October 27, 1962. Nouvelle Serie, No. 294. Rabat (Weekly).

Jeune Moghreb (October 20, 1962.) Casablanca (Weekly).

JULIEN, CH.-ANDRE (1961) *Histoire de l'Afrique du Nord*. 2 vol. Paris: Payot.

IBN KHALDOUN. *Histoire des Berbères et des Dynasties Musulmans*. Vol. II. Traduite par Baron de Slane (1834). Algiers.

The Koran. Translated from the Arabic by the Rev. J. M. Rodwell (1909). New York: Dutton.

The Koran. Translated from the Arabic by George Sale. New York: Warne.

LACOUTURE, JEAN and SIMONNE (1958) *Le Maroc à l'Epreuve*. Paris: Editions du Seuil.

LANDAU, ROM (1961) *Hassan II*. London: Allen and Unwin.

———— (1959) *Islam and the Arabs*. New York: Macmillan.

———— (1957) *Mohammed V, King of Morocco*. Rabat: "Morocco" Publishers.

———— (1956) *Moroccan Drama 1900–1955*. San Francisco: The American Academy of Asian Studies.

———— (1961) *Morocco Independent and Mohammed V*. London: Allen and Unwin.

LANE-POOLE, STANLEY (1886) *The Story of the Moors in Spain* (with the collaboration of Arthur Gilman). New York: Putnam.

LANGER, WILLIAM L. (1956) *An Encyclopaedia of World History*. Boston: Houghton Mifflin.

LEAKEY, LOUIS SEYMOUR BAZETT (1936) *Stone Age of Africa*. London: Oxford.

LEEDER, S. H. (1910) *The Desert Gateway. Biskra and Thereabouts*. London: Nelson.

LEGLAY, MAURICE (1922) *Recits Marocains de la Plaine et des Monts*. Paris: Berger Levrault.

LEMPRIÈRE, G. (1801) *Voyage dans l'empire de Maroc et le royaume de Fes 1790–1791*. Traduit de l'anglais par M. de Sainte Suzanne. Paris.

LEON L'AFRICAIN, JEAN (Rome, 1526) *Description de l'Afrique*. Traduite de l'Italien par A. Epaulard. Annotée par A. E. Th. Monod, H. Lhote et R. Mauny. Paris: Adrien Maisonneuve.

LHOTE, HENRI (1959) *Search for the Tassili Frescoes*. Translated from the French. New York: Dutton.

LODWICK, JOHN (1956) *The Forbidden Coast*. London: The Travel Book Club.

LOTI, PIERRE (1890) *Morocco*. Paris: Calmann-Levy.

MACAULAY, THOMAS BABINGTON. *A History of England*. New York: John Wortele Lovell.

MAHDI, MUHSIN (1957) *Ibn Khaldoun's Philosophy of History*. London: George Allen and Unwin.

Maroc Tourisme (1962) No. 10. Office National Marocain du Tourisme, Rabat.

Le Mali en Marche (1962) Republic of Mali, Secretariat of Information, Bamako.

MAUGHAM, ROBERT CECIL ROMER (1961) *The Slaves of Timbuctu*. New York: Harper.

MAUROIS, ANDRÉ (1931) *Lyautey*. Paris: Librairie Plon.

MEAKIN, BUDGETT (1901) *Land of the Moors*. London: S. Sonnenschein & Co.; New York: Macmillan.

———— (1899) *The Moorish Empire*. London: S. Sonnenschein & Co.; New York: Macmillan.

MINER, HORACE (1953) *The Primitive City of Timbuctu*. Published for the American Philosophical Society by Princeton University Press.

Ministère de l'Information et du Tourisme, Royaume du Maroc, Rabat:

(a) *Documents sur la Constitution et l'Action du Gouvernement de sa Majesté du 26 mai au 26 août 1960.*

(b) *Sa Majesté Mohammed V. Le Maroc à l'Heure de l'Indépendence.* Tome I, 1955–1957.

(c) *Le Maroc VI année d'indépendence.*

(d) *Réalizations et Perspectives.* 16 novembre 1955–18 novembre 1957.

(e) *Le Sucre Marocain* (1959) Conference Internationale du Sucre, Tanger, 23–28 novembre, 1959.

MONTAGU, ASHLEY (1951) *An Introduction to Physical Anthropology.* Springfield, Ill.: Charles C Thomas.

———— (1957) *Man: His First Million Years.* Cleveland and New York: World.

MOUETTE, SIEUR GERMAIN DE. *The Travels of the Sieur de Mouette in the Kingdoms of Fez and Morocco.*

EN NASIRI. *Kitab el Istiqsa.* Traduite par E. Fumey (1907). Archives Marocaines. Paris: Leroux.

New York Times. Western Edition, November, 1962–January, 1964.

NICKERSON, JANE SOAMES (1961) *A Short History of North Africa.* New York: Devin-Adair.

OBERMAIER, HUGO (1924) *Fossil Man in Spain.* New Haven: Yale University Press.

O'CONNOR, V. SCOTT (1932) "Morocco Beyond the Grand Atlas," *National Geographic Magazine,* Vol. LXI, No. 3.

OSBORN, HENRY FAIRFIELD (1928) *Men of the Old Stone Age.* New York: Scribner.

OUFRANI, NOZHAT EL HADJ. *Histoire de la Dynastie Saadienne au Maroc de 1511 à 1670 traduite par O. Houdas.* Collection des langues orientales, 3ième serie, Vol. III, 1889. Paris: Leroux.

PACHECO, F. HERNANDEZ Y TORRES, J. M. CORDERO (1962) *El Sahara espanol.* Madrid: Instituto de Estudios Politicos.

PECHKOFF, ZINOVI (1929) *La Légion Etrangère au Maroc.* Paris: Marcelle Lesage Editeur.

PELLOW, THOMAS (1736) *Adventures of Thomas Pellow.* London.

POND, ALONZO W. (1928) *A Contribution to the Study of Prehistoric Man in Algeria, North Africa.* With supplementary papers by Alfred S. Romes and Fay-Cooper Cole. *Logan Museum Bulletin,* Beloit, Wisconsin. Vol. I, No. 2. Vol. XXVI, No. 5.

———— (1962) *The Desert World.* New York: Nelson.

POWELL, ALEXANDER. *In Barbary.* New York: Century.

PREVILLE-ORTON, C. W. (1953) *The Shorter Cambridge Medieval History.* New York: Cambridge University Press.

RAWLINSON, GEORGE (1889) *Phoenicia.* New York: Putnam.

RICARD, PROSPER (1919) *Dynasties Marocaines.* Casablanca.

———— (1924) *Pour Comprendre l'Art Musulman dans l'Afrique du Nord et en Espagne.* Paris: Hachette.

ROOSEVELT, ELLIOTT (1946) *As He Saw It.* New York: Duell, Sloan and Pearce.

SCOTT, SAMUEL PARSONS (1904) *History of the Moorish Empire in Europe.* Philadelphia: Lippincott.

SEABROOK, WILLIAM (1934) *The White Monk of Timbuctoo.* New York: Harcourt Brace.

SEDGWICK, HENRY DWIGHT (1926) *A Short History of Spain.* Boston: Little Brown.

SHEIK, ABDUL GHAFUR (1953) "From America to Mecca on Airborne Pilgrimage," *National Geographic Magazine,* Vol. CIV, No. 1.

SHEPHERD, WILLIAM R. (1911) *Historical Atlas.* New York: Holt; 8th rev. ed., Barnes & Noble.

SHOR, JEAN and FRANC (1955) "From Sea to Sahara in French Morocco," *National Geographic Magazine*, Vol. CVII, No. 2.

SITWELL, SACHEVERELL (1958) *Arabesque and Honeycomb*. New York: Random House.

—— (1940) *Mauretania. Warrior, Man, and Woman*. London: Gerald Duckworth.

SKOLLE, JOHN (1956) *Azalai*. New York: Harper.

STEVENS, EDMUND (1955) *North African Powder Keg*. New York: Coward-McCann.

STUART, GRAHAM H. (1955) *The International City of Tangier*. Stanford, Calif.: Stanford University Press.

TERASSE, HENRI and HAINAUT, JEAN (1925) *Les Arts Decoratifs au Maroc*. Paris: Laurens.

THARAUD, JEROME, and JEAN (1930) *Fez ou les Bourgeois de l'Islam*. Paris: Librairie Plon.

—— — —— (1920) *Marrakech ou Les Seigneurs de l'Atlas*. Paris: Librairie Plon.

THILLY, FRANK (1914) *A History of Philosophy*. New York: Holt.

Time Magazine, 1955–1963.

THOMASSY, R. (1859) *Le Maroc. Relations de la France avec cet Empire*. Paris: F. Didot.

WELCH, GALBRAITH (1939) *North African Prelude*. New York: Morrow.

—— (1949) *The Unveiling of Timbuctu. The Astounding Adventures of Caillié*. New York: Morrow.

WELLS, H. G. (1921) *The Outline of History*. New York: Macmillan.

WESTERMARCK, EDWARD (1926) *Ritual and Belief in Morocco*. 2 Vols. London: Macmillan.

WHARTON, EDITH (1920) *In Morocco*. New York: Scribner.

WINDUS, JOHN (1725) *A Journey to Mequinez*. London.

EZ ZIANI, ABOULHASAN BEN AHMED (1886) *Le Maroc de 1631 à 1812*. Traduite par O. Houdas (1886). Paris: Leroux.

INDEX

Eleanor Hoffmann, who has written sixteen books and numerous articles, was born in Belmont, Massachusetts, in 1895. Her father was Ralph Hoffmann, author of **Birds of the Pacific Coast** and director of the Santa Barbara Museum of Natural History.

From 1924 to 1932 Miss Hoffmann spent most of her time in Europe and what was then French North Africa—Morocco, Algeria and Tunisia. In Morocco she began what was to become an extensive collection of Berber rugs, jewelry and other handicrafts, often exhibited in the United States. In the summer of 1931 she lived in a house within the walls of Old Fez. There the extraordinary hospitality of the Moroccan people, many of whom became her close friends, gave her an unforgettable insight into Moroccan life.

In 1962 Miss Hoffmann returned to the land of the burnous and the minaret—this time to an independent Morocco. She traveled beyond to Timbuctu, reached Bamako, the capital of Mali, by Niger riverboat, and flew the Sahara—all of this devoted to thorough research for **Realm of the Evening Star.**

ATLANTIC OCEAN

MOHAMMED
CASABLANCA

AZEMMOUR
EL-JADIDA
DAOURAT
SETT
FOUT

OUALIDIA

SAFI
YOUSOUFIA
HEMAIA

MARRAKESH
CHICHAOUA
AIT OURIR
ESSAOUIRA
AMIZMIZ
MASN
IMI N TANOUTE
OUKAIMEDEN

TAMANAR
AGADIR
IMMOUZER DES IDA OUTANANE
TAFINEGOULT

TAROUDANNT
TALIOUINE

AGADIR
INEZGANE

AIT BAHA
TIMKITE
TAT
TAFRAOUTE

INRITEK
AMIZ
MRIMIN
TIZNIT

AKKA
BOU IZAKARN
TARJICHT

GOULIMINE
TOUM EL HASSAINE
ASSA

TINDOUF

TARFAYA